PLINY

LETTERS AND PANEGYRICUS

II

PLINY

LETTERS AND PANEGYRICUS

IN TWO VOLUMES

II
LETTERS, BOOKS VIII–X AND PANEGYRICUS

WITH AN ENGLISH TRANSLATION BY
BETTY RADICE

LONDON
WILLIAM HEINEMANN LTD
CAMBRIDGE, MASSACHUSETTS
HARVARD UNIVERSITY PRESS
MCMLXIX

Printed in Great Britain

CONTENTS

V

THE LETTERS OF PLINY

BOOK VIII

C. PLINII CAECILII SECUNDI
EPISTULARUM

LIBER OCTAVUS

I

C. PLINIUS SEPTICIO SUO S.

1 ITER commode explicui, excepto quod quidam ex
meis adversam valetudinem ferventissimis aestibus
2 contraxerunt. Encolpius quidem lector, ille seria
nostra ille deliciae, exasperatis faucibus pulvere
sanguinem reiecit. Quam triste hoc ipsi, quam
acerbum mihi, si is cui omnis ex studiis gratia in-
habilis studiis fuerit! Quis deinde libellos meos sic
3 leget, sic amabit? Quem aures meae sic sequentur?
Sed di laetiora promittunt. Stetit sanguis, resedit
dolor. Praeterea continens ipse, nos solliciti, medici
diligentes. Ad hoc salubritas caeli, secessus quies
tantum salutis quantum otii pollicentur. Vale.

II

C. PLINIUS CALVISIO SUO S.

1 ALII in praedia sua proficiscuntur ut locupletiores
revertantur, ego ut pauperior. Vendideram vinde-

---

¹ Evidently Tifernum. See V. 6. 6: 45-6.

2

THE LETTERS OF PLINY

BOOK VIII

I

To Septicius Clarus

I HAD an easy journey, apart from the fact that some of my people were taken ill in the intense heat. Indeed, my reader Encolpius (the one who is our joy for work or play) found the dust so irritating to his throat that he spat blood, and it will be a sad blow to him and a great loss to me if this makes him unfit for his services to literature when they are his main recommendation. Who else will read and appreciate my efforts or hold my attention as he does? But the gods promise happier things. The haemorrhage has stopped and the pain is less severe; and he is a good patient, we are taking every care of him, and the doctors are attentive. In addition, the healthy climate here[1] and the complete rest and quiet can provide as much for a cure as for a holiday.

II

To Calvisius Rufus

OTHER people visit their estates to come away richer than before, but I go only to return the

mias certatim negotiatoribus ementibus. Invitabat
2 pretium, et quod tunc et quod fore videbatur. Spes
fefellit. Erat expeditum omnibus remittere aequaliter, sed non satis aequum. Mihi autem egre-
gium in primis videtur ut foris ita domi, ut in magnis
ita in parvis, ut in alienis ita in suis agitare iustitiam.
3 Nam si paria peccata, pares etiam laudes. Itaque
omnibus quidem, ne quis " mihi non donatus abiret,"
partem octavam pretii quo quis emerat concessi;
deinde iis, qui amplissimas summas emptionibus
occupaverant, separatim consului. Nam et me magis
4 iuverant, et maius ipsi fecerant damnum. Igitur iis
qui pluris quam decem milibus emerant, ad illam communem et quasi publicam octavam addidi decimam
5 eius summae, qua decem milia excesserant. Vereor
ne parum expresserim: apertius calculo ostendam.
Si qui forte quindecim milibus emerant, hi et quindecim milium octavam et quinque milium decimam
6 tulerunt. Praeterea, cum reputarem quosdam ex
debito aliquantum, quosdam aliquid, quosdam nihil
reposuisse, nequaquam verum arbitrabar, quos non
aequasset fides solutionis, hos benignitate remissionis
7 aequari. Rursus ergo iis qui solverant eius quod
solverant decimam remisi. Per hoc enim aptissime

---

[1] *Aeneid* V. 305.

poorer. I had sold my grape harvest to the dealers, who were eager to buy, when the price quoted at the time was tempting and prospects seemed good. Their hopes were frustrated. It would have been simple to give them all the same rebate, but hardly fair, and I hold the view that one of the most important things in life is to practise justice in private as in public life, in small matters as in great, and apply it to one's own affairs no less than to other people's. For if we say with the Stoics that " all offences are equal " the same applies to merits. Accordingly I returned to everyone an eighth of the sum he had spent so that " none should depart without a gift of mine."[1] Then I made a special provision for those who had invested very large sums in their purchase, since they had been of greater service to me and theirs was the greater loss. I therefore allowed everyone whose purchases had cost him more than 10,000 sesterces a tenth of anything he had spent above the 10,000, in addition to the original eighth which was a sort of general grant.

I am afraid I have put it badly; let me try to make my calculations clearer. Suppose someone had offered the sum of 15,000 sesterces; he would receive an eighth of 15,000, plus a tenth of 5,000. Moreover, in view of the fact that some people had paid down large instalments of what they owed, while others had paid little or nothing, I thought it most unfair to treat them all with the same generosity in granting a rebate when they had not been equally conscientious in discharging their debts. Once more, then, I allowed another tenth of the sum received to those who had paid. This seemed a

et in praeteritum singulis pro cuiusque merito gratia referri, et in futurum omnes cum ad emendum tum
8 etiam ad solvendum allici videbantur. Magno mihi seu ratio haec seu facilitas stetit, sed fuit tanti. Nam regione tota et novitas remissionis et forma laudatur. Ex ipsis etiam quos non una, ut dicitur, pertica sed distincte gradatimque tractavi, quanto quis melior et probior, tanto mihi obligatior abiit expertus non esse apud me ⟨ἐν δὲ ἰῇ τιμῇ ἠμὲν κακὸς ἠδὲ καὶ ἐσθλός⟩.[1] Vale.

III

C. Plinius Sparso Suo S.

1 Librum quem novissime tibi misi, ex omnibus meis vel maxime placere significas. Est eadem opinio
2 cuiusdam eruditissimi. Quo magis adducor ut neutrum falli putem, quia non est credibile utrumque falli, et qui tamen [2] blandior mihi. Volo enim proxima quaeque absolutissima videri, et ideo iam nunc contra istum librum faveo orationi, quam nuper in publicum dedi communicaturus tecum, ut primum
3 diligentem tabellarium invenero. Erexi exspectationem tuam, quam vereor ne destituat oratio in manus sumpta. Interim tamen tamquam placituram (et fortasse placebit) exspecta. Vale.

---

[1] ἐν . . . ἐσθλός ai, om. Mθ.
[2] tantum Stout.

---

[1] Iliad IX. 319.

6

suitable way both of expressing my gratitude to each
individual according to his past merits, and of encouraging them all not only to buy from me in the
future but also to pay their debts.

My system—or my good nature—has cost me a lot,
but it has been worth it. The whole district is praising
the novelty of my rebate and the way in which it
was carried out, and the people I classified and
graded instead of measuring all with the same rod, so
to speak, have departed feeling obliged to me in proportion to their honest worth and satisfied that I am
not a person who " holds in equal honour the wicked
and the good." [1]

III

To Julius Sparsus

You say that the book I sent you the other day has
given you more pleasure than any of my other works.
A learned friend of mine is of the same opinion, and
this encourages me to think that neither of you is
mistaken; for it is unlikely that you would both be
wrong, and I like to flatter myself. In fact I always
want my latest work to be thought my masterpiece;
consequently I have turned against the one you have
in favour of a speech which I have just published,
and which you shall see as soon as I can find someone reliable to bring it. Now I have roused your
expectations, but I fear they may be disappointed
when you have the speech in your hands. Meanwhile wait for its arrival with the intention of liking
it, and you may find you do so after all.

THE LETTERS OF PLINY

IV

C. PLINIUS CANINIO SUO S.

1 OPTIME facis, quod bellum Dacicum scribere paras. Nam quae tam recens tam copiosa tam elata, quae denique tam poetica et quamquam in verissimis rebus 2 tam fabulosa materia? Dices immissa terris nova flumina, novos pontes fluminibus iniectos, insessa castris montium abrupta, pulsum regia pulsum etiam vita regem nihil desperantem; super haec actos bis triumphos, quorum alter ex invicta gente primus, 3 alter novissimus fuit. Una sed maxima difficultas, quod haec aequare dicendo arduum immensum, etiam tuo ingenio, quamquam altissime adsurgat et amplissimis operibus increscat. Non nullus et in illo labor, ut barbara et fera nomina, in primis regis 4 ipsius, Graecis versibus non resultent. Sed nihil est quod non arte curaque, si non potest vinci, mitigetur. Praeterea, si datur Homero et mollia vocabula et Graeca ad levitatem versus contrahere extendere inflectere, cur tibi similis audentia praesertim 5 non delicata sed necessaria non detur? Proinde iure vatum invocatis dis, et inter deos ipso, cuius res opera consilia dicturus es, immitte rudentes, pande

---

¹ Trajan held triumphs in the winters of 102/3 and 106/7 to celebrate the ends of the two Dacian wars. Decebalus King of Dacia died by suicide in 106 after his capital, Sarmizegethusa, was captured. See *Pan.* 17, Dio, LXVIII. 14–15, and the scenes on Trajan's Column.

IV

To CANINIUS RUFUS

IT is an excellent idea of yours to write about the Dacian war. There is no subject which offers such scope and such a wealth of original material, no subject so poetic and almost legendary although its facts are true. You will describe new rivers set flowing over the land, new bridges built across rivers, and camps clinging to sheer precipices; you will tell of a king driven from his capital and finally to death, but courageous to the end; you will record a double triumph,[1] one the first over a nation hitherto unconquered, the other a final victory.

There is only one difficulty, but a serious one. To find a style of expression worthy of the subject is an immense undertaking, difficult even for a genius like yours, though this is capable of attaining supreme heights and surpasses itself in each magnificent work you have produced. Another problem arises out of the barbaric names, especially that of the king himself where the uncouth sounds will not fit into Greek verse; but every difficulty can be reduced by skill and application even if it cannot be entirely resolved. Besides, if Homer is permitted to contract, lengthen, and modify the flexible syllables of the Greek language to suit the even flow of his verse, why should you be denied a similar licence, especially when it is a necessity and no affectation? So call the gods to your aid, as a poet may, without forgetting that divine hero whose exploits, achievements and wisdom you are going to celebrate; slacken your sheets, spread sail,

9

vela ac, si quando alias, toto ingenio vehere. Cur
6 enim non ego quoque poetice cum poeta? Illud iam
nunc paciscor: prima quaeque ut absolveris mittito,
immo etiam ante quam absolvas, sicut erunt recentia
7 et rudia et adhuc similia nascentibus. Respondebis
non posse perinde carptim ut contexta, perinde
incohata placere ut effecta. Scio. Itaque et a me
aestimabuntur ut coepta, spectabuntur ut membra,
extremamque limam tuam opperientur in scrinio
nostro. Patere hoc me super cetera habere amoris
tui pignus, ut ea quoque norim quae nosse neminem
8 velles. In summa potero fortasse scripta tua magis
probare laudare, quanto illa tardius cautiusque, sed
ipsum te magis amabo magisque laudabo, quanto
celerius et incautius miseris. Vale.

V

C. Plinius Gemino Suo S.

1 Grave vulnus Macrinus noster accepit: amisit
uxorem singularis exempli, etiam si olim fuisset.
Vixit cum hac triginta novem annis sine iurgio sine
offensa. Quam illa reverentiam marito suo praestitit, cum ipsa summam mereretur! quot quantasque
virtutes, ex diversis aetatibus sumptas, collegit et
2 miscuit! Habet quidem Macrinus grande solacium,
quod tantum bonum tam diu tenuit, sed hinc magis

---

[1] Probably Minicius Macrinus, father of Acilianus mentioned
in I. 14.

and now, if ever, let the full tide of your genius carry
you along. (Why shouldn't I be poetical with a
poet?)

Now I have a stipulation to make; send me each
section in turn as you finish it, or better still send it
unfinished in its rough draught as it is first put together. You will object that a collection of incom-
plete fragments cannot give the same pleasure as the
finished whole. But knowing this I shall judge them
only as a beginning, examine them as parts of a
whole, and keep them in my desk to await your final
revision. Give me this further pledge of your affection—let me into the secrets you would prefer no
one to know. To sum up, I may perhaps be better
able to approve and admire your work if you are
slow and cautious about sending it, but I shall love
and value yourself the more if you can send it without delays and misgivings.

V

To Rosianus Geminus

Our friend Macrinus[1] has had a terrible blow;
he has lost his wife, one who would have been
exemplary even in former times, after they had lived
together for thirty-nine years without a quarrel or
misunderstanding. She always treated her husband
with the greatest respect, while deserving the highest
regard herself, and she seemed to have assembled in
herself the virtues of every stage of life in the highest
degree. Macrinus has indeed the great consolation
of having possessed such a treasure so long, though

exacerbatur quod amisit; nam fruendis voluptatibus
3 crescit carendi dolor. Ero ergo suspensus pro homine amicissimo, dum admittere avocamenta et
cicatricem pati possit, quam nihil aeque ac necessitas
ipsa et dies longa et satietas doloris inducit. Vale.

VI

C. Plinius Montano Suo S.

1 Cognovisse iam ex epistula mea debes, adnotasse
me nuper monumentum Pallantis sub hac inscrip-
tione: " Huic senatus ob fidem pietatemque erga
patronos ornamenta praetoria decrevit et sestertium
centies quinquagies, cuius honore contentus fuit."
2 Postea mihi visum est pretium operae ipsum senatus
consultum quaerere. Inveni tam copiosum et effu-
sum, ut ille superbissimus titulus modicus atque
etiam demissus videretur. Conferant se misceant-
que, non dico illi veteres, Africani Achaici Numantini,
sed hi proximi Marii Sullae Pompei (nolo progredi
3 longius): infra Pallantis laudes iacebunt. Urbanos
qui illa censuerunt putem an miseros? Dicerem
urbanos, si senatum deceret urbanitas; miseros, sed
nemo tam miser est ut illa cogatur. Ambitio ergo
et procedendi libido? Sed quis adeo demens, ut per
suum, per publicum dedecus procedere velit in ea

---

[1] VII. 29.
[2] P. Cornelius Scipio Africanus, victor over Hannibal in
202 B.C.; L. Mummius Achaicus, captor of Corinth in 146 B.C.;
Scipio Aemilianus Africanus Numantinus, victor at the siege
of Numantia in Spain in 133 B.C.

it is this which makes his loss so hard to bear; for our enjoyment of pleasure increases the pain of deprivation. So I shall continue to be anxious about him, for I love him dearly, until he can permit himself some distraction and allow his wound to heal; nothing can do this but acceptance of the inevitable, lapse of time, and surfeit of grief.

VI

To MONTANUS

You should have heard from my last letter[1] that I had recently seen a monument to Pallas with this inscription: "To him the Senate decreed in return for his loyal services to his patrons, the insignia of a praetor and the sum of fifteen million sesterces, but he thought fit to accept the distinction only." I thought it worth while afterwards to look up the actual decree of the Senate, and found it so verbose and fulsome in tone that the insolence of this inscription seemed modest and positively humble by comparison. All our national heroes put together—and I don't mean those of the past, with their titles of Africanus, Achaicus, and Numantinus,[2] but the Marii, Sullas, and Pompeys of recent times, to name no more—would still fall short of Pallas's fame. Am I to suppose this decree expresses the wit or the misery of its authors? Wit is unbecoming to the Senate; and no man's misery need bring him to this extremity. Then was it self-interest or desire for advancement? But who is so crazy as to desire advancement won through his own and his country's

civitate, in qua hic esset usus florentissimae dignitatis,
4 ut primus in senatu laudare Pallantem posset?
Mitto quod Pallanti servo praetoria ornamenta
offeruntur (quippe offeruntur a servis), mitto quod
censent non exhortandum modo verum etiam com-
pellendum ad usum aureorum anulorum; erat enim
contra maiestatem senatus, si ferreis praetorius
5 uteretur. Levia haec et transeunda, illa memoranda
quod nomine Pallantis senatus (nec expiata postea
curia est), Pallantis nomine senatus gratias agit
Caesari, quod et ipse cum summo honore mentionem
eius prosecutus esset et senatui facultatem fecisset
6 testandi erga eum benevolentiam suam. Quid enim
senatui pulchrius, quam ut erga Pallantem satis
gratus videretur? Additur: "Ut Pallas, cui se
omnes pro virili parte obligatos fatentur, singularis
fidei singularis industriae fructum meritissimo ferat."
Prolatos imperi fines, redditos exercitus rei publicae
7 credas. Adstruitur his: "Cum senatui populoque
Romano liberalitatis gratior repraesentari nulla
materia posset, quam si abstinentissimi fidelissimique
custodis principalium opum facultates adiuvare
contigisset." Hoc tunc votum senatus, hoc praecipuum gaudium populi, haec liberalitatis materia
gratissima, si Pallantis facultates adiuvare publicarum
8 opum egestione contingeret. Iam quae sequuntur?
Voluisse quidem senatum censere dandum ex aerario

---

[1] A rhetorical exaggeration: Pallas was a freedman and
some members of the Senate could have been sons of freedmen.

dishonour, in a State where the chief privilege of its highest office is that of being the first to pay compliments to Pallas in the Senate?

I say nothing of this offer of the praetorian insignia to a slave,[1] for they were slaves themselves who made the offer, nothing of the resolution that he should not only be begged but even compelled to wear a gold ring (it would lower the prestige of the Senate for a praetorian to wear the slave's iron one); these are trivial details which may well be set aside. This is what must stand on record; on behalf of Pallas the Senate (and the House has not been subsequently purged of its shame) — on behalf of Pallas the Senate thanked the Emperor for his own recognition of the man in bestowing high honour, and for giving them the opportunity of testifying their appreciation. For what could be more splendid for the Senate than to show suitable gratitude to Pallas? The resolution continues: ". . . that Pallas, to whom all to the utmost of their ability acknowledge their obligation, should reap the just reward of his outstanding loyalty and devotion to duty." (One might suppose he had extended the boundaries of the Empire or brought home the armies he had commanded.) Then follows: " Since the Senate and the Roman people could have no more gratifying occasion for liberality than the opportunity to add to the means of this self-denying and faithful custodian of the imperial finances. . . ." This then was the will of the Senate, the chief pleasure of the people, the highly gratifying occasion for liberality—to add to Pallas's fortune by squandering public funds.

What next? The Senate wished to vote him a

sestertium centies quinquagies et quanto ab eius
modi cupiditatibus remotior eius animus esset, tanto
impensius petere a publico parente, ut eum com-
9 pelleret ad cedendum senatui. Id vero deerat, ut
cum Pallante auctoritate publica ageretur, Pallas
rogaretur ut senatui cederet, ut illi superbissimae
abstinentiae Caesar ipse patronus, ipse advocaretur,[1]
ne sestertium centies quinquagies sperneret. Sprev-
it, quod solum potuit tantis opibus publice oblatis
10 adrogantius facere, quam si accepisset. Senatus
tamen id quoque similis querenti laudibus tulit, his
quidem verbis: sed cum princeps optimus parensque
publicus rogatus a Pallante eam partem sententiae,
quae pertinebat ad dandum ei ex aerario sestertium
centies quinquagies, remitti voluisset, testari senatum, et se libenter ac merito hanc summam inter
reliquos honores ob fidem diligentiamque Pallanti
decernere coepisse, voluntati tamen principis sui,
cui in nulla re fas putaret repugnare, in hac quoque
11 re obsequi. Imaginare Pallantem velut interce-
dentem senatus consulto moderantemque honores
suos et sestertium centies quinquagies ut nimium
recusantem, cum praetoria ornamenta tamquam minus recepisset; imaginare Caesarem liberti precibus
vel potius imperio coram senatu obtemperantem
(imperat enim libertus patrono, quem in senatu
12 rogat); imaginare senatum usquequaque testantem
merito libenterque se hanc summam inter reliquos

[1] advocaretur *a*: advocatus esset *Mθ*.

grant of fifteen million sesterces from the Treasury,
and, knowing how far removed he was from all desires of this kind, the more urgently besought the
Father of the State to compel him to comply with
their wishes.   In fact the only thing lacking was for
Pallas to be officially approached and begged to
comply, for the Emperor himself to champion the
cause, and plead with that insolent self-denial in order
that the fifteen million should not be rejected.   But
Pallas did reject it; a great fortune had been offered
him in the name of the State, and this was his only
means of showing greater contempt than if he had
accepted it.   Yet even this the Senate met with
further compliments, this time in a reproachful tone:
" But inasmuch as the noble Emperor and Father of
the State at Pallas's request has expressed his wish
that the clause referring to the grant of fifteen million sesterces from the Treasury should be rescinded,
the Senate declares that though it had freely and
justly taken steps to grant this sum to Pallas among
the other distinctions offered him on account of his
loyalty and devotion to duty, yet since it holds that
in nothing is it lawful to oppose the Emperor, in this
matter also it must bow to his wishes."

Picture Pallas interposing his veto, as it were, on
the Senate's decree, setting limits to his own honours,
and refusing fifteen million as excessive while accepting the praetorian insignia as if they meant less!
Picture the Emperor before the assembled Senate
carrying out his freedman's request or rather command—for this is what such a request made before
the Senate amounts to.   Picture the Senate going
so far as to declare that it had freely and justly taken

honores Pallanti coepisse decernere et persever-
aturum fuisse, nisi obsequeretur principis voluntati,
cui non esset fas in ulla re repugnare. Ita ne sestertium centies quinquagies Pallas ex aerario ferret,
verecundia ipsius obsequio senatus opus fuit in hoc
praecipue non obsecuturi, si in ulla re putasset fas
esse non obsequi.

13 Finem existimas? Mane dum et maiora accipe:
" Utique, cum sit utile principis benignitatem promp-
tissimam ad laudem praemiaque merentium inlustrari
ubique et maxime iis locis, quibus incitari ad imi-
tationem praepositi rerum eius curae possent, et
Pallantis spectatissima fides atque innocentia exemplo
provocare studium tam honestae aemulationis posset,
ea quae x kal. Februarias quae proximae fuissent in
amplissimo ordine optimus princeps recitasset sena-
tusque consulta de iis rebus facta in aere inciderentur,
idque aes figeretur ad statuam loricatam divi Iulii."[1]

14 Parum visum tantorum dedecorum esse curiam tes-
tem: delectus est celeberrimus locus, in quo legenda
praesentibus, legenda futuris proderentur. Placuit
aere signari omnes honores fastidiosissimi mancipî,
quosque repudiasset quosque quantum ad decernentes

---

[1] This seems to be the only reference to this statue; it presumably stood outside the Temple of Divus Iulius where the
offices of the *fiscus* were probably housed. An official of the
fiscus was called the *procurator a loricata*.

steps to grant Pallas this sum among his other
honours, and that it would have carried out its intention but for the need of bowing to the Emperor's
wishes which could not on any point be lawfully opposed. Thus, to permit Pallas to decline this fifteen
million from the Treasury, it took the combined
forces of his own discretion and the Senate's obedience, which it would never have shown on this occasion had it believed that disobedience were lawful
on any point.

Is this all, do you think? Wait and hear something better still. "Inasmuch as it is expedient that
the Emperor's generous promptitude to praise and
reward merit should everywhere be published and
particularly in places where those entrusted with the
administration of his affairs may be encouraged to
follow the example set them, and where the example
of Pallas's proved loyalty and integrity may inspire
others to honourable rivalry, it is resolved that the
statement made by the noble Emperor before this
distinguished House on 23 January, together with
the resolutions passed by the Senate concerning this
matter, shall be engraved on a bronze tablet and that
tablet shall be affixed to the mailed statue of the
deified Julius Caesar."[1] So it was not enough for
these disgraceful proceedings to be witnessed by the
walls of the Senate house; the most frequented spot
in Rome was chosen to display them, where they
could be read by everyone, today and ever after.
A resolution was passed that all the honours of this
insolent slave should be inscribed on bronze, both
those he had refused and those he had accepted as
far as those who conferred them had the power to do

pertinet gessit. Incisa et insculpta sunt publicis aeternisque monumentis praetoria ornamenta Pallantis, sic quasi foedera antiqua, sic quasi sacrae leges.

15 Tanta principis, tanta senatus, tanta Pallantis ipsius —quid dicam nescio, ut vellent in oculis omnium figi Pallas insolentiam suam, patientiam Caesar, humilitatem senatus. Nec puduit rationem turpitudini obtendere, egregiam quidem pulchramque rationem, ut exemplo Pallantis praemiorum ad studium aemu-

16 lationis ceteri provocarentur. Ea honorum vilitas erat, illorum etiam quos Pallas non dedignabatur. Inveniebantur tamen honesto loco nati, qui peterent cuperentque quod dari liberto promitti servis videbant.

17 Quam iuvat quod in tempora illa non incidi, quorum sic me tamquam illis vixerim pudet! Non dubito similiter adfici te. Scio quam sit tibi vivus et ingenuus animus: ideo facilius est ut me, quamquam indignationem quibusdam in locis fortasse ultra epistulae modum extulerim, parum doluisse quam nimis credas. Vale.

VII

C. PLINIUS TACITO SUO S.

1 NEQUE ut magistro magister neque ut discipulo discipulus (sic enim scribis), sed ut discipulo magister (nam tu magister, ego contra; atque adeo tu in

so. The praetorian insignia granted to Pallas were engraved and cut on a public monument for all time as if they were an ancient covenant or a sacred law. To such lengths did the Emperor, the Senate, and Pallas himself push their—I can't think of a word to express their conduct—as if they intended to set up a record in the sight of all, Pallas of his insolence, the Emperor of his complaisance, the Senate of its degradation! Nor were they ashamed to find a reason to justify their disgrace, and a splendid reason too, " so that by the reward given to Pallas others might be inspired to rival him "! Honours were then to be so cheap, the honours which Pallas did not disdain; and yet people of good family could be found who were fired by ambition for distinctions which they saw granted to freedmen and promised to slaves.

How glad I am that my lot did not fall in those days —for which I blush as if I had lived in them. I am sure you will feel the same, knowing your lively sympathy and honest mind; so that, though in some passages I may have let my indignation carry me beyond the bounds of a letter, you will readily believe that I have suppressed my feelings rather than exaggerated them.

VII

To Cornelius Tacitus

It was not as one master to another, nor, as you say, as one pupil to another, but as a master to his pupil (for you are master, I am pupil, and so you call me back to school while I am still keeping the

scholam revocas, ego adhuc Saturnalia extendo)
2 librum misisti. Num potui longius hyperbaton facere;
atque hoc ipso probare eum esse me qui non modo
magister tuus, sed ne discipulus quidem debeam dici?
Sumam tamen personam magistri, exseramque in
librum tuum ius quod dedisti, eo liberius quod nihil
ex meis interim missurus sum tibi in quo te ulciscaris.
Vale.

VIII

C. PLINIUS ROMANO SUO S.

1 VIDISTINE aliquando Clitumnum fontem? Si nondum (et puto nondum: alioqui narrasses mihi), vide;
2 quem ego (paenitet tarditatis) proxime vidi. Modicus collis adsurgit, antiqua cupressu nemorosus et
opacus. Hunc subter exit fons et exprimitur pluribus
venis sed imparibus, eluctatusque quem facit gurgitem[1] lato gremio patescit, purus et vitreus, ut numerare iactas stipes et relucentes calculos possis.
3 Inde non loci devexitate, sed ipsa sui copia et quasi
pondere impellitur, fons adhuc et iam amplissimum
flumen, atque etiam navium patiens; quas obvias
quoque et contrario nisu in diversa tendentes trans-
mittit et perfert, adeo validus ut illa qua properat
ipse, quamquam per solum planum, remis non adiu-

---

[1] eluctatusque (-que *om. θ,add. i*) quem *Mθ*: eluctatusque
facit gurgitem qui *a*.

---

[1] See VII. 20. This could be the *Dialogus* (the tone of the
letter suggests a work on oratory) or a second roll of the *Histories*.

Saturnalia) that you sent me your book.[1]   Could I
write a longer hyperbaton than that, and thereby
prove that so far from being your master I do not
even deserve to be called your pupil?   But I will
play the part of master and exercise the authority
you have given me over your book; the more freely
as for the moment I have nothing of my own to send
you on which you can take your revenge.

VIII

To Voconius Romanus

Have you ever seen the source of the Clitumnus?[2]
If not (and I fancy not, or you would have told me)
do visit it as I did the other day.   I am only sorry
I put off seeing it so long.

There is a fair-sized hill which is densely wooded
with ancient cypresses; at the foot of this the spring
rises and gushes out through several channels of
different size, and when its eddies have subsided it
broadens out into a pool as clear as glass.   You can
count the coins which have been thrown in and the
pebbles shining at the bottom.   Then it is carried on,
not by any downward slope of the land but by its
own volume and weight of water: one minute it is
still a spring and the next a broad river navigable for
boats to which it can give a passage even when two
are moving in opposite directions and must pass each

[2] In Umbria, between Trevi and Spoleto (Clitunno).   Cf.
Virgil, *Georgics*, II. 146; Propertius, *Elegies*, II. 19. 25; Statius,
Silvae, I. 4. 128 ff.

23

vetur, idem aegerrime remis contisque superetur
4 adversus. Iucundum utrumque per iocum ludum-
que fluitantibus, ut flexerint cursum, laborem otio
otium labore variare. Ripae fraxino multa, multa
populo vestiuntur, quas perspicuus amnis velut
mersas viridi imagine adnumerat. Rigor aquae
5 certaverit nivibus, nec color cedit. Adiacet templum priscum et religiosum. Stat Clitumnus ipse
amictus ornatusque praetexta; praesens numen atque
etiam fatidicum indicant sortes. Sparsa sunt circa
sacella complura, totidemque di. Sua cuique veneratio suum nomen, quibusdam vero etiam fontes.
Nam praeter illum quasi parentem ceterorum sunt
minores capite discreti; sed flumini miscentur, quod
6 ponte transmittitur. Is terminus sacri profanique:
in superiore parte navigare tantum, infra etiam
natare concessum. Balineum Hispellates, quibus
illum locum divus Augustus dono dedit, publice praebent, praebent et hospitium. Nec desunt villae
quae secutae fluminis amoenitatem margini insistunt.
7 In summa nihil erit, ex quo non capias voluptatem.
Nam studebis quoque: leges multa multorum omnibus columnis omnibus parietibus inscripta, quibus fons
ille deusque celebratur. Plura laudabis, non nulla

---

[1] Spello.

other. The current is so strong that although the ground remains level, a boat travelling downstream is hurried along without needing its oars, while it is very difficult to make any headway upstream with oars and poles combined. Anyone boating for pleasure can enjoy hard work alternating with easy movement simply by a change of course.

The banks are thickly clothed with ash trees and poplars, whose green reflections can be counted in the clear stream as if they were planted there. The water is as cold and as sparkling as snow. Close by is a holy temple of great antiquity in which is a standing image of the god Clitumnus himself clad in a magistrate's bordered robe; the written oracles lying there prove the presence and prophetic powers of his divinity. All round are a number of small shrines, each containing its god and having its own name and cult, and some of them also their own springs, for as well as the parent stream there are smaller ones which have separate sources but afterwards join the river. The bridge which spans it marks the sacred water off from the ordinary stream: above the bridge boats only are allowed, while below bathing is also permitted. The people of Hispellum,[1] to whom the deified Emperor Augustus presented the site, maintain a bathing place at the town's expense and also provide an inn; and there are several houses picturesquely situated along the river bank. Everything in fact will delight you, and you can also find something to read: you can study the numerous inscriptions in honour of the spring and the god which many hands have written on every pillar and wall. Most of them you will admire, but some will make

ridebis; quamquam tu vero, quae tua humanitas,
nulla ridebis. Vale.

IX

C. Plinius Urso Suo S.

1   Olim non librum in manus, non stilum sumpsi, olim
nescio quid sit otium quid quies, quid denique illud
iners quidem, iucundum tamen nihil agere nihil esse:
adeo multa me negotia amicorum nec secedere nec
2 studere patiuntur. Nulla enim studia tanti sunt,
ut amicitiae officium deseratur, quod religiosissime
custodiendum studia ipsa praecipiunt. Vale.

X

C. Plinius Fabato Prosocero Suo S.

1   Quo magis cupis ex nobis pronepotes videre, hoc
tristior audies neptem tuam abortum fecisse, dum se
praegnantem esse puellariter nescit, ac per hoc quaedam custodienda praegnantibus omittit, facit omit-
tenda. Quem errorem magnis documentis expiavit,
2 in summum periculum adducta. Igitur, ut necesse
est graviter accipias senectutem tuam quasi paratis
posteris destitutam, sic debes agere dis gratias, quod
ita tibi in praesentia pronepotes negaverunt, ut
servarent neptem, illos reddituri, quorum nobis spem

you laugh—though I know you are really too chari-
table to laugh at any of them.

IX

To Cornelius Ursus

It is a long time since I have had a book or a pen
in my hand, a long time since I have known what
peace and quiet are or even known that lovely,
lazy state of doing and being nothing; so completely
has the pressure of my friends' business kept me from
either leaving Rome or working at my books. For
no such work is important enough to justify neglect
of the claims of friendship, a duty which these same
books tell us to observe with scrupulous care.

X

To Calpurnius Fabatus, his Wife's Grandfather

I know how anxious you are for us to give you a
great-grandchild, so you will be all the more sorry
to hear that your granddaughter has had a miscarriage. Being young and inexperienced she did not
realize she was pregnant, failed to take proper pre-
cautions, and did several things which were better
left undone. She has had a severe lesson, and paid
for her mistake by seriously endangering her life;
so that although you must inevitably feel it hard for
your old age to be robbed of a descendant already on
the way, you should thank the gods for sparing your
granddaughter's life even though they denied you

27

certiorem haec ipsa quamquam parum prospere ex-
3 plorata fecunditas facit. Isdem nunc ego te quibus
ipsum me hortor moneo confirmo. Neque enim
ardentius tu pronepotes quam ego liberos cupio, quibus videor a meo tuoque latere pronum ad honores
iter et audita latius nomina et non subitas imagines
relicturus. Nascantur modo et hunc nostrum dolorem gaudio mutent. Vale.

XI

C. Plinius Hispullae Suae S.

1 Cum adfectum tuum erga fratris filiam cogito
etiam materna indulgentia molliorem, intellego prius
tibi quod est posterius nuntiandum, ut praesumpta
laetitia sollicitudini locum non relinquat. Quamquam vereor ne post gratulationem quoque in metum
redeas, atque ita gaudeas periculo liberatam, ut simul
2 quod periclitata sit perhorrescas. Iam hilaris, iam
sibi iam mihi reddita incipit refici, transmissumque
discrimen convalescendo metiri. Fuit alioqui in
summo discrimine (impune dixisse liceat), fuit nulla
sua culpa, aetatis aliqua. Inde abortus et ignorati
3 uteri triste experimentum. Proinde etsi non contigit
tibi desiderium fratris amissi aut nepote eius aut
nepte solari, memento tamen dilatum magis istud
28

the child for the present. They will surely grant us children later on, and we may take hope from this evidence of her fertility though the proof has been unfortunate.

I am giving you the same advice and encouragement as I use on myself, for your desire for great-grandchildren cannot be keener than mine for children. Their descent from both of us should make their road to office easy; I can leave them a well-known name and an established ancestry, if only they may be born and turn our present grief to joy.

XI

To Calpurnia Hispulla

Remembering how you love your brother's daughter more tenderly than a mother, I feel that I ought to begin with the second half of my news, so that happiness may come first and leave no room for anxiety. And yet I am afraid your relief will turn to fear again, and your joy at hearing that your niece is out of danger will be tempered by your alarm at her narrow escape. By now her good spirits are returning as she feels herself restored to herself and to me, and she is beginning to measure the danger she has been through by her progress towards recovery. The danger was indeed grave—I hope I may safely say so now—through no fault of her own, but perhaps of her youth. Hence her miscarriage, a sad proof of unsuspected pregnancy. So though you are still without a grandchild of your brother's to comfort you for his loss, you must remember that this

29

quam negatum, cum salva sit ex qua sperari potest. Simul excusa patri tuo casum, cui paratior apud feminas venia. Vale.

XII

C. PLINIUS MINICIANO SUO S.

1 Hunc solum diem excuso: recitaturus est Titinius Capito, quem ego audire nescio magis debeam an cupiam. Vir est optimus et inter praecipua saeculi ornamenta numerandus. Colit studia, studiosos amat fovet provehit, multorum qui aliqua componunt portus sinus gremium,[1] omnium exemplum, ipsarum denique litterarum iam senescentium reductor ac 2 reformator. Domum suam recitantibus praebet, auditoria non apud se tantum benignitate mira frequentat; mihi certe, si modo in urbe, defuit numquam. Porro tanto turpius gratiam non referre, 3 quanto honestior causa referendae. An si litibus tererer, obstrictum esse me crederem obeunti vadimonia mea, nunc, quia mihi omne negotium omnis in studiis cura, minus obligor tanta sedulitate celebranti, in quo obligari ego, ne dicam solo, certe 4 maxime possum? Quod si illi nullam vicem nulla quasi mutua officia deberem, sollicitarer tamen vel

---

[1] gremium *G. H. Schaefer*: praemium *MaI*.

---

[1] Hopes that were never realized. The contrast in tone between the two letters is striking.

consolation is postponed, not denied us. We build
our hopes[1] on her, and she has been spared. Meanwhile, explain this accident to your father, as it is the
sort women can more easily understand.

XII

To Cornelius Minicianus

TODAY is the one day I must be free: Titinius
Capito is giving a reading, which it is my duty—
or perhaps my urgent desire—to attend. He is a
splendid personality who should be numbered among
the shining lights of our generation; a patron of
literature and admirer of literary men, whom he
supports and helps in their careers. To many who
are authors he is a haven of refuge and protection,
while he is an example to all; it is he in fact who has
restored and reformed literature itself when it was
on the decline. He lends his house for public readings, and is wonderfully generous about attending
those which are held elsewhere; at any rate he has
never missed one of mine, provided that he was in
Rome at the time. It would then be all the more
disgraceful in me to fail to show the gratitude I have
every good reason to feel. If I were engaged in a
lawsuit I should feel bound to the man who stood bail
for me; so now when literature is absorbing all my
thoughts, shall I feel less bound to the one whose
unfailing attentiveness to me gives him a special—
if I mayn't say a sole—claim on me? But even if I
owed Capito no return, no exchange of services, I
should still be persuaded by the greatness of his noble

ingenio hominis pulcherrimo et maximo et in summa
severitate dulcissimo, vel honestate materiae.   Scri-
bit exitus inlustrium virorum, in his quorundam mihi
5 carissimorum.   Videor ergo fungi pio munere,
quorumque exsequias celebrare non licuit, horum
quasi funebribus laudationibus seris quidem sed tanto
magis veris interesse.   Vale.

XIII

C. Plinius Geniali Suo S.

1   Probo quod libellos meos cum patre legisti.   Pertinet ad profectum tuum a disertissimo viro discere,
quid laudandum quid reprehendendum, simul ita
institui, ut verum dicere adsuescas.   Vides quem
2 sequi, cuius debeas implere vestigia.   O te beatum,
cui contigit unum atque idem optimum et coniunctissimum exemplar, qui denique eum potissimum
imitandum habes, cui natura esse te simillimum voluit!
Vale.

XIV

C. Plinius Aristoni Suo S.

1   Cum sis peritissimus et privati iuris et publici,
cuius pars senatorium est, cupio ex te potissimum
audire, erraverim in senatu proxime necne, non ut

---

¹ In I. 17. 3 Capito writes in verse on the lives of the republican heroes, but the present work may be in prose.   For the
theme, cf. C. Fannius's work described in V. 5. 3.

genius which can combine tenderness with austerity, or else by the dignity of his theme. He is writing on the deaths of famous men,[1] some of whom were very dear to me; so I feel that I am performing a pious duty in being present at something like their funeral orations when I could not attend their funerals: a tribute no less sincere for being thus delayed.

XIII

To Genialis

I am glad to hear that you have been reading my published speeches with your father. It will help your own progress if you learn from a man of his accomplishments what to admire and what to criticize, and at the same time are taught the habit of speaking the truth. You have your model before you, in whose footsteps you should tread, and are fortunate indeed to be blessed with a living example who is both the best possible and your close relative: in short, to have for imitation the very man whom Nature intended you to resemble most.

XIV

To Titius Aristo

As you are such an authority on civil and constitutional law, including senatorial procedure, I am particularly anxious to hear whether or not you think I made a mistake at a recent meeting of the Senate. It is too late to be put right about past events, but I

in praeteritum (serum enim), verum ut in futurum si
2 quid simile inciderit erudiar. Dices: " Cur quaeris
quod nosse debebas? "[1] Priorum temporum servitus ut aliarum optimarum artium, sic etiam iuris
senatorii oblivionem quandam et ignorantiam induxit.
3 Quotus enim quisque tam patiens, ut velit discere,
quod in usu non sit habiturus? Adde quod difficile
est tenere quae acceperis nisi exerceas. Itaque
reducta libertas rudes nos et imperitos deprehendit;
cuius dulcedine accensi, cogimur quaedam facere
4 ante quam nosse. Erat autem antiquitus institutum,
ut a maioribus natu non auribus modo verum etiam
oculis disceremus, quae facienda mox ipsi ac per
vices quasdam tradenda minoribus haberemus.
5 Inde adulescentuli statim castrensibus stipendiis
imbuebantur ut imperare parendo, duces agere dum
sequuntur adsuescerent; inde honores petituri ad-
sistebant curiae foribus, et consilii publici spectatores
6 ante quam consortes erant. Suus cuique parens pro
magistro, aut cui parens non erat maximus quisque et
vetustissimus pro parente. Quae potestas referenti-
bus, quod censentibus ius, quae vis magistratibus,
quae ceteris libertas, ubi cedendum ubi resistendum,
quod silentii tempus, quis dicendi modus, quae dis-
tinctio pugnantium sententiarum, quae exsecutio

---

[1] debebas *Gronovius*: debeas *MaI*.

should like to know what to do in future should any similar situation arise. You will wonder why I am asking a question I should have been able to answer myself. The fact is we have forgotten our knowledge of senatorial procedure, as of other honest practices, in the servitude of former times; very few people have the patience and will-power to learn what is never likely to be of any practical use, and it is besides difficult to remember what you have learned unless you put it into practice. So, now that Liberty is restored, she finds us awkward and inexperienced; carried away by her charms we are compelled to act in certain ways before we understand them.

In ancient times it was the recognized custom for us to learn from our elders by watching their behaviour as well as listening to their advice, thus acquiring the principles on which to act subsequently ourselves and to hand on in our turn to our juniors. Hence young men began their early training with military service, so that they might grow accustomed to command by obeying, and learn how to lead by following others; hence as candidates for office they stood at the door of the Senate house and watched the course of State councils before taking part in them. Everyone had a teacher in his own father, or, if he was fatherless, in some older man of distinction who took his father's place. Thus men learned by example (the surest method of instruction) the powers of the proposer, the rights of expressing an opinion, the authority of office, and the privileges of ordinary members; they learned when to give way and when to stand firm, how long to speak and when to keep silence, how to distinguish between conflicting

prioribus aliquid addentium, omnem denique senatorium morem (quod fidissimum percipiendi genus)
7 exemplis docebantur.   At nos iuvenes fuimus quidem
in castris; sed cum suspecta virtus, inertia in pretio,
cum ducibus auctoritas nulla, nulla militibus verecundia, nusquam imperium nusquam obsequium,
omnia soluta turbata atque etiam in contrarium
versa, postremo obliviscenda magis quam tenenda.
8 Iidem prospeximus curiam, sed curiam trepidam et
elinguem, cum dicere quod velles periculosum, quod
nolles miserum esset.   Quid tunc disci potuit, quid
didicisse iuvit, cum senatus aut ad otium summum
aut ad summum nefas vocaretur, et modo ludibrio
modo dolori retentus numquam seria, tristia saepe
9 censeret?   Eadem mala iam senatores, iam participes
malorum multos per annos vidimus tulimusque;
quibus ingenia nostra in posterum quoque hebetata
10 fracta contusa sunt. Breve tempus (nam tanto
brevius omne quanto felicius tempus) quo libet scire
quid simus, libet exercere quod scimus.[1]   Quo iustius
peto primum ut errori, si quis est error, tribuas
veniam, deinde medearis scientia tua cui semper fuit
curae, sic iura publica ut privata sic antiqua ut re-
11 centia sic rara ut adsidua tractare.   Atque ego arbitror illis etiam, quibus plurimarum rerum agitatio

---

[1] scimus *Reifferscheid*: sumus *MaI*.

---

[1] Cf. *Pan.* 18. 1.
[2] Cf. *Pan.* 76. 3 and Tacitus, *Agr.* 44–5.

proposals and how to introduce an amendment, in short the whole of senatorial procedure. For our own generation it was different. Though our early manhood was spent in camp, it was at a time when merit was under suspicion and apathy an asset, when officers lacked influence and soldiers respect, when there was neither authority nor obedience, and the whole system was slack, disorganized and chaotic, better forgotten than remembered.[1] We too were spectators in the Senate, but in a Senate which was apprehensive and dumb, since it was dangerous to voice a genuine opinion and pitiable to express a forced one.[2] What could be learned at that time, what profit could there be in learning, when the Senate was summoned to idle away its time or to perpetrate some vile crime, and was kept sitting for a joke or its own humiliation; when it could never pass a serious resolution, though often one with tragic consequences? On becoming senators we took part in these evils and continued to witness and endure them for many years, until our spirits were blunted, broken and destroyed with lingering effect; so that it is only a short time (the happier the time the shorter it seems) since we began to want to know our own powers and put our knowledge into practice.

I have then all the more reason to ask you first to forgive any mistake I may have made, and then to remedy it with your expert knowledge; for you have always made a special study of civil and constitutional law, ancient and modern, with reference to exceptional as well as current problems. Personally I think that the kind of question I am putting to you would be unfamiliar even to people whose constant

frequens nihil esse ignotum patiebatur, genus quaestionis quod adfero ad te aut non satis tritum aut etiam inexpertum fuisse. Hoc et ego excusatior si forte sum lapsus, et tu dignior laude, si potes id quoque docere quod in obscuro est an didiceris.

12 Referebatur de libertis Afrani Dextri consulis incertum sua an suorum manu, scelere an obsequio perempti. Hos alius (Quis?[1] Ego; sed nihil refert) post quaestionem supplicio liberandos, alius in insulam relegandos, alius morte puniendos arbitrabatur. Quarum sententiarum tanta diversitas erat, ut non
13 possent esse nisi singulae. Quid enim commune habet occidere et relegare? Non hercule magis quam relegare et absolvere; quamquam propior aliquanto est sententiae relegantis, quae absolvit, quam quae occidit (utraque enim ex illis vitam relinquit, haec adimit), cum interim et qui morte puniebant et qui relegabant, una sedebant et temporaria simula-
14 tione concordiae discordiam differebant. Ego postulabam, ut tribus sententiis constaret suus numerus, nec se brevibus indutiis duae iungerent. Exigebam ergo ut qui capitali supplicio adficiendos putabant, discederent a relegante, nec interim contra abso-

---

[1] alius quis *I* (*in margine*) *a*: alioquis *I*: alius inquis *M*: alius. Quis? inquis. *Guillemin, Schuster.*

---

[1] The date is given in the consular *Fasti* as 24 June 105.

[2] Compare the case of the City Prefect Pedanius in 61, when his 400 slaves were executed, but his freedmen spared by order of Nero (Tacitus, *Ann.* XIV. 42–5).

dealing with large numbers of cases makes them conversant with most possibilities; it might be entirely outside their experience. So there will be the more excuse for me, if perhaps I was at fault, and the more credit to you if you can instruct me on a point on which you may not have been informed yourself.

The case at issue concerned the freedmen of the consul Afranius Dexter, who had been found dead;[1] it was not known whether he had killed himself or his servants were responsible, and, if the latter, whether they acted criminally or in obedience to their master. After the proceedings one opinion (whose? —mine, but that is irrelevant) was that they should be acquitted, another that they should be banished to an island, and a third that they should be put to death.[2] Such diversity of sentences meant that they had to be considered singly; for what have death and banishment in common? Obviously no more than banishment and acquittal, though a vote for acquittal is much nearer one for banishment than is a vote for death, for the first two leave a man his life while death removes it. Meanwhile those who voted for the death penalty and banishment respectively were sitting together and shelving their differences by a temporary show of unity.

My own proposal was that the three sentences should be reckoned as three, and that two should not join forces under a momentary truce. Therefore I insisted that the supporters of the death penalty should move away from the proposer of banishment, and that the two parties should not combine to oppose those asking for acquittal when they would afterwards

39

lventes mox dissensuri congregarentur, quia parvolum referret an idem displiceret, quibus non idem
15 placuisset. Illud etiam mihi permirum videbatur,
eum quidem qui libertos relegandos, servos supplicio
adficiendos censuisset, coactum esse dividere sententiam; hunc autem qui libertos morte multaret, cum
relegante numerari. Nam si oportuisset dividi
sententiam unius, quia res duas comprehendebat,
non reperiebam quamadmodum posset iungi sententia duorum tam diversa censentium.

16 Atque adeo permitte mihi sic apud te tamquam
ibi, sic peracta re tamquam adhuc integra rationem
iudicii mei reddere, quaeque tunc carptim multis
17 obstrepentibus dixi, nunc per otium iungere. Fin-
gamus tres omnino iudices in hanc causam datos esse;
horum uni placuisse perire libertos, alteri relegari,
tertio absolvi. Utrumne sententiae duae collatis
viribus novissimam periment, an separatim una
quaeque tantundem quantum altera valebit, nec
magis poterit cum secunda prima conecti quam sec-
18 unda cum tertia? Igitur in senatu quoque numerari
tamquam contrariae debent, quae tamquam diversae
dicuntur. Quodsi unus atque idem et perdendos
censeret et relegandos, num ex sententia unius et
perire possent et relegari? Num denique omnino
una sententia putaretur, quae tam diversa coniun-
19 geret? Quemadmodum igitur, cum alter puniendos,
alter censeat relegandos, videri potest una sententia

disagree among themselves; for it mattered little that they took the same negative view when their positive proposals were so different. Another point I found extraordinary was that the member who proposed banishment for the freedmen and death for the slaves should have been obliged to divide his vote, while one who was for executing the freedmen could be counted as voting with the proposer of banishment. For if one person's vote had to be divided because it covered two distinct sentences, I could not see how the votes of two people making such different proposals could be taken together.

Now, although the case is over let me treat it as still open; let me explain to you, as I did to the Senate, why I held this view; and let me assemble now in my own time the points I had then to make piecemeal amidst considerable interruption. Let us suppose that three judges only have been appointed for this case, one of whom has said that the freedmen should die, the second that they should be banished, and the third that they should be acquitted. Is the combined weight of the first two sentences to defeat the third, or is each one to be weighed against the others and the first and second to be combined no more than the second and third? Similarly, in the Senate, all different opinions expressed ought to be counted as conflicting. But if one and the same person proposed both death and banishment, could the prisoners suffer both punishments by one person's sentence alone? Could it be considered as one sentence at all when it combined such different proposals? Then, when one person proposes death and another banishment, how can these be held to be a

quae dicitur a duobus, quae non videretur una, si ab
uno diceretur? Quid? lex non aperte docet dirimi
debere sententias occidentis et relegantis, cum ita
discessionem fieri iubet: " Qui haec censetis,[1]
in hanc partem, qui alia omnia, in illam partem ite qua
sentitis "? Examina singula verba et expende: " qui
haec censetis," hoc est qui relegandos putatis, " in
hanc partem," id est in eam in qua sedet qui censuit
20 relegandos. Ex quo manifestum est non posse in
eadem parte remanere eos, qui interficiendos arbi-
trantur. " Qui alia omnia ": animadvertis, ut non
contenta lex dicere " alia " addiderit " omnia."
Num ergo dubium est alia omnia sentire eos qui
occidunt quam qui relegant? " In illam partem
ite qua sentitis ": nonne videtur ipsa lex eos qui
dissentiunt in contrariam partem vocare cogere im-
pellere? Non consul etiam, ubi quisque remanere,
quo transgredi debeat, non tantum sollemnibus verbis,
21 sed manu gestuque demonstrat? At enim futurum
est ut si dividantur sententiae interficientis et relegantis, praevaleat illa quae absolvit. Quid istud ad
censentes? quos certe non decet omnibus artibus,
omni ratione pugnare, ne fiat quod est mitius.
Oportet tamen eos qui puniunt et qui relegant,
absolventibus primum, mox inter se comparari.

[1] censetis *Mommsen*: sentis *MaI.*

single sentence because expressed by two people when they were not a single sentence if expressed by one person?

Well; the law clearly states that sentences of death and banishment should be considered separately, in its formula for taking a division: " All who agree go to this side, all who support any other proposal to the side you support." Take the words one by one and consider them. " Who agree " means " Who think the prisoners should be banished "; " to this side " is the side of the House where the proposer of banishment is sitting. It is clear from this that those who want death for the prisoners cannot stay on that side. " Who support any other proposal "—you will observe that the law is not content with saying " other " but has added the word " any." Can it be doubted that those who would put the prisoners to death " support any other proposal " in comparison with those who would banish them? " Go to the side you support "; surely the wording of the law seems to summon and positively compel those who disagree to take different sides? The consul also indicates not only by the established formula, but by a movement of the hand where everyone is to remain or to what side to cross.

But it can be argued that if the sentences of death and banishment are taken separately it will result in the acquittal having a majority. That is no concern of the voters, and it certainly ill becomes them to use every weapon and device to defeat a more lenient sentence. Or, again, it can be said that those voting for death and banishment should first be matched against those supporting acquittal, and

43

Scilicet ut in spectaculis quibusdam sors aliquem sep-
onit ac servat, qui cum victore contendat, sic in senatu sunt aliqua prima, sunt secunda certamina, et ex
duabus sententiis eam, quae superior exstiterit, tertia
22 exspectat. Quid, quod prima sententia comprobata
ceterae perimuntur? Qua ergo ratione potest esse
non unus atque idem locus sententiarum, quarum
23 nullus est postea? Planius repetam. Nisi dicente
sententiam eo qui relegat, illi qui puniunt capite initio
statim in alia discedant, frustra postea dissentient ab
24 eo cui paulo ante consenserint. Sed quid ego similis
docenti? cum discere velim, an sententias dividi an
iri in singulas oportuerit. Obtinui quidem quod
postulabam; nihilo minus tamen quaero, an postu-
lare debuerim. Quemadmodum obtinui? Qui ulti-
mum supplicium sumendum esse censebat, nescio an
iure, certe aequitate postulationis meae victus, omissa
sententia sua accessit releganti, veritus scilicet ne, si
dividerentur sententiae, quod alioqui fore videbatur,
ea quae absolvendos esse censebat numero praeva-
25 leret. Etenim longe plures in hac una quam in duabus singulis erant. Tum illi quoque qui auctoritate
eius trahebantur, transeunte illo destituti reliquerunt
sententiam ab ipso auctore desertam, secutique
sunt quasi transfugam quem ducem sequebantur.

then against each other. In some of the public
games one gladiator draws a lot which entitles him
to stand aside and wait to fight the victor; so I
suppose there are to be first and second rounds in
the Senate, too, and the third sentence is to wait
and meet the victor of the other two. What about
the rule that if the first sentence is approved all
the others are defeated? On what principle can
these sentences not start on the same footing, seeing that they may all subsequently cease to count?
I will put this again more clearly. As soon as
the proposal of banishment is made, unless those
in favour of execution immediately cross over to
the other side, it will be useless their afterwards
opposing what they agreed with a short time before.

But I should not be the one to give instruction,
when I really wanted to learn whether the two sentences should have been subsequently divided, or all
three voted on separately. I carried my point, but
none the less I want to know whether I should have
made it. How did I manage this? The proposer
of the death sentence was convinced by the justice
of my request (whether or not it was legal), dropped
his own proposal, and supported that of banishment.
He was afraid, no doubt, that if the sentences were
taken separately (which seemed likely if he did not
act) the acquittal would have a majority, for there
were many more people in favour of this than of
either of the other two proposals. Then, when those
who had been influenced by him found themselves
abandoned by his crossing the floor and the proposal
thrown over by its author, they dropped it too, and
deserted after their leader. So the three sentences

45

26 Sic ex tribus sententiis duae factae, tenuitque ex
duabus altera tertia expulsa, quae, cum ambas
superare non posset, elegit ab utra vinceretur. Vale.

XV

C. Plinius Iuniori Suo S.

1 Oneravi te tot pariter missis voluminibus, sed
oneravi primum quia exegeras, deinde quia scrip-
seras tam graciles istic vindemias esse, ut plane
scirem tibi vacaturum, quod vulgo dicitur, librum
2 legere. Eadem ex meis agellis nuntiantur. Igitur
mihi quoque licebit scribere quae legas, sit modo unde
chartae emi possint;[1] aut necessario quidquid
scripserimus boni malive delebimus. Vale.

XVI

C. Plinius Paterno Suo S.

1 Confecerunt me infirmitates meorum, mortes
etiam, et quidem iuvenum. Solacia duo nequaquam
paria tanto dolori, solacia tamen: unum facilitas
manumittendi (videor enim non omnino immaturos
perdidisse, quos iam liberos perdidi), alterum quod
permitto servis quoque quasi testamenta facere,
2 eaque ut legitima custodio. Mandant rogantque
quod visum; pareo ut iussus. Dividunt donant relin-
quunt, dumtaxat intra domum; nam servis res

---

[1] *post* possint *add.* quae si scabrae, bibulaeve sint, aut non
scribendum *a*.

became two, and the second carried the day by elimination of the third which could not defeat both the others, and therefore chose to submit to one.

XV

To Terentius Junior

I MUST be overwhelming you by sending so many books at once; but you asked for them, and, as you write that your grape harvest is so poor, I can be sure that if you can't be picking grapes you will have time, as they say, to pick up a book. I have the same news from my own farms, so I shall have time, too, to write something for your "picking" so long as I can still afford to buy paper. Otherwise I shall have to erase all I write, good or bad, and use the paper again.

XVI

To Plinius Paternus

I HAVE been much distressed by illness among my servants, the deaths, too, of some of the younger men. Two facts console me somewhat, though inadequately in trouble like this: I am always ready to grant my slaves their freedom, so I don't feel their death is so untimely when they die free men, and I allow even those who remain slaves to make a sort of will which I treat as legally binding. They set out their instructions and requests as they think fit, and I carry them out as if acting under orders. They can

3 publica quaedam et quasi civitas domus est. Sed
quamquam his solaciis adquiescam, debilitor et
frangor eadem illa humanitate, quae me ut hoc ipsum
permitterem induxit. Non ideo tamen velim durior
fieri. Nec ignoro alios eius modi casus nihil amplius
vocare quam damnum, eoque sibi magnos homines et
sapientes videri. Qui an magni sapientesque sint,
4 nescio; homines non sunt. Hominis est enim adfici
dolore sentire, resistere tamen et solacia admittere,
5 non solaciis non egere. Verum de his plura fortasse
quam debui; sed pauciora quam volui. Est enim
quaedam etiam dolendi voluptas, praesertim si in
amici sinu defleas, apud quem lacrimis tuis vel laus
sit parata vel venia. Vale.

XVII

C. PLINIUS MACRINO SUO S.

1 NUM istic quoque immite et turbidum caelum?
Hic adsiduae tempestates et crebra diluvia. Tiberis
alveum excessit et demissioribus ripis alte super-
2 funditur; quamquam fossa quam providentissimus
imperator fecit exhaustus, premit valles, innatat

---

[1] For Tiber floods and damage in Rome, see Tac. *Hist.* I. 86.
[2] For Trajan's public works, see *Pan.* 29. This drainage
canal is confirmed by an inscription from Ostia, if correctly
restored (R. Meiggs, *Roman Ostia*, p. 488).

distribute their possessions and make any gifts and bequests they like, within the limits of the household: for the house provides a slave with a country and a sort of citizenship.

But though I can take comfort from these thoughts, I still find my powers of resistance weakened by the very feelings of humanity which led me to grant this privilege. Not that I would wish to be harder of heart; and I am well aware that some people look upon misfortunes of this kind as no more than a monetary loss, and think themselves fine men and philosophers for doing so. Whether they are in fact fine and philosophic I can't say, but they are certainly not men. A true man is affected by grief and has feelings, though he may fight them; he allows himself to be consoled, but is not above the need of consolation. I may perhaps have said more on this subject than I ought, but not so much as I would like. Even grief has its pleasure, especially if you can weep in the arms of a friend who is ready with approval or sympathy for your tears.

XVII

To Caecilius Macrinus

Can the weather be as bad and stormy where you are? Here we have nothing but gales and repeated floods. The Tiber has overflowed its bed and deeply flooded its lower banks,[1] so that although it is being drained by the canal cut by the Emperor,[2] with his usual foresight, it is filling the valleys and inundating

campis, quaque planum solum, pro solo cernitur.
Inde quae solet flumina accipere et permixta deve-
here, velut obvius retro[1] cogit, atque ita alienis aquis
3 operit agros, quos ipse non tangit. Anio, delicatissi-
mus amnium ideoque adiacentibus villis velut invi-
tatus retentusque, magna ex parte nemora quibus
inumbratur fregit et rapuit; subruit montes, et
decidentium mole pluribus locis clausus, dum amissum iter quaerit, impulit tecta ac se super ruinas
4 eiecit atque extulit. Viderunt quos excelsioribus
terris illa tempestas deprehendit, alibi divitum adparatus et gravem supellectilem, alibi instrumenta
ruris, ibi boves aratra rectores, hic soluta et libera
armenta, atque inter haec arborum truncos aut
villarum trabes atque culmina[2] varie lateque
5 fluitantia. Ac ne illa quidem malo vacaverunt, ad
quae non ascendit amnis. Nam pro amne imber
adsiduus et deiecti nubibus turbines, proruta opera
quibus pretiosa rura cinguntur, quassata atque etiam
decussa monumenta. Multi eius modi casibus de-
bilitati obruti obtriti, et aucta luctibus damna.
6 Ne quid simile istic, pro mensura periculi vereor,
teque rogo, si nihil tale, quam maturissime sollicitudini meae consulas, sed et si tale, id quoque nunties.
Nam parvolum differt, patiaris adversa an exspectes;

---

[1] retro *aI*: sistere *M*.
[2] atque culmina *a et I in margine: om. MI*.

the fields, and wherever there is level ground there is nothing to be seen but water. Then the streams which it normally receives and carries down to the sea are forced back as it spreads to meet them, and so it floods with their water the fields it does not reach itself. The Anio, most delightful of rivers— so much so that the houses on its banks seem to beg it not to leave them—has torn up and carried away most of the woods which shade its course. High land nearby has been undermined, so that its channel is blocked in several places with the resultant land-slides; and in its efforts to regain its lost course it has wrecked buildings and forced out its way over the debris.

People who were hit by the storm on higher ground have seen the valuable furniture and fittings of wealthy homes, or else all the farm stock, yoked oxen, ploughs and ploughmen, or cattle left free to graze, and among them trunks of trees or beams and roofs of houses, all floating by in widespread confu-sion. Nor have the places where the river did not rise escaped disaster, for instead of floods they have had incessant rain, gales and cloudbursts which have destroyed the walls enclosing valuable properties, rocked public buildings, and brought them crashing to the ground. Many people have been maimed, crushed, and buried in such accidents, so that grievous loss of life is added to material damage.

My fears that you have been through something like this are proportionate to the danger—if I am wrong, please relieve my anxiety as soon as possible; and let me know in any case. Whether disaster is actual or expected the effect is much the same, except

nisi quod tamen est dolendi modus, non est timendi.
Doleas enim quantum scias accidisse, timeas quantum possit accidere. Vale.

XVIII

C. Plinius Rufino Suo S.

1 Falsum est nimirum quod creditur vulgo, testamenta hominum speculum esse morum, cum Domitius Tullus longe melior adparuerit morte quam vita.
2 Nam cum se captandum praebuisset, reliquit filiam heredem, quae illi cum fratre communis, quia genitam fratre adoptaverat. Prosecutus est nepotes plurimis iucundissimisque legatis, prosecutus etiam proneptem. In summa omnia pietate plenissima ac tanto
3 magis inexspectata sunt. Ergo varii tota civitate sermones: alii fictum ingratum immemorem loquuntur, seque ipsos dum insectantur illum turpissimis confessionibus produnt, ut qui de patre avo proavo quasi de orbo querantur; alii contra hoc ipsum laudibus ferunt, quod sit frustratus improbas spes hominum, quos sic decipi pro moribus temporum est. Addunt etiam non fuisse ei liberum alio testamento mori: neque enim reliquisse opes filiae sed reddi-
4 disse, quibus auctus per filiam fuerat. Nam Curtilius [1] Mancia perosus generum suum Domitium Lucanum (frater is Tulli) sub ea condicione filiam

---

[1] Curtilius *Casaubon*: Curtius *MaI*.

---

[1] Domitia Lucilla. Her daughter of the same name was the mother of the Emperor Marcus Aurelius. (See Syme, pp. 792-3.)

that suffering has its limits but apprehension has none; suffering is confined to the known event, but apprehension extends to every possibility.

XVIII

To Fadius Rufinus

THERE is certainly no truth in the popular belief that a man's will is a mirror of his character, for Domitius Tullus has proved himself to be much better in death than life. Although he had encouraged legacy hunters, he left as heiress the daughter [1] he shared with his brother (he had adopted his brother's child). He also left a great many welcome legacies to his grandsons and to his great-granddaughter; in fact the whole will is ample proof of his affection for his family, and so all the more unexpected.

Consequently the city is full of conflicting opinions; some accuse him of hypocrisy, ingratitude, and fickleness, and in attacking him betray themselves by their own disgraceful admissions, for they complain about a man who was a father, grandfather, and great-grandfather as if he were childless. Others applaud him for the very reason that he has disappointed the shameless expectations of men whose frustration in this way accords with the spirit of the times. They also say that Tullus was not free to leave any other will, for he did not bequeath his wealth to his daughter so much as restore what he had acquired through her. For when Curtilius Mancia took a violent dislike to his son-in-law Domitius Lucanus (brother of Tullus), he made his

eius neptem suam instituerat heredem, si esset manu
patris emissa. Emiserat pater, adoptaverat patruus,
atque ita circumscripto testamento consors frater in
fratris potestatem emancipatam filiam adoptionis
fraude revocaverat et quidem cum opibus amplissimis.
5 Fuit alioqui fratribus illis quasi fato datum ut divites
fierent, invitissimis a quibus facti sunt. Quin etiam
Domitius Afer, qui illos in nomen adsumpsit, reliquit
testamentum ante decem et octo annos nuncupatum,
adeoque postea improbatum sibi, ut patris eorum
6 bona proscribenda curaverit. Mira illius asperitas,
mira felicitas horum: illius asperitas, qui numero
civium excidit, quem socium etiam in liberis habuit;
felicitas horum, quibus successit in locum patris, qui
7 patrem abstulerat. Sed haec quoque hereditas Afri,
ut reliqua cum fratre quaesita, transmittenda erant
filiae fratris, a quo Tullus ex asse heres institutus
praelatusque filiae fuerat, ut conciliaretur. Quo
laudabilius testamentum est, quod pietas fides pudor
scripsit, in quo denique omnibus adfinitatibus pro
cuiusque officio gratia relata est, relata et uxori.
8 Accepit amoenissimas villas, accepit magnam pecuniam uxor optima et patientissima ac tanto melius de
viro merita, quanto magis est reprehensa quod nupsit.

---

[1] Sextus Curvius Tullus.
[2] His second wife, name unknown.

granddaughter, Lucanus's daughter, his heiress on condition that she was freed from her father's control. The father set her free, but the uncle adopted her; thus the purpose of the will was defeated, for, as the brothers held their property jointly, the daughter, once freed, was brought back under her father's control by the device of adoption, and with her came a large fortune. Indeed, these brothers seemed destined to be made rich by people who intended otherwise. Even Domitius Afer, who adopted them into his family, left a will which had been drawn up eighteen years previously and was subsequently so far removed from his intentions that he had taken steps to procure the confiscation of their father's [1] property. His severity in removing from the citizen roll the man whose children he had shared is no less remarkable than their good fortune in finding a second father in the man who ruined their first. However, this inheritance from Afer was also destined to go to Lucanus's daughter along with the rest of the brothers' joint acquisitions; for Lucanus had made Tullus his sole heir in preference to his own daughter, with the idea of bringing them together.

So this will is all the more creditable for being dictated by family affection, honesty and feelings of shame; and in it Tullus acknowledges his obligations to all his relatives in return for their services to him, as he does to the excellent wife [2] who had borne with him so long. She has inherited his beautiful country houses and a large sum of money, and deserved all the more from her husband for having been so severely criticized for marrying him. It was

55

Nam mulier natalibus clara, moribus proba, aetate
declivis, diu vidua mater olim, parum decore secuta
matrimonium videbatur divitis senis ita perditi
morbo, ut esse taedio posset uxori, quam iuvenis
9 sanusque duxisset. Quippe omnibus membris ex-
tortus et fractus, tantas opes solis oculis obibat, ac ne
in lectulo quidem nisi ab aliis movebatur; quin etiam
(foedum miserandumque dictu) dentes lavandos fric-
andosque praebebat. Auditum frequenter ex ipso,
cum quereretur de contumeliis debilitatis suae, digi-
10 tos se servorum suorum cotidie lingere. Vivebat
tamen et vivere volebat, sustentante maxime uxore,
quae culpam incohati matrimonii in gloriam perse-
verantia verterat.

11 Habes omnes fabulas urbis; nam sunt omnes
fabulae Tullus. Exspectatur auctio: fuit enim tam
copiosus, ut amplissimos hortos eodem quo emerat
die instruxerit plurimis et antiquissimis statuis;
tantum illi pulcherrimorum operum in horreis quae
neglegebat. Invicem tu, si quid istic epistula
12 dignum, ne gravare. Nam cum aures hominum
novitate laetantur, tum ad rationem vitae exemplis
erudimur. Vale.

thought most unsuitable that a woman of her high birth and blameless character, who was no longer young, had borne children in the past and long been widowed, should marry a wealthy old man and a hopeless invalid, whom even a wife who had known him when young and healthy might have found an object of disgust. Crippled and deformed in every limb, he could only enjoy his vast wealth by contemplating it, and could not even turn in bed without assistance. He also had to have his teeth cleaned and brushed for him—a squalid and pitiful detail—and when complaining about the humiliations of his infirmity was often heard to say that every day he licked the fingers of his slaves. Yet he went on living, and kept his will to live, helped chiefly by his wife, whose devoted care turned the former criticism of her marriage into a tribute of admiration.

That is all the city gossip, as Tullus is all we talk about. We are looking forward to the sale of his effects, for he had so many possessions that on the very day he bought a large garden he was able to beautify it with quantities of antique statues from the splendid works of art he had stored away and forgotten. If you have any local news worth sending in return, don't grudge me it. Not only is it always a pleasure to hear something new, but also through examples we study the art of living.

THE LETTERS OF PLINY

XIX

C. PLINIUS MAXIMO SUO S.

1 ET gaudium mihi et solacium in litteris, nihilque tam laetum quod his laetius, tam triste quod non per has minus triste. Itaque et infirmitate uxoris et meorum periculo, quorundam vero etiam morte turbatus, ad unicum doloris levamentum studia confugi, quae praestant ut adversa magis intellegam sed 2 patientius feram. Est autem mihi moris, quod sum daturus in manus hominum, ante amicorum iudicio examinare, in primis tuo. Proinde si quando, nunc intende libro quem cum hac epistula accipies, quia vereor ne ipse ut tristis parum intenderim. Imperare enim dolori ut scriberem potui; ut vacuo animo laetoque, non potui. Porro ut ex studiis gaudium sic studia hilaritate proveniunt. Vale.

XX

C. PLINIUS GALLO SUO S.

1 AD quae noscenda iter ingredi, transmittere mare solemus, ea sub oculis posita neglegimus, seu quia ita natura comparatum, ut proximorum incuriosi longinqua sectemur, seu quod omnium rerum cupido languescit, cum facilis occasio, seu quod differimus tamquam saepe visuri, quod datur videre quotiens

XIX

To Maximus

Literature is both my joy and my comfort: it can add to every happiness and there is no sorrow it cannot console. So worried as I am by my wife's ill-health and the sickness in my household and death of some of my servants, I have taken refuge in my work, the only distraction I have in my misery. It may make me more conscious of my troubles, but helps me to bear them with patience.

It is, however, my habit to test everything I propose to submit to the general public by the judgement of my friends, especially your own. Will you then give your attention to the book you will receive with this letter, now as never before? I fear my distress will have impaired my own concentration, for I could control my feelings enough to write, but not to write freely and happily, and if one's work is to give pleasure it must have its inspiration in happiness.

XX

To Clusinius (?) Gallus

We are always ready to make a journey and cross the sea in search of things we fail to notice in front of our eyes, whether it is that we are naturally indifferent to anything close at hand while pursuing distant objects, or that every desire fades when it can easily be granted, or that we postpone a visit with the idea that we shall often be seeing what is there to be seen

2 velis cernere. Quacumque de causa, permulta in
urbe nostra iuxtaque urbem non oculis modo sed ne
auribus quidem novimus, quae si tulisset Achaia
Aegyptos Asia aliave quaelibet miraculorum ferax
commendatrixque terra, audita perlecta lustrata
3 haberemus. Ipse certe nuper, quod nec audieram
ante nec videram, audivi pariter et vidi. Exegerat
prosocer meus, ut Amerina praedia sua inspicerem.
Haec perambulanti mihi ostenditur subiacens lacus
nomine Vadimonis; simul quaedam incredibilia
4 narrantur. Perveni ad ipsum. Lacus est in simili-
tudinem iacentis rotae circumscriptus et undique
aequalis: nullus sinus, obliquitas nulla, omnia di-
mensa paria, et quasi artificis manu cavata et exçisa.
Color caerulo albidior; † viridior et pressior † ;[1] sul-
puris odor saporque medicatus; vis qua fracta soli-
dantur. Spatium modicum, quod tamen sentiat
5 ventos, et fluctibus intumescat. Nulla in hoc navis
(sacer enim), sed innatant insulae, herbidae omnes
harundine et iunco, quaeque alia fecundior palus ipsaque illa extremitas lacus effert. Sua cuique figura
ut modus; cunctis margo derasus, quia frequenter vel
litori vel sibi inlisae terunt terunturque. Par omnibus altitudo, par levitas; quippe in speciem carinae
6 humili radice descendunt. Haec ab omni latere

---

[1] viridior *Mθ, om. a*: viridi ora pressior *Schuster*: viridi
lividior et pressior *Stout*.

---

[1] In Umbria (now Amelia).

[2] Lago di Bassano, N.W. of Orte, the site of two Roman

whenever we feel inclined. Whatever the reason, there are a great many things in Rome and near by which we have never seen nor even heard of, though if they were to be found in Greece, Egypt or Asia, or any other country which advertises its wealth of marvels, we should have heard and read about them and seen them for ourselves.

I am a case in point. I have just heard of something (and seen it, too) which I had neither seen nor heard of before. My wife's grandfather had asked me to look at his property in Ameria.[1] While going round I was shown a lake at the foot of the hills called Lake Vadimon,[2] and at the same time told some extraordinary facts about it. I went down to look at it, and found it was perfectly round and regular in shape, like a wheel lying on its side, without a single irregular bend or curve, and so evenly proportioned that it might have been artificially shaped and hollowed out. It is subdued in colour, pale blue with a tinge of green, has a smell of sulphur and a mineral taste, and the property of healing fractures. It is of no great size, but large enough for the wind to raise waves on its surface. There are no boats on it, as the waters are sacred, but floating islands, green with reeds and sedge and the other plants which grow more profusely on the marshy ground at the edge of the lake. Each island has its peculiar shape and size, and all have their edges worn away by friction, as they are constantly knocking against each other and the shore. They all have the same height and buoyancy, each shallow base dipping into the water

victories over the Etruscans (Livy, IX. 39). P.'s interest is scientific, not historic; cf. the Elder Pliny, *NH* II. 209.

perspicitur, eadem aqua pariter suspensa et mersa. Interdum iunctae copulataeque et continenti similes sunt, interdum discordantibus ventis digeruntur, non numquam destitutae tranquillitate singulae fluitant. 7 Saepe minores maioribus velut cumbulae onerariis adhaerescunt, saepe inter se maiores minoresque quasi cursum certamenque desumunt; rursus omnes in eundem locum adpulsae, qua steterunt promovent terram, et modo hac modo illa lacum reddunt auferuntque, ac tum demum cum medium tenuere non contra 8 hunt. Constat pecora herbas secuta sic in insulas illas ut in extremam ripam procedere solere, nec prius intellegere mobile solum quam litori abrepta quasi inlata et imposita circumfusum undique lacum paveant; mox quo tulerit ventus egressa, non magis se descen 9 disse sentire, quam senserint ascendisse. Idem lacus in flumen egeritur, quod ubi se paulisper oculis dedit specu mergitur alteque conditum meat ac, si quid antequam subduceretur accepit, servat et profert. 10 Haec tibi scripsi, quia nec minus ignota quam mihi nec minus grata credebam. Nam te quoque ut me nihil aeque ac naturae opera delectant. Vale.

like the keel of a boat: and this has the same appearance from all sides, both the part above and the part under water. Sometimes the islands join together to look like a continuous piece of land, sometimes they are driven apart by conflicting winds, while in calm weather they are left to float about separately. The smaller islands often attach themselves to the larger, like small boats to a merchant ship, and both large and small sometimes appear to be racing each other; or they are all driven to one side of the lake to create a headland where they cling to the shore; they remove or restore stretches of the lake on one side or the other, so that its size is unaltered only when they all keep to the centre. Cattle are often known to walk on to the islands while grazing, taking them for the edge of the lake, and only realize that they are on moving ground when carried off from the shore as if forcibly put on board ship, and are terrified to find themselves surrounded by water; then, when they land where the wind has carried them, they are no more conscious of having ended their voyage than they were of embarking on it. Another feature of the lake is the river leading from it, which is visible for a short distance before it enters a cave and continues its course at a great depth; anything thrown in before it disappears is carried along and reappears with it.

I have given you these details because I imagine they are as new and interesting to you as they were to me; natural phenomena are always a great source of interest to us both.

THE LETTERS OF PLINY

XXI

C. PLINIUS ARRIANO SUO S.

1 UT in vita sic in studiis pulcherrimum et humanissimum existimo severitatem comitatemque miscere, ne illa in tristitiam, haec in petulantiam excedat.

2 Qua ratione ductus graviora opera lusibus iocisque distinguo. Ad hos proferendos et tempus et locum opportunissimum elegi, utque iam nunc adsuescerent et ab otiosis et in triclinio audiri, Iulio mense, quo maxime lites interquiescunt, positis ante lectos cathe-

3 dris amicos collocavi. Forte accidit ut eodem die mane in advocationem subitam rogarer, quod mihi causam praeloquendi dedit. Sum enim deprecatus, ne quis ut inreverentem operis argueret, quod recitaturus, quamquam et amicis et paucis, id est iterum amicis, foro et negotiis non abstinuissem. Addidi hunc ordinem me et in scribendo sequi, ut necessitates voluptatibus, seria iucundis anteferrem, ac

4 primum amicis tum mihi scriberem. Liber fuit et opusculis varius et metris. Ita solemus, qui ingenio parum fidimus, satietatis periculum fugere. Recitavi biduo. Hoc adsensus audientium exegit; et tamen ut alii transeunt quaedam imputantque quod

XXI

To Maturus Arrianus

In literature, as in life, I think it a becoming sign of humanity to mingle grave and gay, lest the one becomes too austere and the other indelicate; and this is the principle which leads me to intersperse my more serious works with trifles for amusement. Some of these I had ready to bring out, so I chose the most suitable time and place, and to accustom them from now onwards to being received by a leisured audience in the dining-room, I gathered my friends together in the month of July (which is usually a quiet time in the law courts) and settled them with chairs in front of the couches. It so happened that on the morning of that very day I was unexpectedly summoned to court to give legal assistance, and this gave me a subject for my introductory remarks. For I began by hoping that no one would accuse me of irresponsibility when, on the day I was to give a reading (though this was limited to a small circle of friends), I had not kept myself free from professional duties—that is, the claims of other friends. I went on to say that I kept to the same order in my writing; I put duty before pleasure and serious work before amusement, and wrote primarily for my friends and after them for myself.

The work itself consisted of short pieces in different metres, for that is how those of us with no great confidence in our abilities avoid the risk of boring our public. The reading lasted for two days, at the request of my audience, in spite of the fact that, where-

65

transeant, sic ego nihil praetereo atque etiam non praeterire me dico. Lego enim omnia ut omnia emendem, quod contingere non potest electa recitantibus. 5 At illud modestius et fortasse reverentius; sed hoc simplicius et amantius. Amat enim qui se sic amari putat, ut taedium non pertimescat; et alioqui quid praestant sodales, si conveniunt voluptatis suae causa? Delicatus ac similis ignoto est, qui amici 6 librum bonum mavult audire quam facere. Non dubito cupere te pro cetera mei caritate quam maturissime legere hunc adhuc musteum librum. Leges, sed retractatum, quae causa recitandi fuit; et tamen non nulla iam ex eo nosti. Haec emendata postea vel, quod interdum longiore [1] mora solet, deteriora facta quasi nova rursus et rescripta cognosces. Nam plerisque mutatis ea quoque mutata videntur, quae manent. Vale.

XXII

C. PLINIUS GEMINO SUO S.

1 NOSTINE hos qui omnium libidinum servi, sic aliorum vitiis irascuntur quasi invideant, et gravissime puniunt, quos maxime imitantur? cum eos etiam,

---

[1] longiore *Laetus a*: -ori *θ*: -ora *M*.

as other people omit passages and expect credit for doing so, I make it clear that I am leaving nothing out. I read every word so as to correct every word: a thing which is impossible for readers of selected passages. It may be said that theirs is the more restrained and possibly more considerate practice, but mine is more guileless and affectionate; for the confidence in your friends' affection which makes you have no fear of boring them is proof of your own feeling. Besides, what is the good of having friends if they meet only for their own amusement? It is the dilettante and indifferent listener who would rather listen to a good book by his friend instead of helping to make it so. I don't doubt that your affection for me will make you eager to read this work of mine as soon as possible, before it has lost its freshness; and so you shall, but not until after revision, as this was the purpose of my reading it aloud. Parts of it you have seen already, but after these have been corrected (or changed for the worse, as does sometimes happen after a long delay) you will find new life and style in them. For when the greater part of a book is recast the remainder appears to share in the change.

XXII

To Rosianus Geminus

You must know people who are slaves to every sort of passion while they display a sort of jealous resentment against the faults of others, and show least mercy to those they most resemble; though there are

qui non indigent clementia ullius, nihil magis quam
2 lenitas deceat. Atque ego optimum et emendatissi-
mum existimo, qui ceteris ita ignoscit, tamquam ipse
cotidie peccet, ita peccatis abstinet tamquam nemini
3 ignoscat. Proinde hoc domi hoc foris hoc in omni
vitae genere teneamus, ut nobis implacabiles simus,
exorabiles istis etiam qui dare veniam nisi sibi nes-
ciunt, mandemusque memoriae quod vir mitissimus
et ob hoc quoque maximus Thrasea crebro dicere
solebat: " Qui vitia odit, homines odit." Quaeris
4 fortasse quo commotus haec scribam. Nuper quidam—sed melius coram; quamquam ne tunc quidem. Vereor enim ne id quod improbo consectari[1]
carpere referre huic quod cum maxime praecipimus
repugnet. Quisquis ille qualiscumque sileatur, quem
insignire exempli nihil, non insignire humanitatis
plurimum refert. Vale.

XXIII

C. PLINIUS MARCELLINO SUO S.

1 OMNIA mihi studia, omnes curas, omnia avocamenta
exemit excussit eripuit dolor, quem ex morte Iuni
2 Aviti gravissimum cepi. Latum clavum in domo mea
induerat, suffragio meo adiutus in petendis honoribus
fuerat; ad hoc ita me diligebat, ita verebatur, ut me
formatore morum, me quasi magistro uteretur.

---

[1] consectari *C. F. W. Mueller*: eos sectari $a\theta$: eos insectari *M*.

other people who need no man's forgiveness but whose greatest virtue is their tolerance. My own idea of the truly good and faultless man is one who forgives the faults of others as if he was daily committing them himself, and who keeps himself free of faults as if he could never forgive them. This then should be our rule at home and abroad, in every walk of life: to show no mercy to ourselves and be ready with it for others, even for those who can excuse no failings but their own. Let us always remember what was so often said by Thrasea, whose gift of sympathy made him the great man he was: "Anyone who hates faults hates mankind."

You may wonder what has provoked me to write like this. Someone recently—but I can tell you better when we meet, or better still, not at all, for I am afraid that if I offer any hostile criticism or even tell you what I dislike, it will conflict with this principle to which I attach such importance. The man and his character shall not be told; to expose him would point no moral, but not to do so is a true sign of generosity.

XXIII

To Aefulanus Marcellinus

Work, cares, and distractions—all are interrupted, cut short, and driven out of my mind, for the death of Junius Avitus has been a terrible blow. He had assumed the broad stripe of the senator in my house and had my support when standing for office, and such moreover was his affectionate regard for me that

3 Rarum hoc in adulescentibus nostris. Nam quotus
quisque vel aetati alterius vel auctoritati ut minor
cedit? Statim sapiunt, statim sciunt omnia, neminem verentur, neminem [1] imitantur, atque ipsi sibi
exempla sunt. Sed non Avitus, cuius haec praecipua
prudentia, quod alios prudentiores arbitrabatur, haec
4 praecipua eruditio quod discere volebat. Semper ille
aut de studiis aliquid aut de officiis vitae consulebat,
semper ita recedebat ut melior factus; et erat factus
vel eo quod audierat, vel quod omnino quaesierat.
5 Quod ille obsequium Serviano exactissimo viro
praestitit! quem legatum tribunus ita et intellexit
et cepit, ut ex Germania in Pannoniam transeuntem
non ut commilito sed ut comes adsectatorque sequeretur. Qua industria qua modestia quaestor,
consulibus suis (et plures habuit) non minus iucun-
dus et gratus quam utilis fuit! Quo discursu, qua
vigilantia hanc ipsam aedilitatem cui praereptus est
petiit! Quod vel maxime dolorem meum exulcerat.
6 Obversantur oculis cassi labores, et infructuosae
preces, et honor quem meruit tantum; redit animo
ille latus clavus in penatibus meis sumptus, redeunt
illa prima illa postrema suffragia mea, illi sermones
7 illae consultationes. Adficior adulescentia ipsius,
adficior necessitudinum casu. Erat illi grandis natu

---

[1] verentur nem. *om. Mθ*: nem. verentur imitantur nem. *a*.

---

[1] For Julius Ursus Servianus, see Index.
[2] *i.e.* the *consules ordinarii* and *suffecti* of his year in office.

he took me for his moral guide and mentor. This is
rare in the young people of today, few of whom will
yield to age or authority as being their superior.
They are born with knowledge and understanding of
everything; they show neither respect nor desire to
imitate, and set their own standards.

Avitus was not like this. His wisdom consisted in
his belief that others were wiser than himself, his
learning in his readiness to be taught. He always
sought advice for his studies or his duties in life, and
always went away feeling he was made better; and
indeed he *was* better, either from the advice given
him or from the very fact that he had asked for it.
What deference he showed to the high standards of
Servianus! They first met when Servianus[1] was
legate of Germany, and Avitus, when serving as military tribune, so won his heart that on his transfer to
Pannonia he took the young man with him, not as a
serving soldier so much as a companion and member
of his personal staff. Think of the industry and unassuming manner which won him the liking and
affection of the many consuls[2] who found him so use-
ful as a quaestor, and the energy and concentration
he applied to canvassing for the office of aedile, from
which he has been thus prematurely taken away.
This is what I find most painful to bear; his useless
efforts, his fruitless prayers, the position he deserved
but never held, are always in my mind's eye; the
senator's stripe he assumed in my home, the first
time, and now this last time I supported his election,
our talks and discussions, all come back to me.

I mourn his youth and the plight of his family, for
he leaves an elderly mother, a wife he married only a

parens, erat uxor quam ante annum virginem acceperat, erat filia quam paulo ante sustulerat. Tot
8 spes tot gaudia dies unus in diversa convertit. Modo designatus aedilis, recens maritus recens pater intactum honorem, orbam matrem, viduam uxorem, filiam pupillam ignaram[1] patris reliquit. Accedit lacrimis meis quod absens et impendentis mali nescius, pariter aegrum pariter decessisse cognovi, ne gravissimo dolori timore consuescerem. In tantis tormentis eram cum scriberem haec ⟨ut haec⟩[2] scriberem sola; neque enim nunc aliud aut cogitare aut loqui possum. Vale.

XXIV

C. Plinius Maximo Suo S.

1 Amor in te meus cogit, non ut praecipiam (neque enim praeceptore eges), admoneam tamen, ut quae
2 scis teneas et observes, aut nescire melius. Cogita te missum in provinciam Achaiam, illam veram et meram Graeciam, in qua primum humanitas litterae, etiam fruges inventae esse creduntur; missum ad ordinandum statum liberarum civitatum, id est ad homines maxime homines, ad liberos maxime

---

[1] ignaram *Keil*: ignaram avi *Mθ*: ignaramque *a*.
[2] ut haec scrib. sola *D. S. Robertson*: scrib. sola *Mθ*, om. *a*.

---

[1] He is to act (together with the annual proconsul) as a *corrector*, a special commissioner appointed by the Emperor.

year ago, and a daughter not long born. So many hopes and joys are thus reversed in a single day. He had just been elected aedile, and for a short time he was husband and father: now he has left the post he never held, his mother is childless and his wife a widow, and his daughter is left an orphan, never to know a father's love. I weep the more to think that I was away and knew nothing of the fate hanging over him—the news of his illness and death reached me at the same moment, before apprehension could accustom me to this cruel sorrow. I am in such anguish as I write that this must be all; I can think and speak of nothing else just now.

XXIV

To Valerius (?) Maximus

I know you need no telling, but my love for you prompts me to remind you to keep in mind and put into practice what you know already, or else it would be better for you to remain ignorant. Remember that you have been sent to the province of Achaia, to the pure and genuine Greece, where civilization and literature, and agriculture, too, are believed to have originated; and you have been sent to set in order the constitution of free cities,[1] and are going to free men who are both men and free in the fullest sense, for they have maintained their natural rights

---

Civitates liberae were normally exempt from the governor's authority (cf. X. 47 and 92), as were *civitates foederatae* which had separate treaties with Rome guaranteeing their rights and privileges.

liberos, qui ius a natura datum virtute meritis amici-
3 tia, foedere denique et religione tenuerunt.   Reverere conditores deos et nomina deorum reverere
gloriam veterem et hanc ipsam senectutem, quae in
homine venerabilis, in urbibus sacra. Sit apud te
honor antiquitati, sit ingentibus factis, sit fabulis
quoque. Nihil ex cuiusquam dignitate, nihil ex
4 libertate, nihil etiam ex iactatione decerpseris. Habe
ante oculos hanc esse terram, quae nobis miserit iura,
quae leges non victis sed petentibus dederit, Athenas
esse quas adeas, Lacedaemonem esse quam regas;
quibus reliquam umbram et residuum libertatis nom-
5 en eripere durum ferum barbarum est. Vides a medicis, quamquam in adversa valetudine nihil servi ac
liberi differant, mollius tamen liberos clementiusque
tractari. Recordare quid quaeque civitas fuerit,
non ut despicias quod esse desierit; absit superbia
6 asperitas. Nec timueris contemptum. An con-
temnitur qui imperium qui fasces habet, nisi humilis
et sordidus, et qui se primus ipse contemnit? Male
vim suam potestas aliorum contumeliis experitur,
male terrore veneratio adquiritur, longeque valentior
amor ad obtinendum quod velis quam timor. Nam
timor abit si recedas, manet amor, ac sicut ille in
7 odium hic in reverentiam vertitur. Te vero etiam
atque etiam (repetam enim) meminisse oportet officii
tui titulum ac tibi ipsum interpretari, quale quantum-

by their courage, merits, and friendly relationships, and finally by treaty and sanction of religion. Respect the gods their founders and the names they bear, respect their ancient glory and their very age, which in man commands our veneration, in cities our reverence. Pay regard to their antiquity, their heroic deeds, and the legends of their past. Do not detract from anyone's dignity, independence, or even pride, but always bear in mind that this is the land which provided us with justice and gave us laws, not after conquering us but at our request; that it is Athens you go to and Sparta you rule, and to rob them of the name and shadow of freedom, which is all that now remains to them, would be an act of cruelty, ignorance and barbarism. (Illness is the same in a slave as in a free man, but you will have observed how a doctor will treat the free man with more kindness and consideration.) Remember what each city was once, but without looking down on it for being so no longer; do not allow yourself to be hard or domineering, and have no fear that you will be despised for this. No one who bears the insignia of supreme authority is despised unless his own meanness and ignobility show that he must be the first to despise himself. It is a poor thing if authority can only test its powers by insults to others, and if homage is to be won by terror; affection is far more effective than fear in gaining you your ends. Fear disappears at your departure, affection remains, and, whereas fear engenders hatred, affection develops into genuine regard.

Never, never forget (I must repeat this) the official title you bear, and keep clearly in mind what it means to establish order in the constitution of free

que sit ordinare statum liberarum civitatum. Nam quid ordinatione civilius, quid libertate pretiosius?

8 Porro quam turpe, si ordinatio eversione, libertas servitute mutetur! Accedit quod tibi certamen est tecum: onerat te quaesturae tuae fama, quam ex Bithynia optimam revexisti; onerat testimonium principis; onerat tribunatus, praetura atque haec

9 ipsa legatio quasi praemium data. Quo magis nitendum est ne in longinqua provincia quam suburbana, ne inter servientes quam liberos, ne sorte quam iudicio missus, ne rudis et incognitus quam exploratus probatusque humanior melior peritior fuisse videaris, cum sit alioqui, ut saepe audisti saepe legisti, multo deformius amittere quam non adsequi laudem.

10 Haec velim credas, quod initio dixi, scripsisse me admonentem, non praecipientem; quamquam praecipientem quoque. Quippe non vereor, in amore ne modum excesserim. Neque enim periculum est ne sit nimium quod esse maximum debet. Vale.

cities, for nothing can serve a city like ordered rule and nothing is so precious as freedom; nor can anything equal the disgrace should order be overthrown and freedom give place to servitude. You are moreover your own rival; you bring with you the excellent reputation you won during your quaestorship in Bithynia, you bring the Emperor's recognition and your experience as tribune, praetor, and holder of your present office, given you as a reward for your services. You must then make every effort not to let it appear that you were a better, kinder, and more experienced administrator in a remote province than in one nearer Rome, and when dealing with servile rather than free men, when you were elected by lot instead of being the Emperor's choice, and at a time when you were raw and unknown before being tested and proved by experience. And, besides, as you have often heard and read, it is far more shameful to lose a reputation than not to win one.

Please believe, as I said at the start, that this letter was intended not to tell, but to remind you of your duties—though I know I am really telling you as well, as I am not afraid of letting my affection carry me too far; there is no danger of excess where there ought to be no limits.

BOOK IX

LIBER NONUS

I

C. PLINIUS MAXIMO SUO S.

1 SAEPE te monui, ut libros quos vel pro te vel in
Plantam, immo et pro te et in illum (ita enim materia
cogebat), composuisti quam maturissime emitteres;
quod nunc praecipue morte eius audita et hortor et
2 moneo. Quamvis enim legeris multis legendosque
dederis, nolo tamen quemquam opinari defuncto
demum incohatos, quos incolumi eo peregisti. Salva
3 sit tibi constantiae fama. Erit autem, si notum
aequis iniquisque fuerit non post inimici mortem
scribendi tibi natam esse fiduciam, sed iam paratam
4 editionem morte praeventam. Et simul vitabis illud
οὐχ ὁσίη φθιμένοισι. Nam quod de vivente scriptum de vivente recitatum est,[1] in defunctum quoque
tamquam viventem adhuc editur, si editur statim.
Igitur si quid aliud in manibus, interim differ; hoc

---

[1] de vivente recitatum *a et (post* est) *i: om. Mγ, Stout.*

---

[1] Pompeius Planta, prefect of Egypt 98–100. This letter
is unlikely to be addressed to his successor, Vibius Maximus, as
he was condemned for malpractices in 107. If the recipient
is Novius M., cf. IV. 20 and V. 5 (S-W). Planta was the

BOOK IX

I

To Novius (?) Maximus

I HAVE often urged you to be as quick as you can about publishing the articles you wrote in your own defence or against Planta[1]—or rather, with both ends in view as the subject demanded. Now that I have news of his death, I really do beg you to do this. I know you have read them to a number of people and lent them to others to read, but I don't want anyone to imagine that you waited for his death to begin what you had in fact completed during his lifetime. You must keep up your reputation for standing by your convictions, and can do so if it is known to your friends and enemies alike that you did not pluck up courage to write as a result of your enemy's death, but that your work was already finished for publication when his death intervened. At the same time you will avoid Homer's "impiety of boasting over the dead,"[2] for anything written and read about a man in his lifetime can still be published against him after death as if he were still alive, so long as it is published at once. So, if you have anything else in hand, lay it aside for the present and put

author of a work on the Civil Wars of 69 (Schol. to Juv. *Sat.* II. 99) possibly the reason for Maximus's attack.
[2] Odyssey XXII, 412.

perfice, quod nobis qui legimus olim absolutum videtur. Sed iam videatur et tibi, cuius cunctationem nec res ipsa desiderat, et temporis ratio praecidit. Vale.

II

C. PLINIUS SABINO SUO S.

1 FACIS iucunde quod non solum plurimas epistulas meas verum etiam longissimas[1] flagitas; in quibus parcior fui partim quia tuas occupationes verebar, partim quia ipse multum distringebar plerumque frigidis negotiis quae simul et avocant animum et comminuunt. Praeterea nec materia plura scri-2 bendi dabatur. Neque enim eadem nostra condicio quae M. Tulli, ad cuius exemplum nos vocas. Illi enim et copiosissimum ingenium, et par ingenio qua varietas rerum qua magnitudo largissime suppetebat; 3 nos quam angustis terminis claudamur etiam tacente me perspicis, nisi forte volumus scholasticas tibi atque, 4 ut ita dicam, umbraticas litteras mittere. Sed nihil minus aptum arbitramur, cum arma vestra cum castra, cum denique cornua tubas sudorem pulverem soles 5 cogitamus. Habes, ut puto, iustam excusationem, quam tamen dubito an tibi probari velim. Est enim summi amoris negare veniam brevibus epistulis amicorum, quamvis scias illis constare rationem. Vale.

---

[1] n. s. plurimas epistulas meas v. e. longissimas γ: n. s. epistulas v. e. plurimas M, *Stout*.

---

[1] Tacitus expresses the same regret in *Ann.* IV. 32.

the finishing touch to these speeches; although those of us who have read them think they reached perfection long ago. You should think the same, for the subject calls for action and the circumstances should cut short your hesitation.

II

To Statius Sabinus

It is kind of you to ask me to make my letters long as well as frequent. I have been rather doubtful about doing so, partly out of consideration for your busy life, partly because my own time has been much taken up, mostly with trivial duties which interrupt concentration and make it difficult to resume it. Besides, I lacked subject-matter for writing more. You want me to follow Cicero's example, but my position is very different from his. He was not only richly gifted but was supplied with a wealth of varied and important topics to suit his abilities, though you know without my telling you the narrow limits confining me.[1] I might decide to send you a sort of schoolboy's exercise for a letter, but I can imagine nothing less suitable, when I think of your life under arms, the camps, bugles and trumpets, sweat and dust and heat of the sun.

There is my excuse, a reasonable one I think, though I'm not sure if I want you to accept it; it is a sign of true affection to refuse to forgive a friend for the shortness of his letters although you know he has good reason for them.

III

C. PLINIUS PAULINO SUO S.

1 ALIUS aliud:[1] ego beatissimum existimo, qui bonae
mansuraeque famae praesumptione perfruitur, certus-
que posteritatis cum futura gloria vivit. Ac mihi
nisi praemium aeternitatis ante oculos, pingue illud
2 altumque otium placeat. Etenim omnes homines
arbitror oportere aut immortalitatem suam aut
mortalitatem cogitare, et illos quidem contendere
eniti, hos quiescere remitti, nec brevem vitam caducis
laboribus fatigare, ut video multos misera simul et ingrata imagine industriae ad vilitatem sui pervenire.
3 Haec ego tecum quae cotidie mecum, ut desinam mecum, si dissenties tu; quamquam non dissenties, ut
qui semper clarum aliquid et immortale meditere.
Vale.

IV

C. PLINIVS MACRINO SVO S.

1 VERERER ne immodicam orationem putares, quam
cum hac epistula accipies, nisi esset generis eius ut
saepe incipere saepe[2] desinere videatur. Nam singulis criminibus singulae velut causae continentur.
2 Poteris ergo, undecumque coeperis ubicumque
desieris, quae deinceps sequentur et quasi incipientia

---

[1] aliud *Mγ*: alium *ai, Guillemin, Schuster.*
[2] incipere saepe *ai*: om. *Mγ, Stout.*

---

[1] This fits the case of Classicus and his accomplices, III. 9.

III

To Valerius Paulinus

Opinions differ, but my idea of the truly happy man is of one who enjoys the anticipation of a good and lasting reputation, and, confident in the verdict of posterity, lives in the knowledge of the fame that is to come. Were my own eyes not fixed on the reward of immortality I could be happy in an easy life of complete retirement, for everyone, I think, must choose between two considerations: that fame is imperishable or man is mortal. The former will lead him to a life of toil and effort, the latter will teach him to relax quietly and not to wear out his short existence with vain endeavours, as I see many doing, though their semblance of industry, as wretched as it is unrewarding, only brings them to despise themselves. I tell you this as I tell it to myself every day, so that I can stop if you disagree; but I doubt if you will, when you have some great and immortal project always in mind.

IV

To Caecilius Macrinus

With this letter I am sending a speech which I might fear you would find too long, were it not the kind which gives the impression of repeated starts and conclusions; for each separate charge is treated as a separate case.[1] So, wherever you begin and leave off, you will be able to read what follows either

85

legere et quasi cohaerentia, meque in universitate
longissimum, brevissimum in partibus iudicare. Vale.

V

C. PLINIUS TIRONI SUO S.

1 EGREGIE facis (inquiro enim) et persevera, quod
iustitiam tuam provincialibus multa humanitate com-
mendas; cuius praecipua pars est honestissimum
quemque complecti, atque ita a minoribus amari, ut
2 simul a principibus diligare. Plerique autem dum
verentur, ne gratiae potentium nimium impertire
videantur, sinisteritatis atque etiam malignitatis
3 famam consequuntur. A quo vitio tu longe recessis-
ti, scio, sed temperare mihi non possum quominus
laudem similis monenti, quod eum modum tenes ut
discrimina ordinum dignitatumque custodias; quae
si confusa turbata permixta sunt, nihil est ipsa
aequalitate inaequalius. Vale.

VI

C. PLINIUS CALVISIO SUO S.

1 OMNE hoc tempus inter pugillares ac libellos iucun-
dissima quiete transmisi. " Quemadmodum " inquis
" in urbe potuisti? " Circenses erant, quo genere
spectaculi ne levissime quidem teneor. Nihil novum

---

[1] Tiro is now in Baetica, of which P. was patron (III. 4. 5–6).

as a new subject or as part of the whole, and judge me long-winded over the complete speech but brief enough in each section.

V

To Calestrius Tiro

I HEAR on enquiry that you are doing splendidly (and I hope this will continue) in your administration of justice in your province;[1] by your tact you make it accepted by the people, a tact which consists mainly in making every honest man your friend, and winning the affection of the humble without losing the regard of their superiors. Yet most people in their fear of appearing to allow too many concessions to the influence of the great, acquire the reputation of being clumsy and even offensive. You are quite free from this fault I know, but I cannot help sounding as if I were proffering advice when I meant to congratulate you on the way in which you preserve the distinctions of class and rank; once these are thrown into confusion and destroyed, nothing is more unequal than the resultant " equality."

VI

To Calvisius Rufus

I HAVE been spending all the last few days among my notes and papers in most welcome peace. How could I—in the city? The Races were on, a type of spectacle which has never had the slightest attraction for me. I can find nothing new or different in

nihil varium, nihil quod non semel spectasse sufficiat.
2 Quo magis miror tot milia virorum tam pueriliter
identidem cupere currentes equos, insistentes curri-
bus homines videre. Si tamen aut velocitate equo-
rum aut hominum arte traherentur, esset ratio non
nulla; nunc favent panno pannum amant, et si in
ipso cursu medioque certamine hic color illuc ille
huc transferatur, studium favorque transibit, et
repente agitatores illos equos illos, quos procul nosci-
3 tant, quorum clamitant nomina relinquent. Tanta
gratia tanta auctoritas in una vilissima tunica, mitto
apud vulgus, quod vilius tunica, sed apud quosdam
graves homines; quos ego cum recordor, in re inani
frigida adsidua, tam insatiabiliter desidere, capio
aliquam voluptatem, quod hac voluptate non capior.
4 Ac per hos dies libentissime otium meum in litteris
colloco, quos alii otiosissimis occupationibus perdunt.
Vale.

VII

C. PLINIUS ROMANO SUO S.

1 AEDIFICARE te scribis. Bene est, inveni patroci-
ium; aedifico enim iam ratione quia tecum. Nam
hoc quoque non dissimile quod ad mare tu, ego ad
2 Larium lacum. Huius in litore plures meae villae,
3 sed duae maxime ut [1] delectant ita exercent. Altera

---

[1] maxime ut *M*: ut maxime *γ*.

them: once seen is enough, so it surprises me all the more that so many thousands of adult men should have such a childish passion for watching galloping horses and drivers standing in chariots, over and over again. If they were attracted by the speed of the horses or the drivers' skill one could account for it, but in fact it is the racing-colours they really support and care about, and if the colours were to be exchanged in mid-course during a race, they would transfer their favour and enthusiasm and rapidly desert the famous drivers and horses whose names they shout as they recognize them from afar. Such is the popularity and importance of a worthless shirt —I don't mean with the crowd, which is worth less than the shirt, but with certain serious individuals. When I think how this futile, tedious, monotonous business can keep them sitting endlessly in their seats, I take pleasure in the fact that their pleasure is not mine. And I have been very glad to make good use of my idle hours with literary work during these days which others have wasted in the idlest of occupations.

VII

To Voconius Romanus

I AM delighted to hear you are building; now I can count on you to plead my case, and be justified in my own plans if you are building too. We have a further point in common—you are building by the sea and I on the shores of Lake Como. There I have several houses, two of which give me a lot of pleasure but a

imposita saxis more Baiano lacum prospicit, altera aeque more Baiano lacum tangit. Itaque illam tragoediam, hanc adpellare comoediam soleo, illam quod quasi cothurnis, hanc quod quasi socculis sustinetur. Sua utrique amoenitas, et utraque possi-
4 denti ipsa diversitate iucundior. Haec lacu propius, illa latius utitur; haec unum sinum molli curvamine amplectitur, illa editissimo dorso duos dirimit; illic recta gestatio longo limite super litus extenditur, hic spatiosissimo xysto leviter inflectitur; illa fluctus non sentit haec frangit; ex illa possis despicere piscantes, ex hac ipse piscari, hamumque de cubiculo ac paene etiam de lectulo ut e naucula iacere. Hae mihi causae utrique quae desunt adstruendi ob ea quae
5 supersunt. Etsi quid ego rationem tibi? apud quem pro ratione erit idem facere. Vale.

VIII

C. Plinius Augurino Suo S.

1 Si laudatus a te laudare te coepero, vereor ne non tam proferre iudicium meum quam referre gratiam videar. Sed licet videar, omnia scripta tua pulcher-
2 rima existimo, maxime tamen illa de nobis. Accidit

---

[1] The popular resort on the coast of Campania.
[2] See IV. 27. 4.

corresponding amount of work. One is built on the rocks with a view over the lake, like the houses at Baiae,[1] the other stands on the very edge of the water in the same style, and so I have named one Tragedy, because it seems to be raised on actor's boots, and the other Comedy, because it wears low shoes. Each has its special charm and seems the more attractive to the occupant by contrast with the other. The former has a wider view of the lake, the latter a closer one, as it is built to curve gradually round a single bay, following its line by a broad terrace; while the other stands on a high ridge dividing two bays, where a straight drive extends for some distance above the shore. One is untouched by the water and you can look down from its height to the fishermen below, while the waves break against the other and you can fish from it yourself, casting your line from your bedroom window and practically from your bed as if you were in a boat. All these existing amenities give me a reason for building necessary additions on to both houses; though I know I need not explain myself to you, when this is no more than you are doing yourself.

VIII

To Sentius Augurinus

If I begin praising you after your praise of me,[2] I fear I shall look as though I am only showing gratitude instead of giving a true opinion. All the same, I do think all your written works are very fine, but especially those which deal with me. For this there

hoc una eademque de causa. Nam et tu, quae de
amicis, optime scribis, et ego, quae de me, ut optima
lego. Vale.

IX

C. PLINIUS COLONO SUO S.

1 UNICE probo quod Pompei Quintiani morte tam
dolenter adficeris, ut amissi caritatem desiderio ex-
tendas, non ut plerique qui tantum viventes amant
seu potius amare se simulant, ac ne simulant quidem
nisi quos florentes vident; nam miserorum non secus
ac defunctorum obliviscuntur. Sed tibi perennis
fides tantaque in amore constantia, ut finiri nisi tua
2 morte non possit. Et hercule is fuit Quintianus,
quem diligi deceat ipsius exemplo. Felices amabat,
miseros tuebatur, desiderabat amissos. Iam illa
quanta probitas in ore, quanta in sermone cunctatio,
quam pari libra gravitas comitasque! quod studium
litterarum, quod iudicium! qua pietate cum dissimillimo patre vivebat! quam non obstabat illi, quo minus
3 vir optimus videretur, quod erat optimus filius! Sed
quid dolorem tuum exulcero? Quamquam sic amasti
iuvenem ut hoc potius quam de illo sileri velis, a me
praesertim cuius praedicatione putas vitam eius

is one and the same reason—you are at your best in writing about your friends, and I find it your best when it is about myself.

IX

To Colonus

I VERY much appreciate your grief at the death of Pompeius Quintianus, and can understand how your love for him is increased by your sense of loss; unlike most people who feel affection only for the living, or rather make a show of doing so, and not even that unless they see their friends prospering: the unfortunate they forget as quickly as the dead. But your loyalty is unfailing, and your constancy in love too great for anything short of your own death to end it; and Quintianus was indeed a man who deserved affection through the example he gave of it. He loved his friends in success, helped them in misfortune, and mourned them in death. Think, too, of his honest countenance and deliberate speech, the happy balance he kept between reserve and friendliness, and his enthusiasm for literature combined with his critical powers: think how he lived dutifully with a father very unlike himself, and though an excellent son was never prevented from showing his merits as a man!

But I must not aggravate your suffering, though I know you loved the young man so dearly that you find suffering preferable to silence about him; and least of all do you want silence from me, when I can voice the praise which you feel can do honour to his

ornari, memoriam prorogari, ipsamque illam qua est
raptus aetatem posse restitui. Vale.

X

C. Plinius Tacito Suo S.

1 Cupio praeceptis tuis parere; sed aprorum tanta
penuria est, ut Minervae et Dianae, quas ais pariter
2 colendas, convenire non possit. Itaque Minervae
tantum serviendum est, delicate tamen ut in secessu
et aestate. In via plane non nulla leviora statimque
delenda ea garrulitate qua sermones in vehiculo
seruntur extendi. His quaedam addidi in villa, cum
aliud non liberet. Itaque poemata quiescunt, quae
tu inter nemora et lucos commodissime perfici putas.
3 Oratiunculam unam alteram retractavi; quamquam
id genus operis inamabile inamoenum, magisque
laboribus ruris quam voluptatibus simile. Vale.

XI

C. Plinius Gemino Suo S.

1 Epistulam tuam iucundissimam accepi,[1] eo maxime
quod aliquid ad te scribi volebas, quod libris inseri

---

[1] accepi M: recepi γ.

---

[1] Written from his Tuscan estate. There is a possible reference to Tacitus, *Dial.* 9. 6 in s. 2. Cf. R. T. Bruyère, *Class.
Phil.* XLIX, p. 166.

life, prolong his memory, and give back to him the years taken from him.

X

To Cornelius Tacitus

I SHOULD like to obey your orders, but when you tell me I ought to honour Diana along with Minerva I find it impossible—there is such a shortage of boars. So I can only serve Minerva, and even her in the lazy way to be expected during a summer holiday. On my way here I made up some bits of nonsense (not worth keeping) in the conversational style one uses when travelling, and I added something to them once I was here and had nothing better to do; but peace reigns over the poems which you fancy are only too easy to finish in the woods and groves.[1] I have revised one or two short speeches, though this is the sort of disagreeable task I detest and is more like one of the hardships of country life than its pleasures.

XI

To Rosianus Geminus

I HAVE your letter, a specially welcome one as you want me to write you something which can be included in your[2] published work. I will find a subject,

---

[2] This could equally refer to P.'s own work, in which case Geminus wants a letter addressed to him in P.'s next volume.

posset. Obveniet materia vel haec ipsa quam mon-
stras, vel potior alia. Sunt enim in hac offendicula
2 non nulla: circumfer oculos et occurrent. Biblio-
polas Lugduni esse non putabam ac tanto libentius
ex litteris tuis cognovi venditari libellos meos, quibus
peregre manere gratiam quam in urbe collegerint
delector. Incipio enim satis absolutum existimare,
de quo tanta diversitate regionum discreta hominum iudicia consentiunt. Vale.

XII

C. Plinius Iuniori Suo S.

1 Castigabat quidam filium suum quod paulo sump-
tuosius equos et canes emeret. Huic ego iuvene
digresso: "Heus tu, numquamne fecisti, quod a
patre corripi posset? 'Fecisti' dico? Non interdum facis quod filius tuus, si repente pater ille tu
filius, pari gravitate reprehendat? Non omnes
homines aliquo errore ducuntur? Non hic in illo
2 sibi, in hoc alius indulget?" Haec tibi admonitus
immodicae severitatis exemplo, pro amore mutuo
scripsi, ne quando tu quoque filium tuum acerbius
duriusque tractares. Cogita et illum puerum esse et
te fuisse, atque ita hoc quod es pater utere, ut memi-
neris et hominem esse te et hominis patrem. Vale.

---

¹ Lyon was the capital of the Three Gauls and a town of
some culture; Caligula had held a contest in oratory there
(Suet. *Cal.* 20). Cf. Martial's pleasure in hearing that his
verses are read at Vienne (Martial VII. 88).
² For Pliny's tolerance, cf. VIII. 22.

either the one you suggest or something preferable, for yours may give offence in certain quarters—use your eyes and you will see. I didn't think there were any booksellers in Lugdunum,[1] so I was all the more pleased to learn from your letter that my efforts are being sold. I'm glad they retain abroad the popularity they won in Rome, and I'm beginning to think my work must really be quite good when public opinion in such widely different places is agreed about it.

XII

To Terentius Junior

SOMEONE was reproving his son for spending rather too much buying horses and dogs. When the young man had left us I said to his father: "Well, have *you* never done anything your father could complain about? Or rather, don't you still sometimes do things which your son could criticize as severely if he suddenly became father and you his son? Surely everyone is liable to make mistakes and everyone has his own foibles?" I took warning myself from this instance of undue severity, and am writing to you as one friend to another so that you, too, may never be too harsh and strict with your son. Remember that he is a boy and you have been a boy yourself, and use your rights as a father without forgetting that you are only human and so is your son.[2]

XIII

C. PLINIUS QUADRATO SUO S.

1 QUANTO studiosius intentiusque legisti libros quos
de Helvidi ultione composui, tanto impensius postulas,
ut perscribam tibi quaeque extra libros quaeque
circa libros, totum denique ordinem rei cui per aetatem non interfuisti.

2 Occiso Domitiano statui mecum ac deliberavi, esse
magnam pulchramque materiam insectandi nocentes,
miseros vindicandi, se proferendi. Porro inter multa
scelera multorum nullum atrocius videbatur, quam
quod in senatu senator senatori, praetorius consulari,

3 reo iudex manus intulisset. Fuerat alioqui mihi cum
Helvidio amicitia, quanta potuerat esse cum eo, qui
metu temporum nomen ingens paresque virtutes
secessu tegebat; fuerat cum Arria et Fannia, quarum
altera Helvidi noverca, altera mater novercae. Sed
non ita me iura privata, ut publicum fas et indignitas

4 facti et exempli ratio incitabat. Ac primis quidem
diebus redditae libertatis pro se quisque inimicos suos,
dumtaxat minores, incondito turbidoque clamore

---

¹ The younger Helvidius Priscus. See Index, and Introduction, p. xiv.

² Publicius Certus, active at the trial of Senecio and Helvidius in 93; cf. III. 11 and VII. 19; Tac. *Agr.* 45.

³ Coins of Nerva for 96 show *libertas publica* on the reverse
(S.27b).

⁴ P. had originally intended to attack Regulus, but perhaps
found him too powerful; see I. 5. 15–16.

XIII

To Ummidius Quadratus

THE more thoroughly you apply yourself to reading my speeches in vindication of Helvidius,[1] the more pressing becomes your demand that I should give you a full account of the particulars not covered by the speeches as well as those arising out of them—in fact you want the whole sequence of the events which you were too young to witness yourself.

Once Domitian was killed I decided on reflection that this was a truly splendid opportunity for attacking the guilty, avenging the injured, and making oneself known. Moreover, though many crimes had been committed by numerous persons, none seemed so shocking as the violent attack in the Senate-house made by a senator on a fellow senator, by a praetorian[2] acting as judge on a consular who had been brought to trial. I had also been the friend of Helvidius, as far as friendship was possible with one who had been driven through fear of the times to hide his famous name and equally famous virtues in retirement, and the friend of his stepmother Fannia and her mother Arria. But I was not moved to act so much by personal obligations as by the demands of common justice, the enormity of the deed, and the thought of establishing a precedent. Now, in the early days after liberty was restored,[3] everyone had acted for himself, brought his personal enemies to trial (if they were not too powerful),[4] and had them condemned amid the general confusion and chaos. By contrast I believed that the proper course, as well

99

postulaverat simul et oppresserat. Ego et modestius
et constantius arbitratus immanissimum reum non
communi temporum invidia, sed proprio crimine
urgere, cum iam satis primus ille impetus defremuisset[1] et languidior in dies ira ad iustitiam redisset,
quamquam tum maxime tristis amissa nuper uxore,
mitto ad Anteiam (nupta haec Helvidio fuerat); rogo
ut veniat, quia me recens adhuc luctus limine conti-
5 neret. Ut venit, " Destinatum est " inquam " mihi
maritum tuum non inultum pati. Nuntia Arriae et
Fanniae " (ab exsilio redierant), " consule te, consule
illas, an velitis adscribi facto, in quo ego comite non
egeo; sed non ita gloriae meae faverim, ut vobis
societate eius invideam." Perfert Anteia mandata,
nec illae morantur.
6 Opportune senatus intra diem tertium. Omnia
ego semper ad Corellium rettuli, quem providentis-
simum aetatis nostrae sapientissimumque cognovi:
in hoc tamen contentus consilio meo fui veritus ne
vetaret; erat enim cunctantior cautiorque. Sed
non sustinui inducere in animum, quominus illi
eodem die facturum me indicarem, quod an facerem
non deliberabam, expertus usu de eo quod desti-
naveris non esse consulendos quibus consultis obsequi
7 debeas. Venio in senatum, ius dicendi peto, dico

---

¹ defremuisset *M*: defervisset γ.

---

¹ His second wife, daughter of Pompeia Celerina.
² *i.e.* permission to raise a point for discussion before the
formal session opened. This is later withdrawn (s. 9).

as the more effective, was to deal with this atrocious
criminal not through the universal hatred of Domitian's time, but by bringing a specific charge against
him at a moment when the first outburst had spent
itself and the fury which was daily abating had
yielded to justice. So though I was greatly distressed at the time by the recent death of my wife,[1]
I sent a message to Anteia (widow of Helvidius)
asking her to visit me, as I was kept indoors by my
recent bereavement. When she came I told her I
had determined not to leave her husband unavenged.
" Tell this to Arria and Fannia," I said (for they were
back from exile). " Talk it over with them and see
whether you wish to be associated with this case. I
don't need support, but I am not so jealous for my
own glory as to grudge you a share in it." Anteia
did as I asked and the women acted promptly.

Fortunately the Senate met on the next day but
one. I was in the habit of referring everything to
Corellius Rufus, whom I knew to possess the greatest
foresight and wisdom of our time, but on this occasion I was satisfied with my own judgement; for I was
afraid he might forbid me to proceed, being rather
cautious and hesitant. However, I could not bring
myself not to tell him of my intended action on the
actual day, when my decision was made. (I have
learned from experience that, if your mind is already
made up, you should not consult people whose advice you should take if you ask for it.) I entered
the Senate, asked for permission to speak,[2] and for a
while won warm approval for what I was saying,
but as soon as I mentioned the charge and indicated
(though not yet by name) who was to be accused,

paulisper maximo adsensu. Ubi coepi crimen attingere, reum destinare, adhuc tamen sine nomine, undique mihi reclamari. Alius: " Sciamus, quis sit de quo extra ordinem referas ", alius: " Quis est
8 ante relationem reus? ", alius: " Salvi simus, qui supersumus." Audio imperturbatus interritus: tantum susceptae rei honestas valet, tantumque ad fiduciam vel metum differt, nolint homines quod facias an non probent. Longum est omnia quae tunc hinc
9 inde iacta sunt recensere. Novissime consul: " Secunde, sententiae loco dices, si quid volueris." " Permiseras " inquam " quod usque adhuc omnibus
10 permisisti." Resido; aguntur alia. Interim me quidam ex consularibus amicis, secreto curatoque sermone, quasi nimis fortiter incauteque progressum corripit revocat, monet ut desistam, adicit etiam:
11 " Notabilem te futuris principibus fecisti." " Esto " inquam " dum malis." Vix ille discesserat, rursus alter: " Quid audes? quo ruis? quibus te periculis obicis? quid praesentibus confidis incertus futurorum? Lacessis hominem iam praefectum aerarii et brevi consulem, praeterea qua gratia quibus amicitiis fultum!" Nominat quendam, qui tunc ad orientem amplissimum [1] exercitum non sine magnis dubiisque
12 rumoribus obtinebat. Ad haec ego: " ' Omnia praecepi atque animo mecum ante peregi ' nec

[1] *post* amplissimum *add.* et famosissimum *a: om. γ.*

---

[1] An indication of the general feeling of insecurity in the early days of Nerva's reign, before the mutiny of the praetorian guard and Trajan's adoption; cf. *Pan.* 5–6.

there was a general outcry against me. " Tell us who
is the object of this irregular attack! " " Who is being charged before notice is served? " " Let us
survivors remain alive! " and so on. I listened, calm
and unafraid; such is the strength to be won from an
honest cause, and so much does confidence or fear
depend on whether one's conduct meets with active
opposition or no more than disapproval. It would
take too long to recount all the arguments on both
sides, but finally the consul told me that if I had anything to say I could speak in my proper turn. I
pointed out that I had only been granted the permission which was never refused anyone, and then
sat down while other business was dealt with.
Meanwhile, one of my friends among the consulars
took me aside privately and rebuked me in carefully
chosen words for coming forward so rashly and reck-
lessly, advised me to desist, and added that I had
made myself a marked man in the eyes of future
Emperors.[1] " Never mind," said I, " as long as they
are bad ones." Scarcely had he left me when another began: " What are you trying to do? Where
are you heading? What about the risks you are run-
ning? Why such confidence in the present when the
future is uncertain? You are challenging a man who
is already a Treasury official and will soon be consul,
and has besides such influence and friends to support
him! " (He named someone[2] who was then in the
east, at the head of a powerful and celebrated army,
and about whom serious though unconfirmed ru-
mours were circulating.) To this I replied, " ' All
have I foreseen and gone through in my mind;'[3]

[2] Unidentified.　　　　　　[3] *Aeneid* VI. 105.

recuso, si ita casus attulerit, luere poenas ob honestissimum factum, dum flagitiosissimum ulciscor."

13   Iam censendi tempus. Dicit Domitius Apollinaris
consul designatus, dicit Fabricius Veiento, Fabius
Postuminus,[1] Bittius Proculus collega Publici Certi,
de quo agebatur, uxoris autem meae quam amiseram
vitricus, post hos Ammius Flaccus. Omnes Certum
nondum a me nominatum ut nominatum defendunt
crimenque quasi in medio relictum defensione
14 suscipiunt. Quae praeterea dixerint, non est necesse
narrare: in libris habes; sum enim cuncta ipsorum
15 verbis persecutus. Dicunt contra Avidius Quietus,
Cornutus Tertullus: Quietus, iniquissimum esse
querelas dolentium excludi, ideoque Arriae et Fanniae ius querendi non auferendum, nec interesse cuius
16 ordinis quis sit, sed quam causam habeat; Cornutus,
datum se a consulibus tutorem Helvidi filiae petentibus matre eius et vitrico; nunc quoque non sustinere
deserere officii sui partes, in quo tamen et suo dolori
modum imponere et optimarum feminarum perferre
modestissimum adfectum; quas contentas esse ad-
monere senatum Publici Certi cruentae adulationis et
petere, si poena flagitii manifestissimi remittatur, nota
17 certe quasi censoria inuratur. Tum Satrius Rufus
medio ambiguoque sermone " Puto " inquit " iniu-

---

[1] Posthuminus *a*: Postumius *γ*: Maximinus *M*.

if it is to be my fate, I am prepared to face the penalty for an honest deed while punishing a criminal one."

By now it was time for members to give their opinions. Domitius Apollinaris the consul-elect, Fabricius Veiento, Fabius Postuminus, Bittius Proculus, colleague of Publicius Certus (the subject of the debate) and stepfather of my late wife, all spoke, and were followed by Ammius Flaccus. All defended Certus as if I had named him (though I had not yet done so), and set about refuting a charge as yet unspecified. What else they said I needn't tell you, as you have it all in the published speeches—I gave it all in full, in the words of the speakers.

Avidius Quietus and Cornutus Tertullus then spoke on the opposite side. Quietus argued that it was quite unjust to refuse to hear the complaints of injured parties, and that therefore Arria and Fannia should not be denied their right of protest; what mattered was not a man's position but the case he had to answer. Cornutus said that the consuls had appointed him guardian to Helvidius's daughter at the request of her mother and stepfather, and even at the present time he could not think of giving up his responsibilities; however, he would set a limit to his personal indignation and comply with the very moderate sentiments of these excellent women, who asked no more than to remind the Senate of the bloodstained servility of Publicius Certus and to petition that if such flagrant crime were to go unpunished, he might at least be branded with some degradation like the former censors' mark. Then Satrius Rufus made a vague and ambiguous sort of

riam factam Publicio Certo, si non absolvitur; nominatus est ab amicis Arriae et Fanniae, nominatus ab amicis suis. Nec debemus solliciti esse; idem enim nos, qui bene sentimus de homine, et iudicaturi sumus. Si innocens est, sicut et spero et malo et, donec aliquid probetur, credo, poteritis absolvere."

18 Haec illi quo quisque ordine citabantur. Venitur ad me. Consurgo, utor initio quod in libro est, respondeo singulis. Mirum qua intentione, quibus clamoribus omnia exceperint, qui modo reclamabant: tanta conversio vel negotii dignitatem vel proventum orationis vel actoris constantiam subsecuta est.

19 Finio. Incipit respondere Veiento; nemo patitur; obturbatur obstrepitur, adeo quidem ut diceret: " Rogo, patres conscripti, ne me cogatis implorare auxilium tribunorum." Et statim Murena tribunus: " Permitto tibi, vir clarissime Veiento, dicere."

20 Tunc quoque reclamatur. Inter moras consul citatis nominibus et peracta discessione mittit senatum, ac paene adhuc stantem temptantemque dicere Veientonem reliquit. Multum ille de hac (ita vocabat) contumelia questus est Homerico versu: Ὦ γέρον,

21 ἦ μάλα δή σε νέοι τείρουσι μαχηταί. Non fere quisquam in senatu fuit, qui non me complecteretur

---

1 He had already spoken in his proper turn.
2 Possibly to be identified with Pompeius Falco; see Index.
3 *Iliad* VIII. 102. Veiento is first heard of in 62, accused of bribery and libellous writing (Tacitus, *Ann.* XIV. 50).

speech. "In my opinion," he said, "injustice will be done to Publicius Certus if he is not acquitted; for his name was only mentioned by the friends of Arria and Fannia, and by his own friends. We need not be apprehensive, for it is we, who have confidence in the man, who will be his judges. If he is innocent, as I hope and wish and shall continue to believe until something is proved against him, you will be able to acquit him."

These were the views expressed as the speakers were called upon in order. Then my turn came. I rose to my feet with the opening words you see in the published speech, and replied to them one by one. It was remarkable to see the attention and applause with which all I said was received by those who had previously shouted me down: a change of front produced either by the importance of the issue, the success of the speech, or the firmness of the speaker. I came to an end, and Veiento began to reply. No one would allow it,[1] and the interruption and uproar increased until he said, " I beg you, Conscript Fathers, not to compel me to appeal for the protection of the tribunes." At once the tribune Murena[2] retorted, "The honourable member has my permission to proceed." Again there was an outcry, and meanwhile the consul called out names, took a division, and dismissed the Senate, leaving Veiento still standing and trying to speak. He has complained bitterly about this insult (as he calls it) in a line of Homer's: " My lord, the young fighters are surely too much for your age."[3]

Almost the entire Senate embraced me with open arms and overwhelmed me with enthusiastic con-

exoscularetur certatimque laude cumularet, quod
intermissum iam diu morem in publicum consulendi
susceptis propriis simultatibus reduxissem; quod
denique senatum invidia liberassem, qua flagrabat
apud ordines alios, quod severus in ceteros senatoribus
solis dissimulatione quasi mutua parceret.

22   Haec acta sunt absente Certo; fuit enim seu tale
aliquid suspicatus sive, ut excusabatur, infirmus.   Et
relationem quidem de eo Caesar ad senatum non
23 remisit; obtinui tamen quod intenderam: nam
collega Certi consulatum, successorem Certus accepit,
planeque factum est quod dixeram in fine: " Reddat
praemium sub optimo principe, quod a pessimo
accepit." Postea actionem meam utcumque potui
24 recollegi, addidi multa.   Accidit fortuitum, sed non
tamquam fortuitum, quod editis libris Certus intra
25 paucissimos dies implicitus morbo decessit.   Audivi
referentes hanc imaginem menti eius hanc oculis
oberrasse, tamquam videret me sibi cum ferro imminere. Verane haec, adfirmare non ausim; interest
tamen exempli, ut vera videantur.

26   Habes epistulam, si modum epistulae cogites, libris
quos legisti non minorem; sed imputabis tibi qui
contentus libris non fuisti.   Vale.

gratulations for having revived the practice, long fallen into disuse, of bringing measures for the public good before the Senate at the risk of incurring personal enmities; I had in fact freed the Senate from the odium in which it was held among the other classes for showing severity to others while sparing its own members by a sort of mutual connivance. Certus was not present at these proceedings; either he suspected something of the sort or he was ill— the excuse he gave. It is true that the Emperor brought no motion against him before the Senate, but I won my point. The consulship was given to Certus's colleague, and Certus was removed from his Treasury post, so that my concluding demand was fulfilled that " he should give back under the best of Emperors the reward he received from the worst."

Afterwards I set down what I could remember of my speech, and made several additions. By coincidence, though it seemed no mere coincidence, a few days after the speech was published Certus fell ill and died. I have heard it said that always in his mind's eye he had a vision of me threatening him with a sword. Whether this is true I shouldn't like to say, but it helps to point a moral if it is accepted as true.

Here you have a letter as long as the speeches you have read, if you think what the length of a letter should be—but you weren't satisfied with the speeches and have only yourself to blame.

THE LETTERS OF PLINY

XIV

C. PLINIUS TACITO SUO S.

NEC ipse tibi plaudis, et ego nihil magis ex fide quam de te scribo. Posteris an aliqua cura nostri, nescio; nos certe meremur, ut sit aliqua, non dico ingenio (id enim superbum), sed studio et labore et reverentia posterorum. Pergamus modo itinere instituto, quod ut paucos in lucem famamque provexit, ita multos e tenebris et silentio protulit. Vale.

XV

C. PLINIUS FALCONI SUO S.

1 REFUGERAM in Tuscos, ut omnia ad arbitrium meum facerem. At hoc ne in Tuscis quidem: tam multis undique rusticorum libellis et tam querulis inquietor, quos aliquanto magis invitus quam meos 2 lego; nam et meos invitus. Retracto enim actiunculas quasdam, quod post intercapedinem temporis et frigidum et acerbum est. Rationes quasi absente me 3 negleguntur. Interdum tamen equum conscendo et patrem familiae hactenus ago, quod aliquam partem praediorum, sed pro gestatione percurro. Tu consuetudinem serva, nobisque sic rusticis urbana acta perscribe. Vale.

XIV

To CORNELIUS TACITUS

You are never satisfied with yourself, but I never write with such confidence as when I write about you. Whether posterity will give us a thought I don't know, but surely we deserve one—I don't say for our genius, which sounds like boasting, but for our application, hard work, and regard for future generations. Only let us continue along the path we have chosen; if it leads few to the full light of fame, it brings many out of the shades of obscurity.

XV

To POMPEIUS FALCO

I TOOK refuge in Tuscany to be free to do as I liked, but even there it has been impossible. I am beset on all sides by the peasants with all their petitions full of complaints, and these I read rather more unwillingly than my own writings, which I really have no wish to read either. (I am revising some minor speeches of mine, and after a lapse of time it is a tedious and exasperating task.) My accounts are neglected, as if I had not come here to do them. I do, however, mount a horse sometimes and play the part of proprietor, but only to the extent of riding round part of the estate for exercise. Don't you drop your habit of sending me the city news while I am rusticating in this way!

XVI

C. Plinius Mamiliano Suo S.

1 Summam te voluptatem percepisse ex isto copiosissimo genere venandi non miror cum historicorum more scribas numerum iniri non potuisse. Nobis venari nec vacat nec libet: non vacat quia vindemiae 2 in manibus, non libet quia exiguae. Devehimus tamen pro novo musto novos versiculos tibique iucundissime exigenti ut primum videbuntur defervisse mittemus. Vale.

XVII

C. Plinus Genitori Suo S.

1 Recepi litteras tuas quibus quereris taedio tibi fuisse quamvis lautissimam cenam, quia scurrae 2 cinaedi moriones mensis inerrabant. Vis tu remittere aliquid ex rugis? Equidem nihil tale habeo, habentes tamen fero. Cur ergo non habeo? Quia nequaquam me ut inexspectatum festivumve delectat, si quid molle a cinaedo, petulans a scurra, stultum a 3 morione profertur. Non rationem sed stomachum tibi narro. Atque adeo quam multos putas esse, quos ea quibus ego et tu capimur et ducimur, partim ut inepta partim ut molestissima offendant! Quam multi, cum lector aut lyristes aut comoedus inductus est, calceos poscunt aut non minore cum taedio recubant, quam tu ista (sic enim adpellas) prodigia

---

¹ Literally, "demand their shoes." P. himself enjoys music and acting in I. 15. 2.

XVI

To Pomponius Mamilianus

I'm not surprised you enjoyed your hunting so much, with all that in the bag—you write as the historians do that the numbers couldn't be counted. Personally I have neither time nor inclination for hunting; no time because I am busy with the grape harvest, and no inclination because it is a bad one. But I am bringing in some new verses instead of new wine, and, as you are kind enough to ask for them, I will send them when the fermenting stage is over.

XVII

To Julius Genitor

Thank you for your letter. You complain about a dinner party, a grand affair which filled you with disgust at the mimes and clowns and the male " dancers " going the round of the tables. Please don't be for ever frowning—I have nothing of that kind in my own house, but I can put up with those who do. The reason why I don't have them is that I find nothing novel or amusing to attract me in that sort of " dancer's " charms, in a mime's impudence, or a clown's folly. But you see I am not pleading my principles but my personal taste; and think how many people there are who dislike the entertainments which you and I find fascinating, and think them either pointless or boring. How many take their leave[1] at the entry of a reader, a musician, or an actor, or else lie back in disgust, as you did when you

4 perpessus es! Demus igitur alienis oblectationibus veniam, ut nostris impetremus. Vale.

XVIII

C. PLINIUS SABINO SUO S.

1 QUA intentione, quo studio, qua denique memoria legeris libellos meos, epistula tua ostendit. Ipse igitur exhibes negotium tibi qui elicis et invitas, ut 2 quam plurima communicare tecum velim. Faciam, per partes tamen et quasi digesta, ne istam ipsam memoriam, cui gratias ago, adsiduitate et copia turbem oneratamque et quasi oppressam cogam pluribus singula posterioribus priora dimittere. Vale.

XIX

C. PLINIUS RUSONI SUO S.

1 SIGNIFICAS legisse te in quadam epistula mea iussisse Verginium Rufum inscribi sepulcro suo:

Hic situs est Rufus, pulso qui Vindice quondam imperium adseruit non sibi sed patriae.

Reprehendis quod iusserit, addis etiam melius rectiusque Frontinum, quod vetuerit omnino monumentum sibi fieri, meque ad extremum quid de utroque

---

[1] See II.1, VI. 10 and notes.

had to endure those monstrosities as you call them!
Let us then be tolerant of other people's pleasures
so as to win indulgence for our own.

XVIII

To Statius Sabinus

THE devoted concentration with which you read
and remember my small efforts is clear from your
letter; so you are to blame for the task you set
yourself by begging and coaxing me to send you as
much of my work as I can.   I can't refuse, but I shall
send it bit by bit in small doses—grateful though I
am to that memory of yours, I don't want to confuse
it by application to too much material at a time and
leave it overwhelmed and surfeited, so that it has to
sacrifice the parts for the whole and the earlier items
for the later.

XIX

To Cremutius Ruso

You say you have read in a letter of mine[1] that
Verginius Rufus ordered this inscription for his tomb:

Here lies Rufus, who once defeated Vindex and
    set free the imperial power
Not for himself, but for his country.

You dislike his doing so; Frontinus, you say, showed
a better and nobler spirit in forbidding any monument
at all to be set up to himself; finally, you want my
opinion on both men.

2 sentiam consulis. Utrumque dilexi, miratus sum magis quem tu reprehendis, atque ita miratus ut non putarem satis umquam posse laudari, cuius nunc mihi 3 subeunda defensio est. Omnes ego qui magnum aliquid memorandumque fecerunt, non modo venia verum etiam laude dignissimos iudico, si immortalitatem quam meruere sectantur, victurique nominis famam supremis etiam titulis prorogare nituntur. 4 Nec facile quemquam nisi Verginium invenio, cuius tanta in praedicando verecundia quanta gloria ex 5 facto. Ipse sum testis, familiariter ab eo dilectus probatusque, semel omnino me audiente provectum, ut de rebus suis hoc unum referret, ita secum aliquando Cluvium locutum: "Scis, Vergini, quae historiae fides debeatur; proinde si quid in historiis meis legis aliter ac velis rogo ignoscas." Ad hoc ille: "Tune ignoras, Cluvi, ideo me fecisse quod feci, ut 6 esset liberum vobis scribere quae libuisset?" Age dum, hunc ipsum Frontinum in hoc ipso, in quo tibi parcior videtur et pressior, comparemus. Vetuit exstrui monumentum, sed quibus verbis? "Impensa monumenti supervacua est; memoria nostri durabit, si vita meruimus." An restrictius arbitraris per orbem terrarum legendum dare duraturam memoriam suam quam uno in loco duobus versiculis signare

---

¹ Cluvius Rufus, the historian of the early Empire, and one of Tacitus's sources. As a supporter of Galba he may have

I loved them both, but I admired more the man you criticize, admired him so much that I thought he could never be praised enough. Yet now the time has come when I must undertake his defence. Everyone who has done some great and memorable deed should, I think, not only be excused but even praised if he wishes to ensure the immortality he has earned, and by the very words of his epitaph seeks to perpetuate the undying glory of his name. And I cannot easily think of anyone except Verginius whose fame in action is matched by his modesty in speaking of it. I can bear witness to this myself; I enjoyed his confidence and close friendship, but only once in my hearing did he go so far as to make a single reference to what he had done. This was the occasion when Cluvius[1] said, " You know how a historian must be faithful to facts, Verginius, so, if you find anything in my histories which is not as you like it, please forgive me." To this he replied, " Don't you realize, Cluvius, that I did what I did so that the rest of you should be at liberty to write as you please ? "

Now let us consider Frontinus, on the very point in which you find him more moderate and restrained. Frontinus forbade any monument to be set up, but what were his words? " A monument is money wasted; my memory will live on if my life has deserved it." Do you really think that it shows more reticence to publish throughout the world that your memory will live on, than to record your achievement in a single place in a mere couple of lines ? However,

criticized Verginius for remaining loyal to Nero and defeating Vindex, whom Galba supported. Cf. Tacitus, *Hist.* I. 8.

7 quod feceris? Quamquam non habeo propositum illum reprehendendi, sed hunc tuendi; cuius quae potest apud te iustior esse defensio, quam ex colla-
8 tione eius quem praetulisti? Meo quidem iudicio neuter culpandus, quorum uterque ad gloriam pari cupiditate, diverso itinere contendit, alter dum expetit debitos titulos, alter dum mavult videri contempsisse. Vale.

XX

C. Plinius Venatori Suo S.

1 Tua vero epistula tanto mihi iucundior fuit quanto longior erat, praesertim cum de libellis meis tota loqueretur; quos tibi voluptati esse non miror, cum
2 omnia nostra perinde ac nos ames. Ipse cum maxime vindemias graciles quidem, uberiores tamen quam exspectaveram colligo, si colligere est non numquam decerpere uvam, torculum invisere, gustare de lacu mustum, obrepere urbanis, qui nunc rusticis praesunt meque notariis et lectoribus reliquerunt. Vale.

XXI

C. Plinius Sabiniano Suo S.

1 Libertus tuus, cui suscensere te dixeras, venit ad me advolutusque pedibus meis tamquam tuis haesit. Flevit multum, multum rogavit, multum etiam

my intention was not to criticize Frontinus but to defend Verginius; though there could be no better defence of him for your ears than a comparison with the man you prefer. My own feeling is that neither should be blamed, for both hoped for fame though they sought it by different roads, one by claiming the epitaph which was his due, the other by professing to despise it.

XX

To Venator

Your letter pleased me all the more for being a long one, especially as it was all about my own books. I can't be surprised that you enjoy them, since you care almost as much for my efforts as you do for myself. As for me, at this very moment I am gathering in the grape harvest, which is poor, but better than I had expected; if you can call it " gathering " to pick an occasional grape, look at the press, taste the fermenting wine in the vat, and pay a surprise visit to the servants I brought from the city—who are now standing over the peasants at work and have abandoned me to my secretaries and readers.

XXI

To Sabinianus

The freedman of yours with whom you said you were angry has been to me, flung himself at my feet, and clung to me as if I were you. He begged my help with many tears, though he left a good deal

tacuit, in summa fecit mihi fidem paenitentiae verae:
2 credo emendatum quia deliquisse se sentit. Irasceris,
scio, et irasceris merito, id quoque scio; sed tunc
praecipua mansuetudinis laus, cum irae causa
iustissima est. Amasti hominem et, spero, amabis:
interim sufficit ut exorari te sinas. Licebit rursus
irasci, si meruerit, quod exoratus excusatius facies.
Remitte aliquid adulescentiae ipsius, remitte lacrimis, remitte indulgentiae tuae. Ne torseris illum,
ne torseris etiam te; torqueris enim cum tam lenis
3 irasceris. Vereor ne videar non rogare sed cogere, si
precibus eius meas iunxero; iungam tamen tanto
plenius et effusius, quanto ipsum acrius severiusque
corripui, destricte minatus numquam me postea
rogaturum. Hoc illi, quem terreri oportebat, tibi
non idem; nam fortasse iterum rogabo, impetrabo
iterum: sit modo tale, ut rogare me, ut praestare te
deceat. Vale.

XXII

C. Plinius Severo Suo S.

1 MAGNA me sollicitudine adfecit Passenni Pauli
valetudo, et quidem plurimis iustissimisque de causis.
Vir est optimus honestissimus, nostri amantissimus;
praeterea in litteris veteres aemulatur exprimit

---

[1] See VI. 15 and Index.

unsaid; in short, he convinced me of his genuine penitence. I believe he has reformed, because he realizes he did wrong. You are angry, I know, and I know too that your anger was deserved, but mercy wins most praise when there was just cause for anger. You loved the man once, and I hope you will love him again, but it is sufficient for the moment if you allow yourself to be appeased. You can always be angry again if he deserves it, and will have more excuse if you were once placated. Make some concession to his youth, his tears, and your own kind heart, and do not torment him or yourself any longer —anger can only be a torment to your gentle self.

I'm afraid you will think I am using pressure, not persuasion, if I add my prayers to his—but this is what I shall do, and all the more freely and fully because I have given the man a very severe scolding and warned him firmly that I will never make such a request again. This was because he deserved a fright, and is not intended for your ears; for maybe I *shall* make another request and obtain it, as long as it is nothing unsuitable for me to ask and you to grant.

XXII

To Herennius (?) Severus

I HAVE been very worried about the illness of Passennus Paulus[1]—and with every just reason, for he is the best of men, the soul of honesty, and my devoted friend. His literary work is modelled on that of the ancients whom he imitates and brings

reddit, Propertium in primis, a quo genus ducit, vera
2 suboles eoque simillima illi in quo ille praecipuus. Si
elegos eius in manus sumpseris, leges opus tersum
molle iucundum, et plane in Properti domo scriptum.
Nuper ad lyrica deflexit, in quibus ita Horatium ut in
illis illum alterum effingit: putes si quid in studiis
cognatio valet, et huius propinquum. Magna
varietas magna mobilitas: amat ut qui verissime,
dolet ut qui impatientissime, laudat ut qui benignis-
sime, ludit ut qui facetissime, omnia denique tam-
3 quam singula absolvit. Pro hoc ego amico, pro hoc
ingenio non minus aeger animo quam corpore ille,
tandem illum tandem me recepi. Gratulare mihi,
gratulare etiam litteris ipsis, quae ex periculo eius
tantum discrimen adierunt, quantum ex salute gloriae
consequentur. Vale.

XXIII

C. PLINIUS MAXIMO SUO S.

1 FREQUENTER agenti mihi evenit, ut centumviri cum
diu se intra iudicum auctoritatem gravitatemque
tenuissent, omnes repente quasi victi coactique
2 consurgerent laudarentque; frequenter e senatu
famam qualem maxime optaveram rettuli: numquam tamen maiorem cepi voluptatem, quam nuper

back to life, Propertius in particular, from whom he
traces his descent; and he is indeed a true descendant, resembling the poet most in the qualities which
were his greatest. Take up his elegiacs and you
will find them exquisitely finished, full of sensuous
charm, and truly in Propertius's style. He has lately
turned to lyric poetry, and here he recalls Horace as
successfully as he does Propertius elsewhere: if kinship has any influence on literature, you would think
he was related to Horace too. He is highly versa-
tile, with many changes of mood; he can love like a
true lover and portray grief in all its passion; his
tributes are generous and his wit is brilliant: in fact
everything he does is perfected as a whole and in part.

This is the friend and genius for whom I have been
as sick at heart as he was in body, but now at last he
is restored, and I with him. Congratulate me, congratulate literature itself, for the danger to his life
has brought it through hazards as great as the glory
his recovery will ensure for it.

XXIII

To Maximus

It has often happened to me when speaking in the
Centumviral Court that my hearers have preserved
their judicial dignity and impassivity for a while and
then suddenly jumped to their feet with one accord
to congratulate me as if driven by some compelling
force. From the Senate, too, I have often had all
the applause my heart could desire; but never have
I felt such pleasure as I did recently at something

ex sermone Corneli Taciti. Narrabat sedisse secum
circensibus proximis equitem Romanum. Hunc post
varios eruditosque sermones requisisse: "Italicus es
3 an provincialis?" Se respondisse: "Nosti me, et
quidem ex studiis." Ad hoc illum: "Tacitus es an
Plinius?" Exprimere non possum, quam sit
iucundum mihi quod nomina nostra quasi litterarum
propria, non hominum, litteris redduntur, quod
uterque nostrum his etiam ex studiis notus, quibus
aliter ignotus est.
4 Accidit aliud ante pauculos dies simile. Recum-
bebat mecum vir egregius, Fadius[1] Rufinus, super
eum municeps ipsius, qui illo die primum venerat in
urbem; cui Rufinus demonstrans me: "Vides
hunc?" Multa deinde de studiis nostris; et ille
5 "Plinius est" inquit. Verum fatebor, capio magnum laboris mei fructum. An si Demosthenes iure
laetatus est, quod illum anus Attica ita noscitavit:
Οὗτός ἐστι Δημοσθένης, ego celebritate nominis
mei gaudere non debeo? Ego vero et gaudeo et
6 gaudere me dico. Neque enim vereor ne iactantior
videar, cum de me aliorum iudicium non meum
profero, praesertim apud te qui nec ullius invides
laudibus et faves nostris. Vale.

[1] fadius *M*: fidius *a*: fabius *γ*.

---

[1] Cf. Tacitus, *Dial.* 7. 4.   [2] Cicero, *Tusc. Disp.* V. 103.

Tacitus said. He was describing how at the last Races he had sat next to a Roman knight who engaged him in conversation on several learned subjects and then asked if he came from Italy or the provinces. "You know me," said Tacitus, "from your reading." At which the man said, "Then are you Tacitus or Pliny?" I can't tell you how delighted I am to have our names assigned to literature as if they belonged there and not to individuals, and to learn that we are both known by our writing to people who would otherwise not have heard of us.[1]

A similar thing happened to me a day or two ago. I had a distinguished neighbour at dinner, Fadius Rufinus, and on his other side was someone from his native town who had come to Rome on his first visit that same day. Pointing to me, Rufinus said to him, "Do you see my friend here?" Then he spoke at length about my work, and the man exclaimed, "It must be Pliny!"

I confess I feel well rewarded for my labours. If Demosthenes had the right to be pleased when the old woman of Attica recognized him with the words "That's Demosthenes!"[2] I may surely be glad when my name is well known. In fact I *am* glad and admit it. For I'm not afraid of appearing too boastful when I have other people's opinions to quote and not only my own, especially when talking to you: for you are never envious of anyone's reputation and are always furthering mine.

XXIV

C. PLINIUS SABINIANO SUO S.

BENE fecisti quod libertum aliquando tibi carum reducentibus epistulis meis in domum in animum recepisti. Iuvabit hoc te; me certe iuvat, primum quod te tam tractabilem video, ut in ira regi possis, deinde quod tantum mihi tribuis, ut vel auctoritati meae pareas vel precibus indulgeas. Igitur et laudo et gratias ago; simul in posterum moneo, ut te erroribus tuorum, etsi non fuerit qui deprecetur, placabilem praestes. Vale.

XXV

C. PLINIUS MAMILIANO SUO S.

1 QUERERIS de turba castrensium negotiorum et, tamquam summo otio perfruare, lusus et ineptias nostras legis amas flagitas, meque ad similia con-
2 denda non mediocriter incitas. Incipio enim ex hoc genere studiorum non solum oblectationem verum etiam gloriam petere, post iudicium tuum viri
3 eruditissimi gravissimi ac super ista verissimi. Nunc me rerum actus modice sed tamen distringit; quo finito aliquid earundem Camenarum in istum benignissimum sinum mittam. Tu passerculis et

---

[1] Cf. Letter 21.

XXIV

To Sabinianus [1]

You have done the right thing in taking back into your home and favour the freedman who was once dear to you, with my letter to mediate between you both. You will be glad of this, and I am certainly glad, first because I see you are willing to be reasonable and take advice when angry, and then because you have paid me the tribute of bowing to my authority, or, if you prefer, granting my request. So accept my compliments as well as my thanks, but, at the same time, a word of advice for the future: be ready to forgive the faults of your household even if there is no one there to intercede for them.

XXV

To Pomponius Mamilianus

You grumble about being beset with military affairs, and yet you can read my bits of nonsense as if you had all the leisure in the world—you even enjoy them, clamour for them, and are insistent that I produce more like them. I am in fact beginning to think that I can look for more than mere amusement from this kind of writing, and now that I have the opinion of one who is both learned and serious, and above all sincere, I may even think of fame.

At the moment I have some legal work to do, not much, but enough to occupy my time. When this is finished I will entrust something inspired by the same

columbulis nostris inter aquilas vestras dabis pennas,
si tamen et tibi placebunt; si tantum sibi, con-
tinendos cavea nidove curabis. Vale.

XXVI

C. PLINIUS LUPERCO SUO S.

1 DIXI de quodam oratore saeculi nostri recto
quidem et sano, sed parum grandi et ornato, ut
opinor, apte: " Nihil peccat, nisi quod nihil peccat."
2 Debet enim orator erigi attolli, interdum etiam
effervescere ecferri, ac saepe accedere ad praeceps;
nam plerumque altis et excelsis adiacent abrupta.
Tutius per plana sed humilius et depressius iter; fre-
quentior currentibus quam reptantibus lapsus, sed his
non labentibus nulla, illis non nulla laus etiamsi
3 labantur. Nam ut quasdam artes ita eloquentiam
nihil magis quam ancipitia commendant. Vides qui
per funem in summa nituntur, quantos soleant
excitare clamores, cum iam iamque casuri videntur.
4 Sunt enim maxime mirabilia quae maxime insperata,
maxime periculosa utque Graeci magis exprimunt,
παράβολα. Ideo nequaquam par gubernatoris est
virtus, cum placido et cum turbato mari vehitur: tunc

---

1 The legionary standards.
2 See II. 5, and for the theme, I. 20, where P. also shows he
prefers something less austere than the Attic style.
3 Cf. Horace, *Ars Poet.* 28.

Muse to your kindly care. If you think well of my little sparrows and doves, as they do of themselves, let them fly among your eagles;[1] and if you don't, please shut them in a cage or keep them in their nest.

XXVI

To Lupercus

One of our contemporary orators is a sound and sober speaker while lacking in grandeur and eloquence, so that I think my comment on him has point: his only fault is that he is faultless.

The orator [2] ought in fact to be roused and heated, sometimes even to boiling-point, and to let his feelings carry him on till he treads the edge of a precipice; for a path along the heights and peaks often skirts the sheer drop below. It may be safer to keep to the plain, but the road lies too low to be interesting. [3] A runner risks more falls than a man who keeps to a snail's pace, but he wins praise in spite of a stumble, whereas there is no credit in walking without a fall. Eloquence is in fact one of the skills which gain most from the risks they run. You have seen tightrope walkers and the applause they win as they move along the length of the rope and every minute look as though they are going to fall; for it is the most unexpected and dangerous feats which win most admiration: ventures which the Greeks can define so well in a single word. Consequently the courage demanded of a helmsman to steer his course through a stormy sea is quite different from what he needs when the sea is calm and he

129

admirante nullo, inlaudatus inglorius subit portum,
at cum stridunt funes curvatur arbor gubernacula
gemunt, tunc ille clarus et dis maris proximus.

5 Cur haec? Quia visus es mihi in scriptis meis
adnotasse quaedam ut tumida quae ego sublimia, ut
improba quae ego audentia, ut nimia quae ego plena
arbitrabar. Plurimum autem refert, reprehendenda
6 adnotes an insignia. Omnis enim advertit, quod
eminet et exstat; sed acri intentione diiudicandum
est, immodicum sit an grande, altum an enorme.
Atque ut Homerum potissimum attingam, quem
tandem alterutram in partem potest fugere ἀμφὶ δὲ
σάλπιγξεν μέγας οὐρανός, ἠέρι δ᾽ ἔγχος ἐκέκλιτο et
7 totum illud οὔτε θαλάσσης κῦμα τόσον βοάᾳ? Sed
opus est examine et libra, incredibilia sint haec et
inania an magnifica caelestia. Nec nunc ego me
his similia aut dixisse aut posse dicere puto (non ita
insanio), sed hoc intellegi volo, laxandos esse elo-
quentiae frenos, nec angustissimo gyro ingeniorum
impetus refringendos.

8 "At enim alia condicio oratorum, alia poetarum."
Quasi vero M. Tullius minus audeat! Quamquam
hunc omitto; neque enìm ambigi puto. Sed

---

[1] *Iliad*, XXI. 388; V. 356; XIV. 394.

reaches harbour unnoticed, to find no praise and congratulations awaiting him. It is when the sheets creak, the mast bends, and the rudder groans that he is covered with glory and stands almost equal to the gods of the sea!

I write as I do because I had an idea that you had criticized some passages in my writings for being pompous, though I thought them splendid, and what I imagined to be a full treatment of a bold enterprise you dismissed as redundant and exaggerated. But it is important to determine whether you are attacking genuine faults or only striking phrases; for, though anyone can see what stands out above the average, it needs a keen judgement to decide whether this is extravagant and disproportionate or lofty and sublime. Homer provides the best examples; no one can fail to notice (whatever he feels about them) such expressions as " high heaven's trumpet rang out," " his spear rested on a cloud," and the whole passage " neither the sea's breakers roar so loud,"[1] but they must be weighed with care before judging if they are meaningless phantasies or noble creations of a divine inspiration. Not that I think that these are the times and I am the person to have written words like these, nor that I have the ability to do so; I am not so foolish. But I want to make the point that eloquence should be given its head, and the pace of genius should not be confined within too narrow a ring.

You may say that orators are different from poets— as if indeed Cicero lacked daring! However, let us leave out Cicero, since in his case I think there is no dispute. But there is surely no curb nor restraint

Demosthenes ipse, ille norma oratoris et regula, num se cohibet et comprimit, cum dicit illa notissima: ἄνθρωποι μιαροί, κόλακες καὶ ἀλάστορες et rursus οὐ λίθοις ἐτείχισα τὴν πόλιν οὐδὲ πλίνθοις ἐγώ et statim οὐκ ἐκ μὲν θαλάττης τὴν Εὔβοιαν προβαλέσθαι πρὸ τῆς Ἀττικῆς et alibi: ἐγὼ δὲ οἶμαι μέν, ὦ ἄνδρες Ἀθηναῖοι, νὴ τοὺς θεοὺς ἐκεῖνον 9 μεθύειν τῷ μεγέθει τῶν πεπραγμένων? Iam quid audentius illo pulcherrimo ac longissimo excessu: νόσημα γάρ . . .? Quid haec breviora superioribus, sed audacia paria: τότε ἐγὼ μὲν τῷ Πύθωνι θρασυνομένῳ καὶ πολλῷ ῥέοντι καθ᾽ ἡμῶν? Ex eadem nota ὅταν δὲ ἐκ πλεονεξίας καὶ πονηρίας ⟨τις⟩[1] ὥσπερ οὗτος ἰσχύσῃ, ἡ πρώτη πρόφασις καὶ μικρὸν πταῖσμα ἅπαντα ἀνεχαίτισε καὶ διέλυσε. Simile his ἀπεσχοινισμένος ἅπασι τοῖς ἐν τῇ πόλει δικαίοις et ibidem σὺ τὸν εἰς ταῦτα ἔλεον προὔδωκας, Ἀριστόγειτον, μᾶλλον δ᾽ ἀνῄρηκας ὅλως. μὴ δή, πρὸς οὓς αὐτὸς ἔχωσας λιμένας καὶ προβόλων ἐνέπλησας, πρὸς τούτους ὁρμίζου. Et dixerat: τούτῳ δ᾽ οὐδένα ὁρῶ τῶν τόπων τούτων βάσιμον ὄντα, ἀλλὰ πάντα ἀπόκρημνα, φάραγγας, βάραθρα. Et deinceps: δέδοικα, μὴ δόξητέ τισι τὸν ἀεὶ βουλόμενον εἶναι πονηρὸν τῶν ἐν τῇ πόλει παιδοτριβεῖν, nec satis: οὐδὲ γὰρ τοὺς προγόνους ὑπολαμβάνω τὰ δικαστήρια ταῦτα ὑμῖν οἰκοδομῆσαι, ἵνα τοὺς τοιούτους ἐν αὐτοῖς μοσχεύητε, ad hoc: εἰ δὲ κάπηλός ἐστι πονηρίας καὶ παλιγκάπηλος καὶ μεταβολεύς et mille

---

[1] ΤΙΣ *om. γα: supp. II Olynth. 9.*

[1] *De Corona,* 296, 299, and 301.
[2] *Philippic,* I. 49.   [3] *De Falsa Legatione,* 259.
[4] *De Cor.* 136.   [5] *Olynthiac,* II. 9.
[6] *In Aristogeitonem,* I. 28, 84, 76, 7, 48, and 46.

holding back Demosthenes, the true model and
exemplar of oratory, when he delivers the famous
" Abominable men, flatterers and evil spirits " and
again " neither with stones nor bricks did I fortify
this city," and later, " Was it not to make Euboea
the bulwark of Attica on the seaward side ? "[1] Elsewhere he says, " For my part, men of Athens, by the
gods I believe that Philip is drunk with the magni-
tude of his achievements,"[2] and there can hardly be
anything bolder than the magnificent long digres-
sion beginning " For a disease . . ."[3] The following passage may be shorter but is no less daring:
" Then when Python swaggered and poured out a
torrent of abuse on us, I stood firm,"[4] and this bears
the same stamp : " But when a man has grown strong
as Philip has, by rapacity and crime, then the first
pretext, some trifling slip, overthrows and shatters
all."[5] In the same style are the expressions " Cor-
doned off from every right which holds sacred in
the city " and in the same speech, " You have thrown
away their claim to pity, Aristogeiton, indeed you
have destroyed it once and for all. Do not then seek
anchorage in harbours which you have yourself
blocked up and filled with stakes." He had already
said " But I cannot see that any one of these topics
gives a sure foothold to the defendant; he has
nothing before him but precipices, gulfs and pitfalls,"
and also " I am afraid that to some you will appear
to have set up as a trainer of any citizen with a taste
for wickedness." There is also " I cannot believe
that your ancestors built you these law courts as a
hotbed for rascals of this sort " and " If he is a job-
bing dealer, a pedlar, and retailer of wickedness,"[6]

talia, ut praeteream quae ab Aeschine θαύματα, non ῥήματα vocantur.

10 In contrarium incidi: dices hunc quoque ob ista culpari. Sed vide, quanto maior sit, qui reprehenditur, ipso reprehendente et maior ob haec quoque; in aliis enim vis, in his granditas eius elucet.

11 Num autem Aeschines ipse eis, quae in Demosthene carpebat, abstinuit? ⟨Χρὴ γάρ, ὦ ἄνδρες Ἀθηναῖοι, τὸ αὐτὸ⟩[1] φθέγγεσθαι τὸν ῥήτορα καὶ τὸν νόμον· ὅταν δὲ ἑτέραν μὲν φωνὴν ἀφιῇ ὁ νόμος, ἑτέραν δὲ ὁ ῥήτωρ .... Alio loco: ἔπειτα ἀναφαίνεται περὶ πάντων ἐν τῷ ψηφίσματι. Iterum alio: ἀλλ' ἐγκαθήμενοι καὶ ἐνεδρεύοντες ἐν τῇ ἀκροάσει εἰσελαύνετε αὐτὸν εἰς τοὺς παρανόμους λόγους.

12 Quod adeo probavit, ut repetat: ἀλλ' ὥσπερ ἐν ταῖς ἱπποδρομίαις εἰς τὸν τοῦ πράγματος αὐτὸν δρόμον εἰσελαύνετε. Iam illa custoditius pressiusque: σὺ δὲ ἑλκοποιεῖς, ⟨καὶ μᾶλλόν σοι μέλει τῶν αὐθημέρων λόγων ἢ τῆς σωτηρίας τῆς πόλεως, altius illa: οὐκ ἀποπέμψεσθε τὸν ἄνθρωπον ὡς κοινὴν τῶν Ἑλλήνων συμφοράν; ἢ συλλαβόντες ὡς⟩[2] λῃστὴν τῶν πραγμάτων ⟨ἐπ' ὀνομάτων⟩[3] διὰ τῆς πολιτείας πλέοντα

---

[1] ΧΡΗ . . . ΑΥΤΟ *Catanaeus a, om. γ.*
[2] ΚΑΙ ΜΑΛΛΟΝ . . . ΣΥΛΛΑΒΟΝΤΕΣ ΩΣ *Cat. a: om. γ.*
[3] ΕΠ ΟΝΟΜΑΤΩΝ *om. Cat. a et γ.*

---

[1] *In Ctesiphontem,* 167.   [2] *In Ctes.,* 16, 101, 206.

and innumerable such instances, not counting those
which Aeschines called " not words but wonders." [1]

Here I am up against an argument on the other
side, and you will retort that Demosthenes is at fault
in the same way as you say I am. But you must see
how much greater he is than Aeschines, his critic, and
greater in these very passages; he can show vigour
elsewhere, but here he stands out as sublime.   Besides, was Aeschines himself free from the faults he
finds in Demosthenes ? " For it is essential, men of
Athens, that the orator and the law should speak the
same language; but when the law says one thing,
and the orator another . . ."   Elsewhere he says that
" Then he displays himself as especially concerned
with the decree," and again, " But keep watch and
lie in ambush as you listen to him, so that you drive
him to keep within the limits of the charge of ille-
gality," [2] and he is so pleased with this metaphor that
he repeats it: " But as in the race track, drive him
to keep to the relevant course." [3]   Nor [4] is his style
any more controlled and restrained in this example:
" But you reopen old wounds, and are more concerned
with today's speeches than with the welfare of the
State "; and he aims high when he asks: " Will
you not dismiss this man as a public menace to
Greece ? Or arrest him as a pirate who infests
politics by cruising around the State in his brig of
words, and then bring him to justice ? " [5]

[3] *In Timarchum*, 176.
[4] The logic of the argument demands a rhetorical question
(" Is his style any more . . .? ") which is more clearly translated by a negative.
[5] *In Ctes.*, 208 and 253.

13 ⟨τιμωρήσεσθε⟩;[1] Exspecto, ut quaedam ex hac
epistula ut illud "gubernacula gemunt" et "dis maris
proximus" isdem notis quibus ea, de quibus scribo,
confodias; intellego enim me, dum veniam prioribus
peto, in illa ipsa quae adnotaveras incidisse. Sed
confodias licet, dum modo iam nunc destines diem,
quo et de illis et de his coram exigere possimus.
Aut enim tu me timidum aut ego te temerarium
faciam. Vale.

XXVII

C. Plinius Paterno Suo S.

1 Quanta potestas, quanta dignitas, quanta maiestas,
quantum denique numen sit historiae, cum frequenter
alias tum proxime sensi. Recitaverat quidam veris-
simum librum, partemque eius in alium diem reser-
2 vaverat. Ecce amici cuiusdam orantes obsecran-
tesque, ne reliqua recitaret. Tantus audiendi
quae fecerint pudor, quibus nullus faciendi quae
audire erubescunt. Et ille quidem praestitit quod
rogabatur (sinebat fides); liber tamen ut factum
ipsum manet manebit legeturque semper, tanto
magis quia non statim. Incitantur enim homines ad
noscenda quae differuntur. Vale.

[1] ΤΙΜΩΡΗΣΑΣΘΕ *Cat. a* (*om. γ*).

---

[1] For the embarrassments of recent history, see V. 8. 12.

I am waiting for you to strike out certain expressions in this letter (such as " the rudder groans " and " equal to the gods of the sea ") by the same rule as you attack the passages I am quoting; for I am well aware that in seeking indulgence for my past offences I have fallen into the very errors you condemn. Strike then—as long as you will fix an early date for us to discuss both past and present in person. Then you can make me more cautious or I shall teach you to be venturesome.

XXVII

To Plinius Paternus

I have often been conscious of the powers of history, its dignity and majesty and inspired authority, but never more so than on a recent occasion. An author had begun a reading of a work of exceptional candour, and had left part to be read another day. Up came the friends of someone I won't name, begging and praying him not to read the remainder; such is the shame people feel at hearing about their conduct, though they felt none at the time of doing what they blush to hear.[1] The author complied with their request, as he could well do without loss of sincerity, but the book, like their deeds, remains and will remain; it will always be read, and all the more for this delay, for information withheld only sharpens men's curiosity to hear it.

THE LETTERS OF PLINY

XXVIII

C. Plinius Romano Suo S.

1 Post longum tempus epistulas tuas, sed tres pariter recepi, omnes elegantissimas amantissimas, et quales a te venire praesertim desideratas oportebat. Quarum una iniungis mihi iucundissimum ministerium, ut ad Plotinam sanctissimam feminam litterae tuae perferantur: perferentur. Eadem com-

2 mendas Popilium Artemisium: statim praestiti quod petebat. Indicas etiam modicas te vindemias collegisse: communis haec mihi tecum, quamquam in diversissima parte terrarum, querela est. Altera

3 epistula nuntias multa te nunc dictare nunc scribere, quibus nos tibi repraesentes. Gratias ago; agerem magis si me illa ipsa, quae scribis aut dictas, legere voluisses. Et erat aequum ut te mea ita me tua scripta cognoscere, etiamsi ad alium quam ad me

4 pertinerent. Polliceris in fine, cum certius de vitae nostrae ordinatione aliquid audieris, futurum te fugitivum rei familiaris statimque ad nos evolaturum,[1] qui iam tibi compedes nectimus, quas perfringere[2]

5 nullo modo possis. Tertia epistula continebat esse tibi redditam orationem pro Clario[3] eamque visam

---

[1] evolaturum a: advolaturum γ.
[2] perfringere a: effringere γ.
[3] pro Clario a: proclamo γ.

---

[1] Trajan's wife, the Empress. See *Pan.* 83.
[2] Voconius Romanus (see Index) was a native of Hither

XXVIII

To Voconius Romanus

YOUR letters have reached me after a long delay, three in fact at once, all beautifully expressed, warmly affectionate, and such as I ought to have from you, especially when I have been waiting for them. In one you entrust me with the very welcome commission of forwarding your letter to the august lady Plotina:[1] it shall be done. The same letter introduces Popilius Artemisius. I carried out his request at once. You also say that you have had a poor grape harvest, and I can join you in this complaint, although we live so far from each other.[2]

The second letter tells me you are setting down or dictating your impressions of myself. Thank you— I would thank you more if you had been willing for me to read the actual pages as they are finished; as you read my work, in common justice I should read yours, even when someone else is the subject. At the end you promise that, once you have some definite news of my arrangements,[3] you will escape from your domestic affairs and take refuge here with me, where I am already forging you fetters which you will never manage to break.

Your third letter mentions that you have received my speech on behalf of Clarius and thought it seemed fuller than when you heard me deliver it. It *is* fuller,

Spain, but it is not clear here or in IX. 7 whether he had retired there or was living in Italy.

[3] This could be taken as generally meant, or as suggesting that P. was expecting some consular post (though he did not go to Bithynia until 109/10). See Syme, p. 659.

uberiorem, quam dicente me audiente te fuerit.
Est uberior; multa enim postea inserui. Adicis
alias te litteras curiosius scriptas misisse; an ac-
ceperim quaeris. Non accepi et accipere gestio.
Proinde prima quaque occasione mitte adpositis
quidem usuris, quas ego (num parcius possum?)
centesimas computabo. Vale.

XXIX

C. Plinius Rustico Suo S.

1 Ut satius unum aliquid insigniter facere quam plura
mediocriter, ita plurima mediocriter, si non possis
unum aliquid insigniter. Quod intuens ego variis me
studiorum generibus nulli satis confisus experior.
2 Proinde, cum hoc vel illud leges, ita singulis veniam
ut non singulis dabis. An ceteris artibus excusatio in
numero, litteris durior lex, in quibus difficilior effectus
est? Quid autem ego de venia quasi ingratus?
Nam si ea facilitate proxima acceperis qua priora,
laus potius speranda quam venia obsecranda est.
Mihi tamen venia sufficit. Vale.

XXX

C. Plinius Gemino Suo S.

1 Laudas mihi et frequenter praesens et nunc per
epistulas Nonium tuum, quod sit liberalis in quosdam:

---

[1] Possibly the historian. See Index.

for I made several additions afterwards. You then want to know if I have had the other letter you sent, which was composed with special care. No, I haven't, and I can't wait for it. So send it as soon as you can, and pay me full interest: I work it out at twelve per cent per annum, and can't be expected to let you off more lightly than that.

XXIX

To Fabius (?) Rusticus[1]

It is better to excel in one thing than do several moderately well, but moderate skill in several things is better if you lack ability to excel in one. Bearing this in mind, I have tried my hand at various styles of composition as I have never felt confident in any one. So when you read anything of mine you must be indulgent to each style I use in consideration of its not being my only one; quantity is an excuse for lack of quality in the other arts, so why should there be a harsher law for literature where success is even more difficult? But I mustn't talk about indulgence as if I were ungrateful—if you receive my latest efforts as kindly as you did my earlier work I should be looking for praise rather than begging indulgence, though this would be enough for me.

XXX

To Rosianus Geminus

I have often heard you praise your friend Nonius in person, as you do in your last letter, for his generosity

et ipse laudo, si tamen non in hos solos. Volo enim
eum, qui sit vere liberalis, tribuere patriae propinquis,
adfinibus amicis, sed amicis dico pauperibus, non ut
isti qui iis potissimum donant, qui donare maxime
2 possunt. Hos ego viscatis hamatisque muneribus non
sua promere puto sed aliena corripere. Sunt ingenio
simili qui quod huic donant auferunt illi, famamque
3 liberalitatis avaritia petunt. Primum est autem suo
esse contentum, deinde, quos praecipue scias indi-
gere, sustentantem foventemque orbe quodam socia-
litatis ambire. Quae cuncta si facit iste, usquequaque laudandus est; si unum aliquid, minus
4 quidem, laudandus tamen: tam rarum est etiam
imperfectae liberalitatis exemplar. Ea invasit homines habendi cupido, ut possideri magis quam possi-
dere videantur. Vale.

XXXI

C. PLINIUS SARDO SUO S.

1 POSTQUAM a te recessi, non minus tecum, quam cum
ad te fui. Legi enim librum tuum identidem
repetens ea maxime (non enim mentiar), quae de me
scripsisti, in quibus quidem percopiosus fuisti. Quam
multa, quam varia, quam non eadem de eodem nec

to certain people, and I will add my own praises if his generosity is not confined to these individual cases. I should like to see the truly generous man giving to his country, neighbours, relatives, and friends, but by them I mean his friends without means; unlike the people who mostly bestow their gifts on those best able to make a return. Such persons do not seem to me to part with anything of their own, but use their gifts as baits to hook other people's possessions. Other smart characters rob one person to give to another, hoping their rapacity will bring them a reputation for generous giving. But the first essential is to be content with your own lot, the second to support and assist those you know to be most in need, embracing them all within the circle of your friendship.

If your friend can achieve all this he is wholly to be praised, if part only he is still praiseworthy in a lesser degree; so few instances are there even of partial generosity. Greed for ownership has taken such a hold of us that we seem to be possessed by wealth rather than to possess it.

XXXI

To Sardus

I am still enjoying your company as much as before we parted, for I have been reading your book, and, to be honest, rereading again and again the passages about myself, where you have indeed been eloquent! The wealth of your material and variety of treatment, and the skill whereby you avoid repetition without

2 tamen diversa dixisti! Laudem pariter et gratias
agam? Neutrum satis possum et, si possem, timerem
ne adrogans esset ob ea laudare, ob quae gratias
agerem. Unum illud addam, omnia mihi tanto
laudabiliora visa quanto iucundiora, tanto iucundiora
quanto laudabiliora erant. Vale.

XXXII

C. Plinius Titiano Suo S.

Quid agis, quid acturus es? Ipse vitam iucundissimam (id est, otiosissimam) vivo. Quo fit, ut
scribere longiores epistulas nolim, velim legere, illud
tamquam delicatus, hoc tamquam otiosus. Nihil est
enim aut pigrius delicatis aut curiosius otiosis. Vale.

XXXIII

C. Plinius Caninio Suo S.

1 Incidi in materiam veram sed simillimam fictae,
dignamque isto laetissimo altissimo planeque poetico
ingenio; incidi autem, dum super cenam varia mira-
cula hinc inde referuntur. Magna auctori fides:
tametsi quid poetae cum fide? Is tamen auctor,
2 cui bene vel historiam scripturus credidisses. Est in

---

[1] The poet of VIII. 4.

loss of consistency, makes me wonder whether I should mingle congratulations with my thanks. I do neither adequately, and if I could I should be afraid it would look conceited to congratulate you on the very thing for which I am thanking you. I will only add that my pleasure in your work increased its merit for me, while its merit added to my pleasure.

XXXII

To Cornelius Titianus

What are you doing, and what are your plans? As for me, I'm enjoying life to the full, which means I am thoroughly idle. Consequently I can't be bothered with writing longer letters in my pampered state, though I should welcome some to read in my idle hours. Nothing is so lazy as a pampered man, and nothing so inquisitive as a man with nothing to do.

XXXIII

To Caninius Rufus [1]

I have come across a true story which sounds very like fable, and so ought to be a suitable subject for your abundant talent to raise to the heights of poetry. I heard it over the dinner table when various marvellous tales were being circulated, and I had it on good authority—though I know that doesn't really interest poets. However, it was one which even a historian might well have trusted.

145

Africa Hipponensis colonia mari proximà. Adiacet navigabile stagnum; ex hoc in modum fluminis aestuarium emergit, quod vice alterna, prout aestus aut repressit aut impulit, nunc infertur mari, nunc 3 redditur stagno. Omnis hic aetas piscandi navigandi atque etiam natandi studio tenetur, maxime pueri, quos otium lususque sollicitat. His gloria et virtus altissime provehi: victor ille, qui longissime ut litus 4 ita simul natantes reliquit. Hoc certamine puer quidam audentior ceteris in ulteriora tendebat. Delphinus occurrit, et nunc praecedere puerum nunc sequi nunc circumire, postremo subire deponere iterum subire, trepidantemque perferre primum in altum, mox flectit ad litus, redditque terrae et 5 aequalibus. Serpit per coloniam fama; concurrere omnes, ipsum puerum tamquam miraculum adspicere, interrogare audire narrare. Postero die obsident litus, prospectant mare et si quid est mari simile. Natant pueri, inter hos ille, sed cautius. Delphinus rursus ad tempus, rursus ad puerum. Fugit ille cum ceteris. Delphinus, quasi invitet et revocet, exsilit mergitur, variosque orbes implicat expeditque. 6 Hoc altero die, hoc tertio, hoc pluribus, donec homines innutritos mari subiret timendi pudor. Accedunt et adludunt et adpellant, tangunt etiam

---

[1] Hippo Diarrhytus (now Bizerta), N.W. of Carthage.

The Roman colony of Hippo[1] is situated on the
coast of Africa. Near by is a navigable lagoon, with
an estuary like a river leading from it which flows
into the sea or back into the lagoon according to the
ebb and flow of the tide. People of all ages spend
their time here to enjoy the pleasures of fishing,
boating, and swimming, especially the boys who
have plenty of time to play. It is a bold feat with
them to swim out into deep water, the winner being
the one who has left the shore and his fellow-swim-
mers farthest behind. In one of these races a particularly adventurous boy went farther out than the
rest. A dolphin met him and swam now in front,
now behind him, then played round him, and finally
dived to take him on its back, then put him off, took
him on again, and first carried him terrified out to
sea, then turned to the shore and brought him back
to land and his companions.

The tale spread through the town; everyone ran
up to stare at the boy as a prodigy, ask to hear his
story and repeat it. The following day crowds
thronged the shore, watched the sea, and anything
like the sea, while the boys began to swim out,
among them the same boy, but this time more
cautious. The dolphin punctually reappeared and
approached the boy again, but he made off with the
rest. Meanwhile the dolphin jumped and dived,
coiled and uncoiled itself in circles as if inviting and
calling him back. This was repeated the next day,
the day after, and on several more occasions, until
these people, who are bred to the sea, began to be
ashamed of their fears. They went up to the dolphin and played with it, called it, and even touched

pertrectantque praebentem. Crescit audacia experimento. Maxime puer, qui primus expertus est,
adnatat nanti, insilit tergo, fertur referturque,
agnosci se amari putat, amat ipse; neuter timet,
neuter timetur; huius fiducia, mansuetudo illius
7 augetur. Nec non alii pueri dextra laevaque simul
eunt hortantes monentesque. Ibat una (id quoque
mirum) delphinus alius, tantum spectator et comes.
Nihil enim simile aut faciebat aut patiebatur, sed
alterum illum ducebat reducebat, ut puerum ceteri
8 pueri. Incredibile, tam verum tamen quam priora,
delphinum gestatorem collusoremque puerorum in
terram quoque extrahi solitum, harenisque siccatum,
9 ubi incaluisset in mare revolvi. Constat Octavium
Avitum, legatum proconsulis, in litus educto religione
prava superfudisse unguentum, cuius illum novitatem
odoremque in altum refugisse, nec nisi post multos
dies visum languidum et maestum, mox redditis
viribus priorem lasciviam et solita ministeria repe-
10 tisse. Confluebant omnes ad spectaculum magistratus, quorum adventu et mora modica res publica
novis sumptibus atterebatur. Postremo locus ipse
quietem suam secretumque perdebat: placuit occulte
11 interfici, ad quod coibatur. Haec tu qua misera-

---

¹ The elder Pliny tells the story briefly in *NH* IX. 26, and
names the proconsul, Tampius Flavianus.

and stroked it when they found it did not object,
and their daring increased with experience. In particular the boy who first met it swam up when it was
in the water, climbed on its back, and was carried
out to sea and brought back; he believed it knew and
loved him, and he loved it. Neither was feared nor
afraid, and the one grew more confident as the other
became tamer. Some of the other boys used to go
with him on either side, shouting encouragement and
warnings, and with it swam another dolphin (which
is also remarkable), but only to look on and escort
the other, for it did not perform the same feats or
allow the same familiarities, but only accompanied
its fellow to shore and out to sea as the boys did their
friend. It is hard to believe, but as true as the rest
of the story, that the dolphin who carried and played
with the boys would even let itself be pulled out on to
the shore, dry itself in the sand, and roll back into the
sea when it felt hot.

Then, as is generally known,[1] the governor's legate,
Octavius Avitus, was moved by some misguided
superstition to pour scented oil on the dolphin as it
lay on the shore, and the strange sensation and smell
made it take refuge in the open sea. It did not re-
appear for many days, and then seemed listless and
dejected; but as it regained strength it returned to
its former playfulness and usual tricks. All the local
officials used to gather to see the sight, and their
arrival to stay in the little town began to burden it
with extra expense, until finally the place itself was
losing its character of peace and quiet. It was then
decided that the object of the public's interest should
be quietly destroyed.

tione, qua copia deflebis ornabis attolles! Quamquam non est opus adfingas aliquid aut adstruas; sufficit ne ea quae sunt vera minuantur. Vale.

XXXIV

C. Plinius Tranquillo Suo S.

1 Explica aestum meum: audio me male legere, dumtaxat versus; orationes enim commode, sed tanto minus versus. Cogito ergo recitaturus familiaribus amicis experiri libertum meum. Hoc quoque familiare, quod elegi non bene sed melius (scio) lecturum, 2 si tamen non fuerit perturbatus. Est enim tam novus lector quam ego poeta. Ipse nescio, quid illo legente interim faciam, sedeam defixus et mutus et similis otioso an, ut quidam, quae pronuntiabit, murmure oculis manu prosequar. Sed puto me non minus male saltare quam legere. Iterum dicam, explica aestum meum vereque rescribe, num sit melius pessime legere quam ista vel non facere vel facere. Vale.

---

[1] See T. F. Higham, *Greece and Rome*, VII. 1. pp. 82 ff., for a verified account of a dolphin playing with children.

I can imagine how sadly you will lament this ending and how eloquently you will enrich and adorn
this tale—though there is no need for you to add any
fictitious details; it will be enough if the truth is told
in full.[1]

XXXIV

To Suetonius Tranquillus

PLEASE settle my doubts. I am told that I read
badly—I mean when I read verse, for I can manage
speeches, though this seems to make my verse reading all the worse. So, as I am planning to give an
informal reading to my personal friends, I am thinking of making use of one of my freedmen. This is
certainly treating them informally, as the man I have
chosen is not really a good reader, but I think he will
do better than I can as long as he is not nervous.
(He is in fact as inexperienced a reader as I am a
poet.) Now, I don't know what I am to do myself
while he is reading, whether I am to sit still and
silent like a mere spectator, or do as some people and
accompany his words with low voice, eye, and gesture.
But I don't believe I am any better at mime than at
reading aloud. Once more, then, settle my doubts
and give me a straight answer whether it would be
better to read myself, however badly, than to do or
leave undone what I have just said.

XXXV

C. Plinius †Atrio†[1] Suo S.

1 Librum, quem misisti, recepi et gratias ago. Sum tamen hoc tempore occupatissimus. Ideo nondum eum legi, cum alioqui valdissime cupiam. Sed eam reverentiam cum litteris ipsis tum scriptis tuis debeo, ut sumere illa nisi vacuo animo inreligiosum 2 putem. Diligentiam tuam in retractandis operibus valde probo. Est tamen aliquis modus, primum quod nimia cura deterit magis quam emendat, deinde quod nos a recentioribus revocat simulque nec absolvit priora et incohare posteriora non patitur. Vale.

XXXVI

C. Plinius Fusco Suo S.

1 Quaeris, quemadmodum in Tuscis diem aestate disponam. Evigilo cum libuit, plerumque circa horam primam, saepe ante, tardius raro. Clausae fenestrae manent; mire enim silentio et tenebris ab iis quae avocant abductus et liber et mihi relictus, non oculos animo sed animum oculis sequor, qui eadem 2 quae mens vident, quotiens non vident alia. Cogito si quid in manibus, cogito ad verbum scribenti

---

[1] Atrio *aut* Appio γ: Oppio *a*: "*fortasse* Attio" *Keil*.

XXXV

To Atrius (?)

I HAVE received the book you sent, for which many thanks. I am very busy just now, so I haven't read it yet in spite of my impatience. But I hold literature in general and your writings in particular in such high regard that I should feel it sacrilege to handle them, unless I could give my undivided attention.

I very much approve of the trouble you take over revising your work, but there should be a limit to this; first because too much application blurs the outline instead of improving the details, and then because it distracts us from more recent subjects and prevents us from starting on new work and also from finishing off the old.

XXXVI

To Fuscus Salinator

You want to know how I plan the summer days I spend in Tuscany. I wake when I like, usually about sunrise, often earlier but rarely later. My shutters stay closed, for in the stillness and darkness I feel myself surprisingly detached from any distractions and left to myself in freedom; my eyes do not determine the direction of my thinking, but, being unable to see anything, they are guided to visualize my thoughts. If I have anything on hand I work it out in my head, choosing and correcting the wording,

THE LETTERS OF PLINY

emendantique similis, nunc pauciora nunc plura, ut
vel difficile vel facile componi tenerive potuerunt.
Notarium voco et die admisso quae formaveram dicto;
3 abit rursusque revocatur rursusque dimittitur. Ubi
hora quarta vel quinta (neque enim certum dimen-
sumque tempus), ut dies suasit, in xystum me vel
cryptoporticum confero, reliqua meditor et dicto.
Vehiculum ascendo. Ibi quoque idem quod ambu-
lans aut iacens; durat intentio mutatione ipsa refecta.
Paulum redormio, dein ambulo, mox orationem
Graecam Latinamve clare et intente non tam vocis
causa quam stomachi lego; pariter tamen et illa
4 firmatur. Iterum ambulo ungor exerceor lavor.
Cenanti mihi, si cum uxore vel paucis, liber legitur;
post cenam comoedia aut lyristes; mox cum meis
ambulo, quorum in numero sunt eruditi. Ita variis
sermonibus vespera extenditur, et quamquam longis-
5 simus dies bene[1] conditur. Non numquam ex hoc
ordine aliqua mutantur; nam, si diu iacui vel ambu-
lavi, post somnum demum lectionemque non vehiculo
sed, quod brevius quia velocius, equo gestor. Inter-
veniunt amici ex proximis oppidis, partemque diei ad
se trahunt interdumque lasso mihi opportuna inter-
6 pellatione subveniunt. Venor aliquando, sed non

[1] bene γ: cito θ.

---

[1] As Zosimus (V. 19) and Encolpius (VIII. 1).

and the amount I achieve depends on the ease or difficulty with which my thoughts can be marshalled and kept in my head. Then I call my secretary, the shutters are opened, and I dictate what I have put into shape; he goes out, is recalled, and again dismissed. Three or four hours after I first wake (but I don't keep to fixed times) I betake myself according to the weather either to the terrace or the covered arcade, work out the rest of my subject, and dictate it. I go for a drive, and spend the time in the same way as when walking or lying down; my powers of concentration do not flag and are in fact refreshed by the change. After a short sleep and another walk I read a Greek or Latin speech aloud and with emphasis, not so much for the sake of my voice as my digestion, though of course both are strengthened by this. Then I have another walk, am oiled, take exercise, and have a bath. If I am dining alone with my wife or with a few friends, a book is read aloud during the meal and afterwards we listen to a comedy or some music; then I walk again with the members of my household, some of whom are well educated.[1] Thus the evening is prolonged with varied conversation, and, even when the days are at their longest, comes to a satisfying end.

Sometimes I vary this routine, for, if I have spent a long time on my couch or taking a walk, after my siesta and reading I go out on horseback instead of in a carriage so as to be quicker and take less time. Part of the day is given up to friends who visit me from neighbouring towns, and sometimes come to my aid with a welcome interruption when I am tired. Occasionally I go hunting, but not without my note-

sine pugillaribus, ut quamvis nihil ceperim non nihil referam. Datur et colonis, ut videtur ipsis, non satis temporis, quorum mihi agrestes querelae litteras nostras et haec urbana opera commendant. Vale.

XXXVII

C. PLINIUS PAULINO SUO S.

1 NEC tuae naturae est translaticia haec et quasi publica officia a familiaribus amicis contra ipsorum commodum exigere, et ego te constantius amo quam ut verear, ne aliter ac velim accipias, nisi te kalendis statim consulem videro, praesertim cum me necessitas locandorum[1] praediorum plures annos ordinatura detineat, in qua mihi nova consilia sumenda 2 sunt. Nam priore lustro, quamquam post magnas remissiones, reliqua creverunt: inde plerisque nulla iam cura minuendi aeris alieni, quod desperant posse persolvi; rapiunt etiam consumuntque quod natum 3 est, ut qui iam putent se non sibi parcere. Occurrendum ergo augescentibus vitiis et medendum est. Medendi una ratio, si non nummo sed partibus locem ac deinde ex meis aliquos operis exactores,

---

[1] locandorum a: tuscianorum γ (-canorum θ).

---

[1] Cf. I. 6 and IX. 10.
[2] He was suffect consul September–December 107. See Index.

books so that I shall have something to bring home even if I catch nothing.[1] I also give some time to my tenants (they think it should be more) and the boorishness of their complaints gives fresh zest to our literary interests and the more civilized pursuits of town.

XXXVII

To Valerius Paulinus

It is not your nature to demand the conventional formalities from your personal friends when they are likely to be inconvenienced, and I love you too surely to fear you will misinterpret my intentions if I am not present when you take up your consulship on the first of the month;[2] especially when I must stay here to arrange for letting my farms on long leases and I shall have to adopt a new system for this. During the past five years, despite the large reductions I made in the rents, the arrears have increased and as a result most of my tenants have lost interest in reducing their debt because they have no hope of being able to pay off the whole; they even seize and consume the produce of the land in the belief that they will gain nothing themselves by conserving it.

I must therefore face this growing evil and find a remedy. One way would be to let the farms not for a money rent but for a fixed share of the produce,[3] and then make some of my servants overseers to

---

[3] This is the *mezzadria* system still in use in Tuscany and northern Italy. Cf. the similar one followed on the imperial estates in N. Africa described in inscriptions (S. 463 and 464).

custodes fructibus ponam. Et alioqui nullum iustius genus reditus, quam quod terra caelum annus refert.
4 At hoc magnam fidem acres oculos numerosas manus poscit. Experiundum tamen et quasi in veteri morbo quaelibet mutationis auxilia temptanda sunt.
5 Vides, quam non delicata me causa obire primum consulatus tui diem non sinat; quem tamen hic quoque ut praesens votis gaudio gratulatione celebrabo. Vale.

XXXVIII

C. PLINIUS SATURNINO SUO S.

Ego vero Rufum nostrum laudo, non quia tu ut ita facerem petisti sed quia est ille dignissimus. Legi enim librum omnibus numeris absolutum, cui multum apud me gratiae amor ipsius adiecit. Iudicavi tamen; neque enim soli iudicant qui maligne legunt. Vale.

XXXIX

C. PLINIUS MUSTIO SUO S.

1 Haruspicum monitu reficienda est mihi aedes Cereris in praediis in melius et in maius, vetus sane et angusta, cum sit alioqui stato die frequentissima.

---

[1] Possibly the poet Caninius Rufus of VIII. 4 and IX. 33.
[2] Probably that near Tifernum; Mustius appears to be at Rome.

keep a watch on the harvest. There is certainly no more just return than what is won from the soil, climate and seasons, but this method requires strict honesty, keen eyes, and many pairs of hands. However, I must make the experiment and try all possible changes of remedy for an obstinate complaint.

You see that it is not pure selfishness on my part which prevents my attending you on the first day of your consulship, and I shall celebrate it here with prayers, rejoicing and congratulations as if I were with you.

XXXVIII

To Pompeius Saturninus

I DO indeed congratulate our friend Rufus,[1] not at your request but because he merits praise. I have read his book, a finished performance in every way, my pleasure in which was much increased by my affection for its author. I did however read it critically; for criticism is not confined to those who read only to find fault.

XXXIX

To Mustius

I AM told by the soothsayers that I must rebuild the temple of Ceres which stands on my property;[2] it needs enlarging and improving, for it is certainly very old and too small considering how crowded it is on its special anniversary, when great crowds gather

2 Nam idibus Septembribus magnus e regione tota coit
populus, multae res aguntur, multa vota suscipiuntur,
multa redduntur; sed nullum in proximo suffugium
3 aut imbris aut solis. Videor ergo munifice simul
religioseque facturus, si aedem quam pulcherrimam
exstruxero, addidero porticus aedi, illam ad usum
4 deae has ad hominum. Velim ergo emas quattuor
marmoreas columnas, cuius tibi videbitur generis,
emas marmora quibus solum, quibus parietes exco-
lantur. Erit etiam faciendum [1] ipsius deae signum,
quia antiquum illud e ligno quibusdam sui partibus
5 vetustate truncatum est. Quantum ad porticus,
nihil interim occurrit, quod videatur istinc esse
repetendum, nisi tamen ut formam secundum
rationem loci scribas. Neque enim possunt circum-
dari templo: nam solum templi hinc flumine et
6 abruptissimis ripis, hinc via cingitur. Est ultra
viam latissimum pratum, in quo satis apte contra
templum ipsum porticus explicabuntur; nisi quid tu
melius invenies, qui soles locorum difficultates arte
superare. Vale.

XL

C. Plinius Fusco Suo S.

1 Scribis pergratas tibi fuisse litteras meas, quibus
cognovisti quemadmodum in Tuscis otium aestatis
exigerem; requiris quid ex hoc in Laurentino hieme
2 permutem. Nihil, nisi quod meridianus somnus

---

[1] faciendum γ: vel faciendum vel emendum *a Guillemin.*

there from the whole district on 13 September and many ceremonies are performed and vows made and discharged. But there is no shelter near by from rain or sun, so I think it will be an act of generosity and piety alike to build as fine a temple as I can and add porticoes—the temple for the goddess and the porticoes for the public.

Will you then please buy me four marble columns, any kind you think suitable, and marble for improving the floor and walls; and we shall also have to have made a statue of the goddess, for several pieces are broken off the original wooden one as it is so old. As for the porticoes, at the moment I can't think of anything I want from you, unless you will draw me a plan suitable for the position.[1] They cannot be built round the temple, for the site has a river with steep banks on one side and a road on the other. On the far side of the road is a large meadow where they might quite well stand facing the temple; unless you can think of a better solution from your professional experience of overcoming difficulties of terrain.

XL

To Fuscus Salinator

You say you were delighted with my letter describing how I spend my summer holidays in Tuscany, and you want to know what changes I make at Laurentum in winter. None, except that I cut out

---

[1] As in III. 6, P. has removed the essential details of measurement before publication.

eximitur multumque de nocte vel ante vel post diem sumitur, et, si agendi necessitas instat, quae frequens hieme, non iam comoedo vel lyristae post cenam locus, sed illa, quae dictavi, identidem retractantur, ac simul memoriae frequenti emenda-

3 tione proficitur. Habes aestate hieme consuetudinem; addas[1] huc licet ver et autumnum,[2] quae inter hiemem aestatemque media,[3] ut nihil de die perdunt, de nocte parvolum adquirunt. Vale.

[1] addas *R. Agricola*: non addas γα: nunc addas *Guillemin*.

[2] ver et autumnum quae *R. Agricola*: vere (*om. a*) tantum numquae γα.

[3] aestatemque media *R. Agricola*: statim (*om. a*) aestatemque mediam γα.

my siesta and shorten my nights a good deal by using the hours before dawn or after sunset; and, if I have an urgent case pending, as often happens in winter, instead of having comedy or music after dinner I work again and again over what I have dictated, and so fix it in my memory by repeated revision.

Now that you have my habits in summer and winter you can add spring and autumn, the intermediate seasons, during which none of the day is wasted and so very little is stolen from the night.

BOOK X

LIBER DECIMUS

AD TRAIANUM IMPERATOREM
CUM EIUSDEM RESPONSIS

I

C. Plinius Traiano Imperatori

1 Tua quidem pietas, imperator sanctissime, optaverat, ut quam tardissime succederes patri; sed di immortales festinaverunt virtutes tuas ad gubernacula rei publicae quam susceperas admovere.
2 Precor ergo ut tibi et per te generi humano prospera omnia, id est digna saeculo tuo contingant. Fortem te et hilarem, imperator optime, et privatim et publice opto.

II

C. Plinius Traiano Imperatori

1 Exprimere, domine, verbis non possum, quantum mihi gaudium attuleris, quod me dignum putasti iure trium liberorum. Quamvis enim Iuli Serviani, optimi viri tuique amantissimi, precibus indulseris, tamen etiam ex rescripto intellego libentius hoc ei te

---

[1] Cf. *Pan.* 8 and 10. Nerva adopted Trajan in October 97 and died 27/28 January 98. This letter was written soon after his death.

BOOK X

ADDRESSED TO THE EMPEROR TRAJAN AND INCLUDING HIS REPLIES

I

PLINY TO THE EMPEROR TRAJAN

YOUR filial feelings, august Emperor, prompted your desire to succeed your father at the latest possible moment, but the immortal gods have hastened to put our country in your hands, a task to which you had already been assigned.[1] Therefore I pray that you, and through you all mankind, may enjoy every prosperity, as befits your reign; and as an individual no less than as an official, noble Emperor, I wish you health and happiness.

II

PLINY TO THE EMPEROR TRAJAN

I HAVE no words to tell you, Sir, how much pleasure you have given me by thinking me fit for the privileges granted to parents of three children.[2] I know that you have granted this at the request of your worthy and devoted servant Julius Servianus, but from the wording of your decision I understand that

[2] For these privileges see II. 13. 8 and note.

2 praestitisse, quia pro me rogabat. Videor ergo
summam voti mei consecutus, cum inter initia
felicissimi principatus tui probaveris me ad pecu-
liarem indulgentiam tuam pertinere; eoque magis
liberos concupisco, quos habere etiam illo tristissimo
saeculo volui, sicut potes duobus matrimoniis meis
3 credere. Sed di melius, qui omnia integra bonitati
tuae reservarunt; malui hoc potius tempore me
patrem fieri, quo futurus essem et securus et felix.

III A

C. PLINIUS TRAIANO IMPERATORI

1 UT primum me, domine, indulgentia vestra pro-
movit ad praefecturam aerarii Saturni, omnibus
advocationibus, quibus alioqui numquam eram
promiscue functus, renuntiavi, ut toto animo delegato
2 mihi officio vacarem. Qua ex causa, cum patronum
me provinciales optassent contra Marium Priscum,
et petii veniam huius muneris et impetravi. Sed
cum postea consul designatus censuisset agendum [1]
nobiscum, quorum erat excusatio recepta, ut essemus
in senatus potestate pateremurque nomina nostra in
urnam conici, convenientissimum esse tranquillitati

---

[1] censuisset agendum *Gruter*: -ses tacendum *a*.

---

[1] Pliny's second wife died in early 97: cf. IX. 13. 4. He
does not appear to have married Calpurnia till after 100.
[2] See V. 14. 5, X. 8. 3 and *Pan.* 91. 1 with note. Pliny
was nominated before Nerva's death 27/28 January 98.

you were the more willing to do so as his petition was on my behalf. For you to think me worthy of your personal favour at the opening of your auspicious reign is, I feel, the realization of my highest hopes. Still more now do I long for children of my own, though I wanted them even during those evil days now past, as you may know from my having married twice.[1] The gods knew better when they reserved my good fortune wholly for your generosity. Now is the time I would wish to be a father, when my happiness need know no fear.

III A

PLINY TO THE EMPEROR TRAJAN

WHEN the kind interest of your father and yourself, Sir, promoted me to take charge of the Treasury of Saturn,[2] I gave up my practice in the courts (though I had never taken on cases indiscriminately) so that I could be free to give my whole attention to the duties assigned to me. Thus when the province of Africa asked me to act for them against Marius Priscus,[3] I begged to be excused the honour, and my excuse was accepted. Subsequently the consul-elect proposed that those of us who had been granted exemption should be prevailed on to remain at the Senate's disposal and to permit our names to be included in the ballot for advocates.[4] I then thought I

[3] In late 98. This refers to the first proceedings against Marius Priscus, II. 11. 2.

[4] An advocate was assigned to a province by *sortitio* if it had not asked for someone by name, as Baetica asked for Pliny in the case of Classicus, III. 4. 2.

saeculi tui putavi praesertim tam moderatae voluntati
3 amplissimi ordinis non repugnare. Cui obsequio meo
opto ut existimes constare rationem, cum omnia facta
dictaque mea probare sanctissimis moribus tuis
cupiam.

III B

TRAIANUS PLINIO

ET civis et senatoris boni partibus functus es
obsequium amplissimi ordinis, quod iustissime exige-
bat, praestando. Quas partes impleturum te secundum susceptam fidem confido.

IV

C. PLINIUS TRAIANO IMPERATORI

1 INDULGENTIA tua, imperator optime, quam plenis-
simam experior, hortatur me, ut audeam tibi etiam
pro amicis obligari; inter quos sibi vel praecipuum
locum vindicat Voconius Romanus, ab ineunte aetate
2 condiscipulus et contubernalis. Quibus ex causis et a
divo patre tuo petieram, ut illum in amplissimum
ordinem promoveret. Sed hoc votum meum bonitati
tuae reservatum est, quia mater Romani liberalitatem
sestertii quadragies,[1] quod conferre se filio codicillis

---

[1] quadragiens I (*in margine* vel quadragies vel quadringenties).

---

[1] For Voconius Romanus, see Index and II. 13. There is
no indication that this petition succeeded.

should best accord with the peaceful atmosphere of
your reign if I did not oppose that distinguished
body, especially when they were so reasonable in
their request. I trust that you will think my obedience was correct, for I am anxious for every word
and deed of mine to receive the sanction of your own
supreme standards.

III B

TRAJAN TO PLINY

You have acted rightly both as a citizen and as a
member of the Senate in obeying the just demands
of that distinguished body, and I am sure that you
will perform the duties you have undertaken in accordance with the trust placed in you.

IV

PLINY TO THE EMPEROR TRAJAN

YOUR kindness, noble Emperor, of which I have
full personal experience, encourages me to venture
to ask you to extend it to my friends, among whom
Voconius Romanus[1] has the highest claim. He has
been my friend from our early years when we were
at school together, and for this reason I petitioned
your deified father, the late Emperor, to raise him to
the dignity of senatorial rank. However, I await your
generosity for my wish to be granted; for, although
Romanus's mother had written to your father to state
that she was making a gift of four million sesterces to

ad patrem tuum scriptis professa fuerat, nondum
satis legitime peregerat; quod postea fecit admonita
3 a nobis. Nam fundos emancipavit, et cetera quae in
emancipatione implenda solent exigi consummavit.
4 Cum sit ergo finitum, quod spes nostras morabatur,
non sine magna fiducia subsigno apud te fidem pro
moribus Romani mei, quos et liberalia studia exornant
et eximia pietas, quae hanc ipsam matris liberalitatem
et statim patris hereditatem et adoptionem a vitrico
5 meruit. Auget haec et natalium et paternarum
facultatium splendor; quibus singulis multum com-
mendationis accessurum etiam ex meis precibus
6 indulgentiae tuae credo. Rogo ergo, domine, ut me
exoptatissimae mihi gratulationis compotem facias et
honestis, ut spero, adfectibus meis praestes, ut non in
me tantum verum et in amico gloriari iudiciis tuis
possim.

V

C. PLINIUS TRAIANO IMPERATORI

1 PROXIMO anno, domine, gravissima valetudine
usque ad periculum vitae vexatus iatralipten ad-
sumpsi; cuius sollicitudini et studio tuae tantum
indulgentiae beneficio referre gratiam parem possum.
2 Quare rogo des ei civitatem Romanam. Est enim

---

1 This illness is dated in X. 8. 3 to the period in 97 before
Nerva's last illness.

her son, she had failed to complete the legal formalities. She has since done so after a reminder from me, has transferred some property to him, and completed the usual necessary forms for the conveyance.

Now that the obstacle to our hopes is removed, I can vouch for the character of my friend Romanus with complete confidence, a character signalized by his cultivated interests and the devotion to his parents to which he owes this gift from his mother, as well as his inheritance from his father soon afterwards and his adoption by his stepfather. He comes, moreover, from a distinguished family, and his father was a wealthy man. In addition to this I trust that my own plea on his behalf will be a further recommendation to your kind interest. I pray you then, Sir, to enable me to congratulate Romanus as I so much wish to do, and to gratify what I hope is a worthy affection. I can then be proud to think that your recognition of myself extends to my friend.

V

PLINY TO THE EMPEROR TRAJAN

WHEN I was seriously ill last year,[1] Sir, and in some danger of my life, I called in a medical therapist [2] whose care and attentiveness I cannot adequately reward without the help of your kind interest in the man. I pray you therefore to grant him Roman citizenship. He is a resident alien, Arpocras by

[2] An *iatraliptes* was superior to a γυμναστής but inferior to an ἰατρός, his treatment depending on massage, exercise and diet. Cf. Juvenal, *Sat.* III. 76. Petronius, *Satyricon* 28.

peregrinae condicionis manumissus a peregrina.
Vocatur ipse Arpocras,[1] patronam habuit Thermuthin
Theonis, quae iam pridem defuncta est. Item rogo
des ius Quiritium libertis Antoniae Maximillae,
ornatissimae feminae, Hediae et Antoniae Harmeridi;
quod a te petente patrona peto.

VI

C. PLINIUS TRAIANO IMPERATORI

1 AGO gratias, domine, quod et ius Quiritium libertis
necessariae mihi feminae et civitatem Romanam
Arpocrati, iatraliptae meo, sine mora indulsisti. Sed
cum annos eius et censum sicut praeceperas ederem,
admonitus sum a peritioribus debuisse me ante ei
Alexandrinam civitatem impetrare, deinde Roma-
2 nam, quoniam esset Aegyptius. Ego autem, quia
inter Aegyptios ceterosque peregrinos nihil interesse
credebam, contentus fueram hoc solum scribere tibi,
esse eum a peregrina manumissum patronamque eius
iam pridem decessisse. De qua ignorantia mea non
queror, per quam stetit ut tibi pro eodem homine
saepius obligarer. Rogo itaque, ut beneficio tuo
legitime frui possim, tribuas ei et Alexandrinam
civitatem [et Romanam[2]]. Annos eius et censum, ne

---

[1] Arpocras *I*: Harp. *a* (*idem in* X. 6, 7, 10).
[2] et Romanam *seclusit Böhm.*

---

[1] The *Ius Quiritium* granted full civil status to freedmen of
inferior status (*Latini Iuniani*: cf. X. 104).
[2] The man was evidently resident in the Greek city of Alex-

name, and was given his freedom by his patron, also
alien. She was Thermuthis, wife of Theon, and
died some time ago.

I also pray you to grant full Roman citizenship [1]
to Hedia and Antonia Harmeris, the freedwomen of
the noble lady Antonia Maximilla. It is at her
desire that I make the request.

VI

PLINY TO THE EMPEROR TRAJAN

THANK you, Sir, for your promptitude in granting
full citizenship to the freedwomen of my relative
Antonia, and Roman citizenship to my therapist
Arpocras. But when I was supplying his age and
property according to your instructions, I was re-
minded by people more experienced than I am that,
since the man is an Egyptian, I ought not to have
asked for Roman citizenship for him before he became a citizen of Alexandria. [2] I had not realized
that there was any distinction between Egyptians
and other aliens, so I had thought it sufficient to inform you only that he had been given his freedom by
an alien and that his patron had died some time ago.
I shall not regret my ignorance if it means that I can
be further indebted to you on behalf of the same
person; I pray you therefore to make him a citizen
of Alexandria too so that I may lawfully enjoy the
favour you have conferred. To prevent any further

andria, and so eligible for Roman citizenship; unlike the
majority of Egyptians who could never become Roman
citizens and were ineligible for legionary service.

quid rursus indulgentiam tuam moraretur, libertis
tuis quibus iusseras misi.

VII

TRAIANUS PLINIO

CIVITATEM Alexandrinam secundum institutionem
principum non temere dare proposui. Sed cum
Arpocrati, iatraliptae tuo, iam civitatem Romanam
impetraveris, huic quoque petitioni tuae negare non
sustineo. Tu, ex quo nomo sit, notum mihi facere
debebis, ut epistulam tibi ad Pompeium Plantam
praefectum Aegypti amicum meum mittam.

VIII

C. PLINIUS TRAIANO IMPERATORI

1 CUM divus pater tuus, domine, et oratione pulcher-
rima et honestissimo exemplo omnes cives ad munifi-
centiam esset cohortatus, petii ab eo, ut statuas
principum, quas in longinquis agris per plures suc-
cessiones traditas mihi quales acceperam custodie-
bam, permitteret in municipium transferre adiecta
2 sua statua. Quod quidem [1] ille mihi cum plenissimo
testimonio indulserat; ego statim decurionibus

---

[1] quod quidem *Keil* [1]: quodque *Ia*: quod cum *Gruter*:
quod *Keil,* [2] *Stout.*

---

[1] Egypt was divided into 47 *nomoi* each under a *strategos*
responsible to one of three *epistrategoi* and through him to the
equestrian prefect. For Planta, see IX. 1.

delay to your generous interest I have given the details of his age and property to your freedmen, as instructed.

VII

TRAJAN TO PLINY

FOLLOWING the rule of my predecessors, I do not intend to grant Alexandrian citizenship except in special cases; but as you have already obtained Roman citizenship for your medical therapist Arpocras, I cannot refuse this further request. You must inform me of the man's district[1] so that I can write you a letter for my friend Pompeius Planta, the prefect of Egypt.

VIII

PLINY TO THE EMPEROR TRAJAN

YOUR late father, Sir, the deified Emperor, had encouraged liberal giving among his subjects in his fine public speeches and by his own noble example. I therefore sought his permission to transfer to the town of Tifernum the statues of former Emperors which I had inherited through various bequests and had kept as I received them on my estate some distance away; I also asked if I might add to them a statue of himself. He had given his permission with his full approval. I had then written at once to the town council to ask them to allocate me a site where

scripseram, ut adsignarent solum in quo templum pecunia mea exstruerem; illi in honorem[1] operis
3 ipsius electionem loci mihi obtulerant. Sed primum mea, deinde patris tui valetudine, postea curis delegati a vobis officii retentus, nunc videor commodissime posse in rem praesentem excurrere. Nam et menstruum meum kalendis Septembribus finitur, et sequens mensis complures dies feriatos habet.
4 Rogo ergo ante omnia permittas mihi opus quod incohaturus sum exornare et tua statua; deinde, ut hoc facere quam maturissime possim, indulgeas com-
5 meatum. Non est autem simplicitatis meae dissimulare apud bonitatem tuam obiter te plurimum collaturum utilitatibus rei familiaris meae. Agrorum enim, quos in eadem regione possideo, locatio, cum alioqui cccc excedat, adeo non potest differri, ut proximam putationem novus colonus facere debeat. Praeterea continuae sterilitates cogunt me de remissionibus cogitare; quarum rationem nisi prae-
6 sens inire non possum. Debebo[2] ergo, domine, indulgentiae tuae et pietatis[3] meae celeritatem et status ordinationem, si mihi ob utraque haec dederis commeatum xxx dierum. Neque enim angustius tempus praefinire possum, cum et municipium et agri de quibus loquor sint ultra centesimum et quinquagesimum lapidem.

[1] honorem *Cortius*: honore *Ia*.
[2] debebo *Gronovius*: debeo *Ia*.
[3] pietatis *Gronovius*: -tati *Ia*.

[1] See III. 4 and IV. 1.

I could set up a temple[1] at my own expense, and they had honoured my proposal by leaving the choice of a site to me. But first my own ill-health, then your father's illness, and subsequently the responsibilities of the post you have both assigned me,[2] have caused delays, so that this seems the first convenient opportunity for me to go there in person. My month on duty finishes at the end of August, and there are a great many public holidays in September.

I pray you then first to permit me to add your statue to the others which will adorn the temple I propose to build, then to grant me leave of absence so that it can be built as soon as possible. But I should fail in sincerity if I concealed from your kindness the fact that my personal affairs will incidentally benefit very much. The farms I own in the district bring in more than 400,000 sesterces, and I cannot postpone letting them, especially as the new tenants should be there to see to the pruning of the vines, and this must be done soon. Moreover, the series of bad harvests we have had are forcing me to consider reducing rents, and I cannot calculate these unless I am on the spot.

If then, Sir, you will grant me thirty days' leave of absence on both accounts, I shall be indebted to your generosity both for the speedy accomplishment of my act of loyalty and the setting in order of my private affairs. I cannot manage with less than a month, as the town and farms I am talking about are more than 150 miles from Rome.

[2] The letter must be written in summer 98 or 99, when Pliny was *praefectus aerarii Saturni* and Trajan was absent in Germany and Pannonia.

IX

Traianus Plinio

Et multas et omnes[1] publicas causas petendi commeatus reddidisti; mihi autem vel sola voluntas tua suffecisset. Neque enim dubito te, ut primum potueris, ad tam districtum officium reversurum. Statuam poni mihi a te eo quo desideras loco, quamquam eius modi honorum parcissimus tamen patior, ne impedisse cursum erga me pietatis tuae videar.

X

C. Plinius Traiano Imperatori

1 Exprimere, domine, verbis non possum, quanto me gaudio adfecerint epistulae tuae, ex quibus cognovi te Arpocrati, iatraliptae meo, et Alexandrinam civitatem tribuisse, quamvis secundum institutionem principum non temere eam dare proposuisses. Esse autem Arpocran νομοῦ Μεμφίτου indico tibi. 2 Rogo ergo, indulgentissime imperator, ut mihi ad Pompeium Plantam praefectum Aegypti amicum tuum, sicut promisisti, epistulam mittas. Obviam iturus, quo maturius, domine, exoptatissimi[2] adventus tui gaudio frui possim, rogo permittas mihi quam longissime occurrere tibi.

---

[1] et multas et omnes *Ia*: et privatas multas *Cat.*[2].
[2] exoptatissimi *Gronovius*: -ime *Ia*.

---

[1] For Trajan's reluctance to permit statues of himself, see *Pan.* 52. 3.
[2] From Germany and Pannonia in late summer 99; cf. *Pan.* 20-2.

IX

Trajan to Pliny

You have given me many reasons, as well as every official explanation, for your application for leave of absence, though I should have been satisfied with the mere expression of your wishes. I do not doubt that you will return as soon as possible to your exacting official duties.

You have my permission to set up my statue in the place you have chosen for it; I am generally very reluctant to accept honours of this kind, but I do not wish it to seem that I have put any check on your loyal feelings towards me.[1]

X

Pliny to the Emperor Trajan

Words cannot express my gratitude, Sir, for your letter telling me that you have given my therapist Arpocras the additional grant of Alexandrian citizenship, although you had intended to follow the rule of your predecessors and grant it only in special cases. I now inform you that his district is Memphis. I pray you then, gracious Emperor, to send me your promised letter to Pompeius Planta, the prefect of Egypt.

I hope to meet you, Sir, to enjoy the sooner the pleasure of your return[2] which is eagerly awaited here; I beg your permission to join you as far out from Rome as I can go.

THE LETTERS OF PLINY

XI

C. PLINIUS TRAIANO IMPERATORI

1 PROXIMA infirmitas mea, domine, obligavit me Postumio Marino medico; cui parem gratiam referre beneficio tuo possum, si precibus meis ex consuetu-
2 dine bonitatis tuae indulseris. Rogo ergo, ut propinquis eius des civitatem, Chrysippo Mithridatis uxorique Chrysippi, Stratonicae Epigoni, item liberis eiusdem Chrysippi, Epigono et Mithridati, ita ut sint in patris potestate utque iis in libertos servetur ius patronorum. Item rogo indulgeas ius Quiritium L. Satrio Abascanto et P. Caesio Phosphoro et Panchariae Soteridi; quod a te volentibus patronis peto.

XII

C. PLINIUS TRAIANO IMPERATORI

1 SCIO, domine, memoriae tuae, quae est bene faciendi tenacissima, preces nostras inhaerere. Quia tamen in hoc quoque indulsisti, admoneo simul et
2 impense rogo, ut Attium[1] Suram praetura exornare digneris, cum locus vacet. Ad quam spem alioqui quietissimum hortatur et natalium splendor et summa integritas in paupertate et ante omnia felicitas

[1] Attium *I*: Accium *a*.

XI

PLINY TO THE EMPEROR TRAJAN

MY recent illness, Sir, put me under an obligation to my doctor, Postumius Marinus, to whom I can make an adequate return with your help, if you will grant my petition with your usual kindness. I pray you therefore to confer citizenship on his relatives, Chrysippus, son of Mithridates, and Stratonice, the wife of Chrysippus, daughter of Epigonus, and on Chrysippus's two sons, Epigonus and Mithridates, while remaining under their father's authority with the further privilege of retaining the rights of a patron over their freedmen. I pray you further to grant full Roman citizenship to Lucius Satrius Abascantus, Publius Caesius Phosphorus, and Pancharia Soteris; I make this request at the desire of their patrons.

XII

PLINY TO THE EMPEROR TRAJAN

I KNOW, Sir, that my petitions are not forgotten, for your memory never lets an opportunity pass for doing good. But as you have hitherto shown me indulgence, may I remind you and at the same time add urgency to my request that you honour Attius Sura with a praetorship now that there is a vacancy? This is his only ambition, and it is fostered by the distinction of his family, his honourable conduct in times of poverty, and, above all, by the happiness of

temporum, quae bonam conscientiam civium tuorum
ad usum indulgentiae tuae provocat et attollit.

XIII

C. PLINIUS TRAIANO IMPERATORI

CUM sciam, domine, ad testimonium laudemque
morum meorum pertinere tam boni principis iudicio
exornari, rogo dignitati, ad quam me provexit indulgentia tua, vel auguratum vel septemviratum, quia
vacant, adicere digneris, ut iure sacerdotii precari
deos pro te publice possim, quos nunc precor pietate
privata.

XIV

C. PLINIUS TRAIANO IMPERATORI

VICTORIAE tuae, optime imperator, maximae,
pulcherrimae, antiquissimae et tuo nomine et rei
publicae gratulor, deosque immortales precor, ut
omnes cogitationes tuas tam laetus sequatur eventus,
cum virtutibus tantis gloria imperii et novetur et
augeatur.

---

[1] Pliny became augur in 103 (cf. IV. 8) so this letter was
addressed to Trajan during his absence in the First Dacian
War.

[2] In Dacia, either in 102 or 106.

your reign which encourages any of your subjects who
know their own merit to hope that they may benefit by your kind interest.

XIII

Pliny to the Emperor Trajan

I am well aware, Sir, that no higher tribute can be
paid to my reputation than some mark of favour from
so excellent a ruler as yourself. I pray you, therefore, to add to the honours to which I have been
raised by your kindness by granting me a priesthood,
either that of augur[1] or member of the septemvirate
as there is a vacancy in both orders. By virtue of
my priesthood I could then add official prayers on
your behalf to those I already offer in private as a
loyal citizen.

XIV

Pliny to the Emperor Trajan

May I congratulate you, noble Emperor, in your
own name and that of the State, on a great and glorious victory[2] in the finest tradition of Rome? I pray
the gods to grant that all your designs meet with
such a happy issue, and that the glory of your Empire
be renewed and enhanced by your outstanding
virtues.

XV

C. Plinius Traiano Imperatori

Quia confido, domine, ad curam tuam pertinere, nuntio tibi me Ephesum cum omnibus meis ὑπὲρ Μαλέαν navigasse quamvis contrariis ventis retentum.[1] Nunc destino partim orariis navibus, partim vehiculis provinciam petere. Nam sicut itineri graves aestus, ita continuae navigationi etesiae reluctantur.

XVI

Traianus Plinio

Recte renuntiasti, mi Secunde carissime. Pertinet enim ad animum meum, quali itinere provinciam pervenias. Prudenter autem constituis interim navibus, interim vehiculis uti, prout loca suaserint.

XVII A

C. Plinius Traiano Imperatori

1 Sicut saluberrimam navigationem, domine, usque Ephesum expertus ita inde, postquam vehiculis iter facere coepi, gravissimis aestibus atque etiam febri-

---

[1] retentum. *H. Stephanus*: retentus, *Ia*.

---

[1] The more usual route to Asia Minor was through the Corinthian Gulf.
[2] *i.e.* the prevailing north winds blowing from July to September.

XV

PLINY TO THE EMPEROR TRAJAN

I FEEL sure, Sir, that you will be interested to hear that I have rounded Cape Malea[1] and arrived at Ephesus with my complete staff, after being delayed by contrary winds. My intention now is to travel on to my province partly by coastal boat and partly by carriage. The intense heat prevents my travelling entirely by road and the prevailing Etesian winds make it impossible to go all the way by sea.[2]

XVI

TRAJAN TO PLINY

You did well to send me news, my dear Pliny, for I am much interested to know what sort of journey you are having to your province. You are wise to adapt yourself to local conditions and travel either by boat or carriage.

XVII A

PLINY TO THE EMPEROR TRAJAN

I KEPT in excellent health, Sir, throughout my voyage to Ephesus, but I found the intense heat very trying when I went on to travel by road and developed a touch of fever which kept me at Pergamum.[3] Then, when I had resumed my journey

[3] Pergamum is about 80 miles N. of Ephesus and over 20 miles from the sea, which suggests that Pliny had originally intended to continue overland to Prusa.

2 culis vexatus Pergami substiti. Rursus, cum transissem in orarias nauculas,[1] contrariis ventis retentus aliquanto tardius quam speraveram, id est xv kal. Octobres, Bithyniam intravi. Non possum tamen de mora queri, cum mihi contigerit, quod erat auspicatis3 simum, natalem tuum in provincia celebrare. Nunc rei publicae Prusensium impendia, reditus, debitores excutio; quod ex ipso tractatu magis ac magis necessarium intellego. Multae enim pecuniae variis ex causis a privatis detinentur; praeterea quaedam 4 minime legitimis sumptibus erogantur. Haec tibi, domine, in ipso ingressu meo scripsi.

XVII B

C. PLINIUS TRAIANO IMPERATORI

1 QUINTO decimo kal. Octob., domine, provinciam intravi, quam in eo obsequio, in ea erga te fide, quam 2 de genere humano mereris, inveni. Dispice, domine, an necessarium putes mittere huc mensorem. Videntur enim non mediocres pecuniae posse revocari a curatoribus operum, si mensurae fideliter agantur. Ita certe prospicio ex ratione Prusensium, quam cum maxime tracto.

---

[1] nauculas *Mynors*: naviculas *Ia*.

---

[1] He would have left this boat at Cyzicus and taken the coastal road via Apollonia to Prusa.

[2] 18 September; cf. *Pan.* 92. 4, and note.

by coastal boat,[1] I was further delayed by contrary winds, so that I did not reach Bithynia until 17 September. I had hoped to arrive earlier, but I cannot complain of the delay as I was in time to celebrate your birthday [2] in my province, and this should be a good omen.

I am now examining the finances of the town of Prusa, expenditure, revenues, and sums owing, and finding the inspection increasingly necessary the more I look into their accounts; large sums of money are detained in the hands of private individuals for various reasons, and further sums are paid out for quite illegal purposes, I am writing this letter, Sir, immediately after my arrival here.[3]

XVII B

PLINY TO THE EMPEROR TRAJAN

I ENTERED my province, Sir, on 17 September, and found there the spirit of obedience and loyalty which is your just tribute from mankind.

Will you consider, Sir, whether you think it necessary to send out a land surveyor? Substantial sums of money could, I think, be recovered from contractors of public works if we had dependable surveys made. I am convinced of this by the accounts of Prusa, which I am handling with all possible care.

[3] Note that on financial matters of this kind Pliny reports progress and seeks no advice.

XVIII

Traianus Plinio

1 CUPEREM sine querela corpusculi tui et tuorum pervenire in Bithyniam potuisses, ac simile tibi iter ab Epheso ei[1] navigationi fuisset, quam expertus 2 usque illo eras. Quo autem die pervenisses in Bithyniam, cognovi, Secunde carissime, litteris tuis. Provinciales, credo, prospectum sibi a me intellegent. Nam et tu dabis operam, ut manifestum sit illis electum te esse, qui ad eosdem mei loco mittereris. 3 Rationes autem in primis tibi rerum publicarum excutiendae sunt; nam et esse eas vexatas satis constat. Mensores vix etiam iis operibus, quae aut Romae aut in proximo fiunt, sufficientes habeo; sed in omni provincia inveniuntur, quibus credi possit, et ideo non deerunt tibi, modo velis diligenter excutere.

XIX

C. Plinius Traiano Imperatori

1 ROGO, domine, consilio me regas haesitantem, utrum per publicos civitatium servos, quod usque

---

[1] ei *Catanaeus*: et *I*: ut *a.*

---

[1] As *legatus propraetore Ponti et Bithyniae consulari potestate*, by direct appointment of Trajan; cf. S. 230. Not to be confused with the post of *corrector* (as Maximus in Achaia, VIII. 24) whose duties were confined to finance, working alongside the regular governor.

XVIII

TRAJAN TO PLINY

I WISH you could have reached Bithynia without any illness yourself or in your party, and that your journey from Ephesus had been as easy as your voyage there. The date of your arrival in Bithynia, my dear Pliny, I have noted from your letter. The people there will appreciate, I think, that I am acting in their own interests, and you too will see that it is made clear to them that you were chosen as my representative for a special mission.[1] Your first task must be to inspect the accounts of the various towns, as they are evidently in confusion.

As for land surveyors, I have scarcely enough for the public works in progress in Rome or in the neighbourhood,[2] but there are reliable surveyors to be found in every province and no doubt you will not lack assistance if you will take the trouble to look for it.

XIX

PLINY TO THE EMPEROR TRAJAN

I PRAY you, Sir, to advise me on the following point. I am doubtful whether I ought to continue using the public slaves[3] in the various towns as prison

[2] This could point to the earlier date (109–11) for Pliny's mission; Trajan's major building programme was probably past its peak in 111. Cf. Pan. 29. 2.

[3] Servi publici (cf. X. 31. 2) performed low-grade duties for the imperial government or the municipality for a small salary.

adhuc factum, an per milites adservare custodias debeam. Vereor enim, ne et per publicos parum fideliter custodiantur, et non exiguum militum nume-
2 rum haec cura distringat. Interim publicis servis paucos milites addidi. Video tamen periculum esse, ne id ipsum utrisque neglegentiae causa sit, dum communem culpam hi in illos, illi in hos regerere posse confidunt.

XX

TRAIANUS PLINIO

1· NIHIL opus sit, mi Secunde carissime, ad conti-nendas custodias plures commilitones converti. Perseveremus in ea consuetudine, quae isti provin-
2 ciae est, ut per publicos servos custodiantur. Ete-nim, ut fideliter hoc faciant, in tua severitate ac diligentia positum est. In primis enim, sicut scribis, verendum est, ne, si permisceantur servis publicis milites, mutua inter se fiducia neglegentiores sint; sed et illud haereat nobis, quam paucissimos a signis avocandos esse.

XXI

C. PLINIUS TRAIANO IMPERATORI

1   GAVIUS[1] BASSUS praefectus orae Ponticae et reverentissime et officiosissime, domine, venit ad me

[1] Gabius *Ia* (*idem* X. 22 *et* 86A).

warders, as hitherto, or to put soldiers on guard-duty in the prisons. I am afraid that the public slaves are not sufficiently reliable, but on the other hand this would take up the time of quite a number of soldiers. For the moment I have put a few soldiers on guard alongside the slaves, but I can see that there is a danger of this leading to neglect of duty on both sides, when each can throw the blame on the other for a fault they may both have committed.

XX

Trajan to Pliny

There is no need, my dear Pliny, for more soldiers to be transferred to guard-duty in the prisons. We should continue the custom of the province and use public slaves as warders. Their reliability depends on your watchfulness and discipline. For, as you say in your letter, if we mix soldiers with public slaves the chief danger is that both sides will become careless by relying on each other. Let us also keep to the general rule that as few soldiers as possible should be called away from active service.

XXI

Pliny to the Emperor Trajan

Gavius Bassus, Sir, the prefect of the Pontic Shore,[1] has called on me with due ceremony and respect, and

---

[1] It is not clear what the duties of this official were, nor why he needed more troops.

et compluribus diebus fuit mecum, quantum pers-
picere potui, vir egregius et indulgentia tua dignus.
Cui ego notum feci praecepisse te ut ex cohortibus,
quibus me praeesse voluisti, contentus esset bene-
ficiariis decem, equitibus duobus, centurione uno.
2 Respondit non sufficere sibi hunc numerum, idque se
scripturum tibi. Hoc in causa fuit, quominus statim
revocandos putarem, quos habet supra numerum.

XXII

Traianus Plinio

1 Et mihi scripsit Gavius Bassus non sufficere sibi
eum militum numerum, qui ut daretur illi, mandatis
meis complexus sum. Cui quae rescripsissem,[1] ut
notum haberes, his litteris subici iussi. Multum
interest, res poscat an hoc nomine eis [2] uti[3] latius
2 uelit.[4] Nobis autem utilitas demum spectanda est,
et, quantum fieri potest, curandum ne milites a signis
absint.

---

[1] cui quae rescripsissem *Keil*: quid quaeris scripsisse me *Ia*.
[2] hoc nomine eis *Sherwin-White*: hoc munere *Keil*: homines
in se *Ia*.
[3] uti *Orelli*: ut *Ia*.
[4] velit *I*: velint *a*: an homines iure uti latius velint *Durry,
Schuster, Stout*.

has been here several days. As far as I could judge
he is an excellent man who merits your kind interest.
I told him that you had given orders that he must
limit himself to ten picked soldiers,[1] two mounted
soldiers, and one centurion from the troops which you
had assigned to my command.[2] He replied that this
number was insufficient and that he would write to
you himself to that effect; so I thought it best not to
recall for the present the soldiers he has in excess of
that number.

XXII

TRAJAN TO PLINY

I HAVE also heard from Gavius Bassus direct that
the number of soldiers assigned him by my order
was inadequate. I have ordered a copy of my
answer to him to be sent with this letter for your
information. It is important to distinguish between
the needs of a situation and the likelihood of his
wishing to extend his privileges because of it. The
public interest must be our sole concern, and as far
as possible we should keep to the rule that soldiers
must not be withdrawn from active service.

---

[1] *Beneficiarii*, soldiers below the rank of centurion exempt
from the usual tasks and given higher pay and special duties
on the governor's staff.

[2] These are auxiliary troops detached from the Danube
areas, but it is not clear why Pliny has more than one cohort
assigned to him.

XXIII

C. Plinius Traiano Imperatori

1 Prusenses, domine, balineum habent; est sordidum et vetus. Itaque magni[1] aestimant[2] novum fieri; quod videris mihi desiderio eorum indulgere posse.
2 Erit enim pecunia, ex qua fiat, primum ea quam revocare a privatis et exigere iam coepi; deinde quam ipsi erogare in oleum soliti parati sunt in opus balinei conferre; quod alioqui et dignitas civitatis et saeculi tui nitor postulat.

XXIV

Traianus Plinio

Si instructio novi balinei oneratura vires Prusensium non est, possumus desiderio eorum indulgere, modo ne quid ideo aut intribuatur aut minus illis in posterum fiat ad necessarias erogationes.

XXV

C. Plinius Traiano Imperatori

Servilius Pudens legatus, domine, VIII kal. Decembres Nicomediam venit meque longae exspectationis sollicitudine liberavit.

---

[1] magni *Sherwin-White*: tamen *Ia*: tamiae *Cuntz*: debere *Stout*: *alii alia*.
[2] aestimant *Hardy*: -mans *Ia*.

---

[1] As in X. 70 and 90, it appears that a licence from the Emperor was needed for works to be build out of public funds.
[2] This suggests that the oil was distributed for consumption by the poor rather than for use at the baths.

XXIII

PLINY TO THE EMPEROR TRAJAN

THE public bath at Prusa, Sir, is old and dilapidated, and the people are very anxious for it to be rebuilt. My own opinion is that you could suitably grant their petition.[1] There will be money available for building it, first from the sums I have begun to call in from private individuals, and secondly because the people are prepared to apply to building the bath the grants they usually make towards financing the distribution of olive oil. This is, moreover, a scheme which is worthy of the town's prestige and the splendour of your reign.

XXIV

TRAJAN TO PLINY

IF building a new bath at Prusa will not strain the city's finances, there is no reason why we should not grant their petition; provided that no new tax is imposed and there is no further diversion of funds of theirs intended for essential services.[2]

XXV

PLINY TO THE EMPEROR TRAJAN

MY assistant,[3] Servilius Pudens, Sir, arrived in Nicomedia on 24 November, to my great relief as I had long been expecting him.

---

[3] As acting in place of the proconsul, Pliny was entitled to one assistant legate, who would be mainly concerned with civil jurisdiction.

XXVI

C. PLINIUS TRAIANO IMPERATORI

1 ROSIANUM GEMINUM, domine, artissimo vinculo
mecum tua in me beneficia iunxerunt; habui enim
illum quaestorem in consulatu. Mei sum[1] observan-
tissimum expertus; tantam mihi post consulatum
reverentiam praestat, et publicae necessitudinis
2 pignera privatis cumulat officiis. Rogo ergo, ut ipse
apud te pro dignitate eius precibus meis faveas. Cui
et, si quid mihi credis, indulgentiam tuam dabis;
dabis ipse operam ut in iis, quae ei mandaveris,
maiora mereatur. Parciorem me in laudando facit,
quod spero tibi et integritatem eius et probitatem et
industriam non solum ex eius honoribus, quos in urbe
sub oculis tuis gessit, verum etiam ex commilitio esse
3 notissimam. Illud unum, quod propter caritatem
eius nondum mihi videor satis plene fecisse, etiam
atque etiam facio teque, domine, rogo, gaudere me
exornata quaestoris mei dignitate, id est per illum
mea, quam maturissime velis.

XXVII

C. PLINIUS TRAIANO IMPERATORI

MAXIMUS libertus et procurator tuus, domine,
praeter decem beneficiarios, quos adsignari a me

---

[1] sum *Gronovius*: summe *Ia.*

---

[1] Rosianus Geminus's military career is unknown, nor is it
clear what post is sought for him. As he was Pliny's quaestor
in 100 he was presumably praetor *c.* 105. He could be seeking

XXVI

PLINY TO THE EMPEROR TRAJAN

As a result of your generosity to me, Sir, Rosianus
Geminus became one of my closest friends; for when
I was consul he was my quaestor. I always found
him devoted to my interests, and ever since then he
has treated me with the greatest deference and increased the warmth of our public relations by many
personal services. I therefore pray you to give your
personal attention to my request for his advancement; if you place any confidence in my advice you
will bestow on him your favour. He will not fail to
earn further promotion in whatever post you place
him. I am sparing in my praises because I trust that
his sincerity, integrity and application are well
known to you already from the high offices he has
held in Rome beneath your own eyes, as well as from
his service in the army under your command.[1]

I still feel that I have not given adequate expression to the warmth of my affection, and so once more
I pray you, Sir, most urgently, to permit me to rejoice
as soon as possible in the due promotion of my
quaestor—that is to say, in my own advancement in
his person.

XXVII

PLINY TO THE EMPEROR TRAJAN

YOUR freedman and procurator Maximus, assures
me, Sir, that he too must have six soldiers, in addi-

a consulship (as Syme thinks) or a legateship or a *cura* (so
S-W).

Gemellino optimo viro iussisti, sibi quoque confirmat necessarios esse milites sex. Hos[1] interim, sicut inveneram, in ministerio eius relinquendos existimavi, praesertim cum ad frumentum comparandum iret in Paphlagoniam. Quin etiam tutelae causa, quia ita desiderabat, addidi duos equites. In futurum, quid servari velis, rogo rescribas.

XXVIII

Traianus Plinio

Nunc quidem proficiscentem ad comparationem frumentorum Maximum libertum meum recte militibus instruxisti. Fungebatur enim et ipse extraordinario munere. Cum ad pristinum actum reversus fuerit, sufficient illi duo a te dati milites et totidem a Virdio Gemellino procuratore meo, quem adiuvat.

XXIX

C. Plinius Traiano Imperatori

1   Sempronius Caelianus, egregius iuvenis, repertos inter tirones duos servos misit ad me; quorum ego supplicium distuli, ut te conditorem disciplinae

---

[1] sex hos *Sherwin-White*: sex tris *Mommsen*: ex his *Ia*.

---

[1] Virdius Gemellinus, with his assistant Maximus (cf. X, 84 and 85), would have taken over the quaestor's financial duties since Bithynia ceased to be a senatorial province, as well as managing those concerned with the *fiscus*. See *Ep.* 21 and note about *beneficiarii*.

tion to the ten picked men whom I had assigned, in accordance with your instructions, to that excellent official Gemellinus.[1] I thought it best to leave him meanwhile the soldiers I found in his service, especially as he was just setting out to collect corn from Paphlagonia,[2] and at his request I also gave him two mounted soldiers as an escort. I pray you to let me know your instructions for the future.

XXVIII

Trajan to Pliny

You did quite right to supply my freedman Maximus with soldiers for his present requirements, when he was setting out to procure corn and so acting on a special mission. When he has returned to his former post the two soldiers you have assigned him should be enough, plus another two from Virdius Gemellinus, the procurator under whom he serves.

XXIX

Pliny to the Emperor Trajan

Sempronius Caelianus, who is an excellent young man, has discovered two slaves among his recruits and has sent them to me.[3] I have postponed judgement on them until I could ask your advice on what

---

[2] Presumably from the coastal plains by the Black Sea. The corn may be for Rome (cf. *Pan.* 29) or for local cities.

[3] No slave could serve in the army in any capacity; the offence was one of seeking citizenship by illegal means and punishable by death.

militaris firmatoremque consulerem de modo poenae.
2 Ipse enim dubito ob hoc maxime quod, ut iam dixer-
ant sacramento, ita nondum distributi in numeros
erant. Quid ergo debeam sequi rogo, domine,
scribas, praesertim cum pertineat ad exemplum.

XXX

Traianus Plinio

1 Secundum mandata mea fecit Sempronius Caelianus
mittendo ad te eos, de quibus cognosci oportebit, an
capitale supplicium meruisse videantur. Refert
autem, voluntarii se obtulerint an lecti sint vel
2 etiam vicarii dati. Lecti ⟨si⟩[1] sunt, inquisitio
peccavit; si vicarii dati, penes eos culpa est qui
dederunt; si ipsi, cum haberent condicionis suae conscientiam, venerunt, animadvertendum in illos erit.
Neque enim multum interest, quod nondum per
numeros distributi sunt. Ille enim dies, quo primum probati sunt, veritatem ab iis originis suae
exegit.

XXXI

C. Plinius Traiano Imperatori

1 Salva magnitudine tua, domine, descendas oportet
ad meas curas, cum ius mihi dederis referendi ad te,

[1] si add. Cat.[2]: om. Ia.

---

[1] It is uncertain whether these recruits are for legions or
auxilia.
[2] Only holders of imperium could conduct a capital trial,
so Caelianus could not act himself.

would be a suitable sentence, knowing that you are the founder and upholder of military discipline. My chief reason for hesitating is the fact that the men had already taken the oath of allegiance but had not yet been enrolled in a unit.[1] I therefore pray you, Sir, to tell me what course to follow, especially as the decision is likely to provide a precedent.

XXX

TRAJAN TO PLINY

SEMPRONIUS CAELIANUS was carrying out my instructions in sending you the slaves.[2] Whether they deserve capital punishment will need investigation; it is important to know if they were volunteers or conscripts, or possibly offered as substitutes. If they are conscripts, then the blame falls on the recruiting officer; if substitutes, then those who offered them as such are guilty; but if they volunteered for service, well aware of their status, then they will have to be executed. The fact that they were not yet enrolled in a legion makes little difference, for the truth about their origin should have come out on the actual day they were accepted for the army.

XXXI

PLINY TO THE EMPEROR TRAJAN

You may stoop when necessary, Sir, to give ear to my problems, without prejudice to your eminent position, seeing that I have your authority to refer to you when in doubt.

2 de quibus dubito. In plerisque civitatibus, maxime
Nicomediae et Nicaeae, quidam vel in opus damnati
vel in ludum similiaque his genera poenarum publi-
corum servorum officio ministerioque funguntur,
atque etiam ut publici servi annua accipiunt. Quod
ego cum audissem, diu multumque haesitavi, quid
3 facere deberem. Nam et reddere poenae post
longum tempus plerosque iam senes et, quantum
adfirmatur, frugaliter modesteque viventes nimis
severum arbitrabar, et in publicis officiis retinere
damnatos non satis honestum putabam; eosdem
rursus a re publica pasci otiosos inutile, non pasci
4 etiam periculosum existimabam. Necessario ergo
rem totam, dum te consulerem, in suspenso reliqui.
Quaeres fortasse, quem ad modum evenerit, ut
poenis in quas damnati erant exsolverentur: et ego
quaesii, sed nihil comperi, quod adfirmare tibi possim. Ut decreta quibus damnati erant proferebantur,
ita nulla monumenta quibus liberati probarentur.
5 Erant tamen, qui dicerent deprecantes iussu proconsulum legatorumve dimissos. Addebat fidem,
quod credibile erat neminem hoc ausum sine auctore.

XXXII

Traianus Plinio

1   Meminerimus idcirco te in istam provinciam missum, quoniam multa in ea emendanda adparuerint.

---

[1] Severe punishments, reducing those condemned to slave
status (*servi poenae*), whereas *servi publici* were a privileged
class of slave. See X. 19 and 32.

In several cities, notably Nicomedia and Nicaea, there are people who were sentenced to service in the mines or the arena,[1] or to other similar punishments, but are now performing the duties of public slaves and receiving an annual salary for their work. Since this was told me I have long been debating what to do. I felt it was too hard on the men to send them back to work out their sentences after a lapse of many years, when most of them are old by now, and by all accounts are quietly leading honest lives, but I did not think it quite right to retain criminals in public service; and though I realized there was nothing to be gained by supporting these men at public expense if they did no work, they might be a potential danger if they were left to starve. I was therefore obliged to leave the whole question in suspense until I could consult you.

You may perhaps want to know how they came to be released from the sentences passed on them. I asked this question myself, but received no satisfactory answer to give you, and although the records of their sentences were produced, there were no documents to prove their release. But people have stated on their behalf that they had been released by order of the previous governors or their deputies, and this is confirmed by the unlikelihood that any unauthorized person would take this responsibility.

XXXII

Trajan to Pliny

Let us not forget that the chief reason for sending you to your province was the evident need for many

Erit autem vel hoc maxime corrigendum, quod qui damnati ad poenam erant, non modo ea sine auctore, ut scribis, liberati sunt, sed etiam in condicionem 2 proborum ministrorum retrahuntur. Qui igitur intra hos proximos decem annos damnati nec ullo idoneo auctore liberati sunt, hos oportebit poenae suae reddi; si qui vetustiores invenientur et senes ante annos decem damnati, distribuamus illos in ea ministeria, quae non longe a poena sint. Solent enim eiusmodi ⟨homines⟩[1] ad balineum, ad purgationes cloacarum, item munitiones viarum et vicorum dari.

XXXIII

C. PLINIUS TRAIANO IMPERATORI

1 CUM diversam partem provinciae circumirem, Nicomediae vastissimum incendium multas privatorum domos et duo publica opera, quamquam via 2 interiacente, Gerusian et Iseon absumpsit. Est autem latius sparsum, primum violentia venti, deinde inertia hominum quos satis constat otiosos et immobiles tanti mali spectatores perstitisse; et alioqui nullus usquam in publico sipo, nulla hama, nullum denique instrumentum ad incendia compescenda. Et haec quidem, ut iam praecepi, para- 3 buntur; tu, domine, dispice an instituendum putes collegium fabrorum dumtaxat hominum CL. Ego

---

[1] enim eiusmodi *a*: et *I, Mynors*: enim eiusmodi ⟨homines⟩ *Sherwin-White*.

---

[1] In X. 39 he is at Claudiopolis.

reforms. Nothing in fact stands more in need of correction than the situation described in your letter, where criminals under sentence have not only been released without authority but are actually restored to the status of honest officials. Those among them who were sentenced within the last ten years and were released by no proper authority must therefore be sent back to work out their sentences. But if the men are elderly and have sentences dating back farther than ten years, they can be employed in work not far removed from penal labour, cleaning public baths and sewers, or repairing streets and highways, the usual employment for men of this type.

XXXIII

PLINY TO THE EMPEROR TRAJAN

WHILE I was visiting another part of the province,[1] a widespread fire broke out in Nicomedia which destroyed many private houses and also two public buildings (the Elder Citizens' Club and the Temple of Isis) although a road runs between them. It was fanned by the strong breeze in the early stages, but it would not have spread so far but for the apathy of the populace; for it is generally agreed that people stood watching the disaster without bestirring themselves to do anything to stop it. Apart from this, there is not a single fire engine anywhere in the town, not a bucket nor any apparatus for fighting a fire. These will now be provided on my instructions.

Will you, Sir, consider whether you think a company of firemen might be formed, limited to 150

attendam, ne quis nisi faber recipiatur neve iure
concesso in aliud utantur;[1] nec erit difficile custodire
tam paucos.

XXXIV

Traianus Plinio

1 Tibi quidem secundum exempla complurium in
mentem venit posse collegium fabrorum apud
Nicomedenses constitui. Sed meminerimus provinciam istam et praecipue eas[2] civitates eius modi
factionibus esse vexatas. Quodcumque nomen ex
quacumque causa dederimus iis, qui in idem contracti
fuerint, hetaeriae eaeque[3] brevi[4] fient. Satius itaque
est comparari ea, quae ad coercendos ignes auxilio
esse possint, admonerique dominos praediorum, ut et
ipsi inhibeant ac, si res poposcerit, adcursu populi ad
hoc uti.

XXXV

C. Plinius Traiano Imperatori

Sollemnia vota pro incolumitate tua, qua publica
salus continetur, et suscepimus, domine, pariter et
solvimus precati deos, ut velint ea semper solvi
semperque signari.

---

[1] utantur *Mommsen*: utatur *Ia*.
[2] eas *Ia*: eius *Hanslik*: ipsas *Sherwin-White*.
[3] eaeque *Schuster*: aeque *J. B. Lightfoot*: utique *Brakman*:
quae *Ia*.   [4] brevi *Orelli*: breves *Ia*.

---

[1] Rome had its 7,000 *vigiles* and the towns of the western
empire their *fabri centonarii*, *dendrophori*, and *tignarii*, but

members?[1] I will see that no one shall be admitted who is not genuinely a fireman, and that the privileges granted shall not be abused: it will not be difficult to keep such small numbers under observation.

XXXIV

TRAJAN TO PLINY

You may very well have had the idea that it should be possible to form a company of firemen at Nicomedia on the model of those existing elsewhere, but we must remember that it is societies like these which have been responsible for the political disturbances in your province, particularly in its towns. If people assemble for a common purpose, whatever name we give them and for whatever reason, they soon turn into a political club. It is a better policy then to provide the equipment necessary for dealing with fires, and to instruct property owners to make use of it, calling on the help of the crowds which collect if they find it necessary.

XXXV

PLINY TO THE EMPEROR TRAJAN

WE have made our annual vows,[2] Sir, to ensure your safety and thereby that of the State, and discharged our vows for the past year, with prayers to the gods to grant that those vows may be always thus discharged and confirmed.

there seems to have been a general ban on any form of *collegium* in the eastern cities.   [2] On 3 January.

XXXVI

Traianus Plinio

Et solvisse vos cum provincialibus dis immortalibus
vota pro mea salute et incolumitate et nuncupasse
libenter, mi Secunde carissime, cognovi ex litteris
tuis.

XXXVII

C. Plinius Traiano Imperatori

1 In aquae ductum, domine, Nicomedenses impen-
derunt HS |xxx| cccxviii, qui imperfectus adhuc
omissus,[1] destructus etiam[2] est; rursus in alium
ductum erogata sunt cc. Hoc quoque relicto novo
impendio est opus, ut aquam habeant, qui tantam
2 pecuniam male perdiderunt. Ipse perveni ad fontem
purissimum, ex quo videtur aqua debere perduci,
sicut initio temptatum erat, arcuato opere, ne tantum
ad plana civitatis et humilia perveniat. Manent
adhuc paucissimi arcus: possunt et erigi quidam
lapide quadrato, qui ex superiore opere detractus est;
aliqua pars, ut mihi videtur, testaceo opere agenda
3 erit, id enim et facilius et vilius. Sed[3] in primis
necessarium est mitti a te vel aquilegem vel architectum, ne rursus eveniat quod accidit. Ego illud
unum adfirmo, et utilitatem operis et pulchritudinem
saeculo tuo esse dignissimam.

---

[1] omissus *Schuster*: emissum *I* (-sus *i*): relictus *a*.
[2] destr. etiam *I*: ac etiam destr. *a*.
[3] sed *G. H. Schaefer*: et *Ia*.

XXXVI

Trajan to Pliny

I was glad to hear from your letter, my dear Pliny, that you and the provincials have discharged your vows to the immortal gods on behalf of my health and safety, and have renewed them for the coming year.

XXXVII

Pliny to the Emperor Trajan

The citizens of Nicomedia, Sir, have spent 3,318,000 sesterces on an aqueduct which they abandoned before it was finished and finally demolished. Then they made a grant of 200,000 sesterces towards another one, but this too was abandoned, so that even after squandering such enormous sums they must still spend more money if they are to have a water supply.

I have been myself to look at the spring which could supply pure water to be brought along an aqueduct, as originally intended, if the supply is not to be confined to the lower-lying parts of the town. There are very few arches still standing, but others could be built out of the blocks of stone taken from the earlier construction, and I think some ought to be made of brick, which would be easier and cheaper.

But the first essential is for you to send out a water-engineer or an architect to prevent a third failure. I will add only that the finished work will combine utility with beauty, and will be well worthy of your reign.

XXXVIII

Traianus Plinio

Curandum est, ut aqua in Nicomedensem civitatem perducatur. Vere credo te ea, qua debebis, diligentia hoc opus adgressurum. Sed medius fidius ad eandem diligentiam tuam pertinet inquirere, quorum vitio ad hoc tempus tantam pecuniam Nicomedenses perdiderint, ne, dum[1] inter se gratificantur, et incohaverint aquae ductus et reliquerint. Quid itaque compereris, perfer in notitiam meam.

XXXIX

C. Plinius Traiano Imperatori

1 Theatrum, domine, Nicaeae maxima iam parte constructum, imperfectum tamen, sestertium (ut audio; neque enim ratio operis[2] excussa est) amplius 2 centies hausit: vereor ne frustra. Ingentibus enim rimis desedit et hiat, sive in causa solum umidum et molle, sive lapis ipse gracilis et putris: dignum est certe deliberatione, sitne faciendum an sit relinquendum an etiam destruendum. Nam fulturae ac substructiones, quibus subinde suscipitur, non tam firmae 3 mihi quam sumptuosae videntur. Huic theatro ex privatorum pollicitationibus multa debentur, ut basilicae circa, ut porticus supra caveam. Quae nunc

---

[1] dum *Gronovius*: cum *Ia*.
[2] operis *C. F. W. Mueller*: plus *Ia*.

XXXVIII

Trajan to Pliny

Steps must be taken to provide Nicomedia with a water supply, and I am sure you will apply yourself to the task in the right way. But for goodness' sake apply yourself no less to finding out whose fault it is that Nicomedia has wasted so much money up to date. It may be that people have profited by this starting and abandoning of aqueducts. Let me know the result of your inquiry.[1]

XXXIX

Pliny to the Emperor Trajan

The theatre at Nicea, Sir, is more than half built but is still unfinished, and has already cost more than ten million sesterces, or so I am told—I have not yet examined the relevant accounts. I am afraid it may be money wasted. The building is sinking and show-ing immense cracks, either because the soil is damp and soft or the stone used was poor and friable. We shall certainly have to consider whether it is to be finished or abandoned, or even demolished, as the foundations and substructure intended to hold up the building may have cost a lot but look none too solid to me. There are many additions to the theatre promised by private individuals, such as a colonnade on either side and a gallery above the auditorium,

---

[1] This sounds like a personal note from Trajan who has not read Pliny's letter carefully. Its main point was the request for an engineer.

omnia differuntur cessante eo, quod ante peragendum
4 est. Iidem Nicaeenses gymnasium incendio amissum ante adventum meum restituere coeperunt, longe numerosius laxiusque quam fuerat, et iam aliquantum erogaverunt; periculum est, ne parum utiliter; incompositum enim et sparsum est. Praeterea architectus, sane aemulus eius a quo opus incohatum est, adfirmat parietes quamquam viginti et[1] duos pedes latos imposita onera sustinere non posse, quia sint caemento medii farti nec testaceo opere praecincti.

5   Claudiopolitani quoque in depresso loco, imminente etiam monte ingens balineum defodiunt magis quam aedificant, et quidem ex ea pecunia, quam buleutae additi beneficio tuo aut iam obtulerunt ob introitum
6 aut nobis exigentibus conferent. Ergo cum timeam ne illic publica pecunia, hic, quod est omni pecunia pretiosius, munus tuum male collocetur, cogor petere a te non solum ob theatrum, verum etiam ob haec balinea mittas architectum, dispecturum utrum sit utilius post sumptum qui factus est quoquo modo consummare opera, ut incohata sunt, an quae videntur emendanda corrigere, quae transferenda transferre, ne dum servare volumus quod impensum est, male impendamus quod addendum est.

---

[1] viginti et *del. Lehmann–Hartleben.*

---

[1] An immense wall, thicker than anything in Rome. But if *caementum* refers to a loose rubble core instead of the strong Roman mortar, it is more intelligible; a brick binding would be needed behind the stone facing.

[2] Cf. 112. 1. This is the *honorarium decurionatus*, more common in the western provinces, and apparently obligatory.

but all these are now held up by the stoppage of work on the main building which must be finished first.

The citizens of Nicaea have also begun to rebuild their gymnasium (which was destroyed by fire before my arrival) on a much larger and more extensive scale than before. They have already spent a large sum, which may be to little purpose, for the buildings are badly planned and too scattered. Moreover, an architect—admittedly a rival of the one who drew up the designs—has given the opinion that the walls cannot support the superstructure in spite of being twenty-two feet thick, as the rubble core has no facing of brick.[1]

The people of Claudiopolis are also building, or rather excavating, an enormous public bath in a hollow at the foot of a mountain. The money for this is coming either from the admission fees already paid by the new members of the town council elected by your gracious favour,[2] or from what they will pay at my demand. So I am afraid there is misapplication of public funds at Nicaea and abuse of your generosity at Claudiopolis, though this should be valued above any money. I am therefore compelled to ask you to send out an architect to inspect both theatre and bath and decide whether it will be more practicable, in view of what has already been spent, to keep to the original plans and finish both buildings as best we can, or to make any necessary alterations and changes of site so that we do not throw away more money in an attempt to make some use of the original outlay.

XL

Traianus Plinio

1 Quid oporteat fieri circa theatrum, quod incohatum apud Nicaeenses est, in re praesenti optime deliberabis et constitues. Mihi sufficiet indicari, cui sententiae accesseris. Tunc autem a privatis exige[1] opera, cum theatrum, propter quod illa promissa sunt, 2 factum erit. Gymnasiis indulgent Graeculi; ideo forsitan Nicaeenses maiore animo constructionem eius adgressi sunt: sed oportet illos eo contentos esse, 3 quod possit illis sufficere. Quid Claudiopolitanis circa balineum quod parum, ut scribis, idoneo loco incohaverunt suadendum sit, tu constitues. Architecti tibi deesse non possunt. Nulla provincia non et peritos et ingeniosos homines habet; modo ne existimes brevius esse ab urbe mitti, cum ex Graecia etiam ad nos venire soliti sint.

XLI

C. Plinius Traiano Imperatori

1 Intuenti mihi et fortunae tuae et animi magnitudinem convenientissimum videtur demonstrari opera non minus aeternitate tua quam gloria digna, quantumque pulchritudinis tantum utilitatis habi-

---

[1] exige Sherwin-White: exigi Ia.

XL

Trajan to Pliny

The future of the unfinished theatre at Nicaea can best be settled by you on the spot. It will be sufficient for me if you let me know your decision. But, once the main building is finished, you will have to see that private individuals carry out their promises of adding to the theatre.

These poor Greeks all love a gymnasium; so it may be that they were too ambitious in their plans at Nicaea. They will have to be content with one which suits their real needs.

As for the bath at Claudiopolis, which you say has been started in an unsuitable site, you must decide yourself what advice to give. You cannot lack architects: every province has skilled men trained for this work. It is a mistake to think they can be sent out more quickly from Rome when they usually come to us from Greece.[1]

XLI

Pliny to the Emperor Trajan

In consideration of your noble ambition which matches your supreme position, I think I should bring to your notice any projects which are worthy of your immortal name and glory and are likely to combine utility with magnificence.

[1] *e.g.* the famous Apollodorus of Damascus who planned the Forum and Basilica of Trajan.

2 tura. Est in Nicomedensium finibus amplissimus
lacus. Per hunc marmora fructus ligna materiae et
sumptu modico et labore usque ad viam navibus, inde
magno labore maiore impendio vehiculis ad mare
devehuntur . . .¹ hoc opus multas manus poscit. At
eae porro non desunt. Nam et in agris magna copia
est hominum et maxima in civitate, certaque spes
omnes libentissime adgressuros opus omnibus fructuo-
3 sum. Superest ut tu libratorem vel architectum si
tibi videbitur mittas, qui diligenter exploret, sitne
lacus altior mari, quem artifices regionis huius
4 quadraginta cubitis altiorem esse contendunt. Ego
per eadem loca invenio fossam a rege percussam, sed
incertum utrum ad colligendum umorem circumia-
centium agrorum an ad committendum flumini
lacum; est enim imperfecta. Hoc quoque dubium,
intercepto rege mortalitate an desperato operis
5 effectu. Sed hoc ipso (feres enim me ambitiosum
pro tua gloria) incitor et accendor, ut cupiam peragi a
te quae tantum coeperant reges.

XLII

TRAIANUS PLINIO

1 POTEST nos sollicitare lacus iste, ut committere
illum mari velimus; sed plane explorandum est

---

¹ *Post* devehuntur *lacunam statuit Ernesti:* negant Durry,
Stout.

---

¹ Lake Sophon (now Lake Sabanja), 18 miles S.E. of Nicomedia. It drained N.E. into the Black Sea via a tributary of
the R. Sangarius. Pliny wishes to connect it by canal with a
navigable river flowing W. into the Gulf of Izmid.

There is a sizeable lake [1] not far from Nicomedia, across which marble, farm produce, wood, and timber for building are easily and cheaply brought by boat as far as the main road; after which everything has to be taken on to the sea by cart, with great difficulty and increased expense. ⟨To connect the lake with the sea [2]⟩ would require a great deal of labour, but there is no lack of it. There are plenty of people in the countryside, and many more in the town, and it seems certain that they will all gladly help with a scheme which will benefit them all.

It remains for you to send an engineer or an architect, if you think fit, to make an accurate survey and determine whether the lake is above sea-level. The local experts say that it is forty cubits [3] above. I have looked at the site myself and find there is a canal dug by one of the former kings of Bithynia, though whether this was intended to drain the surrounding fields or to connect the lake with the river I am not sure; it was left unfinished, and again I cannot say if this was because the king died suddenly or despaired of finishing the work. This, however, only fires me with enthusiasm to see you accomplish what kings could only attempt: you will forgive my ambition for your greater glory.

XLII

Trajan to Pliny

I may perhaps be tempted to think of connecting this lake of yours with the sea, but there must first

---

[2] Something is needed to make the text intelligible.
[3] Now about 120 feet. Nothing is known of this canal.

diligenter, ne si emissus[1] in mare fuerit totus effluat certe, quantum aquarum et unde accipiat. Poteris a Calpurnio Macro petere libratorem, et ego hinc aliquem tibi peritum eius modi operum mittam.

XLIII

C. PLINIUS TRAIANO IMPERATORI

1 REQUIRENTI mihi Byzantiorum rei publicae impendia, quae maxima fecit, indicatum est, domine, legatum ad te salutandum annis omnibus cum psephismate mitti, eique dari nummorum duodena
2 milia. Memor ergo propositi tui legatum quidem retinendum, psephisma autem mittendum putavi, ut simul et sumptus levaretur et impleretur publicum
3 officium. Eidem civitati imputata sunt terna milia, quae viatici nomine annua dabantur legato eunti ad eum qui Moesiae praeest publice salutandum. Haec ego in posterum circumcidenda existimavi.
4 Te, domine, rogo ut quid sentias rescribendo aut consilium meum confirmare aut errorem emendare digneris.

---

[1] emissus *Sherwin-White*: dimissus *A*: immissus *a*: demissus *Cat.*

---

[1] See *Epp.* 61-2. Calpurnius Macer was legate of Lower Moesia 10 Dec. 111–9 Dec. 112 (S. 196). This is the only direct evidence of any date during P.'s mission.

be an accurate survey to find how much water the lake contains and from what source it is filled, or else it might be completely drained once it is given an outlet to the sea. You can apply to Calpurnius Macer[1] for an engineer, and I will send you out someone who has experience of this sort of work.

XLIII

PLINY TO THE EMPEROR TRAJAN

WHEN I was inspecting the accounts of the city of Byzantium,[2] Sir, where expenditure has been very heavy, I was informed that a delegate was sent annually to offer you a loyal address and allow 12,000 sesterces for his expenses. Remembering your wishes, I decided to send on the address but no delegate to convey it, so that the citizens could reduce expenses without failing in their official duty towards you. In the same accounts there is an entry of another 3,000 sesterces under the head of annual travelling expenses for the delegate sent with an official greeting to the governor of Moesia. This, too, I thought should be cut down in future.

I pray you, Sir, to think fit to give me your opinion, and either confirm my decision or correct me if I am at fault.

[2] Byzantium was administered with Bithynia, but as a frontier town and trade junction was protected by the army of Lower Moesia.

XLIV

Traianus Plinio

Optime fecisti, Secunde carissime, duodena ista Byzantiis quae ad salutandum me in legatum impendebantur remittendo. Fungentur[1] his partibus, etsi solum psephisma per te missum fuerit. Ignoscet illis et Moesiae praeses, si minus illum sumptuose coluerint.

XLV

C. Plinius Traiano Imperatori

Diplomata, domine, quorum dies praeterît,[2] an omnino observari et quam diu velis, rogo scribas meque haesitatione liberes. Vereor enim, ne in alterutram partem ignorantia lapsus aut inlicita confirmem aut necessaria impediam.

XLVI

Traianus Plinio

Diplomata, quorum praeteritus est dies, non debent esse in usu. Ideo inter prima iniungo mihi, ut

---

[1] fungentur *Kukula*: fungetur *ai*.
[2] praeteriit an *Orelli* (-ît *Schuster*): praeterita *Aa*: -ita an *Cat.*[2].

---

[1] The imperial courier service (see Tac. *Hist.* II. 54–6, Suet. *Aug.* 49. 3) was maintained along the highways at the expense

XLIV

Trajan to Pliny

You were quite right, my dear Pliny, to remit the 12,000 sesterces which the citizens of Byzantium were spending on a delegate to convey their loyal address to me. Their duty will be fulfilled if their resolution is simply forwarded through you. The governor of Moesia will also forgive them if they spend less on paying their respects to him.

XLV

Pliny to the Emperor Trajan

Are permits to use the Imperial Post [1] valid after their date has expired, and, if so, for how long? I pray you, Sir, to tell me your wishes and settle my doubts. I am anxious not to make the mistake through ignorance of sanctioning illegal documents, or alternatively of holding up essential dispatches.

XLVI

Trajan to Pliny

Permits to use the Post must not be used once their date has expired. I therefore make it a strict

of the provincials and used by the emperors travelling (see *Pan.* 20) and by officials issued with a *diploma* dated and sealed by the issuing emperor. See *Epp.* 64, and 120–1, where it is implied that governors could issue a limited number of permits annually.

per omnes provincias ante mittam nova diplomata, quam desiderari possint.

XLVII

C. PLINIUS TRAIANO IMPERATORI

1 CUM vellem, domine, Apameae cognoscere publicos debitores et reditum et impendia, responsum est mihi cupere quidem universos, ut a me rationes coloniae legerentur, numquam tamen esse lectas ab ullo proconsulum; habuisse privilegium et vetustissimum morem arbitrio suo rem publicam administrare. 2 Exegi ut quae dicebant quaeque recitabant libello complecterentur; quem tibi qualem acceperam misi, quamvis intellegerem pleraque ex illo ad id, de quo 3 quaeritur, non pertinere. Te rogo ut mihi praeire digneris, quid me putes observare debere. Vereor enim ne aut excessisse aut non implesse officii mei partes videar.

XLVIII

TRAIANUS PLINIO

1 LIBELLUS Apamenorum, quem epistulae tuae iunxeras, remisit mihi necessitatem perpendendi qualia essent, propter quae videri volunt eos, qui pro consulibus hanc provinciam obtinuerunt, abstinuisse

---

[1] Colonia Julia Concordia Augusta Apamea (Myrleia) was founded probably by Julius Caesar alongside the Greek city, and the dual community continued to flourish. Cf. Sinope in *Ep.* 90.

rule to see that new permits are sent out to every province before the date they can be needed.

XLVII

PLINY TO THE EMPEROR TRAJAN

WHEN, Sir, I wished to inspect the finances of Apamea, persons owing, revenue, and expenditure, I was told that the citizens were all quite willing for me to see the accounts, but as Apamea was a Roman colony[1] none of the senatorial governors had ever done so; and it was their long-established custom and privilege to manage their internal affairs in their own way. I told them to set down their statements and authorities quoted in the form of a petition, and this I am sending to you just as I received it though I realize that much of it is irrelevant to the point at issue.

I pray you to think fit to instruct me how you judge I ought to act. I am anxious for it not to seem that I have exceeded or fallen short of my duty.

XLVIII

TRAJAN TO PLINY

HAVING received the petition from the citizens of Apamea which you sent with your letter, I think I need not look into the reasons why they wish it to be known that the senatorial governors of the province refrained from inspecting their accounts; seeing that they raise no objection to an inspection by you.

225

inspectatione rationum suarum, cum ipse ut eas
2 inspiceres non recusaverint. Remuneranda est igitur
probitas eorum, ut iam nunc sciant hoc, quod in-
specturus es, ex mea voluntate salvis, quae habent,
privilegiis esse facturum.

XLIX

C. Plinivs Traiano Imperatori

1 Ante adventum meum, domine, Nicomedenses
priori foro novum adicere coeperunt, cuius in angulo
est aedes vetustissima Matris Magnae aut reficienda
aut transferenda, ob hoc praecipue quod est multo
2 depressior opere eo quod cum maxime surgit. Ego[1]
cum quaererem, num esset aliqua lex dicta templo,
cognovi alium hic, alium apud nos esse morem
dedicationis. Dispice ergo, domine, an putes aedem,
cui nulla lex dicta est, salva religione posse transferri;
alioqui commodissimum est, si religio non impedit.

L

Traianus Plinio

Potes, mi Secunde carissime, sine sollicitudine
religionis, si loci positio videtur hoc desiderare, aedem
Matris Deum transferre in eam quae est accom-

---

[1] ego *Cat.*: ergo *Aa.*

---

[1] The Phrygian goddess Cybele.
[2] The dedication of a Roman temple could only be set aside
by the ceremony of *evocatio dei* (Livy, 1. 55), but the authority
of the pontiffs did not extend beyond Italy.

I think then that you should reward their honesty and assure them that on this occasion you are making a special inspection at my express wish, and it will be carried out without prejudice to their existing privileges.

XLIX

PLINY TO THE EMPEROR TRAJAN

BEFORE my arrival, Sir, the citizens of Nicomedia had begun to build a new forum adjacent to their existing one. In one corner of the new area is an ancient temple of the Great Mother,[1] which needs to be rebuilt or moved to a new site, mainly because it is much lower than the buildings now going up. I made a personal inquiry whether the temple was protected by any specific conditions, only to find that the form of consecration practised here is quite different from ours.[2]

Would you then consider, Sir, whether you think that a temple thus unprotected can be moved without loss of sanctity? This would be the most convenient solution if there are no religious objections.

L

TRAJAN TO PLINY

You need have no religious scruple, my dear Pliny, about moving the temple of the Mother of the Gods to a more convenient place if a change of site seems desirable; nor need you worry if you can find no

modatior; nec te moveat, quod lex dedicationis nulla reperitur, cum solum peregrinae civitatis capax non sit dedicationis, quae fit nostro iure.

LI

C. Plinius Traiano Imperatori

1 Difficile est, domine, exprimere verbis, quantam perceperim laetitiam, quod et mihi et socrui meae praestitisti, ut adfinem eius Caelium Clementem in 2 hanc provinciam transferres. Ex illo enim et mensuram beneficii tui penitus intellego, cum tam plenam indulgentiam cum tota domo mea experiar, cui referre gratiam parem ne audeo[1] quidem, quamvis maxime possim.[2] Itaque ad vota confugio deosque precor, ut iis, quae in me adsidue confers, non indignus existimer.

LII

C. Plinius Traiano Imperatori

Diem, domine, quo servasti imperium, dum suscipis, quanta mereris laetitia celebravimus, precati deos ut te generi humano, cuius tutela et securitas saluti tuae innisa est, incolumem florentemque praestarent.

---

[1] ne audeo *Gronovius*: nec audeo *Aa*: ne gaudio *Mommsen*.
[2] maxime possim *A*: Maximo possum *a*: maximo possum *Mommsen*: debeam *Cat*, cum maxime *Sherwin-White*.

conditions laid down for consecration, as the soil of an alien country is not capable of being consecrated according to our laws.

LI

PLINY TO THE EMPEROR TRAJAN

IT is difficult, Sir, to find words to tell you how happy you have made me by your kindness to my mother-in-law and myself in transferring her relative Caelius Clemens to this province.[1] I begin to realize to the full the extent of your generosity when it is thus graciously extended to my whole family: I could not venture to repay it, whatever my ability to do so might be. I can only have recourse to vows taken on your behalf and pray the gods that I may never prove unworthy of the favours you continually bestow.

LII

PLINY TO THE EMPEROR TRAJAN

WE have celebrated with appropriate rejoicing, Sir, the day of your accession[2] whereby you preserved the Empire; and have offered prayers to the gods to keep you in health and prosperity on behalf of the human race, whose security and happiness depends on your safety. We have also administered

---

[1] Clemens, a relative of Pompeia Celerina, probably came as a military tribune.

[2] 28 January. The *dies imperii* was that on which the emperor was hailed as *imperator* by the army.

Praeivimus et commilitonibus ius iurandum more sollemni, eadem provincialibus certatim pietate iurantibus.

LIII

Traianus Plinio

Quanta religione et laetitia commilitones cum provincialibus te praeeunte diem imperii mei celebraverint, libenter, mi Secunde carissime, agnovi litteris tuis.

LIV

C. Plinius Traiano Imperatori

1 Pecuniae publicae, domine, providentia tua et ministerio nostro et iam exactae sunt et exiguntur; quae vereor ne otiosae iaceant. Nam et praediorum comparandorum aut nulla aut rarissima occasio est, nec inveniuntur qui velint debere rei publicae, praesertim duodenis assibus, quanti a privatis mutu-
2 antur. Dispice ergo, domine, numquid minuendam usuram ac per hoc idoneos debitores invitandos putes, et, si nec sic reperiuntur, distribuendam inter decuriones pecuniam, ita ut recte rei publicae caveant; quod quamquam invitis et recusantibus minus acerbum erit leviore usura constituta.

---

¹ The annual *sacramentum* of personal loyalty to the Emperor and his family.
² Per annum, the normal rate of interest for short-term loans.

the oath of allegiance[1] to your fellow-soldiers in the usual form, and found the provincials eager to take it, too, as a proof of their loyalty.

LIII

TRAJAN TO PLINY

I WAS glad to hear from your letter, my dear Pliny, of the rejoicing and devotion with which under your guidance, my fellow-soldiers and the provincials have celebrated the anniversary of my accession.

LIV

PLINY TO THE EMPEROR TRAJAN

THANKS to your foresight, Sir, the sums owed to public funds have been paid in under my administration, or are in process of being so; but I am afraid the money may remain uninvested. There is no opportunity, or practically none, of purchasing landed property, and people cannot be found who will borrow from public funds, especially at the rate of twelve per cent, the same rate as for private loans.[2]

Would you then consider, Sir, whether you think that the rate of interest should be lowered to attract suitable borrowers, and, if they are still not forthcoming, whether the money might be loaned out among the town councillors upon their giving the State proper security? They may be unwilling to accept it, but it will be less of a burden to them if the rate of interest is reduced.

LV

TRAIANUS PLINIO

ET ipse non aliud remedium dispicio, mi Secunde carissime, quam ut quantitas usurarum minuatur, quo facilius pecuniae publicae collocentur. Modum eius, ex copia eorum qui mutuabuntur, tu constitues. Invitos ad accipiendum compellere, quod fortassis ipsis otiosum futurum sit, non est ex iustitia nostrorum temporum.

LVI

C. PLINIUS TRAIANO IMPERATORI

1 SUMMAS, domine, gratias ago, quod inter maximas occupationes ⟨in⟩[1] iis, de quibus te consului, me quoque regere dignatus es; quod nunc quoque 2 facias rogo. Adiit enim me quidam indicavitque adversarios suos a Servilio Calvo, clarissimo viro, in triennium relegatos in provincia morari: illi contra ab eodem se restitutos adfirmaverunt edictumque recitaverunt. Qua causa necessarium credidi rem 3 integram ad te referre. Nam, sicut mandatis tuis cautum est, ne restituam ab alio aut a me relegatos, ita de iis, quos alius et relegaverit et restituerit, nihil

---

[1] in iis *Ernesti*: iis *Aa.*

LV

TRAJAN TO PLINY

NEITHER can I see any other solution myself, my dear Pliny, to the problem of investing public funds, unless the rate of interest on loans is lowered. You can fix the rate yourself, according to the number of potential borrowers. But to force a loan on unwilling persons, who may perhaps have no means of making use of it themselves, is not in accordance with the justice of our times.

LVI

PLINY TO THE EMPEROR TRAJAN

MAY I express my deepest gratitude, Sir, that in the midst of your important preoccupations you have seen fit to direct me on matters on which I have sought your advice; I pray that you will do so once again.

A man has approached me with the information that certain enemies of his, who had been sentenced to three years banishment by the distinguished senator Publius Servilius Calvus, are still in the province. They on the other hand insist that their sentences were reversed by Calvus, and have quoted his edict of restitution. I therefore thought it necessary to refer the whole question to you, seeing that your official instructions were that I should not recall anyone banished by one of the governors or by myself, but I can find no ruling on the situation where a

comprehensum est. Ideo tu, domine, consulendus
fuisti, quid observare me velles, tam hercule quam de
iis qui in perpetuum relegati nec restituti in provincia
4 deprehenduntur. Nam haec quoque species incidit
in cognitionem meam. Est enim adductus ad me in
perpetuum relegatus ⟨a⟩[1] Iulio Basso proconsule.
Ego, quia sciebam acta Bassi rescissa datumque a
senatu ius omnibus, de quibus ille aliquid consti-
tuisset, ex integro agendi, dumtaxat per biennium,
interrogavi hunc, quem relegaverat, an adisset
5 docuissetque proconsulem. ⟨Negavit.[2]⟩ Per quod
effectum est, ut te consulerem, reddendum eum
poenae suae an gravius aliquid et quid potissimum
constituendum putares et in hunc et in eos, si qui
forte in simili condicione invenirentur. Decretum
Calvi et edictum, item decretum Bassi his litteris
subieci.

LVII

TRAIANVS PLINIO

1 QUID in persona eorum statuendum sit, qui a P.
Servilio Calvo proconsule in triennium relegati et
mox eiusdem edicto restituti in provincia reman-
serunt, proxime tibi rescribam, cum causas eius facti

[1] a *Cat.*, a: *om. A.*
[2] negavit *add. Cat.*: *om. Aa.*

---

1 For the trial of Bassus, see IV. 9.
2 As a proconsul, Calvus's acts were not restricted by *mandata* from the Emperor.

governor has passed sentence of banishment and subsequently reversed it. Consequently, Sir, I felt I must ask you what course you wish me to follow, and also what I am to do with people found still to be in the province, although they were sentenced to banishment and never had their sentences reversed.

A further type of case has also come to me for trial. A man was brought before me who had been sentenced to banishment for life by the governor Julius Bassus.[1] Knowing that all Bassus's acts had been annulled, and that the Senate had granted anyone sentenced by him the right to have a new trial so long as the appeal was made within two years, I asked this man if he had brought his case to the notice of the succeeding governor. He said he had not. So now I am obliged to ask you whether you think that the man should be exiled on his original sentence, or if some heavier sentence, and if so, what, should be given him, and any others we may find in a similar situation.

I append copies of the sentence passed by Calvus and his edict of reversal, and the sentence passed by Bassus.

LVII

Trajan to Pliny

I will let you know my decision about the legal position of the persons who were banished for three years by the governor Publius Servilius Calvus and subsequently had their sentences reversed, as soon as I have found out from Calvus the reason why he did this.[2]

2 a Calvo requisiero. Qui a Iulio Basso in perpetuum
relegatus est, cum per biennium agendi facultatem
habuerit, si existimat se iniuria relegatum, neque id
fecerit atque in provincia morari perseverarit,
vinctus mitti ad praefectos praetorii mei debet.
Neque enim sufficit eum poenae suae restitui, quam
contumacia elusit.

LVIII

C. PLINIVS TRAIANO IMPERATORI

1 CUM citarem iudices, domine, conventum incohaturus, Flavius Archippus vacationem petere coepit
2 ut philosophus. Fuerunt qui dicerent non liber-
andum eum iudicandi necessitate, sed omnino
tollendum de iudicum numero reddendumque poenae,
3 quam fractis vinculis evasisset. Recitata est sententia Veli Pauli proconsulis, qua probabatur Archippus crimine falsi damnatus in metallum; ille nihil
proferebat, quo restitutum se doceret; adlegabat
tamen pro restitutione et libellum a se Domitiano
datum et epistulas eius ad honorem suum pertinentes

---

¹ *i.e.* to await trial. It is not clear why, unless the man was
a Roman citizen; as St. Paul in *Acts* XXVIII. 16.

² At Prusa. See *Ep.* 81, 1–3.

³ According to *Digest* L. 4. 18. 30 Vespasian and Hadrian
granted immunity from municipal service *grammaticis et
oratoribus et medicis et philosophis* but this conflates two enact-
ments: Vespasian did not include philosophers (cf. MW 458).

As for the man who was banished for life by Julius Bassus, he had two years in which he could have asked for a re-trial if he thought his sentence was unjust, but, as he took no steps to do so, and remained in the province, he must be sent in chains to the officers in command of my imperial guards.[1] It is not sufficient to restore his former sentence when he evaded it by contempt of court.

LVIII

Pliny to the Emperor Trajan

When, Sir, I was summoning jurors and preparing to hold assizes,[2] Flavius Archippus tried to claim exemption on the grounds that he was a teacher of philosophy.[3] At this some people declared that it was not a question of excusing him from acting as a juror, but of removing his name altogether from the register and sending him back to complete the sentence he had evaded by breaking out of prison. The sentence pronounced by the governor Velius Paulus was quoted, whereby Archippus had been condemned to the mines for forgery.[4] He could produce nothing to prove that this sentence had been reversed, but as evidence of his reinstatement he cited a petition he had presented to Domitian, letters written by Domitian testifying to his character, and a decree voted by

Hadrian did (*Digest* XXVII 1. 6. 8). Was Flavius Archippus " trying it on "?

[4] This is old history. Lappius Maximus (s. 6) is known to have been proconsul soon after 86 and Velius Paulus preceded him.

et decretum Prusensium. Addebat his et tuas
litteras scriptas sibi, addebat et patris tui edictum et
epistulam, quibus confirmasset beneficia a Domitiano
4 data. Itaque, quamvis eidem talia crimina adpli-
carentur, nihil decernendum putavi, donec te
consulerem de eo, quod mihi constitutione tua
dignum videbatur. Ea quae sunt utrimque recitata
his litteris subieci.

EPISTULA DOMITIANI AD TERENTIUM MAXIMUM

5 FLAVIUS Archippus philosophus impetravit a me, ut
agrum ei ad c̄[1] circa † Prusiadam †,[2] patriam suam,
emi iuberem, cuius reditu suos alere posset. Quod ei
praestari volo. Summam expensam liberalitati meae
feres.

EIUSDEM AD LAPPIUM[3] MAXIMUM

6 ARCHIPPUM philosophum, bonum virum et profes-
sioni suae etiam moribus[4] respondentem, com-
mendatum habeas velim, mi Maxime, et plenam ei
humanitatem tuam praestes in iis, quae verecunde
a te desideraverit.

EDICTUM DIVI NERVAE

7 QUAEDAM sine dubio, Quirites, ipsa felicitas temporum edicit, nec exspectandus est in iis bonus

---

[1] ad C̄ *i*: DC. *a*.
[2] Prusiadam *Aa*: Prusiam *Cat.* (*cf. Ep.* 81. 6): Prusam
Sherwin-White.
[3] Lappium *Hanslik e Fastis Ostiensibus*: L. Appium *Aa*.
[4] moribus *Rittershusius*: maioribus *Aa*.

the people of Prusa. To these he added a letter written by him to you, and an edict and letter of your father, all confirming the benefits granted him by Domitian.

Notwithstanding the nature of the charges made against this man, I thought I should make no decision until I had asked your advice; the case seemed to me to need your official ruling. I append the documents cited on both sides.

(a) DOMITIAN'S LETTER TO TERENTIUS MAXIMUS

AT the petition of Flavius Archippus the philosopher, I have given instructions that up to 100,000 sesterces is to be spent on buying him a farm near his native town, Prusa;[1] from the income whereof he may support his family. I wish this to be done on his behalf, and the full cost charged to me as a personal gift to him.

(b) DOMITIAN'S LETTER TO LAPPIUS MAXIMUS

ARCHIPPUS the philosopher is an honest man, his character in accordance with his profession. I wish to recommend him to your notice, my dear Maximus, and trust that you will show him every courtesy in acceding to such modest demands as he may make of you.

(c) EDICT OF THE DEIFIED EMPEROR NERVA[2]

THERE are some matters, citizens, which need no edict in happy times like ours, nor should a good

---

[1] The text is wrong. Pliny means Prusa, not Prusias ad mare. The same mistake appears in *Ep.* 81. 6.

[2] " Pompous, grandiloquent and obscure " (E. G. Hardy).

princeps, quibus illum intellegi satis est, cum hoc
sibi civium meorum spondere possit vel non admonita
persuasio, me securitatem omnium quieti meae
praetulisse, ut et nova beneficia conferrem et ante
8 me concessa servarem. Ne tamen aliquam gaudiis
publicis adferat haesitationem vel eorum qui impetraverunt diffidentia vel eius memoria qui praestitit, necessarium pariter credidi ac laetum obviam
9 dubitantibus indulgentiam meam mittere. Nolo
existimet quisquam quod alio principe vel privatim
vel publice consecutus ⟨sit⟩[1] ideo saltem a me
rescindi, ut potius mihi debeat. Sint rata et certa,
nec gratulatio ullius instauratis egeat precibus, quem
fortuna imperii vultu meliore respexit. Me novis
beneficiis vacare patiantur, et ea demum sciant
roganda esse quae non habent.

EPISTULA EIUSDEM AD TULLIVM IUSTUM

10 CUM rerum omnium ordinatio, quae prioribus
temporibus incohatae consummatae sunt, observanda
sit, tum epistulis etiam Domitiani standum est.

LIX

C. PLINIUS TRAIANO IMPERATORI

FLAVIUS ARCHIPPUS per salutem tuam aeterni-
tatemque petit a me, ut libellum quem mihi dedit

---

[1] sit *add. Orelli*, om. Aa.

ruler have to give evidence of his intentions where
they can be clearly understood. Every one of my
subjects can rest assured without a reminder that,
in sacrificing my retirement to the security of the
State, it was my intention to confer new benefits
and to confirm those already granted. However,
to prevent your public rejoicing being marred by
misgivings, through the doubts of any who have received favours, or the memory of the Emperor who
bestowed them, I have thought it necessary and desirable to meet your anxieties by a proof of my
generosity. It is my wish that no one should think
that I shall withdraw any public or private benefactions conferred by any of my predecessors, so as
to claim credit for restoring them myself. Everything shall be assured and ratified: no one on whom
the fortune of the Empire has smiled, shall need to
renew his petitions in order to confirm his happiness.
Let my subjects then permit me to devote myself to
new benefactions, and be assured that they need ask
only for what they have not hitherto been granted.

(*d*) The Deified Emperor Nerva's Letter to
Tullius Justus

Any regulations laid down for matters begun or
concluded in the last reign are to hold good; consequently letters of Domitian must also remain valid.

LIX

Pliny to the Emperor Trajan

Flavius Archippus has charged me by your prosperity and immortal name, to forward a petition

mitterem tibi. Quod ego sic roganti praestandum putavi, ita tamen ut missurum me notum accusatrici eius facerem, a qua et ipsa acceptum libellum his epistulis iunxi, quo facilius velut audita utraque parte dispiceres, quid statuendum putares.

LX

TRAIANUS PLINIO

1 POTUIT quidem ignorasse Domitianus, in quo statu esset Archippus, cum tam multa ad honorem eius pertinentia scriberet; sed meae naturae accommodatius est credere etiam statui eius subventum interventu principis, praesertim cum etiam statuarum ei honor totiens decretus sit ab iis, qui ⟨non⟩[1] ignorabant, quid de illo Paulus proconsul pronuntias-
2 set. Quae tamen, mi Secunde carissime, non eo pertinent, ut si quid illi novi criminis obicitur, minus de eo audiendum putes. Libellos Furiae Primae accusatricis, item ipsius Archippi, quos alteri epistulae tuae iunxeras, legi.

LXI

C. PLINIUS TRAIANO IMPERATORI

1 TU quidem, domine, providentissime vereris, ne commissus flumini atque ita mari lacus effluat; sed

---

[1] non add. Ernesti, om. Aa.

---

[1] See *Epp.* 41–2.

which he has placed in my hands. I thought it my duty to grant a request made in this way, provided that I informed Furia Prima, his accuser, of my intention. She has also handed me a petition which I am sending with this letter, so that you can hear both sides of the case and be better able to decide what is to be done.

LX

TRAJAN TO PLINY

IT is possible that Domitian was unaware of Archippus's position when he wrote all these letters of recommendation, but I personally find it more natural to believe that Archippus was restored to his former status by the Emperor's intervention. This seems more likely because the people of Prusa several times voted Archippus the honour of having his statue set up, though they must have known about the sentence passed by the governor Paulus. But none of this means, my dear Pliny, that if any new charge is brought against him you must not give it a hearing.

I have read the petitions from Archippus and his accuser, Furia Prima, which you sent me in your second letter.

LXI

PLINY TO THE EMPEROR TRAJAN

You very wisely express the fear, Sir, that the lake near Nicomedia might be drained away if connected with the river and then to the sea,[1] but since I have

ego in re praesenti invenisse videor, quem ad
2 modum huic periculo occurrerem. Potest enim
lacus fossa usque ad flumen adduci nec tamen in
flumen emitti, sed relicto quasi margine contineri
pariter et dirimi. Sic consequemur, ut neque aqua
viduetur flumini mixtus,[1] et sit perinde ac si mis-
ceatur. Erit enim facile per illam brevissimam
terram, quae interiacebit, advecta fossa onera trans-
3 ponere in flumen. Quod ita fiet si necessitas coget,
et (spero) non coget. Est enim et lacus ipse satis
altus et nunc in contrariam partem flumen emittit,
quod interclusum inde et quo volumus aversum, sine
ullo detrimento lacus tantum aquae quantum nunc
portat effundet. Praeterea per id spatium, per quod
fossa fodienda est, incidunt rivi; qui si diligenter
colligantur, augebunt illud quod lacus dederit.
4 Enimvero, si placeat fossam longius ducere et altius[2]
pressam mari aequare nec in flumen, sed in ipsum
mare emittere, repercussus maris servabit et repri-
met, quidquid e lacu veniet. Quorum si nihil nobis
loci natura praestaret, expeditum tamen erat
5 cataractis aquae cursum temperare. Verum et haec
et alia multo sagacius conquiret explorabitque libra-
tor, quem plane, domine, debes mittere, ut polliceris.
Est enim res digna et magnitudine tua et cura. Ego
interim Calpurnio Macro clarissimo viro auctore te
scripsi, ut libratorem quam maxime idoneum mitteret.

---

[1] neque aqua viduetur fl. immixtus *Sherwin-White*: nec
vacue videatur fl. mixtus *Aa*: nec lacus videatur *Stout*.
[2] altius *Gierig*: artius *Aa*.

been on the spot I think I have found a way of meeting this danger. The lake can be brought right up to the river by means of a canal without actually joining it, if a sort of dyke is left between to keep the two apart; it will not actually flow into the river (and so be drained of water) but the effect will be almost the same as if it did. It will be easy to bring cargoes along the canal and then transfer them to the river across the narrow strip of land between.

This would be a solution if necessary, but I am hopeful that it will not be needed; for the lake is in fact fairly deep, and has a river flowing out at the opposite side which can be dammed and diverted wherever we like, so that it would carry off no more water than at present and do no damage to the lake. There are, moreover, several streams along the course of the proposed canal, and if their water is carefully conserved it will augment the supply from the lake. Again, if we decide to cut a longer canal, deepen it and bring it down to sea-level so that the water will flow direct into the sea, instead of via the river, the counter-pressure from the sea will check the outflow from the lake. Even if we had none of these natural advantages we could manage to regulate the flow of water by sluices.

But these and other details can be much more accurately worked out in a survey by the engineer, whom you must assuredly send, Sir, as you promised. The scheme deserves your attention, and will prove worthy of your eminent position. Meanwhile, I have written to the distinguished senator Calpurnius Macer, as you directed, and asked him to send the most suitable engineer he has.

THE LETTERS OF PLINY

LXII

TRAIANUS PLINIO

MANIFESTUM, mi Secunde carissime, nec prudentiam nec diligentiam tibi defuisse circa istum lacum, cum tam multa provisa habeas, per quae nec periclitetur exhauriri et magis in usu nobis futurus sit. Elige igitur id quod praecipue res ipsa suaserit. Calpurnium Macrum credo facturum, ut te libratore instruat, neque provinciae istae his artificibus carent.

LXIII

C. PLINIUS TRAIANO IMPERATORI

SCRIPSIT mihi, domine, Lycormas libertus tuus ut, si qua legatio a Bosporo venisset urbem petitura, usque in adventum suum retineretur. Et legatio quidem, dumtaxat in eam civitatem, in qua ipse sum, nulla adhuc venit, sed venit tabellarius Sauromatae ⟨regis⟩,[1] quem ego usus opportunitate, quam mihi casus obtulerat, cum tabellario qui Lycormam ex itinere praecessit mittendum putavi, ut posses ex Lycormae et regis epistulis pariter cognoscere, quae fortasse pariter scire deberes.

---

[1] Sauromatae (*addito* regis) *A. Schaefer*: Sauromata *Aa.*

---

[1] Evidently some dispute had arisen between Lycormas and the client king of the Crimean principality; the reason is

LXII

Trajan to Pliny

I can see, my dear Pliny, that you are applying all your energy and intelligence to your lake; you have worked out so many ways of avoiding the danger of its water draining away, and so increasing its usefulness to us in future. You choose then the way which best suits the situation. I am sure Calpurnius Macer will not fail to send you an engineer, and there is no lack of such experts in the provinces where you are.

LXIII

Pliny to the Emperor Trajan

I have received a letter, Sir, from your freedman Lycormas, telling me to detain, pending his arrival, any embassy which may come here from the Bosporos on its way to Rome. None has come to Nicaea as yet, at least while I have been here, but a courier has arrived from King Sauromates.[1] I thought I should seize this unforeseen opportunity to send him on with the courier who travelled here ahead of Lycormas, so that you could have both letters together in case they contained news of equal importance to you.

obscure, but unlikely to be connected with Trajan's Parthian projects (see R. P. Longdon in *JRS* XXI, p. 19 ff.).

LXIV

C. Plinius Traiano Imperatori

Rex Sauromates scripsit mihi esse quaedam, quae
deberes quam maturissime scire. Qua ex causa
festinationem tabellarii, quem ad te cum epistulis
misit, diplomate adiuvi.

LXV

C. Plinius Traiano Imperatori

1 Magna, domine, et ad totam provinciam pertinens
quaestio est de condicione et alimentis eorum, quos
2 vocant θρεπτούς. In qua ego auditis constitutioni-
bus principum, quia nihil inveniebam aut proprium
aut universale, quod ad Bithynos referretur, consulendum te existimavi, quid observari velles; neque
putavi posse me in eo, quod auctoritatem tuam
3 posceret, exemplis esse contentum. Recitabatur
autem apud me edictum, quod dicebatur divi Augusti,
ad Andaniam¹ pertinens; recitatae et epistulae divi
Vespasiani ad Lacedaemonios et divi Titi ad eosdem
et Achaeos et Domitiani ad Avidium Nigrinum et
Armenium Brocchum proconsules, item ad Lacedaemonios; quae ideo tibi non misi, quia et parum

---

¹ Andaniam *Cuntz*: Anniam *Aa*: Achaiam *Mommsen*:
Asiam *Hardy*.

---

¹ The courier of the previous letter.
² *i.e.* the *ad hoc* judgements of the proconsuls.

LXIV

PLINY TO THE EMPEROR TRAJAN

KING SAUROMATES has written to me to say that he has news which you should know as soon as possible. I have accordingly given a permit for the Post to the courier who is bringing his letter to you, in order to speed up his journey.[1]

LXV

PLINY TO THE EMPEROR TRAJAN

A SERIOUS problem, Sir, which affects the whole province, concerns the status and cost of maintenance of the persons generally known as foundlings. I have looked at the orders of your predecessors, but was unable to find either a particular case or a general rule which could apply to Bithynia; so I decided I must ask you for directions, as I felt it was not sufficient to be guided only by precedents[2] in a matter which required your authoritative opinion.

An edict referring to Andania[3] was quoted to me, which was said to be one issued by the deified Emperor Augustus, also letters of the deified Emperors Vespasian and Titus to the Spartans, and another from Titus to the Achaeans. There were also letters from Domitian to the governors Avidius Nigrinus and Armenius Brocchus, and yet another to the Spartans from Domitian. I have not sent copies of them to you as they seemed to be inaccurate, and

[3] The former capital of the kings of Messenia in the Peloponnese (now Androssa).

emendata et quaedam non certae fidei videbantur,
et quia vera et emendata in scriniis tuis esse
credebam.

LXVI

Traianus Plinio

1 Quaestio ista, quae pertinet ad eos qui liberi nati
exposti, deinde sublati a quibusdam et in servitute
educati sunt, saepe tractata est, nec quicquam
invenitur in commentariis eorum principum, qui ante
me fuerunt, quod ad omnes provincias sit constitutum.
2 Epistulae sane sunt Domitiani ad Avidium Nigrinum
et Armenium Brocchum, quae fortasse debeant
observari: sed inter eas provincias, de quibus
rescripsit, non est Bithynia; et ideo nec adsertionem
denegandam iis qui ex eius modi causa in libertatem
vindicabuntur puto, neque ipsam libertatem redi-
mendam pretio alimentorum.

LXVII

C. Plinius Traiano Imperatori

1 Legato Sauromatae regis, cum sua sponte Nicaeae,
ubi me invenerat, biduo substitisset, longiorem
moram faciendam, domine, non putavi, primum quod
incertum adhuc erat, quando libertus tuus Lycormas
venturus esset, deinde quod ipse proficiscebar in
diversam provinciae partem, ita officii necessitate

---

[1] In this kind of action (*causa liberalis*) the claimant made
his *assertio* against his master through a representative.
Trajan follows Greek practice in not allowing costs of up-
bringing to the foster-parents.

some of them of doubtful authenticity; and I felt sure that you had accurate and genuine versions among your official files.

LXVI

Trajan to Pliny

THE question you raise of free persons who were exposed at birth, but then brought up in slavery by those who rescued them, has often been discussed, but I can find nothing in the records of my predecessors which could have applied to all provinces. There are, it is true, the letters from Domitian to Avidius Nigrinus and Armenius Brocchus, which ought possibly to give us guidance, but Bithynia is not one of the provinces covered by his ruling. I am therefore of the opinion that those who wish to claim emancipation on this ground should not be prevented from making a public declaration of their right to freedom, nor should they have to purchase their freedom by refunding the cost of their maintenance.[1]

LXVII

Pliny to the Emperor Trajan

AN ambassador from King Sauromates, Sir, saw me at Nicaea, and waited there of his own accord for two days; after which I thought I ought not to delay him further, seeing that I still had no idea when your freedman Lycormas would arrive, and official duties compelled me to leave myself for another part of the

2 exigente. Haec in notitiam tuam perferenda existimavi, quia proxime scripseram petisse Lycormam, ut legationem, si qua venisset a Bosporo, usque in adventum suum retinerem. Quod diutius faciendi nulla mihi probabilis ratio occurrit, praesertim cum epistulae Lycormae, quas detinere, ut ante praedixi, nolui, aliquot diebus hinc legatum antecessurae viderentur.

LXVIII

C. Plinius Traiano Imperatori

Petentibus quibusdam, ut sibi reliquias suorum aut propter iniuriam vetustatis aut propter fluminis incursum aliaque his similia quocumque[1] secundum exemplum proconsulum transferre permitterem, quia sciebam in urbe nostra ex eius modi causa collegium pontificum adiri solere, te, domine, maximum pontificem consulendum putavi, quid observare me velis.

LXIX

Traianus Plinio

Durum est iniungere necessitatem provincialibus pontificum adeundorum, si reliquias suorum propter aliquas iustas causas transferre ex loco in alium locum

---

[1] quocumque *Kukula*: quaec- *Aa*.

---

[1] In *Ep.* 77. 2 he is at Juliopolis.
[2] Pontifical authority did not legally extend beyond Italy (cf. 49) but proconsuls often followed it in their rulings. P.

province.[1] I thought I should bring this to your notice in view of my recent letter saying that Lycormas had asked me to detain pending his arrival any embassy which might come from the Bosporos. I could think of no good reason for keeping him any longer, especially as the letters from Lycormas, which (as I said in my earlier letter) I did not want to delay, seemed likely to reach you some days before this ambassador.

LXVIII

PLINY TO THE EMPEROR TRAJAN

CERTAIN persons have asked me to follow the practice of the senatorial governors and permit them to move to a site of their choice the remains of their deceased relatives, either because their monuments have suffered through lapse of time or the flooding of the river or for other similar reasons. Knowing that when cases of this kind arise in Rome application must be made to the College of Pontiffs, I thought I should consult you, Sir, as Chief Pontiff, to learn what course you wish me to follow.[2]

LXIX

TRAJAN TO PLINY

IT makes things difficult for provincials if we enforce the rule of applying to the Pontiffs when they have good reason for wanting to transfer the remains of their deceased from one site to another. I think

does not, however, suggest referring to the College, and Trajan's answer shows he has read the letter carelessly.

velint. Sequenda ergo potius tibi exempla sunt
eorum, qui isti provinciae praefuerunt, et ut[1] causa
cuique, ita aut permittendum aut negandum.

LXX

C. Plinius Traiano Imperatori

1 Quaerenti mihi, domine, Prusae ubi posset
balineum quod indulsisti fieri, placuit locus in quo fuit
aliquando domus, ut audio, pulchra, nunc deformis
ruinis. Per hoc enim consequemur, ut foedissima
facies civitatis ornetur, atque etiam ut ipsa civitas
amplietur nec ulla aedificia tollantur, sed quae sunt
2 vetustate sublapsa relaxentur in melius. Est autem
huius domus condicio talis: legaverat eam Claudius
Polyaenus Claudio Caesari iussitque in peristylio
templum ei fieri, reliqua ex domo locari. Ex ea
reditum aliquandiu civitas percepit; deinde paulatim
partim spoliata, partim neglecta cum peristylio
domus tota collapsa est, ac iam paene nihil ex ea
nisi solum superest; quod tu, domine, sive donaveris
civitati sive venire iusseris, propter opportunitatem
3 loci pro summo munere accipiet. Ego, si permiseris,
cogito in area vacua balineum collocare, eum autem
locum, in quo aedificia fuerunt, exedra et porticibus
amplecti atque tibi consecrare, cuius beneficio elegans

---

[1] et ut *Keil*: et ex *Cat.*: ex *Aa*.

it would be best to follow the example of former governors of your province and grant or refuse permission on the merits of each individual case.

LXX

PLINY TO THE EMPEROR TRAJAN

I HAVE looked around Prusa, Sir, in search of a possible site for the new bath for which you have graciously given your permission, and chosen one which is occupied at present by the unsightly ruins of what I am told was once a fine house. We could thus remove this eyesore and embellish the city without pulling down any existing structure; indeed, we should be restoring and improving what time has destroyed.

But these are the facts about the house. It was left to the Emperor Claudius by the will of a certain Claudius Polyaenus, who also left instructions that a shrine to the Emperor was to be set up in the garden-court and the rest of the house was to be let. For some time the city drew rent for this; then, partly through pillage and partly through neglect, the whole house, court and garden gradually fell into ruins, so that now little but the site remains. The citizens would esteem it as a great favour, Sir, if you would either make them a present of this or give orders for it to be sold, as it is so conveniently situated. My own plan, if you approve, is to build the bath on what is already an open space, and to use the site of the original buildings for a hall and colonnades, to be dedicated to you as benefactor, for it will be a splen-

4 opus dignumque nomine tuo fiet. Exemplar testamenti, quamquam mendosum, misi tibi; ex quo cognosces multa Polyaenum in eiusdem domus ornatum reliquisse, quae ut domus ipsa perierunt, a me tamen in quantum potuerit requirentur.

LXXI

TRAIANUS PLINIO

POSSUMUS apud Prusenses area ista cum domo collapsa, quam vacare scribis, ad exstructionem balinei uti. Illud tamen parum expressisti, an aedes in peristylio Claudio facta esset. Nam, si facta est, licet collapsa sit, religio eius occupavit solum.

LXXII

C. PLINIUS TRAIANO IMPERATORI

POSTULANTIBUS quibusdam, ut de agnoscendis liberis restituendisque natalibus et secundum epistulam Domitiani scriptam Minicio Rufo et secundum exempla proconsulum ipse cognoscerem, respexi ad senatus consultum pertinens ad eadem genera causarum, quod de iis tantum provinciis loquitur, quibus proconsules praesunt; ideoque rem integram

---

[1] A further problem arising out of the inquiry into the θρεπτοί.

did public monument well worthy of your name. I
am sending a copy of the will, though an imperfect
one, from which you will see that Polyaenus left a
good deal of furniture for the house. This has dis-
appeared as well; but I shall make all possible inquiries about it.

LXXI

Trajan to Pliny

There is no reason why we should not use the open
space and the ruined house, which you say is unoccupied, for building the new bath at Prusa. But
you did not make it clear whether the shrine to
Claudius had actually been set up in the garden-
court. If so, the ground is still consecrated to him
even if the shrine has fallen into ruins.

LXXII

Pliny to the Emperor Trajan

Certain persons have requested that cases concerning acknowledgement of children and granting
of free-born rights to former slaves [1] should come to
me personally for settlement. This, they say,
would be in accordance with a letter written by
Domitian to Minicius Rufus, and with the practice
of former governors. I have looked up the decree of
the Senate referring to cases of these types, but it
covers only provinces under senatorial governors. I

distuli, dum tu,[1] domine, praeceperis, quid observare me velis.

LXXIII

TRAIANUS PLINIO

SI mihi senatus consultum miseris quod haesitationem tibi fecit, aestimabo an debeas cognoscere de agnoscendis liberis et natalibus veris restituendis.

LXXIV

C. PLINIUS TRAIANO IMPERATORI

1 APPULEIUS, domine, miles qui est in statione Nicomedensi, scripsit mihi quendam nomine Callidromum, cum detineretur a Maximo et Dionysio pistoribus, quibus operas suas locaverat, confugisse ad tuam statuam perductumque ad magistratus indicasse, servisse [2] aliquando Laberio Maximo, captumque a Susago in Moesia et a Decibalo muneri missum Pacoro Parthiae regi, pluribusque annis in ministerio eius fuisse, deinde fugisse, atque ita in 2 Nicomediam pervenisse. Quem ego perductum ad

---

[1] tu *add. Cat.:* om. *Aa.*
[2] servisse se *C. F. W. Mueller:* se servisse *Madvig.*

---

[1] *i.e.* he is a *miles stationarius*, like those at Byzantium in *Ep.* 77, to assist the governor in dealing with criminals and runaway slaves.
[2] Trajan's legate: see Index. Susagus must be in the

have therefore left the whole question in suspense until I have received your instructions, Sir, on what course to take.

LXXIII

Trajan to Pliny

IF you will send me the decree of the Senate which is giving you difficulty, I shall be able to judge whether you ought to settle these cases of acknowledging children and restoring genuine free-born rights.

LXXIV

Pliny to the Emperor Trajan

A SOLDIER named Appuleius, Sir, stationed at Nicomedia,[1] has sent me this report about a certain Callidromus. This man had been forcibly detained by his employers, Maximus and Dionysius (who are bakers), but had escaped and taken refuge before one of your statues. When brought before the magistrates, he made the following statement. He had once been a slave of Laberius Maximus,[2] was captured in Moesia by Susagus, and sent by Decebalus as a gift to Pacorus, King of Parthia, in whose service he remained for several years until he escaped and so made his way to Nicomedia.[3]

Dacian army. There is no other literary evidence for the invasion of Moesia in the First Dacian War.

[3] S-W (p. 662) points out that there is no confirmation of this remarkable story, and Nicomedia is suspiciously near Moesia.

me, cum eadem narrasset, mittendum ad te putavi;
quod paulo tardius feci, dum requiro gemmam, quam
sibi habentem imaginem Pacori et quibus ornatus
3 fuisset subtractam indicabat. Volui enim hanc
quoque, si inveniri potuisset, simul mittere, sicut
glebulam misi, quam se ex Parthico metallo attulisse
dicebat. Signata est anulo meo, cuius est aposphra-
gisma quadriga.

LXXV

C. PLINIUS TRAIANO IMPERATORI

1 IULIUS, domine, Largus ex Ponto nondum mihi
visus ac ne auditus quidem (scilicet iudicio tuo
credidit) dispensationem quandam mihi erga te
2 pietatis suae ministeriumque mandavit. Rogavit
enim testamento, ut hereditatem suam adirem cerne-
remque, ac deinde praeceptis [1] quinquaginta milibus
nummum reliquum omne Heracleotarum et Tianorum
civitatibus redderem, ita ut esset arbitrii mei utrum
opera facienda, quae honori tuo consecrarentur,
putarem an instituendos quinquennales agonas, qui
Traiani adpellarentur. Quod in notitiam tuam
perferendum existimavi ob hoc maxime, ut dispiceres
quid eligere debeam.

> [1] praeceptis *Thomas*: perceptis *Aa*.

---

[1] The form of bequest known as *fidei commissum* which
allowed a bequest to pass to a municipality which could not
otherwise inherit. See V. 7. 1.

As he repeated the same story when brought before me, I thought I ought to send him on to you; and I have delayed doing so only while I made inquiries about a jewel engraved with a portrait of Pacorus wearing his royal robes, which the man declared had been stolen from him. I should have liked to send this too, if it could have been found, along with the small nugget of gold I am sending now; he says he brought it from one of the mines in Parthia. I have sealed it with my signet ring, the chariot-and-four.

LXXV

PLINY TO THE EMPEROR TRAJAN

JULIUS LARGUS of Pontus, Sir—a person whom I have never seen nor heard of, but presumably relying on your opinion of me—has entrusted me with the duty of administering, so to speak, his loyal sentiments towards you. He has left a will asking me to take formal possession of his estate [1] and, after deducting 50,000 sesterces for my own use, to pay over the remainder to the cities of Heraclea and Tium, either for the erection of public buildings to be dedicated in your honour or for the institution of five-yearly games to be called by your name, whichever I think best. I thought I should bring this to your notice, mainly because I hope that you will guide my decision.

LXXVI

Traianus Plinio

Iulius Largus fidem tuam quasi te bene nosset elegit. Quid ergo potissimum ad perpetuitatem memoriae eius faciat, secundum cuiusque loci condicionem ipse dispice et quod optimum existimaveris, id sequere.[1]

LXXVII

C. Plinius Traiano Imperatori

1 Providentissime, domine, fecisti, quod praecepisti Calpurnio Macro clarissimo viro, ut legionarium
2 centurionem Byzantium mitteret. Dispice an etiam Iuliopolitanis simili ratione consulendum putes, quorum civitas, cum sit perexigua, onera maxima sustinet tantoque graviores iniurias quanto est
3 infirmior patitur. Quidquid autem Iuliopolitanis praestiteris, id etiam toti provinciae proderit. Sunt enim in capite Bithyniae, plurimisque per eam commeantibus transitum praebent.

LXXVIII

Traianus Plinio

1 Ea condicio est civitatis Byzantiorum confluente undique in eam commeantium turba, ut secundum

1 id sequere *Rivinus*: insequere *Aa*.

LXXVI

TRAJAN TO PLINY

JULIUS LARGUS chose you for your sense of duty as if he had known you personally. Consider what will suit the conditions of both places, and also what will best perpetuate his memory, and make your own decision; you can adopt which ever plan you think best.

LXXVII

PLINY TO THE EMPEROR TRAJAN

IT was a very wise move, Sir, to direct the distinguished senator Calpurnius Macer to send a legionary centurion to Byzantium.[1] Would you now consider giving the same assistance to Juliopolis? Being such a small city it feels its burden heavy, and finds its wrongs the harder to bear as it is unable to prevent them. Any relief you grant to Juliopolis would benefit the whole province, for it is a frontier town of Bithynia with a great deal of traffic passing through it.

LXXVIII

TRAJAN TO PLINY

BYZANTIUM is in an exceptional position, with crowds of travellers pouring into it from all sides.

---

[1] From the Danube armies, as Bithynia had only auxiliary troops, a small force of which would serve under the centurion to control traffic.

consuetudinem praecedentium temporum honoribus
eius praesidio centurionis legionarii consulendum
2 habuerimus. ⟨Si⟩[1] Iuliopolitanis succurrendum
eodem modo putaverimus, onerabimus nos exemplo;
plures enim eo[2] quanto infirmiores erunt idem petent.
Fiduciam ⟨eam⟩[3] diligentiae ⟨tuae⟩[4] habeo, ut
credam te omni ratione id acturum, ne sint obnoxii
3 iniuriis. Si qui autem se contra disciplinam meam
gesserint, statim coerceantur; aut, si plus admiserint
quam ut in re praesenti satis puniantur, si milites
erunt, legatis eorum quod deprehenderis notum facies
aut, si in urbem versus venturi erunt, mihi scribes.

LXXIX

C. PLINIUS TRAIANO IMPERATORI

1 CAUTUM est, domine, Pompeia lege quae Bithynis
data est, ne quis capiat magistratum neve sit in
senatu minor annorum triginta. Eadem lege comprehensum est, ut qui ceperint magistratum sint in
2 senatu. Secutum est dein edictum divi Augusti, quo
permisit minores magistratus ab annis duobus et
3 viginti[5] capere. Quaeritur ergo an, qui minor

---

[1] si *add. hic Cat.*[2], *post* modo *Cat.*[1], *i: om. Aa.*
[2] eo *Kukula:* et *A.*
[3] eam *add. hic Orelli: om. A.*
[4] tuae *add. Cat.: om. Aa.*
[5] duobus et viginti *Aa:* xxv *Nipperdey.*

That is why I thought I ought to follow the practice of previous reigns and give its magistrates support in the form of a garrison under a legionary centurion. If I decide to help Juliopolis in the same way I shall burden myself with a precedent, for other cities, especially the weaker ones, will expect similar help. I rely on you, and am confident that you will be active in every way to ensure that the citizens are protected from injustice.

If people commit a breach of the peace they must be arrested at once; and, if their offences are too serious for summary punishment, in the case of soldiers you must notify their officers of what is found against them, while you may inform me by letter in the case of persons who are passing through on their way back to Rome.

LXXIX

PLINY TO THE EMPEROR TRAJAN

UNDER the code of law, Sir, which Pompey drew up for Bithynia,[1] it was laid down that no one could hold civil office or sit in the senate under the age of thirty. The same law stated that all ex-officials should become members of the local senate. Then followed the edict of the deified Emperor Augustus permitting the minor posts to be held from the age of twenty-two. The question therefore arises whether

---

[1] *Lex Pompeia*, drawn up by Pompey after Bithynia and West Pontus were reorganized as a Roman province in 65 B.C. (cf. *Epp.* 112, 114). Similar regulations for holding office in provincial senates exist in the *Lex Malacitana* § 54. (MW 454)

triginta annorum gessit magistratum, possit a
censoribus in senatum legi, et, si potest, an ii quoque,
qui non gesserint, possint per eandem interpretationem ab ea aetate senatores legi, a qua illis magistratum gerere permissum est; quod alioqui facti-
tatum adhuc et esse necessarium dicitur, quia sit
aliquanto melius honestorum hominum liberos quam
4 e plebe in curiam admitti. Ego a destinatis censoribus quid sentirem interrogatus eos quidem, qui
minores triginta annis gessissent magistratum, putabam posse in senatum et secundum edictum Augusti
et secundum legem Pompeiam legi, quoniam
Augustus gerere magistratus minoribus annis triginta
permisisset, lex senatorem esse voluisset qui gessisset
5 magistratum. De iis autem qui non gessissent,
quamvis essent aetatis eiusdem cuius illi quibus
gerere permissum est, haesitabam; per quod
effectum est ut te, domine, consulerem, quid observari
velles. Capita legis, tum edictum Augusti litteris
subieci.

LXXX

Traianus Plinio

Interpretationi tuae, mi Secunde carissime, idem
existimo: hactenus edicto divi Augusti novatam esse
legem Pompeiam, ut magistratum quidem capere

---

[1] Municipal censors working on Roman lines.

anyone who has held office under the age of thirty
can be admitted to the senate by the censors,[1] and,
if so, whether the law can be similarly interpreted
so that persons who have not actually held office
can be admitted to the senate at the age when they
were eligible to do so. This has been the practice
hitherto, and is considered unavoidable because it is
so much more desirable to choose senators from the
sons of better-class families than from the common
people.

When asked my opinion by the censors-elect, I
told them that I thought it would be in accordance
with both the edict of Augustus and the law of Pompey if anyone who had held civil office under the age
of thirty were admitted to the senate, seeing that
the edict allowed office to be held before the age of
thirty, and the law laid down that all ex-officials
should become senators; but that in the case of
persons who had never held a civil office, although
they had reached an age to make them eligible, I had
some doubts. That is why, Sir, I am asking your
advice on what you wish me to do. I append the
relevant sections of the law of Pompey, and also the
edict of Augustus.

LXXX

TRAJAN TO PLINY

I AGREE with your interpretation, my dear Pliny,
that the law of Pompey was modified by the edict
of Augustus to the extent that any person not under
the age of twenty-two was eligible to hold civil office,

possent ii, qui non minores duorum[1] et viginti annorum essent, et qui cepissent, in senatum cuiusque
civitatis pervenirent. Ceterum non capto magistratu
eos, qui minores triginta annorum sint, quia magistratum capere possint, in curiam etiam loci cuiusque
non existimo legi posse.

LXXXI

C. PLINIUS TRAIANO IMPERATORI

1 CUM Prusae ad Olympum, domine, publicis negotiis
intra hospitium eodem die exiturus vacarem, Asclepiades magistratus indicavit adpellatum me a
Claudio Eumolpo. Cum Cocceianus Dion in bule
adsignari civitati opus cuius curam egerat vellet,
tum Eumolpus adsistens Flavio Archippo dixit
exigendam esse a Dione rationem operis, ante quam
rei publicae traderetur, quod aliter fecisset ac
2 debuisset. Adiecit etiam esse in eodem positam
tuam statuam et corpora sepultorum, uxoris Dionis et
filii, postulavitque ut cognoscerem pro tribunali.
3 Quod cum ego me protinus facturum dilaturumque
profectionem dixissem, ut longiorem diem ad struen-
dam causam darem utque in alia civitate cognoscerem
4 petiit. Ego me auditurum Nicaeae respondi. Ubi
cum consedissem[2] cogniturus, idem Eumolpus tamquam si adhuc parum instructus dilationem petere

---

[1] duorum *Cat.*, *a*: duo *A*: quinque *Nipperdey*.
[2] cum consedissem *Orelli*: cum sed- *a*: consed- *A*.

---

[1] Better known as Dio Chrysostom, the orator and philosopher. His *Or.* XL, XLV, and XLVII refer to his difficulties with public works in Prusa.

and, having done so, could be admitted to the senate of his own town. But no one, I think, under the age of thirty who has not held office, can be elected to the senate of any place merely because he has reached the age of eligibility.

LXXXI

PLINY TO THE EMPEROR TRAJAN

On the last day, Sir, of my stay at Prusa near Mount Olympus, I was finishing my official business in the governor's residence when I was informed by the magistrate Asclepiades that Claudius Eumolpus had a request to make. It seems that at a meeting of the local senate Dio Cocceianus[1] had applied for the transfer to the city of some public work which he had undertaken, but Eumolpus, representing Flavius Archippus, had opposed the transfer until Dio should produce his accounts for the building, as he was suspected of dishonest conduct. He also declared that your statue had been set up in the building although the bodies of Dio's wife and son were buried there, and he requested me to hold a judicial inquiry.

I agreed to postpone my departure and do so immediately, but he then wanted me to give him longer to prepare his case and asked me to hold the inquiry in another town.[2] I arranged to hold it at Nicaea, but, when I took my seat to hear the case, Eumolpus again began to beg for an adjournment on the grounds that he was still insufficiently prepared,

[2] Perhaps for Pliny's convenience, as he was on the point of leaving, or to avoid Dio's influential friends.

5 coepit, contra Dion ut audiretur exigere. Dicta
sunt utrimque multa, etiam de causa. Ego cum dan-
dam dilationem et ⟨te⟩[1] consulendum existimarem
in re ad exemplum pertinenti, dixi utrique parti ut
postulationum suarum libellos darent. Volebam
enim te ipsorum potissimum verbis ea quae erant
6 proposita cognoscere. Et Dion quidem se daturum
dixit. Eumolpus respondit complexurum se libello
quae rei publicae peteret, ceterum quod ad sepultos
pertineret non accusatorem se sed advocatum Flavi
Archippi, cuius mandata pertulisset. Archippus, cui
Eumolpus sicut †Prusiade†[2] adsistebat, dixit se
libellum daturum. At nec Eumolpus nec Archippus
quam⟨quam⟩[3] plurimis diebus exspectati adhuc mihi
libellos dederunt; Dion dedit, quem huic epistulae
7 iunxi. Ipse in re praesenti fui et vidi tuam quoque
statuam in bibliotheca positam, id autem in quo
dicuntur sepulti filius et uxor Dionis in area col-
8 locatum, quae porticibus includitur. Te, domine,
rogo ut me in hoc praecipue genere cognitionis regere
digneris, cum alioqui magna sit exspectatio, ut
necesse est[4] in ea re quae et in confessum venit et
exemplis defenditur.

LXXXII

TRAIANUS PLINIO

1 POTUISTI non haerere, mi Secunde carissime, circa
id de quo me consulendum existimasti, cum pro-

[1] te *add. G. H. Schaefer*: om. *Aa*.
[2] See *Ep* 58. 5 and note. Prusa is the town meant.
[3] quamquam *Keil*: quam *Aa*.
[4] est *Orelli*: sit *A et a*.

whereas Dio demanded an immediate hearing. After much argument on both sides, some of it referring to the actual case, I decided to grant an adjournment in order to ask your advice, as the case is likely to create a precedent. I told both parties to present their demands in writing as I wanted to enable you to judge their statements from their own words. Dio agreed to do this, but Eumolpus said he would confine his written statement to his request for accounts made on behalf of his town; as regards the bodies of Dio's relatives, he said that he was not instigating any charge, but was representing Flavius Archippus and carrying out his instructions. Archippus, who was supported by Eumolpus here as at Prusa, then said that he would draw up the statement himself. I have waited several days, but neither Archippus nor Eumolpus has given me any statement up to now. Dio has handed in the statement which I am sending with this letter.

I have visited the building myself, and have seen your statue in position in a library; the alleged burial-place of Dio's wife and son is in an open space surrounded by a colonnade. I pray you, Sir, to think fit to guide me, especially in an inquiry of this kind; it has aroused great public interest, as is inevitable when the facts are admitted and defended by precedents on both sides.

LXXXII

TRAJAN TO PLINY

You need not have had any doubts, my dear Pliny, about the matter on which you thought it necessary

positum meum optime nosses, non ex metu nec terrore hominum aut criminibus maiestatis reverentiam
2 nomini meo adquiri. Omissa ergo ea quaestione, quam non admitterem etiam si exemplis adiuvaretur, ratio totius operis effecti sub cura[1] Cocceiani Dionis excutiatur, cum et utilitas civitatis exigat nec aut recuset Dion aut debeat recusare.

LXXXIII

C. PLINIUS TRAIANO IMPERATORI

ROGATUS, domine, a Nicaeensibus publice per ea, quae mihi et sunt et debent esse sanctissima, id est per aeternitatem tuam salutemque, ut preces suas ad te perferrem, fas non putavi negare acceptumque ab iis libellum huic epistulae iunxi.

LXXXIV

TRAIANUS PLINIO

NICAEENSIBUS, qui intestatorum civium suorum concessam vindicationem bonorum a divo Augusto adfirmant, debebis vacare contractis omnibus per-

---

[1] cura *Keil*: curatura *Orelli*: cura tua *Aa*.

---

[1] Cf. *Pan.* 42. 1. The charge had not in fact been made under the *lex maiestatis* but had been treated by Pliny as an open problem.
[2] *i.e.* it was to go by the *cursus publicus* to avoid the expense of sending a delegate.

to consult me. You know very well that it is my fixed rule not to gain respect for my name either from people's fears and apprehensions or from charges of treason.[1] You must dismiss this side of the question, which I would not tolerate even if it has precedents to support it, and then see that Dio Cocceianus produces accounts for all the work carried out under his management as the public interest demands. Dio ought not to object and in fact has not done so.

LXXXIII

PLINY TO THE EMPEROR TRAJAN

THE people of Nicaea, Sir, have officially charged me by your immortal name and prosperity, which I must ever hold most sacred, to forward their petition to you. I felt that I could not rightly refuse, and so it has been handed to me to dispatch with this letter.[2]

LXXXIV

TRAJAN TO PLINY

THE Nicaeans state that they have the right granted by the deified Emperor Augustus to claim the property of any of the citizens of Nicaea who die intestate.[3] You must therefore examine this

---

[3] Contrast the law in Rome, where every effort was made to trace heirs, and only when these failed was the property claimed by the *aerarium*.

sonis ad idem negotium pertinentibus, adhibitis Virdio Gemellino et Epimacho liberto meo procuratoribus, ut aestimatis etiam iis, quae contra dicuntur, quod optimum credideritis, statuatis.

LXXXV

C. PLINIUS TRAIANO IMPERATORI

MAXIMUM libertum et procuratorem tuum, domine, per omne tempus, quo fuimus una, probum et industrium et diligentem ac sicut rei tuae amantissimum ita disciplinae tenacissimum expertus, libenter apud te testimonio prosequor, ea fide quam tibi debeo.

LXXXVI A

C. PLINIUS TRAIANO IMPERATORI

GAVIUM BASSUM, domine, praefectum orae Ponticae integrum probum industrium atque inter ista reverentissimum mei expertus, voto pariter et suffragio prosequor, ea fide quam tibi debeo.

---

[1] The procurators are to act as assessors to aid Pliny in the inquiry.

[2] Cf. *Epp.* 27–8 for Maximus. This is his testimonial as he leaves the province.

assertion with care, summon all the persons concerned, and call on the procurators Virdius Gemellinus and Epimachus, my freedman, to help you; so that after weighing their arguments against those on the other side you can reach the best decision.[1]

LXXXV

PLINY TO THE EMPEROR TRAJAN

YOUR freedman and procurator Maximus,[2] throughout the time we have been associated, has always proved honest, hard-working, and conscientious, as devoted to your interests, Sir, as he is a strict maintainer of discipline. I gladly give him this testimonial in all good faith, as demanded by my duty to you.

LXXXVI A

PLINY TO THE EMPEROR TRAJAN

GAVIUS BASSUS,[3] Sir, the prefect of the Pontic Shore, has always proved high-principled, honest, and hard-working in his official duties, and has shown me every respect. I give him my full support and recommendation, in all good faith, as demanded by my duty to you.

[3] Cf. *Ep.* 21 for Gavius Bassus.

LXXXVI B

⟨C. Plinivs Traiano Imperatori⟩

[1]... †quam ea quae speret †instructum commilitio
tuo, cuius disciplinae debet, quod indulgentia tua
dignus est. Apud me et milites et pagani, a quibus
iustitia eius et humanitas penitus inspecta est,
certatim ei qua privatim qua publice testimonium
perhibuerunt.[2] Quod in notitiam tuam perfero, ea
fide quam tibi debeo.

LXXXVII

C. Plinius Traiano Imperatori

1 Nymphidium Lupum, domine, primipilarem com-
militonem habui, cum ipse tribunus essem ille
praefectus: inde familiariter diligere coepi. Crevit
postea caritas ipsa mutuae vetustate amicitiae.
2 Itaque et quieti eius inieci manum et exegi, ut me in
Bithynia consilio instrueret. Quod ille amicissime et
otii et senectutis ratione postposita et iam fecit et
3 facturus est. Quibus ex causis necessitudines eius
inter meas numero, filium in primis, Nymphidium
Lupum, iuvenem probum industrium et egregio patre
dignissimum, suffecturum indulgentiae tuae, sicut
primis eius experimentis cognoscere potes, cum

---

[1] *initium novae epistulae ita constituit Cat.*[1]: Fabium
Valentem instr. comm. tuo valde probo, cuius ...
[2] perhibuerunt *Hardy*: pertrib. *Aa.*

---

[1] Either a substantial part of this letter is lost, or we may
tentatively accept the reading in Catanaeus's 1st edition:

LXXXVI B

PLINY TO THE EMPEROR TRAJAN

I WARMLY recommend. . . .[1] He has served in
the army under you, and to this training he owes
any claim he has on your generosity. While I have
been here both soldiers and civilians, who have had
close experience of his justice and humanity, have
vied with each other to pay personal and public tribute to him. I bring these facts to your notice in
all good faith, as demanded by my duty to you.

LXXXVII

PLINY TO THE EMPEROR TRAJAN

NYMPHIDIUS LUPUS, Sir, the former chief centurion
and I were in the army together, when he was commanding a cohort and I was a tribune. I liked him
very much from the start, and our friendship begun
then has increased in warmth with the passage of
time. I therefore sent him a summons to bring him
out of retirement and induce him to join me in
Bithynia as my assessor. Like a good friend he postponed his plans for a peaceful old age and consented;
and he intends to remain with me. Consequently,
I look upon his relatives as my own, especially his
son Nymphidius Lupus, an honest, hard-working
young man, well worthy of his excellent father. He
will prove equal to any mark of your favour, as you
may judge from his first military appointment as

which S-W (p. 682) thinks is the best reconstruction. For
Fabius Valens, see IV. 24.

praefectus cohortis plenissimum testimonium meruerit Iuli Ferocis et Fusci Salinatoris clarissimorum virorum. Meum gaudium, domine, meamque gratulationem filii honore cumulabis.[1]

LXXXVIII

C. PLINIUS TRAIANO IMPERATORI

OPTO, domine, et hunc natalem et plurimos alios quam felicissimos agas aeternaque laude florentem virtutis tuae gloriam et[2] incolumis et fortis aliis super alia operibus augebis.

LXXXIX

TRAIANUS PLINIO

AGNOSCO vota tua, mi Secunde carissime, quibus precaris, ut plurimos et felicissimos natales florente statu rei publicae nostrae agam.

XC

C. PLINIUS TRAIANO IMPERATORI

1 SINOPENSES, domine, aqua deficiuntur; quae videtur et bona et copiosa ab sexto decimo miliario

---

[1] cumulabis *Maquinness*: continerent *Aa*: -ebis *i Cat.*
[2] et *Cat.*[2]: *del. Keil*: quam *Aa.*

---

[1] The son of a successful leading centurion would start his career with an equestrian military appointment at the age of about 30.

commander of a cohort,[1] for which he has won the highest praise from the distinguished senators, Julius Ferox and Fuscus Salinator. Any promotion which you confer on my friend's son, Sir, will give me also an occasion for personal rejoicing.

LXXXVIII

PLINY TO THE EMPEROR TRAJAN

It is my prayer, Sir, that this birthday[2] and many others to come will bring you the greatest happiness, and that in health and strength you may add to the immortal fame and glory of your reputation by ever new achievements.

LXXXIX

TRAJAN TO PLINY

I write in acknowledgement of your prayers, my dear Pliny, that I may spend many birthdays made happy by the continued prosperity of our country.

XC

PLINY TO THE EMPEROR TRAJAN

The town of Sinope,[3] Sir, is in need of a water supply. I think there is plenty of good water which

[2] 18 September.
[3] The former capital of Mithridates Eupator, King of Pontus, now a *civitas libera* with a Roman colony alongside; cf. Apamea in *Ep.* 47.

279

posse perduci. Est tamen statim ab capite paulo
amplius passus mille locus suspectus et mollis, quem
ego interim explorari[1] modico impendio iussi, an
2 recipere et sustinere opus possit. Pecunia curantibus
nobis contracta non deerit, si tu, domine, hoc genus
operis et salubritati et amoenitati valde sitientis coloniae indulseris.

XCI

TRAIANUS PLINIO

UT coepisti, Secunde carissime, explora diligenter,
an locus ille quem suspectum habes sustinere opus
aquae ductus possit. Neque dubitandum puto, quin
aqua perducenda sit in coloniam Sinopensem, si modo
et viribus suis adsequi potest, cum plurimum ea res et
salubritati et voluptati eius collatura sit.

XCII

C. PLINIUS TRAIANO IMPERATORI

AMISENORUM civitas libera et foederata beneficio
indulgentiae tuae legibus suis utitur. In hac
datum mihi libellum ad ἐράνους pertinentem his
litteris subieci, ut tu, domine, dispiceres quid et

---

[1] explorari *Gesner*: -are *Aa*.

---

[1] Amisus was made *libera* by Caesar, and a *foedus* would
normally date back to an early stage of Roman expansion.

could be brought from a source sixteen miles away,
though there is a doubtful area of marshy ground
stretching for more than a mile from the spring.
For the moment I have only given orders for a survey
to be made, to find out whether the ground can support the weight of an aqueduct. This will not cost
much, and I will guarantee that there will be no lack
of funds so long as you, Sir, will approve a scheme so
conducive to the health and amenities of this very
thirsty city.

XCI

TRAJAN TO PLINY

SEE that the survey you have begun is thoroughly
carried out, my dear Pliny, and find out whether the
ground you suspect can support the weight of an
aqueduct. There can be no doubt, I think, that
Sinope must be provided with a water supply, so long
as the town can meet the expense out of its own
resources. It will contribute a great deal to the
health and happiness of the people.

XCII

PLINY TO THE EMPEROR TRAJAN

THE free and confederate city of Amisus enjoys,
with your permission,[1] the privilege of administering
its own laws. I am sending with this letter a petition
handed to me there which deals with the subject of

Perhaps Trajan confirmed in some way the city's privileges
ensured by this formal treaty of alliance.

quatenus aut permittendum aut prohibendum
putares.

XCIII

Traianus Plinio

Amisenos, quorum libellum epistulae tuae iunxeras,
si legibus istorum, quibus beneficio[1] foederis utuntur,
concessum est eranum habere, possumus quo minus
habeant non impedire, eo facilius si tali collatione non
ad turbas et ad inlicitos coetus, sed ad sustinendam
tenuiorum inopiam utuntur. In ceteris civitatibus,
quae nostro iure obstrictae sunt, res huius modi
prohibenda est.

XCIV

C. Plinius Traiano Imperatori

1 Suetonium Tranquillum, probissimum honestissimum eruditissimum virum, et mores eius secutus et
studia iam pridem, domine, in contubernium ad-
sumpsi, tantoque magis diligere coepi quanto nunc[2]
2 propius inspexi. Huic ius trium liberorum necessarium faciunt duae causae; nam et iudicia amicorum
promeretur et parum felix matrimonium expertus est,
impetrandumque a bonitate tua per nos habet quod

---

[1] beneficio *Kukula*: de officio *Aa*.
[2] nunc *von Winterfeld*: hunc *Aa*: del. *Keil*.

---

[1] The reading *nunc* suggests that he is with P. in Bithynia,
perhaps as a member of his staff.

benefit societies, so that you, Sir, may decide whether and to what extent these clubs are to be permitted or forbidden.

XCIII

TRAJAN TO PLINY

IF the citizens of Amisus, whose petition you send with your letter, are allowed by their own laws, granted them by formal treaty, to form a benefit society, there is no reason why we should interfere: especially if the contributions are not used for riotous and unlawful assemblies, but to relieve cases of hardship among the poor. In all other cities which are subject to our own law these institutions must be forbidden.

XCIV

PLINY TO THE EMPEROR TRAJAN

SUETONIUS TRANQUILLUS, Sir, is not only a very fine scholar but also a man of the highest integrity and distinction. I have long admired his character and literary abilities, and since he became my close friend, and I now have an opportunity to know him intimately,[1] I have learned to value him the more.

There are two reasons why he needs the privileges granted to parents of three children: his friends could then effectively express their recognition of his merits, and, as his marriage has not been blessed with children, he can only look to your generosity, at my suggestion, for the benefits which the cruelty of

3 illi fortunae malignitas denegavit. Scio, domine,
quantum beneficium petam, sed peto a te cuius in
omnibus desideriis meis indulgentiam experior.
Potes enim colligere quanto opere cupiam, quod non
rogarem absens si mediocriter cuperem.

XCV

Traianus Plinio

Quam parce haec beneficia tribuam, utique, mi
Secunde carissime, haeret tibi, cum etiam in senatu
adfirmare soleam non excessisse me numerum, quem
apud amplissimum ordinem suffecturum mihi professus sum. Tuo tamen desiderio subscripsi et
dedisse me ius trium liberorum Suetonio Tranquillo ea
condicione, qua adsuevi, referri in commentarios meos
iussi.

XCVI

C. Plinivs Traiano Imperatori

1 Sollemne est mihi, domine, omnia de quibus
dubito ad te referre. Quis enim potest melius vel
cunctationem meam regere vel ignorantiam in-
struere? Cognitionibus de Christianis interfui num-

---

[1] What exactly these were is not known. Perhaps the
grant was revocable on re-marriage (S-W, p. 691).

[2] For this celebrated exchange of letters, see Tertullian,
Apology II. 6–10, and Eusebius, *Hist. Eccl.* III. 33; for trials
of Christians, see Eusebius, IV. 15, V. 1, etc. Note that P.

fortune has denied him. I know, Sir, what a great
favour I am asking, but remember from experience
your kindness hitherto in granting my wishes; and
you may judge how much this means to me by the
fact that I should not make such a request during my
absence abroad did I not have it much at heart.

XCV

TRAJAN TO PLINY

You are certainly well aware, my dear Pliny, that I
grant these favours sparingly, seeing that I have
often stated in the Senate that I have not exceeded
the number which I said would meet my wishes when
I first addressed its distinguished members. I have,
however, granted your request and issued instructions that it is to be officially recorded that I have
conferred on Suetonius Tranquillus the privileges
granted to parents of three children, on my usual
terms.[1]

XCVI

PLINY TO THE EMPEROR TRAJAN[2]

It is my custom to refer all my difficulties to you,
Sir, for no one is better able to resolve my doubts and
to inform my ignorance.

I have never been present at an examination[3] of

first executes Christians for their *contumacia*, then has doubts
and seeks advice; but the charge is never that of *maiestas*.

[3] The term *cognitio* indicates that this was a formal trial
presided over by the holder of *imperium*, assisted by a *consilium*; cf. the court at Centum Cellae, VI. 31.

quam: ideo nescio quid et quatenus aut puniri soleat
2 aut quaeri. Nec mediocriter haesitavi, sitne aliquod
discrimen aetatum, an quamlibet teneri nihil a robu-
stioribus differant; detur paenitentiae venia, an ei,
qui omnino Christianus fuit, desisse non prosit;
nomen ipsum, si flagitiis careat, an flagitia cohaerentia
nomini puniantur. Interim, ⟨in⟩[1] iis qui ad me
tamquam Christiani deferebantur, hunc sum secutus
3 modum. Interrogavi ipsos an essent Christiani.
Confitentes iterum ac tertio interrogavi supplicium
minatus: perseverantes duci iussi. Neque enim
dubitabam, qualecumque esset quod faterentur,
pertinaciam certe et inflexibilem obstinationem
4 debere puniri. Fuerunt alii similis amentiae, quos,
quia cives Romani erant, adnotavi in urbem remit-
tendos.

Mox ipso tractatu, ut fieri solet, diffundente se
5 crimine plures species inciderunt. Propositus est
libellus sine auctore multorum nomina continens.
Qui negabant[2] esse se Christianos aut fuisse, cum

---

[1] in *add. Cat.*[2]: *om. Aa.*
[2] negabant *Keil*: negant *Aa*: negarent *Casaubon.*

---

[1] Action taken by the Romans against foreign cults was
usually directed against their associated *flagitia*; Pliny's
concern is with what the Christian apologists called *accusatio
nominis*, *i.e.* membership of the cult, approved by Trajan in
his reply. See S-W, Appendix V, pp. 772 ff.
[2] It is not clear whether P. was obliged to do this, whether
or no those charged had (like St. Paul) exercised their right to
appeal (*provocatio*), but it was probably the custom to do so.

Christians. Consequently, I do not know the nature or the extent of the punishments usually meted out to them, nor the grounds for starting an investigation and how far it should be pressed. Nor am I at all sure whether any distinction should be made between them on the grounds of age, or if young people and adults should be treated alike; whether a pardon ought to be granted to anyone retracting his beliefs, or if he has once professed Christianity, he shall gain nothing by renouncing it; and whether it is the mere name of Christian which is punishable, even if innocent of crime, or rather the crimes associated with the name.[1]

For the moment this is the line I have taken with all persons brought before me on the charge of being Christians. I have asked them in person if they are Christians, and if they admit it, I repeat the question a second and third time, with a warning of the punishment awaiting them. If they persist, I order them to be led away for execution; for, whatever the nature of their admission, I am convinced that their stubbornness and unshakeable obstinacy ought not to go unpunished. There have been others similarly fanatical who are Roman citizens. I have entered them on the list of persons to be sent to Rome for trial.[2]

Now that I have begun to deal with this problem, as so often happens, the charges are becoming more widespread and increasing in variety. An anonymous pamphlet has been circulated which contains the names of a number of accused persons. Among these I considered that I should dismiss any who denied that they were or ever had been Christians

praeeunte me deos adpellarent et imagini tuae,
quam propter hoc iusseram cum simulacris numinum
adferri, ture ac vino supplicarent, praeterea male
dicerent Christo, quorum nihil cogi posse dicuntur
6 qui sunt re vera Christiani, dimittendos putavi. Alii
ab indice nominati esse se Christianos dixerunt et
mox negaverunt; fuisse quidem sed desisse, quidam
ante triennium, quidam ante plures annos, non nemo
etiam ante viginti. ⟨Hi⟩ quoque[1] omnes et imaginem tuam deorumque simulacra venerati sunt et
7 Christo male dixerunt. Adfirmabant autem hanc
fuisse summam vel culpae suae vel erroris, quod essent
soliti stato die ante lucem convenire, carmenque
Christo quasi deo dicere secum invicem seque
sacramento non in scelus aliquod obstringere, sed ne
furta ne latrocinia ne adulteria committerent, ne
fidem fallerent, ne depositum adpellati abnegarent.
Quibus peractis morem sibi discedendi fuisse rursusque coeundi ad capiendum cibum, promiscuum
tamen et innoxium; quod ipsum facere desisse post
edictum meum, quo secundum mandata tua hetaerias
8 esse vetueram. Quo magis necessarium credidi ex
duabus ancillis, quae ministrae dicebantur, quid esset
veri, et per tormenta quaerere. Nihil aliud inveni
quam superstitionem pravam et[2] immodicam.

---

[1] viginti. Hi quoque *Keil*: viginti quoque *Aa*.
[2] et *a*: *om. A.*

---

[1] For a full discussion on this evidence for the services of the
early Church, see S-W, pp. 702 ff. The morning service
seems to be one of prayer and reading, the evening one the

when they had repeated after me a formula of invocation to the gods and had made offerings of wine and incense to your statue (which I had ordered to be brought into court for this purpose along with the images of the gods), and furthermore had reviled the name of Christ: none of which things, I understand, any genuine Christian can be induced to do.

Others, whose names were given to me by an informer, first admitted the charge and then denied it; they said that they had ceased to be Christians two or more years previously, and some of them even twenty years ago. They all did reverence to your statue and the images of the gods in the same way as the others, and reviled the name of Christ. They also declared that the sum total of their guilt or error amounted to no more than this:[1] they had met regularly before dawn on a fixed day to chant verses alternately among themselves in honour of Christ as if to a god, and also to bind themselves by oath, not for any criminal purpose, but to abstain from theft, robbery and adultery, to commit no breach of trust and not to deny a deposit when called upon to restore it. After this ceremony it had been their custom to disperse and reassemble later to take food of an ordinary, harmless kind; but they had in fact given up this practice since my edict, issued on your instructions, which banned all political societies. This made me decide it was all the more necessary to extract the truth by torture from two slave-women, whom they call deaconesses. I found nothing but a degenerate sort of cult carried to extravagant lengths.

combined Eucharist and *Agape*. It is the latter which comes under the ban on *collegia* (cf. X. 34).

Ideo dilata cognitione ad consulendum te decucurri.
9 Visa est enim mihi res digna consultatione, maxime
propter periclitantium numerum. Multi enim omnis
aetatis, omnis ordinis, utriusque sexus etiam vocantur
in periculum et vocabuntur. Neque civitates tantum, sed vicos etiam atque agros superstitionis
istius contagio pervagata est; quae videtur sisti et
10 corrigi posse. Certe satis constat prope iam desolata
templa coepisse celebrari, et sacra sollemnia diu
intermissa repeti passimque[1] venire ⟨carnem⟩[2]
victimarum,[3] cuius adhuc rarissimus emptor invenie-
batur. Ex quo facile est opinari, quae turba hominum emendari possit, si sit paenitentiae locus.

XCVII

TRAIANUS PLINIO

1 ACTUM quem debuisti, mi Secunde, in excutiendis
causis eorum, qui Christiani ad te delati fuerant,
secutus es. Neque enim in universum aliquid, quod
quasi certam formam habeat, constitui potest.
2 Conquirendi non sunt; si deferantur et arguantur,
puniendi sunt, ita tamen ut, qui negaverit se Chris-

---

[1] passimque *ai*: passumque *A*: pastumque *Beroaldus*.
[2] carnem *add. Körte post* victimarum: *ita Sherwin-White*.
[3] victimarum cuius *A*: victimas quarum *a*.

---

[1] *i.e.* the charges must be properly made against individuals
by *delatio* and a trial held before the governor. There are to
be no mass prosecutions. Note that Trajan never answers
Pliny's original question on the extent of punishments.

I have therefore postponed any further examination and hastened to consult you. The question seems to me to be worthy of your consideration, especially in view of the number of persons endangered; for a great many individuals of every age and class, both men and women, are being brought to trial, and this is likely to continue. It is not only the towns, but villages and rural districts too which are infected through contact with this wretched cult. I think though that it is still possible for it to be checked and directed to better ends, for there is no doubt that people have begun to throng the temples which had been almost entirely deserted for a long time; the sacred rites which had been allowed to lapse are being performed again, and flesh of sacrificial victims is on sale everywhere, though up till recently scarcely anyone could be found to buy it. It is easy to infer from this that a great many people could be reformed if they were given an opportunity to repent.

XCVII

Trajan to Pliny

You have followed the right course of procedure, my dear Pliny, in your examination of the cases of persons charged with being Christians, for it is impossible to lay down a general rule to a fixed formula. These people must not be hunted out; if they are brought before you and the charge against them is proved, they must be punished,[1] but in the case of anyone who denies that he is a Christian, and makes

tianum esse idque re ipsa manifestum fecerit, id est
supplicando dis nostris, quamvis suspectus in praeteritum, veniam ex paenitentia impetret.   Sine auctore
vero propositi libelli ⟨in⟩ [1] nullo crimine locum habere
debent.   Nam et pessimi exempli nec nostri saeculi
est.

XCVIII

C. Plinius Traiano Imperatori

1 Amastrianorum civitas, domine, et elegans et
ornata habet inter praecipua opera pulcherrimam
eandemque longissimam plateam; cuius a latere per
spatium omne porrigitur nomine quidem flumen, re
vera cloaca foedissima, ac sicut turpis immundissimo
2 adspectu, ita pestilens odore taeterrimo.   Quibus ex
causis non minus salubritatis quam decoris interest
eam contegi; quod fiet si permiseris curantibus nobis,
ne desit quoque pecunia operi tam magno quam
necessario.

XCIX

Traianus Plinio

Rationis est, mi Secunde carissime, contegi aquam
istam, quae per civitatem Amastrianorum fluit, si
intecta salubritati obest.   Pecunia ne huic operi desit,
curaturum te secundum diligentiam tuam certum
habeo.

[1] in add. Gierig: om. Aa.

it clear that he is not by offering prayers to our gods, he is to be pardoned as a result of his repentance however suspect his past conduct may be. But pamphlets circulated anonymously must play no part in any accusation. They create the worst sort of precedent and are quite out of keeping with the spirit of our age.

XCVIII

PLINY TO THE EMPEROR TRAJAN

AMONG the chief features of Amastris, Sir, (a city which is well built and laid out) is a long street of great beauty. Throughout the length of this, however, there runs what is called a stream, but is in fact a filthy sewer, a disgusting eyesore which gives off a noxious stench. The health and appearance alike of the city will benefit if it is covered in, and with your permission this shall be done. I will see that money is not lacking for a large-scale work of such importance.

XCIX

TRAJAN TO PLINY

THERE is every reason, my dear Pliny, to cover the water which you say flows through the city of Amastris, if it is a danger to health while it remains uncovered. I am sure you will be active as always to ensure that there is no lack of money for this work.

293

C

C. Plinius Traiano Imperatori

Vota, domine, priore anno[1] nuncupata alacres laetique persolvimus novaque rursus certante commilitonum et provincialium pietate suscepimus, precati deos ut te remque publicam florentem et incolumem ea benignitate servarent, quam super magnas plurimasque virtutes praecipua sanctitate obsequio deorum honore meruisti.

CI

Traianus Plinio

Solvisse vota dis immortalibus te praeeunte pro mea incolumitate commilitones cum provincialibus laetissimo consensu et in futurum nuncupasse libenter, mi Secunde carissime, cognovi litteris tuis.

CII

C. Plinius Traiano Imperatori

Diem, quo in te tutela generis humani felicissima successione translata est, debita religione celebravimus, commendantes dis imperii tui auctoribus et vota publica et gaudia.

---

[1] priore anno *Mommsen*: priorum annorum *Aa*.

---

[1] 3 January; cf. *Ep.* 55.
[2] 28 January; cf. *Ep.* 52.

C

PLINY TO THE EMPEROR TRAJAN

WE have discharged the vows,[1] Sir, renewed last year, amidst general enthusiasm and rejoicing; and have made those for the coming year, your fellow-soldiers and the provincials vying with one another in loyal demonstrations. We have prayed the gods to preserve you and the State in prosperity and safety, and to show you the favour you deserve for your many great virtues, and above all for your sanctity, reverence, and piety.

CI

TRAJAN TO PLINY

I WAS glad to hear from your letter, my dear Pliny, that the soldiers and provincials, amidst general rejoicing, have discharged under your direction their vows to the immortal gods for my safety, and have renewed them for the coming year.

CII

PLINY TO THE EMPEROR TRAJAN

WE have celebrated with due solemnity the day [2] on which the security of the human race was happily transferred to your care, commending our public vows and thanksgiving to the gods to whom we owe your authority.

CIII

Traianus Plinio

Diem imperii mei debita laetitia et religione commilitonibus et provincialibus praeeunte te celebratum libenter cognovi litteris tuis.

CIV

C. Plinius Traiano Imperatori

Valerius, domine, Paulinus excepto Paulino [1] ius Latinorum suorum mihi reliquit; ex quibus rogo tribus interim ius Quiritium des.   Vereor enim, ne sit immodicum pro omnibus pariter invocare indulgentiam tuam, qua debeo tanto modestius uti, quanto pleniorem experior.   Sunt autem pro quibus peto: C. Valerius Astraeus, C. Valerius Dionysius, C. Valerius Aper.

CV

Traianus Plinio

Cum honestissime iis, qui apud fidem tuam a Valerio Paulino depositi sunt, consultum velis mature per me, iis interim, quibus nunc petisti, dedisse me ius Quiritium referri in commentarios meos iussi idem facturus in ceteris, pro quibus petieris.

---

[1] Paulino *A*: uno *a*.

---

[1] *Latini Iuniani*; cf. VII. 16. 4.   They enjoyed most of the privileges in civil law of full freedmen for their lifetime, but had no power to transmit property, which reverted to their *patronus*.   [2] *Ius Quiritium*; cf. *Ep.* 5, and note.

CIII

Trajan to Pliny

I was glad to hear from your letter that the day of my accession was celebrated under your direction by my fellow-soldiers and the provincials, with due rejoicing and solemnity.

CIV

Pliny to the Emperor Trajan

Valerius Paulinus, Sir, has left a will which passes over his son Paulinus and names me as patron of his Latin freedmen.[1] On this occasion I pray you to grant full Roman citizenship[2] to three of them only; it would be unreasonable, I fear, to petition you to favour all alike, and I must be all the more careful not to abuse your generosity when I have enjoyed it on so many previous occasions. The names of the three are Gaius Valerius Astraeus, Gaius Valerius Dionysius, and Gaius Valerius Aper.

CV

Trajan to Pliny

Your desire to further the interests of the freedmen entrusted to you by Valerius Paulinus does you very great credit. To speed your purpose I have issued instructions that it is to be officially recorded that I have granted full Roman citizenship to the persons mentioned in your letter, and I am prepared to do the same for any others for whom you may ask it.

CVI

C. PLINIUS TRAIANO IMPERATORI

ROGATUS, domine, a P. Accio Aquila, centurione cohortis sextae equestris, ut mitterem tibi libellum per quem indulgentiam pro statu filiae suae implorat, durum putavi negare, cum scirem quantam soleres militum precibus patientiam humanitatemque praestare.

CVII

TRAIANUS PLINIO

LIBELLUM P. Accii Aquilae, centurionis sextae equestris, quem mihi misisti, legi; cuius precibus motus dedi filiae eius civitatem Romanam. Libellum rescriptum,[1] quem illi redderes, misi tibi.

CVIII

C. PLINIUS TRAIANO IMPERATORI

1   QUID habere iuris velis et Bithynas et Ponticas civitates in exigendis pecuniis, quae illis vel ex locationibus vel ex venditionibus aliisve causis debeantur, rogo, domine, rescribas. Ego inveni a plerisque proconsulibus concessam iis protopraxian

---

¹ rescriptum *Vidman*: rescripti *Aa*.

---

¹ Perhaps an illegitimate daughter, or one by a *peregrina*; if the man was a citizen his legitimate children were also citizens.

² Normally the fiscus would have a prior claim on a provincial debtor's assets. As usual, P. wants something more definite than proconsular precedent.

CVI

PLINY TO THE EMPEROR TRAJAN

PUBLIUS ACCIUS AQUILA, Sir, a centurion in the sixth cohort in the auxiliary cavalry, has asked me to send you a petition begging your interest in his daughter's citizen status.[1] It was difficult to refuse, especially as I know how readily you give a sympathetic hearing to your soldiers' requests.

CVII

TRAJAN TO PLINY

I HAVE read the petition which you forwarded on behalf of Publius Accius Aquila, centurion of the sixth cohort of cavalry, and have granted his request. I have accordingly given his daughter Roman citizenship and am sending you a copy of the order to hand to him.

CVIII

PLINY TO THE EMPEROR TRAJAN

I PRAY you, Sir, to tell me what legal rights you wish the cities of Bithynia and Pontus to have in regard to the recovery of money owed to them from contracts for hire or sale, or for any other reason. I find that several of the senatorial governors allowed priority to civic claims, and that this privilege has come to acquire the force of law.[2]

I think, however, that it would be sound policy for

2 eamque pro lege valuisse. Existimo tamen tua
providentia constituendum aliquid et sanciendum per
quod utilitatibus eorum in perpetuum consulatur.
Nam quae sunt ab illis instituta, sint licet sapienter
indulta, brevia tamen et infirma sunt, nisi illis tua
contingit auctoritas.

CIX

TRAIANUS PLINIO

Quo iure uti debeant Bithynae vel Ponticae civitates in iis pecuniis, quae ex quaque causa rei publicae
debebuntur, ex lege cuiusque animadvertendum est.
Nam, sive habent privilegium, quo ceteris creditori-
bus anteponantur, custodiendum est, sive non habent,
in iniuriam privatorum id dari a me non oportebit.

CX

C. PLINIUS TRAIANO IMPERATORI

1 ECDICUS,[1] domine, Amisenorum civitatis petebat
apud me a Iulio Pisone denariorum circiter quadraginta milia donata ei publice ante viginti annos bule
et ecclesia consentiente, utebaturque mandatis tuis,
2 quibus eius modi donationes vetantur. Piso contra
plurima se in rem publicam contulisse ac prope totas
facultates erogasse dicebat. Addebat etiam temporis spatium postulabatque, ne id, quod pro multis et

---

[1] ecdicus *Cat.*[2]: medicus *Aa.*

you to make some permanent regulation to secure their interests for all time; for any previous concession, however wisely granted, remains only a temporary expedient unless confirmed by your authority.

CIX

Trajan to Pliny

The legal rights of the cities of Bithynia and Pontus to recover money owed to them for any reason, can only be determined by reference to their individual laws. For if they already possess the privilege of priority over other creditors, it must be maintained; if not, I have no right to grant them it against the interests of private creditors.[1]

CX

Pliny to the Emperor Trajan

The public prosecutor of Amisus, Sir, has brought a claim before me against Julius Piso, for the sum of about 40,000 denarii granted to the defendant twenty years previously by joint vote of the local senate and assembly. He based his claim on your instructions which forbid donations of this kind. Piso, on the other hand, declared that he had spent large sums of money on his city and had almost exhausted his means. He also pleaded the lapse of time since the grant, and argued that he should not be compelled

---

[1] Trajan, as often, prefers local custom to a general ruling; cf. *Epp.* 66, 69, 113.

olim accepisset, cum eversione reliquae dignitatis reddere cogeretur. Quibus ex causis integram cognitionem differendam existimavi, ut te, domine, consulerem, quid sequendum putares.

CXI

TRAIANUS PLINIO

SICUT largitiones ex publico fieri mandata prohibent, ita, ne multorum securitas subruatur, factas ante aliquantum temporis retractari atque in inritum vindicari non oportet. Quidquid ergo ex hac causa actum ante viginti annos erit, omittamus. Non minus enim hominibus cuiusque loci quam pecuniae publicae consultum volo.

CXII

C. PLINIUS TRAIANO IMPERATORI

1 LEX Pompeia, domine, qua Bithyni et Pontici utuntur, eos, qui in bulen a censoribus leguntur, dare pecuniam non iubet; sed ii, quos indulgentia tua quibusdam civitatibus super legitimum numerum adicere permisit, et singula milia denariorum et bina 2 intulerunt. Anicius deinde Maximus proconsul eos etiam, qui a censoribus legerentur, dumtaxat in paucissimis civitatibus aliud aliis iussit inferre.

---

[1] The *honorarium decurionatus*; cf. the following letter and *Ep.* 39. 5 (Claudiopolis), where Pliny regards it as obligatory.

to refund what had been given him so long ago for his many public services, since it would mean the ruin of his remaining fortunes. I therefore thought that I ought to adjourn the whole case until I could ask you, Sir, for directions on what line to take.

CXI

TRAJAN TO PLINY

It is true that I have issued instructions forbidding public grants of money, but grants made a long time previously ought not to be revoked nor rendered invalid, lest we undermine the position of a great many people. Let us then leave out of consideration any features of this case which date back twenty years, for in every city the interests of individuals are as much my concern as the state of public funds.

CXII

PLINY TO THE EMPEROR TRAJAN

BITHYNIA and Pontus, Sir, are subject to the code of law drawn up by Pompey, which makes no provision for payment of entrance fees by those elected to the local senate by the censors; but in certain cities, where persons in excess of the legal number have been nominated by your special permission, they have been paying fees of one or two thousand denarii.[1] Subsequently the governor Anicius Maximus, made it a rule (though only in a very few places) that persons elected by the censors should also pay an entrance fee, which varied from city to city.

3 Superest ergo, ut ipse dispicias, an in omnibus
civitatibus certum aliquid omnes, qui deinde buleutae
legentur, debeant pro introitu dare. Nam, quod in
perpetuum mansurum est, a te constitui decet, cuius
factis dictisque debetur aeternitas.

CXIII

Traianus Plinio

Honorarium decurionatus omnes, qui in quaque
civitate Bithyniae decuriones fiunt, inferre debeant
necne, in universum a me non potest statui. Id ergo,
quod semper tutissimum est, sequendam cuiusque
civitatis legem puto, sed [1] verius [2] eos, qui invitati [3]
fiunt decuriones, id existimo acturos, ut praestatione [4]
ceteris praeferantur. [5]

CXIV

C. Plinius Traiano Imperatori

1 Lege, domine, Pompeia permissum Bithynicis
civitatibus adscribere sibi quos vellent cives, dum ne
quem earum civitatium, quae sunt in Bithynia.

---

[1] sed *i*: scilicet *Aa*.
[2] verius *Sherwin-White*: adversus *Aa*.
[3] invitati *Sherwin-White*: inviti *Aa*.
[4] praestatione *Hardy*: praefatio *A*: erogatio *Cat. a*.
[5] praeferantur *i*: -atur *Aa*: praefati ceteris praeferantur
Stout.

---

[1] The emendation removes the question of whether this is
an early instance of reluctance to accept municipal office
(*inviti*). Nerva and Trajan increased the size of the municipal
councils of Prusa and Claudiopolis and would hardly have done

It remains then for you to consider whether from now on all persons elected senators should pay a fixed sum as entrance fee; for it is only fitting that a ruling which is to be permanent should come from you, whose deeds and words should live for ever.

CXIII

Trajan to Pliny

It is impossible for me to lay down a general rule whether everyone who is elected to his local senate in every town of Bithynia should pay a fee on entrance or not. I think then that the safest course, as always, is to keep to the law of each city, though as regards fees from senators appointed by invitation,[1] I imagine they will see that they are not left behind the rest in payment.

CXIV

Pliny to the Emperor Trajan

The code of Pompey, Sir, permits the cities of Bithynia to confer their citizenship on anyone they choose, provided that it is not someone who is already a citizen of another Bithynian city.[2] The same law

so if there were a shortage of willing candidates (*Ep.* 112, Dio *Or.* 45. 7–9). But see G. W. Bowersock quoted in *Phoenix*, XVIII, p. 327 in favour of retaining *inviti*.

[2] It was Hellenistic practice to confer citizenship on citizens of other towns; Dio of Prusa was also a citizen of Apamea and Nicomedia (*Or.* 38. 1, 41. 2). The *lex Pompeia* overruled this.

Eadem lege sancitur, quibus de causis e senatu a
2 censoribus eiciantur. Inde me quidam ex censoribus
consulendum putaverunt, an eicere deberent eum
3 qui esset alterius civitatis. Ego quia lex sicut
adscribi civem alienum vetabat, ita eici e senatu ob
hanc causam non iubebat, praeterea, quod adfirma-
batur mihi in omni civitate plurimos esse buleutas ex
aliis civitatibus, futurumque ut multi homines
multaeque civitates concuterentur ea parte legis,[1]
quae iam pridem consensu quodam exolevisset,
necessarium existimavi consulere te, quid servandum
putares. Capita legis his litteris subieci.

CXV

TRAIANUS PLINIO

MERITO haesisti, Secunde carissime, quid a te
rescribi oporteret censoribus consulentibus, an
⟨manere deberent⟩ in senatu[2] aliarum civitatium,
eiusdem tamen provinciae cives. Nam et legis auctoritas et longa consuetudo usurpata contra legem in
diversum movere te potuit. Mihi hoc temperamentum eius placuit, ut ex praeterito nihil novaremus,
sed manerent quamvis contra legem adsciti quarum-
cumque civitatium cives, in futurum autem lex
Pompeia observaretur; cuius vim si retro quoque
velimus custodire, multa necesse est perturbari.

---

[1] ea parte legis *a*: ea pars legis *A*: ea parte legis ⟨reducta⟩
Sherwin-White.
[2] manere deberent in senatu *Hardy*: in sen. manere possent
Cat.: an in senatum *A*: an legerent in senatum *ai.*

---

[1] Cf. 32 and 119 for Trajan's dislike of retrospective rulings.

sets out the reasons for which the censors may remove senators from office. Certain censors have therefore asked my opinion whether or not it is their duty to expel a senator who is a citizen of another city.

But although the law states that such people may not be elected senators, it says nothing about removing them from the senate for this reason. I therefore felt that I must ask you for your view on what ruling I should follow, especially as I am informed that every city has several senators who hold citizenship elsewhere, and many individuals and cities will be seriously affected by the enforcement of a section of the law which by general consent has long since fallen into disuse. I am sending the relevant sections of the law with this letter.

CXV

TRAJAN TO PLINY

You had good reason, my dear Pliny, to be uncertain what answer to give to the censors' question whether senators who are citizens of other cities in the same province should retain their seats in the senate. The authority of the law on the one hand, and the long-established practice against it on the other, would influence you in opposite directions. My own view is that we should compromise; we should make no change in the situation resulting from past practice, so that citizens of any city may remain senators even if their election was not strictly legal; but in future the law of Pompey must be observed. If we tried to enforce it in retrospect it would inevitably lead to great confusion.[1]

CXVI

C. Plinius Traiano Imperatori

1 Qui virilem togam sumunt vel nuptias faciunt vel
ineunt magistratum vel opus publicum dedicant,
solent totam bulen atque etiam e plebe non exiguum
numerum vocare binosque denarios vel singulos dare.
Quod an celebrandum et quatenus putes, rogo scribas.
2 Ipse enim, sicut arbitror, praesertim ex sollemnibus
causis, concedendum ius istud invitationis,[1] ita
vereor ne ii qui mille homines, interdum etiam plures
vocant, modum excedere et in speciem διανομῆς
incidere videantur.

CXVII

Traianus Plinio

Merito vereris, ne in speciem διανομῆς incidat
invitatio, quae et in numero modum excedit et quasi
per corpora, non viritim singulos ex notitia ad sol-
lemnes sportulas contrahit. Sed ego ideo prudentiam tuam elegi, ut formandis istius provinciae
moribus ipse moderareris et ea constitueres, quae ad
perpetuam eius provinciae quietem essent profutura.

---

[1] ius (istud *add. Postgate*) invitationis *Scheffer*: iussi invita-
tiones *Ber. ai*: iussi immutationes *A*.

CXVI

PLINY TO THE EMPEROR TRAJAN

IT is a general practice for people at their coming-of-age or marriage, and on entering upon office or dedicating a public building, to issue invitations to all the local senators and even to quite a number of the common people in order to distribute presents of one or two denarii. I pray you to let me know how far you think this should be allowed, if at all. My own feeling is that invitations of this kind may sometimes be permissible, especially on ceremonial occasions, but the practice of issuing a thousand or even more seems to go beyond all reasonable limits, and could be regarded as a form of corrupt practice.[1]

CXVII

TRAJAN TO PLINY

You have every reason to fear that the issuing of invitations might lead to corrupt practices, if the numbers are excessive and people are invited in groups to a sort of official present-giving rather than individually as personal friends. But I made you my choice so that you could use your good judgement in exercising a moderating influence on the behaviour of the people in your province, and could make your own decisions about what is necessary for their peace and security.

[1] Pliny may be thinking either of political bribery or of riotous assemblies (as at Amisus in *Ep.* 93). Trajan's reply shows some impatience.

CXVIII

C. Plinius Traiano Imperatori

1 ATHLETAE, domine, ea quae pro iselasticis certaminibus constituisti, deberi sibi putant statim ex eo die, quo sunt coronati; nihil enim referre, quando sint patriam invecti, sed quando certamine vicerint, ex quo invehi possint. Ego contra praescribo " iselastici nomen ": [1] itaque †eorum[2] vehementer addubitem an sit potius id tempus, quo εἰσήλασαν, intuendum.
2 Iidem obsonia petunt pro eo agone, qui a te iselasticus factus est, quamvis vicerint ante quam fieret. Aiunt enim congruens esse, sicut non detur sibi pro iis certaminibus, quae esse iselastica postquam vicerunt
3 desierunt, ita pro iis dari quae esse coeperunt. Hic quoque non mediocriter haereo, ne cuiusquam retro habeatur ratio dandumque, quod tunc cum vincerent non debebatur. Rogo ergo, ut dubitationem meam regere, id est beneficia tua interpretari ipse digneris.

CXIX

Traianus Plinio

ISELASTICUM tunc primum mihi videtur incipere deberi, cum quis in civitatem suam ipse εἰσήλασεν.

---

[1] scribo iselastici (-corum *Cat.*) nomine *Aa*: praescribo isel. nomen *Sherwin-White*:

[2] itaque eorum *Aa*: ita ut *Ber.*: ita tamen ut *Cat.*

---

[1] Εἰσελαστικοὶ ἀγῶνες, games in which the winners were privileged to drive in triumph into their native towns, and afterwards received a civic pension.

CXVIII

PLINY TO THE EMPEROR TRAJAN

THE winning athletes in the Triumphal Games,[1] Sir, think that they ought to receive the prizes which you have awarded on the day they are crowned for victory. They argue that the actual date of their triumphal entry into their native towns is irrelevant; the date which matters is that of the victory which entitled them to the triumph. On the other hand, I point out that the name refers to "triumphal entry" and so I am very much inclined to think that their date of entry is the one we should consider.

They also claim awards for previous victories won in Games to which you have subsequently given triumphal privileges, arguing that if they receive nothing in Games which have lost these privileges after their victories it is only fair that they should have something for Games which afterwards acquire them. Here, too, I very much doubt whether any retrospective claim should be allowed and feel that they should not be given anything to which they were not entitled at the time of victory. I pray you, therefore, to think fit to resolve my difficulties and make it clear how your benefactions are to be bestowed.

CXIX

TRAJAN TO PLINY

IN my opinion, awards in these Games should date from the winner's triumphal entry into his city and not before. Prizes awarded in Games to which I

Obsonia eorum certaminum, quae iselastica esse
placuit mihi, si ante iselastica non fuerunt, retro non
debentur. Nec proficere pro desiderio athletarum
potest, quod eorum, quae postea iselastica non esse[1]
constitui, quam vicerunt,[2] accipere desierunt. Mutata enim condicione certaminum nihilo minus, quae
ante perceperant, non revocantur.

CXX

C. Plinius Traiano Imperatori

1 Usque in hoc tempus, domine, neque cuiquam
diplomata commodavi neque in rem ullam nisi tuam
misi. Quam perpetuam servationem meam quaedam
2 necessitas rupit. Uxori enim meae audita morte avi
volenti ad amitam suam excurrere usum eorum
negare durum putavi, cum talis officii gratia in
celeritate consisteret, sciremque te rationem itineris
probaturum, cuius causa erat pietas. Haec tibi
scripsi, quia mihi parum gratus fore videbar, si dis-
simulassem inter alia beneficia hoc unum quoque me
debere indulgentiae tuae, quod fiducia eius quasi
consulto te non dubitavi facere, quem si consuluissem,
sero fecissem.

[1] esse *A. Schaefer*: lege *Aa*.
[2] vicerunt *Hardy*: qui ierant *Aa*: quierant *i*.

have granted triumphal privileges must not be given restrospectively where no such privileges existed previously. Nor does it assist the athletes' claim if they can gain no more awards in the Games from which I have removed triumphal privileges since their victories, for though the Games are now held under different conditions they are not required to hand back prizes previously won.

CXX

PLINY TO THE EMPEROR TRAJAN

Up to now, Sir, I have made it a fixed rule not to issue anyone a permit to use the Imperial Post unless he is travelling on your service, but I have just been obliged to make an exception. My wife had news of her grandfather's death and was anxious to visit her aunt. I thought it would be unreasonable to deny her a permit when promptitude means much in performing a duty of this kind, and I felt sure that you would approve of a journey made for family reasons.

I am writing thus because I should feel myself lacking in gratitude if, among your many acts of kindness, I did not mention this further instance of your generosity whereby I was given confidence to act without hesitation, as if I had asked your permission; but had I waited to receive it, I should have been too late.

CXXI

Traianus Plinio

Merito habuisti, Secunde carissime, fiduciam animi mei nec dubitandum fuisset,[1] si exspectasses donec me consuleres, an iter uxoris tuae diplomatibus, quae officio tuo dedi, adiuvandum esset, cum apud amitam suam uxor tua deberet etiam celeritate gratiam adventus sui augere.

[1] fuisset *ai*: fuisse *A*: fuit ⟨facere quod sero fecisses⟩ *Hanslik.*

---

[1] P. must have died before September 18 of this year. He was succeeded in his post by Cornutus Tertullus (see Index).

CXXI

Trajan to Pliny

You were quite right, my dear Pliny, to feel confident of my response. You need not have had any doubts, even if you had waited to ask me if you could expedite your wife's journey by making use of the permits which I issued to you for official purposes; it is her duty to make her visit doubly welcome to her aunt by her prompt arrival.[1]

PANEGYRICUS

CONTENTS

319

PANEGYRICUS OF PLINIUS SECUNDUS

CONTENTS

PANEGYRICUS PLINII
SECUNDI DICTUS
TRAIANO IMP.

1   1. Bene ac sapienter, patres conscripti, maiores
instituerunt ut rerum agendarum ita dicendi initium
a precationibus capere, quod nihil rite nihil provi-
denter homines sine deorum immortalium ope consilio
2 honore auspicarentur. Qui mos cui potius quam
consuli aut quando magis usurpandus colendusque
est, quam cum imperio senatus, auctoritate rei
publicae ad agendas optimo principi gratias excita-
3 mur? Quod enim praestabilius est aut pulchrius
munus deorum, quam castus et sanctus et dis similli-
4 mus princeps? Ac si adhuc dubium fuisset, forte
casuque rectores terris an aliquo numine darentur,
principem tamen nostrum liqueret divinitus con-
5 stitutum. Non enim occulta potestate fatorum, sed
ab Iove ipso coram ac palam repertus electus est:
quippe inter aras et altaria, eodemque loci quem deus
ille tam manifestus ac praesens quam caelum ac
6 sidera insedit. Quo magis aptum piumque est te,
Iuppiter optime, antea conditorem, nunc conserva-

THE PANEGYRICUS OF PLINIUS SECUNDUS DELIVERED TO THE EMPEROR TRAJAN

1. OUR ancestors in their wisdom, Conscript Fathers, laid down the excellent rule that a speech no less than a course of action should take its start from prayers: thinking that nothing could be properly and prudently begun by mortal men without the aid and counsel of the immortal gods and the honour due to them. Who should duly observe this custom if not the consul? And what occasion could be more appropriate for doing so than the day when by the Senate's command we are called on to express thanks in the name of our country to the best of emperors? For what gift of the gods could be greater and more glorious than a prince whose purity and virtue make him their own equal? If it were still in doubt whether the rulers of the earth were given us by the hazards of chance or by some heavenly power, it would be evident that our emperor at least was divinely chosen for his task; for it was no blind act of fate but Jupiter himself who chose and revealed him in the sight and hearing of us all, among the many altars of the Capitol, in the very place where the god makes his presence as clearly felt as in the heavens and stars. Wherefore, mighty Jupiter, once the founder and now the

torem imperii nostri precari, ut mihi digna consule
digna senatu digna principe contingat oratio, utque
omnibus quae dicentur a me, libertas fides veritas
constet, tantumque a specie adulationis absit
gratiarum actio mea quantum abest a necessitate.

2. Equidem non consuli modo sed omnibus civibus
enitendum reor, ne quid de principe nostro ita dicant,
ut idem illud de alio dici potuisse videatur. Quare
abeant ac recedant voces illae quas metus exprimebat.
Nihil quale ante dicamus, nihil enim quale antea
patimur; nec eadem de principe palam quae prius
praedicemus, neque enim eadem secreto quae prius
loquimur. Discernatur orationibus nostris diversitas
temporum, et ex ipso genere gratiarum agendarum
intellegatur, cui quando sint actae. Nusquam ut deo,
nusquam ut numini blandiamur: non enim de tyranno
sed de cive, non de domino sed de parente loquimur.
Unum ille se ex nobis—et hoc magis excellit atque
eminet, quod unum ex nobis putat, nec minus
hominem se quam hominibus praeesse meminit. In-
tellegamus ergo bona nostra dignosque nos illis usu
probemus, atque identidem cogitemus, quam sit
indignum,[1] si maius principibus praestemus obsequium, qui servitute civium quam qui libertate

---

[1] quam sit indignum: om. M.

---

[1] Cf. Suetonius, *Dom*. 13. and Martial V. 8. 1, VII. 34. 8, etc.
Domitian was addressed as *dominus et deus noster*. The title

preserver of our realm, it is my right and proper
duty to address my prayers to you: grant, I pray
you, that my speech prove worthy of consul, Senate
and prince, that independence, truth, and sincerity
mark my every word, and my vote of thanks be as
far removed from a semblance of flattery as it is from
constraint.

2. It is my view that not only the consul but
every citizen alike should endeavour to say nothing
about our ruler which could have been said of any
of his predecessors. Away, then, with expressions
formerly prompted by fear: I will have none of
them. The sufferings of the past are over: let us
then have done with the words which belong to
them. An open tribute to our Emperor demands a
new form, now that the wording of our private talk
has changed. Times are different, and our speeches
must show this; from the very nature of our thanks
both the recipient and the occasion must be made
clear to all. Nowhere should we flatter him as a
divinity and a god;[1] we are talking of a fellow-
citizen, not a tyrant, one who is our father not our
over-lord. He is one of us—and his special virtue
lies in his thinking so, as also in his never forgetting
that he is a man himself while a ruler of men. Let
us then appreciate our good fortune and prove our
worth by our use of it, and at the same time remember that there can be no merit if greater deference
is paid to rulers who delight in the servitude of their
subjects than to those who value their liberty. The

dominus was retained by the emperors, but without the suggestion of tyranny: it is always used by Pliny in addressing
Trajan, except in *Epp.* X. 1, 4 and 14.

6 laetantur. Et populus quidem Romanus dilectum
principum servat, quantoque paulo ante concentu
formosum alium, hunc fortissimum personat, quibusque aliquando clamoribus gestum alterius et
vocem, huius pietatem abstinentiam mansuetudinem
7 laudat. Quid nos ipsi? Divinitatem principis nostri,
an humanitatem temperantiam facilitatem, ut amor
et gaudium tulit, celebrare universi solemus? Iam
quid tam civile tam senatorium, quam illud additum
a nobis Optimi cognomen? quod peculiare huius et
8 proprium adrogantia priorum principum fecit. Enimvero quam commune quam ex aequo, quod felices
nos felicem illum praedicamus, alternisque votis
"Haec faciat, haec audiat" quasi non dicturi nisi
fecerit comprecamur! Ad quas ille voces lacrimis
etiam ac multo pudore suffunditur; agnoscit enim
sentitque sibi, non principi dici.

3. Igitur quod temperamentum omnes in illo
subito pietatis calore servamus, hoc singuli quoque
meditatique teneamus, sciamusque nullum esse neque
sincerius neque acceptius genus gratiarum, quam
quod illas acclamationes aemulemur, quae fingendi
2 non habent tempus. Quantum ad me pertinet

---

[1] Domitian: cf. Suetonius, *Dom.* 18. 1.

[2] Nero. Cf. Tac. *Ann.* XIV. 15 and Suet. *Nero* 20.

[3] Cf. 88. 4 and 7: *Ep.* II. 13. 8: III. 13. 1. Evidently
Trajan received this title unofficially before October 98 when
he was also called *pater patriae.* From 103 he was *optimus* on

people must have their own ways of distinguishing between their rulers. They all give the same acclamation now to one for his valour as another had a short time ago for his good looks,[1] and the cries which greeted the voice and attitudes of one of his predecessors[2] now serve to praise their present emperor's devotion to duty, his clemency and restraint. What about us? Is it the divine nature of our prince or his humanity, his moderation and his courtesy which joy and affection prompt us to celebrate in a single voice? Surely nothing could reveal him as citizen and senator more appropriately than the title bestowed on him of *Optimus*,[3] Best, one which by contrast with the insolence of some of his predecessors he can claim as his individual right. One and all and all alike we acclaim his good fortune, and with it our own, and beg him to " continue thus " or again, " to hear our prayers," as if forming our requests in the sure knowledge that he will grant these. For his part, he listens with tears in his eyes, and his blushes show his awareness that he is addressed not as the holder of his title of prince but as himself.

3. This moderation, then, which we have all maintained in the sudden surge of our affection, we must individually try to keep in our more studied tributes, remembering that there is no more sincere nor welcome kind of thanks than that which most resembles the spontaneous acclamation which has no time for artifice. For my own part, I shall strive to make my

coins (S. 34–8), and from July 114 he took *optimus* as an *agnomen* in inscriptions. Cf. Dio, LXVIII. 23. 1: S. 99–101, and Durry, *Panégyrique*, Appendix 1.

laborabo, ut orationem meam ad modestiam principis
moderationemque submittam, nec minus considerabo,
quid aures eius pati possint, quam quid virtutibus
3 debeatur. Magna et inusitata principis gloria, cui
gratias acturus non tam vereor ne me in laudibus suis
4 parcum, quam ne nimium putet. Haec me cura haec
difficultas sola circumstat; nam merenti gratias agere
facile est, patres conscripti. Non enim periculum
est ne, cum loquar de humanitate, exprobrari sibi
superbiam credat; cum de frugalitate, luxuriam;
cum de clementia, crudelitatem; cum de liberalitate,
avaritiam; cum de benignitate, livorem; cum de
continentia, libidinem; cum de labore, inertiam;
5 cum de fortitudine, timorem. Ac ne illud quidem
vereor, ne gratus ingratusve videar, prout satis aut
parum dixero. Animadverto enim etiam deos ipsos
non tam accuratis adorantium precibus quam innocentia et sanctitate laetari, gratioremque existimari,
qui delubris eorum puram castamque mentem quam
qui meditatum carmen intulerit.

4. Sed parendum est senatus consulto quod ex
utilitate publica placuit, ut consulis voce sub titulo
gratiarum agendarum boni principes quae facerent
2 recognoscerent, mali quae facere deberent. Id nunc

---

[1] A practice which went back to the time of Augustus, and
before A.D. 8 when Ovid was exiled (*Ep. ex Ponto* IV. 4. 35)
though nothing is known of the decree. Cf. *Ep.* III. 13. 1;

speech conform with the modesty and moderation of my prince, and while paying due tribute to his merits shall remind myself of what his ears can endure to hear. And indeed it does him honour of no ordinary kind if in thanking him my fears are not that he will think I say too little in his praise but that I say too much. This is my sole anxiety, the only difficulty in my path; for it is easy, Conscript Fathers, to render thanks where they are due. There is no danger that in my references to his humanity he will see a reproach for arrogance; that he will suppose I mean extravagance by modest expenditure, and cruelty by forbearance; that I think him covetous and capricious when I call him generous and kind, profligate and idle instead of self-controlled and active, or that I judge him a coward when I speak of him as a brave man. I do not even fear that my gratitude or lack of it will be judged in accordance with the adequacy of my words, for I have noted that the gods themselves delight in the innocence and purity of their worshippers rather than in the elaborate preparation of the prayers they offer, and prefer the man who brings a chaste and sinless heart to their shrines to one who comes with a studied invocation.

4. But now I must bow to the decree of the Senate[1] which in the public interest has declared that under the form of a vote of thanks delivered by the voice of the consul, good rulers should recognize their own deeds and bad ones learn what theirs

III. 18. 1; II. 1. 5 (Verginius Rufus). The *Panegyricus* is greatly enlarged from the original *gratiarum actio*. Cf. III. 13. 1 and note.

eo magis sollemne ac necessarium est, quod parens noster privatas gratiarum actiones cohibet et comprimit, intercessurus etiam publicis, si permitteret

3 sibi vetare quod senatus iuberet. Utrumque, Caesar Auguste, moderate, et quod alibi tibi gratias agi non sinis, et quod hic sinis. Non enim a te ipso tibi honor iste, sed [ab][1] agentibus habetur: cedis adfectibus nostris, nec nobis munera tua praedicare sed audire tibi necesse est.

4 Saepe ego mecum, patres conscripti, tacitus agitavi, qualem quantumque esse oporteret, cuius dicione nutuque maria terrae, pax bella regerentur; cum interea fingenti formantique mihi principem, quem aequata dis immortalibus potestas deceret, numquam voto saltem concipere succurrit similem huic

5 quem videmus. Enituit aliquis in bello, sed obsolevit in pace; alium toga sed non et arma honestarunt; reverentiam ille terrore, alius amorem humilitate captavit; ille quaesitam domi gloriam in publico, hic in publico partam domi perdidit; postremo adhuc nemo exstitit, cuius virtutes nullo vitiorum

6 confinio laederentur. At principi nostro quanta concordia quantusque concentus omnium laudum omnisque gloriae contigit! Ut nihil severitati eius hilaritate, nihil gravitati simplicitate, nihil maiestati

---

[1] ab *M: del. Gesner.*

should be. That is the more necessary and solemn duty today because our Father has banned and forbidden private expressions of thanks and would intervene against public speeches also if he allowed himself to oppose the Senate's will. Both these actions, Caesar Augustus—your refusal of thanks elsewhere and your acceptance here—are proof of your moderation, for you do honour thereby not to yourself but to those who would thank you. You yield to our feelings of affection; and no necessity constrains us to proclaim your good deeds, whereas you have bound yourself to listen to them.

I often used to wonder, Conscript Fathers, what great gifts should be proper to the man whose word or gesture of command could rule land and sea and determine peace or war; but when I tried to picture to myself a ruler worthy of power equalling that of the immortal gods, even in my fondest hopes I never conceived the like of him whom we see before us today. One man may have shone in war, but his glory has grown dim in time of peace, while another has distinguished himself in civil life but not in arms. Some have won respect through men's fear, while others in courting popularity have sunk low. Sometimes the honour gained at home has been thrown away outside it, while at others a public reputation has been lost in private life. In fact there has been no one up till now whose virtues have remained unsullied by the close proximity of his faults. Contrast our prince, in whose person all the merits which win our admiration are found in complete and happy harmony! His essential seriousness and authority lose nothing through his candour and good humour;

331

7 humanitate detrahitur! Iam firmitas, iam proceritas corporis, iam honor capitis et dignitas oris, ad hoc aetatis indeflexa maturitas, nec sine quodam munere deum festinatis senectutis insignibus ad augendam maiestatem ornata caesaries, nonne longe lateque principem ostentant?

5. Talem esse oportuit quem non bella civilia, nec armis oppressa res publica, sed pax et adoptio et 2 tandem exorata terris numina dedissent. An fas erat nihil differre inter imperatorem quem homines et quem di fecissent? quorum quidem in te, Caesar Auguste, iudicium et favor tunc statim, cum ad exercitum proficiscereris, et quidam inusitato ⟨omine⟩[1] 3 enotuit. Nam ceteros principes aut largus cruor hostiarum aut sinister volatus avium consulentibus nuntiavit; tibi ascendenti de more Capitolium quamquam non id agentium civium clamor ut iam principi 4 occurrit, siquidem omnis turba quae limen insederat, ad ingressum tuum foribus reclusis, illa quidem, ut tunc arbitrabatur, deum, ceterum, ut docuit eventus, te consalutavit imperatorem. Nec aliter a cunctis 5 omen acceptum est. Nam ipse intellegere nolebas;

1 omine *add. Keil: om. M.*

---

[1] By Nerva: cf. 7–8.
[2] As legate of Upper Germany (late 96). Cf. SHA *Hadr.* 2. 5. ff.
[3] A statue to *Jupiter Imperator* in the temple on the Capitol had been brought from Praeneste in 380 B.C. by T. Quinctius

he can show humanity but remain a sovereign power. In addition, his splendid bearing and tall stature, his fine head and noble countenance, to say nothing of the firm strength of his maturity and the premature signs of advancing age with which the gods have seen fit to mark his hair and so enhance his look of majesty —are these not sufficient signs to proclaim him far and wide for what he is: our prince?

5. And rightly so: for he was not created for us by civil wars and a country racked by the arms of battle, but in peace, through adoption,[1] by heavenly powers in our lands at long last moved by prayer. How could any man-made emperor ever be permitted to rank equal with the chosen of the gods? Indeed, their choice of you, Caesar Augustus, and their divine favour were made manifest at the very moment of your setting out to join your army[2] by an omen without precedent. The names of all your predecessors were revealed to those who sought the oracles either by a gush of blood from the victims or a flight of birds on the left; but in your case, as you mounted the Capitol, following due precedent, the citizens gathered there for other reasons hailed you with a shout as if you were already emperor: for when the doors of the temple opened for your entry, the entire crowd assembled at the threshold cried *Imperator!* At the time it was thought that they were addressing Jupiter,[3] but events have proved that the title was intended for you, and the omen was thus interpreted by all. You alone were un-

Cincinnatus (Livy VI. 29. 8). This must have been destroyed in the fire of 83 B.C., but this passage shows it had been replaced.

recusabas enim imperare, recusabas, quod erat bene
6 imperaturi. Igitur cogendus fuisti. Cogi porro non
poteras nisi periculo patriae et nutatione rei publicae;
obstinatum enim tibi non suscipere imperium, nisi
7 servandum fuisset. Quare ego illum ipsum furorem
motumque castrensem reor exstitisse, quia magna
vi magnoque terrore modestia tua vincenda erat;
8 ac sicut maris caelique temperiem turbines tem-
pestatesque commendant, ita ad augendam pacis
tuae gratiam illum tumultum praecessisse crediderim.
9 Habet has vices condicio mortalium, ut adversa ex
secundis, ex adversis secunda nascantur. Occultat
utrorumque semina deus, et plerumque bonorum
malorumque causae sub diversa specie latent.

6. Magnum quidem illud saeculo dedecus, magnum
rei publicae vulnus impressum est: imperator et
parens generis humani obsessus captus inclusus,
ablata mitissimo seni servandorum hominum potestas,
ereptumque principi illud in principatu beatissimum,
2 quod nihil cogitur. Si tamen haec sola erat ratio,
quae te publicae salutis gubernaculis admoveret,
prope est ut exclamem tanti fuisse. Corrupta est
disciplina castrorum, ut tu corrector emendatorque

---

¹ The mutiny of the praetorian guard under its commander,
Casperius Aelianus (Dio LXVIII. 3. 3); there was a real
danger of civil war like that of 69. Cf. *Ep.* IX. 13. 11.
(*Nutatio* is used metaphorically only here and in Tac. *Hist.* III.
49. 1, *totius urbis nutatione*.)

willing to accept it, for you were reluctant to assume imperial power, a sure sign that you would use it well. So then you had to be pressed. Even then you could only be persuaded because you saw your country in peril and the whole realm tottering to a fall;[1] for you were resolved only to take up the burden of supreme power when it was threatened with destruction. This, I fancy, explains the rioting and mutiny which had broken out in the army; it was to provide the widespread violence and terror which were needed to overcome your diffidence. Just as a period of calm in sky and sea is welcomed by contrast with storm and tempest, similarly, I think, that earlier season of unrest was designed to increase our appreciation of the peace we owe to you. Such are the vicissitudes of our mortal lot: misfortune is born of prosperity, and good fortune of ill-luck. God conceals their origins in both cases, and the causes of good and evil are hidden for the most part, each behind the other's mask.

6. The great blot on our age, the deadly wound inflicted on our realm, was the time when an emperor and Father of the human race was besieged in his palace, arrested and confined; from the kindest of elderly men was snatched his authority to preserve mankind, from a prince was removed the greatest blessing of princely power, the knowledge that he cannot be forced against his will. Yet if this were the only means whereby you were to be brought to steer the ship of state, I am still ready to declare that the price was not too high. Army discipline broke down so that you could come to correct and improve it; a shocking example was set

335

contingeres; inductum pessimum exemplum, ut
optimum opponeretur; postremo coactus princeps
quos nolebat occidere, ut daret principem, qui cogi
3 non posset. Olim tu quidem adoptari merebare;
sed nescissemus quantum tibi deberet imperium, si
ante adoptatus esses. Exspectatum est tempus quo
liqueret non tam accepisse te beneficium quam
dedisse. Confugit in sinum tuum concussa res
publica, ruensque imperium super imperatorem im-
4 peratoris tibi voce delatum est. Imploratus adoptione et accitus es, ut olim duces magni a peregrinis
externisque bellis ad opem patriae ferendam revocari
solebant. Ita filius ac parens uno eodemque momento rem maximam invicem praestitistis: ille tibi
5 imperium dedit, tu illi reddidisti. Solus ergo ad hoc
aevi pro munere tanto paria accipiendo fecisti, immo
ultra dantem obligasti; communicato enim imperio
sollicitior tu, ille securior factus est.

7. O novum atque inauditum ad principatum iter!
Non te propria cupiditas proprius metus, sed aliena
2 utilitas alienus timor principem fecit. Videaris licet
quod est amplissimum inter homines consecutus,
felicius tamen erat illud quod reliquisti: sub bono

---

[1] Nerva was compelled to punish the murderers of Domitian
(Dio LXVIII. 3. 3).

[2] Perhaps a reference to Hannibal's recall to Carthage (Livy
XXX. 9).

so that you could counter it with a better; finally,
a ruler was forced to put men to death against his
will[1] in order to provide one on whom force should
never prevail. Your merits did indeed call for your
adoption as successor long ago; but had you been
adopted then, we should never have known the empire's debt to you. We had to wait for the moment
which would show you not so much the beneficiary
as the benefactor. The country reeled under its
blows to take refuge in your embrace; the empire
which was falling with its emperor was put into your
hands at the emperor's word; for it was through your
adoption that you yielded to entreaties and allowed
yourself to be recalled, like the great generals of the
past who were summoned from distant wars abroad
to bring aid to their homeland.[2] Thus it was that,
father and son together, at one and the same moment you bestowed on each other the greatest of all
gifts: he gave you supreme power and you returned
it to him. You alone in our time have made proper
return for such a gift, simply by your acceptance of
it; nay, rather, you put the giver in your debt, for
the sharing of authority increased your responsibilities while lessening his cares.

7. This is indeed a novel route to the principate,
unheard of hitherto![3] No ambition of yours, no
fears inspired by you, but another's interests and
another's terrors have made you prince. It may
appear that you have won the highest honour among
men, and yet a greater happiness lay in what you
renounced, namely, your position as subject under

[3] But cf. Galba's speech on adopting Piso (Tac. *Hist.* I.
15–16), a speech with many verbal affinities with *Pan* 7–8.

3 principe privatus esse desisti. Adsumptus es in
laborum curarumque consortium, nec te prospera et
laeta stationis istius, sed aspera et dura ad capessen-
dam eam compulerunt: suscepisti imperium, post-
4 quam alium suscepti paenitebat. Nulla adoptati
cum eo qui adoptabat cognatio, nulla necessitudo,
nisi quod uterque optimus erat, dignusque alter eligi
alter eligere. Itaque adoptatus es non ut prius
alius atque alius in gratiam uxoris. Adscivit enim
te filium non vitricus sed princeps, eodemque animo
divus Nerva pater tuus factus est, quo erat omnium.
5 Nec decet aliter filium adsumi, si adsumatur a
principe. An senatum populumque Romanum, exercitus provincias socios transmissurus uni successorem
e sinu uxoris accipias, summaeque potestatis heredem
tantum intra domum tuam quaeras? non totam per
civitatem circumferas oculos et hunc tibi proximum,
hunc coniunctissimum existimes, quem optimum
6 quem dis simillimum inveneris? Imperaturus omnibus eligi debet ex omnibus; non enim servulis tuis
dominum, ut possis esse contentus quasi necessario
herede, sed principem civibus daturus et imperatorem. Superbum istud et regium, nisi adoptes
eum quem constet imperaturum fuisse, etiamsi non
7 adoptasses. Fecit hoc Nerva nihil interesse arbitratus, genueris an elegeris, si perinde sine iudicio
adoptentur liberi ac nascuntur; nisi quod tamen

---

[1] Augustus and Claudius had adopted their respective
stepsons Tiberius and Nero to please their wives, Livia and
Agrippina (Tac. *Ann.* I. 3, XII. 25).

a good ruler. You were called upon to share his
toils and troubles, nor was it the pleasures and successes of his position which compelled you, but its
difficulties and pains. You assumed authority only
after he wished to be rid of it. No tie of kinship
or relationship bound adopted and adopter; your
only bond was that of mutual excellence, rendering
you worthy either to choose or to be chosen. Thus
you were adopted not as others have been hitherto,
in order to gratify a wife;[1] no stepfather made you
his son, but one who was your prince, and the divine
Nerva became your father in the same sense that he
was father of us all. This is the only fitting way to
adopt a son if the adopter is an emperor; for when
it is a case of transferring the Senate and people of
Rome, armies, provinces, and allies to a single successor, would you look to a wife to provide him, or
seek no further than the four walls of your home?
No indeed, you would search through all your subjects, and judge him the closest and dearest to you
whom you find to be the noblest and dearest to the
gods. If he is destined to rule the people, one and
all, he must be chosen from among them all, for no
natural law can satisfy you when you are not ap-
pointing an overlord for your household of cheap
slaves, but a prince and emperor for the citizens of
Rome. Not to adopt the one man who in the eyes of
all could have proved himself a ruler even without
adoption would indicate the wanton tyranny of power.
Thus Nerva made his choice, realizing that unless
sons are adopted with more judgement than they
are begotten there is little difference between a son
born and a son chosen—but for the fact that men

339

aequiore animo ferunt homines, quem princeps
parum feliciter genuit, quam quem male elegit.

8. Sedulo ergo vitavit hunc casum, nec modo
iudicium hominum sed deorum etiam in consilium
adsumpsit. Itaque non in cubiculo sed in templo,
nec ante genialem torum sed ante pulvinar Iovis
optimi maximi adoptio peracta est, qua tandem non
servitus nostra sed libertas et salus et securitas
2 fundabatur. Sibi enim gloriam illam di vindicaverunt: horum opus, horum illud imperium. Nerva
tantum minister fuit, utque[1] adoptaret, tam paruit
quam tu qui adoptabaris. Adlata erat ex Pannonia
laurea, id agentibus dis ut invicti imperatoris exor-
3 tum victoriae insigne decoraret. Hanc imperator
Nerva in gremio Iovis collocarat, cum repente solito
maior et augustior advocata contione hominum
deorumque te filium sibi, hoc est unicum auxilium
4 fessis rebus, adsumpsit. Inde quasi depositi imperii
qua securitate qua gloria laetus (nam quantulum
refert, deponas an partiaris imperium? nisi quod
difficilius hoc est), non secus ac praesenti tibi innixus,
tuis umeris se patriamque sustentans tua iuventa,
5 tuo robore invaluit. Statim consedit omnis tumultus.

---

[1] utque *Mynors*: ut qui *R*: utque qui *M*.

---

[1] In the second half of October 97.
[2] By the ceremony of *adrogatio*, as in the case of Tiberius's

will more readily forgive a ruler for a son who proves unworthy than for a successor who was a bad choice.

8. He took pains, then, to avoid such a disaster, seeking counsel from gods and men alike; and thus the adoption took place[1] not in his bedroom and by his marriage-bed but in the temple before the couch of Jupiter Best and Highest, the adoption[2] which was to be the basis of no servitude for us, but of security, happiness, and freedom. The gods have claimed the credit for this, since it was carried out at their command. Nerva was no more than their minister, no less obedient as adopter than you who were adopted. Laurels had been brought from Pannonia,[3] at the gods' behest, for the symbol of victory to mark the rise of a ruler who would never know defeat. Nerva laid them in the lap of Jupiter and straightway rose up, taller and nobler than was his wont; before the gathered assembly of gods and men he chose you as his son, his sole support in time of crisis. From that moment onwards he delighted in the happiness and honour he derived from what might be termed his resignation—for there is little to choose between resigning and sharing power, except that the latter is more difficult—leaning on you as if you were there by his side, resting the burden of his person and his country on your shoulders, drawing strength from your youth and vigour. Every disturbance died away at once; though this

adoption (Suet. *Aug.* 65. 1). Contrast Piso's adoption (Tac. *Hist.* I. 16. 9).

[3] Not Trajan's own victory, as he was in Germany. Laurels were sent with bulletins announcing victory (Pliny *N.H.* XV. 133–4).

Non adoptionis opus istud sed adoptati fuit; atque adeo temere fecerat Nerva, si adoptasset alium. Oblitine sumus ut nuper post adoptionem non desierit seditio sed coeperit? Inritamentum istud irarum et fax tumultus fuisset, nisi incidisset in te. 6 An dubium est ut dare posset imperium imperator, qui reverentiam amiserat, auctoritate eius effectum cui dabatur? Simul filius simul Caesar, mox imperator et consors tribuniciae potestatis, et omnia pariter et statim factus es, quae proxime parens verus tantum in alterum filium contulit.

9. Magnum hoc tuae moderationis indicium, quod non solum successor imperii, sed particeps etiam sociusque placuisti. Nam successor etiamsi nolis habendus [est]; [1] non est habendus socius nisi velis. 2 Credentne posteri patricio et consulari et triumphali patre genitum, cum fortissimum amplissimum amantissimum sui exercitum regeret, imperatorem non ab exercitu factum? eidem, cum Germaniae praesi-

---

[1] est *del.* Mynors.

---

[1] Galba's adoption of Piso.

[2] Vespasian shared his power only with Titus (Suet. *Tit.* 6).

[3] Trajan's father was born in Italica, Baetica, where he was afterwards proconsul. He was legate of Leg. X Fretensis during the war in Judaea 67–8, suffect consul between 68 and 71, legate in Syria from 73/4 to 76/7 where he received *ornamenta triumphalia* for some unrecorded success over the Parthians. He was later proconsul of Asia, and probably died there before 100. Trajan was the first provincial aristocrat to become emperor. Note that Pliny says nothing of his Spanish origin.

was the effect not so much of the adoption as the nature of the man adopted, sure indication that Nerva would have been foolish had he chosen otherwise. It is not so long since there was an adoption which failed to check an outbreak of rebellion,[1] and indeed was its occasion; have we forgotten this? Yours too would have inflamed angry feelings and set a torch to insurrection if the choice had not fallen on you. Can it be doubted that if an emperor who had forfeited men's regard was able to bestow the imperial power, it could only be because of the personality of the recipient? At one moment then, you became son and Caesar; soon you were emperor with a share in the tribune's powers, to hold immediately and simultaneously all the titles which in recent times were conferred by an emperor on one only of the sons he had fathered.[2]

9. It is sure proof of your moderation that you have found favour not only as successor to the imperial power but as associate and colleague. A man must have a successor, whether he wants him or not; he need not take a colleague unless he chooses. Posterity may find it hard to believe that one whose father was of noble birth and consular rank and won a triumph,[3] who was himself in command of a mighty army[4] of brave soldiers devoted to their general, could be hailed as *Imperator* by his men and receive from Rome the title of *Germanicus*[5] when governor of Germany, and yet take no steps himself to become

---

[4] Both Upper and Lower Germany had three legions.

[5] The title was assumed by Nerva and Trajan either at the end of 97 or in 98, after Vestricius Spurinna's negotiations with the Bructeri (cf. *Ep.* II. 7. 2).

deret, Germanici nomen hinc missum? nihil ipsum
ut imperator fieret agitasse, nihil fecisse nisi quod
3 meruit et paruit? Paruisti enim, Caesar, et ad
principatum obsequio pervenisti, nihilque magis a te
subiecti animo factum est quam quod imperare
coepisti, iam Caesar iam imperator iam Germanicus
absens et ignarus, et post tanta nomina, quantum
4 ad te pertinet, privatus. Magnum videretur, si
dicerem " Nescisti te imperatorem futurum ": eras
imperator et esse te nesciebas. Ut vero ad te
fortunae tuae nuntius venit, malebas quidem hoc
esse quod fueras, sed non erat liberum. An non
obsequereris principi civis, legatus imperatori, filius
5 patri? Ubi deinde disciplina, ubi mos a maioribus
traditus, quodcumque imperator munus iniungeret,
aequo animo paratoque subeundi? Quid enim, si
provincias ex provinciis ex bellis bella mandaret?
⟨Apparet⟩[1] eodem illo uti iure, cum ad imperium
revocet quo sit usus cum ad exercitum miserit,
nihilque interesse ire legatum an redire principem
iubeat, nisi quod maior sit obsequii gloria in eo, quod
quis minus velit.

10. Augebat auctoritatem iubentis in summum
discrimen auctoritas eius adducta, utque magis
parendum imperanti putares, efficiebatur eo quod ab
2 aliis minus parebatur. Ad hoc audiebas senatus

---

[1] apparet add. Haupt: om. M.

emperor and do nothing in fact except serve as a
soldier and obey. Yes, Caesar, you obeyed, and it
was your obedience which raised you to the principate; nothing is better proof of your sense of discipline than the fact that you started your reign with
these splendid titles of *Caesar*, *Imperator*, and *Germanicus* granted you when you were far from Rome
and unaware of your future, yet still in your own
heart remained a loyal subject. I should be thought
to exaggerate if I said that you did not know you
would be emperor; in fact, you *were* emperor, but
did not know it. And when the news came of your
good fortune, you would have preferred, I think, to
remain as you had been; but you were not free to
decide. You were subject, legate and son: your
duty lay in obedience to your ruler, your general and
your father; else where would military discipline
be, and the tradition of centuries of accepting
readily, without question, whatever charges your
general imposed? He could have assigned you province after province, sent you on campaign after
campaign, for clearly he was exercising the same
authority in recalling you to assume the imperial
power as he did when he sent you out to command
your army. An order is an order, whether it means
a departure as legate or a return as prince, though
there may be greater glory in obedience where the
desire to obey is less.

10. This order was the more authoritative for you
simply because authority was in grave peril; you
thought that obedience was all the more necessary
from you since it was lacking in others. Furthermore, you were told that the Senate and people

populique consensum: non unius Nervae iudicium
illud, illa electio fuit. Nam qui ubique sunt homines,
hoc idem votis expetebant; ille tantum iure principis
occupavit, primusque fecit quod facturi omnes erant.
Nec hercule tanto opere cunctis factum placeret,
3 nisi placuisset ante quam fieret. At quo, di boni,
temperamento potestatem tuam fortunamque
moderatus es! Imperator tu titulis et imaginibus
et signis, ceterum modestia labore vigilantia dux et
legatus et miles, cum iam tua vexilla tuas aquilas
magno gradu anteires, neque aliud tibi ex illa
adoptione quam filii pietatem filii obsequium ad-
sereres, longamque huic nomini aetatem, longam
4 gloriam precarere. Iam te providentia deorum
primum in locum provexerat; tu adhuc in secundo
resistere atque etiam senescere optabas: privatus
tibi videbaris, quam diu imperator et alius esset.
Audita sunt tua vota, sed in quantum optimo illi et
5 sanctissimo seni utile fuit, quem di ideo[1] caelo
vindicaverunt, ne quid post illud divinum et immortale factum mortale faceret: deberi quippe
maximo operi hanc venerationem, ut novissimum
esset, auctoremque eius statim consecrandum, ut
quandoque inter posteros quaereretur, an illud iam
6 deus fecisset. Ita ille nullo magis nomine publicus
parens, quam quia tuus. Ingens gloria ingensque

---

[1] di ideo *Baehrens*: dii de *M*.

---

[1] The medallions showing the head of the emperor fixed
to the standards. (The passage is a verbal echo of Tacitus,
Dialogus 8. 4.)

approved, and this choice and decision were not Nerva's alone, but the heart-felt prayer of the whole country. He did no more than exercise his prerogative as Leader of the State, and anticipate what everyone would have liked to do, nor would his action have been so universally popular if it had not been previously approved. Power and advancement were yours, but heaven may bear witness to the moderate use you made of them. Inscriptions, portraits [1] and the army's standards proclaimed you *Imperator*, but in your self-effacement, activity and vigilance you were soldier, officer and commander in the field; striding ahead of the standards and eagles which were now your own you claimed no benefit from your adoption but the right to show the obedience and devotion of a son, and sought long life and lasting glory only for the name you now bore. The gods in their wisdom had already raised you to the supreme position, but your desire was still to take the second place and grow old there; you felt yourself to be no more than a simple citizen as long as another emperor reigned with you. Your prayers were heard, but only so long as this served the interests of that august and venerable ruler; for the gods claimed him to take his place in the heavens, thinking that nothing merely mortal should follow his godlike and immortal act and that the honour proper to a noble deed was for this deed to be the last of its author, who should then be deified at once so that one day posterity might wonder whether he was already god when his last deed was done. Thus his highest claim to be the Father of his country was his being father to you; and this was his greatest

fama: cum abunde expertus esset, quam bene umeris tuis sederet imperium, tibi terras te terris reliquit, eo ipso carus omnibus ac desiderandus, quod prospexerat ne desideraretur.

11. Quem tu lacrimis primum, ita ut filium decuit, mox templis honestasti, non imitatus illos qui hoc idem sed alia mente fecerunt. Dicavit caelo Tiberius Augustum, sed ut maiestatis crimen induceret; Claudium Nero, sed ut irrideret; Vespasianum Titus, Domitianus Titum, sed ille ut dei filius, hic 2 ut frater videretur. Tu sideribus patrem intulisti non ad metum civium, non in contumeliam numinum, 3 non in honorem tuum, sed quia deum credis. Minus hoc est, cum fit ab iis qui et sese deos putant. Sed licet illum aris pulvinaribus flamine colas, non alio magis tamen deum et facis et probas, quam quod ipse talis es. In principe enim qui electo successore fato concessit, una itemque certissima divinitatis 4 fides est bonus successor. Num ergo tibi ex immortalitate patris aliquid adrogantiae accessit? Num hos proximos divinitate parentum desides ac superbos potius quam illos veteres et antiquos aemuleris, qui hoc ipsum imperium . . .[1] quam

---

[1] *lacuna nondum expleta.*

---

[1] Nerva died 27/8 January 98. The Tacitean epigram is echoed possibly in *Hist.* 1. 16. 3.

[2] There is no record of these apart from a doubtful coin showing a temple of Divus Nerva (Durry, *Pan.* p. 101).

[3] Tac. *Ann.* I. 10. 8; Dio LVI. 46. 1.

[4] Tac. *Ann.* XII. 69; XIII. 2. Suet. *Claud.* 45.

glory and renown: once he had had ample proof that
the Empire rested securely on your shoulders he left
the world to you and you to the world, beloved and
regretted by all for that very act of foresight intended
to ensure that there need be no regrets.[1]

11. He received the proper honours from you, first
the tears which every son should shed, then the
temples[2] you raised to him. Others have done the
same, but with different intent; Tiberius deified
Augustus,[3] but his purpose was to introduce the
charge of high treason; Nero had done the same for
Claudius[4] in a spirit of mockery; Titus had similarly
honoured Vespasian and Domitian Titus, but only
for one to be thought the son and the other the
brother of a god.[5] You gave your father his place
among the stars with no thought of terrorizing your
subjects, of bringing the gods into disrepute, or of
gaining reflected glory, but simply because you
thought he *was* a god. This is an honour which
means less when it is paid by men who believe themselves to be equally divine; unlike you, who set up
his cult with altars, couches and a priest, yet created
and proved his godhead still more by being the man
you are. For there is no more certain proof of
divinity in a ruler who has chosen his successor before
he met his end than the worthiness of his choice.
Consequently, it is inconceivable that knowledge of
your father's immortality would ever make you
proud; you would not take your example from recent times, when sovereigns have grown insolent and
idle just because their parents are divine, instead of
from the rulers of the past who . . . their empire

[5] Suetonius, *Dom.* 2. Martial IX. 101. 22.

imperator cuius pulsi fugatique non aliud maius
5 habebatur indicium, quam si triumpharet. Ergo
sustulerant animos et iugum excusserant, nec iam
nobiscum de sua libertate sed de nostra servitute
certabant, ac ne indutias quidem nisi aequis con-
dicionibus inibant legesque ut acciperent dabant.

12. At nunc rediit omnibus terror, et metus et
votum imperata faciendi. Vident enim Romanum
ducem unum ex illis veteribus et priscis, quibus
imperatorium nomen addebant contecti caedibus
2 campi et infecta victoriis maria. Accipimus obsides
ergo non emimus, nec ingentibus damnis immensisque
muneribus paciscimur ut vicerimus. Rogant sup-
plicant, largimur negamus, utrumque ex imperii
maiestate. Agunt gratias qui impetraverunt, non
3 audent queri quibus negatum est. An audeant, qui
sciant te adsedisse ferocissimis populis, eo ipso
tempore quod amicissimum illis difficillimum nobis,
cum Danubius ripas gelu iungit, duratusque glacie
ingentia tergo bella transportat, cum ferae gentes
non telis magis quam suo caelo, suo sidere armantur ?
4 Sed ubi in proximo tu, non secus ac si mutatae
temporum vices essent, illi quidem latibulis suis

---

[1] The *lacuna* has not been explained. " Our enemies " are
needed as a subject for *sustulerant*; the truce may refer to
Domitian's negotiations with Decebalus of Parthia in 89.
Cf. Dio LXVII. 7.
[2] This must be in the winter of 99, when Trajan passed

. . .[1] an emperor gave no surer proof of his humiliation and defeat than at the very moment of his triumph. Thus our enemies had lifted up their heads and shaken off the yoke; they fought against us, not for their liberty but to enslave us all, accepting no truce save on equal terms, no law before they had made their own.

12. Now once more terror is in their midst; our enemies are afraid, and crave permission to obey commands. They see that Rome has a leader who ranks with her heroes of old, whose title of *Imperator* was on seas stained with the bloodshed of victory and on battlefields piled high with the bodies of the dead. Today, therefore, we are receiving hostages, not paying for them; huge losses and vast sums of money are no longer needed to buy terms of peace which shall name us as the conquerors. The prayers and entreaties are on the other side,[2] for us to grant or refuse at will, so long as we promise our country's sovereign power. They show their gratitude when we will listen, but if we are deaf to their pleas, dare not complain—how could they, when they know how you encamped confronting a dangerous enemy at the very time which was best for them and least favourable to us: when the Danube is bridged by ice from bank to bank and can carry vast preparations for war across its frozen surface, so that its savage peoples can enjoy the double protection of their own arms and the winter weather of their native climate? Once you were on the spot, the seasons might have been reversed; the enemy were

through the Danube regions on his way from Upper Germany to Rome.

clausi tenebantur, nostra agmina percursare ripas et
aliena occasione si permitteres uti, ultroque hiemem
suam barbaris inferre gaudebant.

13. Haec tibi apud hostes veneratio. Quid?
apud milites quam admirationem quemadmodum
comparasti! cum tecum inediam tecum sitim ferrent;
cum in illa meditatione campestri militaribus turmis
imperatorium pulverem sudoremque misceres, nihil
a ceteris nisi robore ac praestantia ⟨differens⟩[1]
libero Marte nunc cominus[2] tela vibrares, nunc
vibrata susciperes, alacer virtute militum et laetus,
quotiens aut cassidi tuae aut clipeo gravior ictus
2 incideret (laudabas quippe ferientes, hortabarisque
ut auderent, et audebant); iam cum spectator
⟨moderator⟩[3] que ineuntium certamina virorum
arma componeres, tela temptares, ac si quod durius
3 accipienti videretur, ipse librares.[4] Quid cum
solacium fessis, aegris opem ferres? Non tibi moris
tua inire tentoria, nisi commilitonum ante lustrasses,
4 nec requiem corpori nisi post omnes dare. Hac mihi
admiratione dignus imperator ⟨vix⟩[5] videretur, si
inter Fabricios et Scipiones et Camillos talis esset;

---

[1] differens *add. Aldus, om. M*: dispar, distans, diversus *alii*.
[2] cominus *M*: eminus G. H. *Schaefer.*
[3] moderatorque *add.* Puteolanus: spectatorque *M*.
[4] librares *codex Vaticanus*: vibrares *M*.
[5] vix *add. C.F. Mueller*: om. *M*.

stopped up inside their lairs, while our armies were eager to cross the river and, if you permitted, adopt the enemy's tactics and launch a winter campaign on them unprovoked.

13. Thus your enemies bowed before your reputation. What shall I say now of the admiration which you won from your own men? They saw how you shared their hunger and thirst on field manoeuvres and how their commander's sweat and dust was mingled with their own; with nothing to mark you out save your height and physique, in open battle you launched your spears at close quarters or received those aimed at you; you delighted in the courage of your soldiers and rejoiced whenever a heavier blow struck you on shield or helmet, praising your assailants and urging them on to greater deeds of daring—which they at once performed. Nothing escaped your direction or your observant eye; it was you who assigned the men their arms before the start of operations, and tested the spears so that when one seemed too heavy for a man you could wield it yourself. Again, it was you who comforted the weary and attended to the sick, for it was your habit to inspect your comrades' tents before you retired to your own; the last man must go off duty before you would take a rest yourself. Such were the great generals of the past, bred in the homes of Fabricius, Scipio, and Camillus;[1] if they have a lesser claim upon my admiration it is because in their day

---

[1] Notably, Gaius Fabricius, hero of the war against Pyrrhus; the Scipios, father and son, who fought against Hannibal in the Second Punic War; and M. Furius Camillus, the saviour of Rome after the Gallic invasion in 387 B.C.

tunc enim illum imitationis ardor semperque melior
5 aliquis accenderet. Postquam vero studium armorum
a manibus ad oculos, ad voluptatem a labore trans-
latum est, postquam exercitationibus nostris non
veteranorum aliquis cui decus muralis aut civica,
sed Graeculus magister adsistit, quam magnum est
unum ex omnibus patrio more patria virtute laetari,
et sine aemulo [ac][1] sine exemplo secum certare,
secum contendere ac, sicut imperet solus, solum ita
esse qui debeat imperare!

14. Non incunabula haec tibi, Caesar, et rudi-
menta, cum puer admodum Parthica lauro gloriam
patris augeres, nomenque Germanici iam tum
mererere, cum ferociam superbiamque Parthorum
ex proximo auditus magno terrore cohiberes,
Rhenumque et Euphratem admirationis tuae societate
coniungeres? cum orbem terrarum non pedibus
magis quam laudibus peragrares, apud eos semper
2 maior et clarior quibus postea contigisses? Et
necdum imperator, necdum dei filius eras. Ger-
maniam ⟨Hispaniam⟩[2] que cum plurimae gentes
ac prope infinita vastitas interiacentis soli, tum
Pyrenaeus Alpes immensique alii montes nisi his
3 comparentur, muniunt dirimuntque. Per hoc omne

[1] ac *M*: *del.* ord. *codex deterior.*
[2] Hispaniamque *add. Keil*: Germaniamque *M.*

---

[1] The *corona muralis* and *corona civica*, awarded for being
the first man over a city-wall, and for saving the life of a citizen
in battle.
[2] Trajan held a military tribunate under his father in Syria,

a man could be inspired by keen rivalry with his betters. But now that interest in arms is displayed in spectacle instead of personal skill, and has become an amusement instead of a discipline, when exercises are no longer directed by a veteran crowned by the mural or civic crown,[1] but by some petty Greek trainer, it is good to find one single man to delight in the traditions and the valour of our fathers, who can strive with none but himself for rival, press on with only his own example before him, and since he is to wield authority alone, will prove that he alone is worthy!

14. Now, Caesar, let us turn to the very cradle and starting point of your career. You were scarcely more than a boy when your successes in Parthia helped to win fame for your father,[2] when you already deserved the name of *Germanicus*,[3] when the mere sound of your approach struck terror into the proud hearts of savage Parthians, when Rhine and Euphrates were united in their admiration for you. Your fame travelled the world ahead of your person, yet always proved less than reality among those who knew you later. And still you were not yet Emperor, not yet the son of a god. Spain and Germany were still divided by the barrier of countless peoples and an almost endless waste of intervening country, to say nothing of the Pyrenees and Alps, and other mountains which seem enormous, though not comparable with these. Throughout the entire journey,

but his part in winning the *ornamenta triumphalia* for his father is not known.

[3] Probably a reference to the part played by Trajan in the revolt of Saturninus, 1 January 89.

spatium cum legiones duceres seu potius (tanta velocitas erat) raperes, non vehiculum umquam, non equum respexisti. Levis hic, non subsidium itineris, sed decus [et cum[1]] subsequebatur, ut cuius tibi nullus usus, nisi cum die stativorum proximum campum alacritate discursus pulvere attolleres. 4 Initium laboris mirer an finem? Multum est quod perseverasti, plus tamen quod non timuisti ne per- 5 severare non posses. Nec dubito quin ille qui te inter ipsa Germaniae bella ab Hispania usque ut validissimum praesidium exciverat, iners ipse alien- isque virtutibus tunc quoque invidus imperator, cum ope earum indigeret, tantam admirationem tui non sine quodam timore conceperit, quantam ille genitus Iove post saevos labores duraque imperia regi suo indomitus semper indefessusque referebat, cum aliis super alias expeditionibus itinere illo dignus inveni- reris.

15. Tribunus vero disiunctissimas terras teneris adhuc annis viri firmitate lustrasti, iam tunc prae- monente fortuna, ut diu penitusque perdisceres,

---

[1] et cum M: del. Haupt.

[1] Trajan was commanding the Leg. VII Gemina (*one* legion only) in Hispania Tarraconensis, and was summoned to bring it to Upper Germany.

[2] In fact, Domitian left Rome with the Guard for Germany on 12 January (Dio LXVII. 11. 5) and Saturninus was defeated on 25 January by Lappius Maximus, legate of Lower Germany.

[3] Hercules and Eurystheus. Trajan is also compared with

as you led, or rather, hurried along your legions[1] in your urgent haste, you never thought of horse or carriage. Your charger followed, unmounted, more for propriety's sake than to help you on your way: you made use of it only at the rest camps, raising the dust as you worked off your energy galloping over the countryside. Which am I to admire more, the start of your undertaking or its end? It was a great thing to carry it out, but even greater to have had no doubts that you could do so. This much is certain of the man who had called you from Spain to be his surest support during those very German wars, unwilling as he was to bestir himself and jealous[2] of another's virtues even when he was in dire need of them: you must have filled him with the same admiration (not unmixed with fear) as Jupiter's great son inspired in his king[3] when he remained forever unwearied and undaunted after the cruel labours demanded by the latter's harsh commands; for after that journey he judged you worthy to conduct a series of campaigns.[4]

15. Indeed, as tribune in the army and still of tender age, you had served and proved your manhood at the far-flung boundaries of the empire, for even then Fortune set you to study closely, without haste, the lessons which later you would have to

Hercules in 82. 7. Coins of 100 show "Hercules Gaditanus" and the cult was a special interest of Trajan's, perhaps because he had also come from S. Spain.

[4] Nothing is known of Trajan's military activities between 89 and 96, nor is there any mention of a consulship or proconsular post. Either Pliny glosses over his employment by the hated Domitian, or he prefers to imply that Trajan's career —like his own—was retarded (cf. 95. 3).

2 quae mox praecipere deberes. Neque enim pro-
spexisse castra brevemque militiam quasi transisse
contentus, ita egisti tribunum ut esse dux statim
posses, nihilque discendum haberes tempore docendi :
3 cognovisti per stipendia decem mores gentium
regionum situs opportunitates locorum, et diversam
aquarum caelique temperiem ut patrios fontes
patriumque sidus ferre consuesti. Quotiens equos,
4 quotiens emerita arma mutasti ! Veniet ergo tempus
quo posteri visere visendumque tradere minoribus
suis gestient, quis sudores tuos hauserit campus,
quae refectiones tuas arbores, quae somnum saxa
praetexerint, quod denique tectum magnus hospes
impleveris, ut tunc ipsi tibi ingentium ducum sacra
5 vestigia isdem in locis monstrabantur. Verum haec
olim; in praesentia quidem, quisquis paulo vetustior
miles, hic te commilitone censetur. Quotus enim
quisque, cuius tu non ante commilito quam imperator? Inde est, quod prope omnes nomine
adpellas, quod singulorum fortia facta commemoras,
nec habent adnumeranda tibi pro re publica vulnera,
quibus statim laudator et testis contigisti.

16. Sed tanto magis praedicanda est moderatio
tua, quod innutritus bellicis laudibus pacem amas,
nec quia vel pater tibi triumphalis vel adoptionis

---

[1] Ten years as *tribunus militaris laticlavius* is without precedent, and must be an exaggeration. Possibly Pliny is
exploiting the period between assuming the *toga virilis* at 15

teach. A distant look at a camp, a stroll through a short term of service was not enough for you; your time as tribune must qualify you for immediate command, with nothing left to learn when the moment came for passing on your knowledge. Ten years of service[1] taught you customs of peoples, locality of countries, lie of the land, and accustomed you to enduring every kind of river and weather as if these were the springs and climate of your native land. Many were the times when you changed your mount and the arms worn out with service! The day will come when posterity will clamour to see and show their youngers the earth which was soaked in your sweat, the trees and rocks which sheltered your moments of sleep and repose, the roof which gave hospitality to your noble person, as in your time you were shown the cherished traces left by the great generals of the past. But this is for the future; meanwhile, any soldier who is not too young can gain glory from having served with you. How many do you suppose there are who did not know you as comrade in arms before you were their emperor? Thus you can call nearly all your soldiers by name, and know the deeds of bravery of each one, while they need not recount the wounds they received in their country's service, since you were there to witness and applaud.

16. But nurtured though you were on the glories of war, you have remained a lover of peace, and for this your moderation commands our greater praise. Your own father had been granted triumphal

---

[1] and holding the quaestorship at 25. The normal age for the *laticlavius* was 19–20.

tuae die dicata Capitolino Iovi laurus, idcirco ex
2 occasione omni quaeris triumphos. Non times bella
nec provocas. Magnum est, imperator auguste,
magnum est stare in Danubii ripa, si transeas certum triumphi, nec decertare cupere cum recusantibus; quorum alterum fortitudine, alterum modera-
3 tione efficitur. Nam ut ipse nolis pugnare moderatio,
fortitudo tua praestat ut neque hostes tui velint.
Accipiet ergo aliquando Capitolium non mimicos
currus nec falsae simulacra victoriae, sed imperatorem veram ac solidam gloriam reportantem, pacem[1]
tranquillitatem et tam confessa hostium obsequia, ut
4 vincendus nemo fuerit. Pulchrius hoc omnibus
triumphis; neque enim umquam nisi ex contemptu
5 imperii nostri factum est ut vinceremus. Quodsi
quis barbarus rex eo insolentia furorisque processerit,
ut iram tuam indignationemque mereatur, ne ille
sive interfuso mari seu fluminibus immensis seu
praecipiti monte defenditur, omnia haec tam prona
tamque cedentia virtutibus tuis sentiet, ut subsedisse
montes, flumina exaruisse, interceptum mare in-
latasque sibi non classes nostras sed terras ipsas
arbitretur.

[1] pacem H: om. X.

---

[1] In winter, 98–9.
[2] Evidently an addition made to the speech during the
Dacian war of 101.
[3] Cf. Dio LXVII. 7. 4. Pliny consistently plays down
Domitian's military exploits.

honours, and on the day of your adoption laurels
were dedicated to Capitoline Jupiter, but you did
not seek opportunity for triumphs of your own. You
have neither fear of war, nor any desire to cause one.
How magnificent it was, august Emperor, to stand
on the Danube's bank[1] knowing that a triumph was
certain did you but cross, and yet have no urge to
press on against a foe who refused battle, proof alike
of valour and of moderation, the one denying battle
to the enemy wanting it, the other denying battle to
yourself. And so the day will come[2] when the Capitol
shall see no masquerade of triumph,[3] the chariots and
sham trappings of false victory, but an emperor coming
home with true and genuine honour, bringing peace
and the end of strife, and the submission of his enemies so evident that none shall be left to conquer.
Here is an achievement which is nobler than any
triumph! For hitherto our victories have been won
only after our sovereignty has been slighted; but
now, if some native king[4] shall presume so far in his
folly as to call down your just wrath and indignation
on his head, though he be defended by the seas between, the mighty rivers or sheer mountains, he
will surely find that all these barriers yield and fall
away before your prowess, and will fancy that the
mountains have subsided, the rivers dried up and
the sea drained off, while his country falls a victim
not only to our fleets[5] but to the natural forces of
the earth!

[4] Decebalus, king of Parthia.
[5] The Danube fleet, consisting of the *classis Pannonica* and
classis Moesica.

17. Videor iam cernere non spoliis provinciarum
et extorto sociis auro, sed hostilibus armis capto-
2 rumque regum catenis triumphum gravem; videor
ingentia ducum nomina nec indecora nominibus
corpora noscitare; videor intueri immanibus ausis
barbarorum onusta fercula et sua quemque facta
vinctis manibus sequentem, mox ipsum te sublimem
instantemque curru domitarum gentium tergo, ante
3 currum autem clipeos quos ipse perfoderis. Nec
tibi opima defuerint, si quis regum venire in manus
audeat, nec modo telorum tuorum, sed oculorum
etiam minarumque coniectum, toto campo totoque
4 exercitu opposito perhorrescat. Meruisti proxima
moderatione, ut quandoque te vel inferre vel pro-
pulsare bellum coegerit imperi dignitas, non ideo
vicisse videaris ut triumphares, sed triumphare quia
viceris.

18. Aliud ex alio mihi occurrit. Quam speciosum
est enim quod disciplinam castrorum lapsam exstinc-
tam refovisti, depulso prioris saeculi malo inertia et
2 contumacia et dedignatione parendi! Tutum est
reverentiam, tutum caritatem mereri, nec ducum
quisquam aut non amari a militibus aut amari timet;
exinde[1] offensae pariter gratiaeque securi, instant

---

[1] exinde *Baehrens*: inde *Keil*: et inde *M*.

---

[1] The triumph for the First Dacian War, held during the
winter of 102–3. Cf. *Ep*. VIII. 4. 2.
[2] *i.e.* on painted scenes, or tableaux, mounted on wagons.
These are shown on Trajan's column (for which see C. A. H.
Plates V, pp. 36–40, 84).

17. Already I seem to see before me a triumph[1] piled high not with the spoils of plundered provinces and gold wrung from our allies, but with our enemies' arms and the chains of captured kings. I can recognise the high-sounding titles of chieftains whose persons are not unworthy of such names, and watch the wagons pass with their loads to show the fearful ventures of the savage foe, each prisoner following, hands bound, the scene of his own deeds;[2] then, close behind the conquered nations your own self standing high in your chariot, before which are the shields pierced by your own hand. The spoils of supreme honour would be yours if any king would dare to match himself against you, shuddering with terror though the whole field of battle and army might lie between, when confronted not only by your weapons but by a glance from your threatening eye. And your recent moderation has ensured that whenever you are compelled to war, offensive or defensive, for the honour of your realm, you will be known to win triumph through victory, not to seek victory in order to triumph.

18. How wonderful it was of you (for one idea suggests another) to rekindle the dying flame of military discipline by destroying the indifference, insolence and contempt for obedience, those evils of the preceding regime![3] Today it is safe to earn respect and affection, and no one in command need fear to be unpopular—or popular—with his men. Thus freed from the anxiety alike of incurring favour or giving offence, he can press on with constructive

---

[3] Cf. *Ep.* VIII. 14. 7; X. 29. 1.

operibus, adsunt exercitationibus, arma moenia viros
3 aptant. Quippe non is princeps qui sibi imminere
sibi intendi putet, quod in hostes paretur; quae
persuasio fuit illorum qui hostilia cum facerent
timebant. Iidem ergo torpere militaria studia nec
animos modo sed corpora ipsa languescere, gladios
etiam incuria hebetari retundique gaudebant. Duces
porro nostri non tam regum exterorum quam suorum
principum insidias, nec tam hostium quam commilitonum manus ferrumque metuebant.

19. Est haec natura sideribus, ut parva et exilia
validorum exortus obscuret: similiter imperatoris
2 adventu legatorum dignitas inumbratur. Tu tamen
maior quidem omnibus eras, sed sine ullius deminutione maior: eandem auctoritatem praesente
te quisque quam¹ absente retinebat; quin etiam
plerisque ex eo reverentia accesserat, quod tu
3 quoque illos reverebare. Itaque perinde summis
atque infimis carus, sic imperatorem commilito-
nemque miscueras, ut studium omnium laboremque
et tamquam exactor intenderes et tamquam particeps
4 sociusque relevares. Felices illos, quorum fides et
industria non per internuntios et interpretes, sed ab
ipso te nec auribus tuis sed oculis probabantur!

---

¹ quisque quam *Puteolanus*: quisquam *M*.

---

¹ Between his adoption (or Nerva's death) and his recall to
Rome in the Spring of 99, Trajan carried out a tour of inspec-

work, conduct manoeuvres, make all arrangements
for fortifications, weapons and his men. For ours
is not a prince who sees in preparations against his
enemies a threat directed at himself, after the fashion
of his predecessors, who feared to fall victim to their
own harsh practices and so were glad to see a falling
off of interest in the soldier's life, slack training and
lowered morale, while swords grew dull and blunted
through disuse. Thus our generals had less to fear
from foreign foes than from their masters' treachery,
and more from the swords their own men held than
from their enemies'.

19. In the heavens it is natural that the smaller
and weaker stars should be overshadowed by the
rising of the greater ones, and in the same way an
emperor's legates can feel their prestige dimmed
when he appears.[1] But you could be greater than all
without anyone's suffering from your majesty; no
one lost in your presence the authority he had enjoyed before you came, and many found men's regard for them the greater because you shared it too.
So you were beloved by all, the highest and the
lowest; the emperor and the comrade-in-arms so
combined in your person that you could fire men's
ardour and endurance by your supervision, while re-
lieving their hardships by sharing the common lot,
Happy those whose seal and loyalty were known
to you not at second-hand, by word of mouth, but
through the first-hand evidence of your own eyes!

tion of the troops on the Rhine and in Pannonia. The legates
are either the governors of the imperial provinces (*legati
Augusti propraetore*) or the commanders of the legions (*legati
Augusti legionis*).

Consecuti sunt ut absens quoque de absentibus nemini magis quam tibi crederes.

20. Iam te civium desideria revocabant, amoremque castrorum superabat caritas patriae. Iter inde placidum ac modestum et plane a pace redeuntis. 2 Nec vero ego in laudibus tuis ponam, quod adventum tuum non pater quisquam, non maritus expavit: adfectata aliis castitas, tibi ingenita et innata, 3 interque ea quae imputare non possis. Nullus in exigendis vehiculis tumultus, nullum circa hospitia fastidium; annona quae ceteris; ad hoc comitatus accinctus et parens. Diceres magnum aliquem ducem ac te potissimum ad exercitus ire: adeo nihil aut certe parum intererat inter imperatorem factum 4 et futurum. Quam dissimilis nuper alterius principis transitus! si tamen transitus ille, non populatio fuit, cum abactus hospitium[1] exsereret, omniaque dextera laevaque perusta et attrita, ut si vis aliqua vel ipsi illi barbari quos fugiebat inciderent. Persuadendum provinciis erat illud iter Domitiani fuisse, non princi- 5 pis. Itaque non tam pro tua gloria quam pro utilitate communi edicto subiecisti, quid in utrumque vestrum esset impensum. Adsuescat imperator cum imperio calculum ponere; sic exeat sic redeat

---

[1] abactus hospicium exereret *M, quod tuetur Haupt*: exerceret *codex deterior.*

---

[1] Cf. 5. 2, and note.

It was also their good fortune that when you were not with them you trusted no man's judgement of them but your own.

20. But now your people's prayers were calling you home; affection for your country heard them, and love of army life had to stand aside. Your journey was quiet and undemanding, truly that of one returning from a settled peace. It is not for me to call it a virtue in you if neither father nor husband dreaded your approach; others have made a point of cultivating moral purity, but in you it is natural and inborn, and not something to be counted to your credit. Carriages were requisitioned without fuss, no difficulties were raised over lodgings, rations were the same for all, and your staff was alert and disciplined. It might have been some great general, most likely yourself, travelling to join his army,[1] for there was no difference, or practically none, between the high authority you held then and what it was to be. It was not long since another Emperor had passed that way[2] in very different fashion, and his progress was better called a plundering foray, when houses were forcibly emptied to provide lodgings, and right and left the land was burnt and trampled as if struck by some disaster or the very barbarian hordes from whom he fled. The provinces had to be convinced it was only Domitian, and not every emperor who travelled in this fashion, and so you published a statement contrasting his expenditure with your own. Here your chief concern was the public interest and not your reputation, for an emperor must

[2] Domitian, returning from the Suebian–Sarmatic war, in December 92.

tamquam rationem redditurus; edicat quid absump-
6 serit. Ita fiet ut non absumat quod pudeat edicere.
Praeterea futuri principes, velint nolint, sciant:
"Tanti ⟨. . ., tanti⟩[1] tuum constat", propositisque
duobus exemplis meminerint perinde coniecturam
de moribus suis homines esse facturos, prout hoc vel
illud elegerint.

21. Nonne his tot tantisque meritis novos aliquos
honores, novos titulos merebare? At tu etiam patris
patriae recusabas. Quam longa nobis cum modestia
2 tua pugna, quam tarde vicimus! Nomen illud, quod
alii primo statim principatus die ut imperatoris et
Caesaris receperunt, tu usque eo distulisti, donec tu
quoque, beneficiorum tuorum parcissimus aestimator,
3 iam te mereri fatereris. Itaque soli omnium contigit tibi, ut pater patriae esses ante quam fieres.
Eras enim in animis in iudiciis nostris, nec publicae
pietatis intererat quid vocarere, nisi quod ingrata
sibi videbatur, si te imperatorem potius vocaret et
4 Caesarem, cum patrem experiretur. Quod quidem
nomen qua benignitate qua indulgentia exerces! ut
cum civibus tuis quasi cum liberis parens vivis! ut
reversus imperator, qui privatus exieras, agnoscis
agnosceris! Eosdem nos eundem te putas, par
omnibus et hoc tantum ceteris maior quod melior.

---

[1] tanti tuum constat *M* : *lacunam indicat Mynors addito* tanti.

---

[1] The text is very uncertain.
[2] 57. 5 shows that Trajan already had the title of *pater patriae* before the consular elections of 98.
[3] Pliny is doubtless thinking of Domitian, but the only emperor whose inscriptions show this title from the start is Nerva.

learn to balance accounts with his empire, to go abroad and return with the knowledge that he must publish his expenses and account for his movements, so that he will not spend what he is ashamed to make known to all. Moreover your successors will be obliged willy-nilly to know the cost of your respective journeys[1] and with both examples before them must realize that they will be judged according to which they elect to follow.

21. Although your many outstanding merits surely called for you to assume some new title and honour, you refused the title of Father of your country,[2] and it was only after a prolonged struggle between us and your modesty that in the end you were persuaded. Others[3] accepted that title from the start along with that of Emperor and Caesar, on the first day of their principate, but you waved it away until even in your own grudging estimate of your services, you had to admit it was your due. Thus you alone have been Father of the country in fact before you were in name. In our hearts, in our minds we knew you as this; the title made no difference to the devotion of your people, except for our feeling of ingratitude if we addressed you only as Emperor and Caesar when we felt we had a Father in you. And now that you bear the name, how kind and considerate you show yourself, living with your subjects as a father with his children! You left us as an ordinary citizen, you return as emperor, knowing your subjects as you are known to them; in your thoughts we have not changed, nor in ours have you; you are one among us all, the greatest of us simply because you are the best.

22. Ac primum qui dies ille, quo exspectatus desideratusque urbem tuam ingressus es! Iam hoc ipsum, quod ingressus es, quam mirum laetumque! Nam priores invehi et importari solebant, non dico quadriiugo curru et albentibus equis sed umeris

2 hominum, quod adrogantius erat. Tu sola corporis proceritate elatior aliis et excelsior, non de patientia nostra quendam triumphum, sed de superbia principum egisti. Ergo non aetas quemquam non valetudo, non sexus retardavit, quo minus oculos insolito

3 spectaculo impleret. Te parvuli noscere, ostentare iuvenes, mirari senes, aegri quoque neglecto medentium imperio ad conspectum tui quasi ad salutem sanitatemque prorepere. Inde alii se satis vixisse te viso te recepto, alii nunc magis esse vivendum praedicabant. Feminas etiam tunc fecunditatis suae maxima voluptas subiit, cum cernerent cui principi cives, cui imperatori milites peperissent.

4 Videres referta tecta ac laborantia, ac ne eum quidem vacantem locum qui non nisi suspensum et instabile vestigium caperet, oppletas undique vias angustumque tramitem relictum tibi, alacrem hinc atque inde populum, ubique par gaudium paremque

5 clamorem. Tam aequalis ab omnibus ex adventu tuo laetitia percepta est, quam omnibus venisti; quae tamen ipsa cum ingressu tuo crevit, ac prope in singulos gradus aucta est.

23. Gratum erat cunctis, quod senatum osculo

---

[1] Late summer 99; the occasion marked by the absence of Silius Italicus (*Ep.* III. 7. 6–7).

22. Now first of all, think of the day when you entered your city,[1] so long awaited and so much desired! The very method of your entry won delight and surprise, for your predecessors chose to be borne, or carried in, not satisfied even to be drawn by four white horses in a triumphal carriage, but lifted up on human shoulders in their overbearing pride. You towered above us only because of your own splendid physique; your triumph did not rest on our humiliation, won as it was over imperial arrogance. Thus neither age, health nor sex held your subjects back from feasting their eyes on this unexpected sight: small children learned who you were, young people pointed you out, old men admired: even the sick disregarded their doctors' orders and dragged themselves out for a glimpse of you as if this could restore their health. There were some who cried that they had lived long enough now they had seen and welcomed you, others that this was a reason for longer life. Women rejoiced as never before to bear children now that they knew they had brought forth citizens and soldiers to live and serve under your rule and command. Roofs could be seen sagging under the crowds they bore, not a vacant inch of ground was visible except under a foot poised to step, streets were packed on both sides leaving only a narrow passage for you, on every side the excited populace, cheers and rejoicing everywhere. All felt the same joy at your coming, when you were coming to be the same for all, joy which could still grow as you moved forward, and (one might say) swell with every step.

23. There was general delight when you embraced

371

exciperes, ut dimissus osculo fueras; gratum, quod equestris ordinis decora honore nominum sine monitore signares; gratum, quod tantum ⟨non⟩[1] ultro clientibus salutatis quasdam familiaritatis notas 2 adderes; gratius tamen, quod sensim et placide et quantum respectantium turba pateretur incederes, quod occursantium populus te quoque, et immo maxime artaret,[2] quod primo statim die latus tuum 3 crederes omnibus. Neque enim stipatus satellitum manu sed circumfusus undique nunc senatus, nunc equestris ordinis flore, prout alterutrum frequentiae genus invaluisset, silentes quietosque lictores tuos subsequebare; nam milites nihil a plebe habitu 4 tranquillitate modestia differebant. Ubi vero coepisti Capitolium ascendere, quam laeta omnibus adoptionis tuae recordatio, quam peculiare gaudium eorum, qui te primi eodem loco salutaverant imperatorem! Quin etiam deum ipsum tuum ⟨patrem⟩[3] praecipuam voluptatem operis sui percepisse credi- 5 derim. Ut quidem isdem vestigiis institisti, quibus parens tuus ingens illud deorum prolaturus arcanum, quae circumstantium gaudia, quam recens clamor, quam similis illi dies, qui hunc diem genuit! ut plena altaribus angusta victimis cuncta, ut in unius salutem collata omnium vota, cum sibi se ac liberis suis intellegerent precari, quae pro te precarentur!

[1] tantum ultro *M*: non *add. edd*: tantus ultro *Brakman*.
[2] artaret *edd*: astaret *M*.
[3] patrem *add. Beroaldus ante* tuum: *om. M*.

the members of the Senate, as they had embraced you when you went away, when you singled out the leading knights for the honour of being greeted by name without an official intermediary, when you not only took the first step in greeting your clients but added some touches of friendliness, and still greater delight when you moved slowly and quietly forward where the crowds of spectators fell back, letting yourself be jostled as one of the people, though in fact the crowds pressed thickest where you were. On that very first day you made yourself accessible to all, for no party of satellites attended you; you moved in the midst of the élite of the senators or knights, as the numbers of either party prevailed as they gathered round you, and your lictors quietly and courteously cleared your path. As for the soldiers present, they differed from the civilians in neither dress, propriety, nor discipline. But when you proceeded to mount the Capitol, how gladly everyone remembered your adoption,[1] and what special joy it was for those who had first hailed you as *Imperator* in that very place! But the greatest pleasure of all, I fancy, was that of the god who was your father in his own creation. Above all, as you trod in the same steps as your father when he prepared to reveal the mighty secret of the gods, how the crowd rejoiced with fresh outbursts of cheering, as this day recalled that other which had brought it into being! Everywhere there were altars, but still not enough for their victims; everyone's prayers were for your safety alone, since each man knew they would be answered for himself and his children if they were granted for you.

[1] Cf. 8.

6 Inde tu in palatium quidem, sed eo vultu ea moderatione, ut si privatam domum peteres; ceteri ad penates suos quisque iteraturus gaudii fidem, ubi nulla necessitas gaudendi est.

24. Onerasset alium eius modi introitus; tu cotidie admirabilior et melior, talis denique quales alii principes futuros se tantum pollicentur. Solum ergo te commendat augetque temporis spatium: iunxisti enim ac miscuisti res diversissimas, securitatem olim 2 imperantis et incipientis pudorem. Non tu civium amplexus ad pedes tuos deprimis, nec osculum manu reddis; manet imperatori quae prior oris humanitas, dexterae verecundia.[1] Incedebas pedibus, incedis; laetabaris labore, laetaris, eademque illa omnia circa 3 te, nihil ⟨in⟩[2] ipso te fortuna mutavit. Liberum est ingrediente per publicum principe subsistere occurrere, comitari praeterire: ambulas inter nos non quasi contingas, et copiam tui non ut imputes facis. Haeret lateri tuo quisquis accessit, finemque sermoni 4 suus cuique pudor, non tua superbia facit. Regimur quidem a te et subiecti tibi, sed quemadmodum legibus sumus: nam et illae cupiditates nostras libidinesque moderantur, nobiscum tamen et inter nos versantur. Emines excellis ut Honor, ut Potestas, quae super homines quidem, hominum 5 sunt tamen. Ante te principes fastidio nostri et

[1] dextrae verecundia *Cuspinianus*: *om. M.*
[2] in *add. Lipsius*: *om. M.*

Then you walked to the palace, with the same modest demeanour as if it had been a private house, and everyone returned home to repeat the sincere expression of a happiness which was wholly spontaneous.

24. Such an entry would have overwhelmed another; but you became daily more admirable, more perfect, such a prince in fact as others can only promise to be. You alone have gained and grown in reputation through passage of time, for you have two extremes combined and blended in your person, a beginner's modesty and the assurance of one long accustomed to command. You do not direct your subjects to grovel at your feet, returning a kiss with no more than a proffered hand; your lips keep their old courtesy now you are emperor, your hand respects its proper use. You used to go on foot before, you still do now; you delighted in hard work, and still delight; though fortune has changed all around you, she changed nothing in yourself. When the prince moves among his subjects they are free to stand still or approach him, to accompany him or pass ahead, for you do not walk in our midst to confer a benefit by your presence, nor put us in your debt if we enjoy your company. Anyone who approaches you can stay at your side, and conversation lasts till it is ended by his discretion, not by any loftiness of yours. We are ruled by you and subject to you, but no more than we are to the laws, for these too must regulate our desires and passions, always with us and among us. You shine out in splendour like Honour, like Sovereignty, for these are always above mortal men and yet inseparable from them. Previous

quodam aequalitatis metu usum pedum amiserant.
Illos ergo umeri cervicesque servorum super ora
nostra, te fama te gloria te civium pietas, te libertas
super ipsos principes vehunt; te ad sidera tollit
humus ista communis et confusa principis vestigia.

25. Non vereor, patres conscripti, ne longior
videar, cum sit maxime optandum, ut ea pro quibus
aguntur principi gratiae multa sint; quae quidem
reverentius fuerit integra inlibataque cogitationibus
vestris reservari quam carptim breviterque per-
stringi, quia fere sequitur ut illa quidem de quibus
2 taceas, tanta quanta sunt esse videantur—nisi vero
leviter attingi placet locupletatas tribus datumque
congiarium populo et datum totum, cum donativi
partem milites accepissent. An mediocris animi est
his potius repraesentare, quibus magis negari potest?
quamquam in hac quoque diversitate aequalitatis
ratio servata est. Aequati sunt enim populo milites
eo quod partem sed priores, populus militibus quod
3 posterior sed totum statim accepit. Enimvero qua

---

¹ These were (1) the *frumentationes* given monthly from the
fiscus to the *plebs urbana frumentaria*, on the basis of a fixed
number of 200,000 recipients; names could be added only
when there were vacancies (cf. 25. 3). Trajan added 5,000
children to the list (28. 4). (2) the *congiarium*, money dis-
tributions to the *populus* at irregular intervals. Domitian
in his early years gave 3 *congiaria* of 225 denarii a head.
Nerva's lavish donations look like bribery, and Trajan paid
out 650 denarii a head, a vast sum. See Syme, *JRS* XX.
Note that Pliny says nothing about the alimentary system
instituted by Nerva and revised by Trajan in 101 (S. 435–6,

rulers in their scorn for us, and, it may be, through fear of being brought down to our level, had lost the use of their legs; carried on the shoulders and bowed backs of slaves they rose above our heads. But you are borne aloft by your own renown and glory, by freedom and your subjects' love, far above those self-same rulers; you are lifted to the heavens by the very ground we all tread, where your imperial footsteps are mingled with our own.

25. I am not afraid of seeming long-winded, Conscript Fathers, since nothing is more desirable than that we should have much to offer thanks for to our prince. And rather than run quickly through a selection of his merits, we should show more respect if we left everything unspoken and implicit in our hearts: for what is left untouched is more likely to be judged at its true worth. Nevertheless, I should like to say a word about his gifts to enrich the urban population,[1] the largess distributed to civilians in its entirety, whereas the military received only half of their bonus.[2] This is sure indication of no ordinary spirit—to make a donation to those who could more easily have been refused—though in spite of this distinction, the rule of parity was not neglected, and the army was put on the same footing as the civilians in that it received its half-donation first, while the people who had the whole at once took second place. How generous

the " Veleian Table "); perhaps this was still being reorganized when the speech was delivered.

[2] The *donativum* to each soldier, paid in cash. Nerva had evidently paid it in full on his accession, or Pliny would not make much of Trajan's policy.

benignitate divisum est, quantaeque tibi curae fuit
ne quis expers liberalitatis tuae fieret! Datum est
his qui post edictum tuum in locum erasorum subditi
fuerant, aequatique sunt ceteris illi etiam quibus non
4 erat promissum. Negotiis aliquis valetudine alius,
hic mari ille fluminibus distinebatur: exspectatus
est, provisumque, ne quis aeger ne quis occupatus
ne quis denique longe fuisset; veniret quisque cum
5 vellet, veniret quisque cum posset. Magnificum,
Caesar, et tuum disiunctissimas terras munificentiae
ingenio velut admovere, immensaque spatia liberalitate contrahere, intercedere casibus occursare fortunae, atque ope adniti, ne quis e plebe Romana
dante congiarium te hominem se magis sentiret
fuisse quam civem.

26. Adventante congiarii die observare principis
egressum in publicum, insidere vias examina infantium futurusque populus solebat. Labor parentibus erat ostentare parvulos impositosque cervicibus
2 adulantia verba blandasque voces edocere: redde-
bant illi quae monebantur, ac plerique inritis precibus
surdas principis aures adstrepebant, ignarique quid
rogassent quid non impetrassent, donec plane scirent
3 differebantur. Tu ne rogari quidem sustinuisti et
quamquam laetissimum oculis tuis esset conspectu
Romanae sobolis impleri, omnes tamen ante quam
te viderent adirentve, recipi incidi iussisti, ut iam
inde ab infantia parentem publicum munere educa-

you were in your distribution, and what care you took
to include everyone in your bounty! It was bestowed even on those whose names were listed after
your edict, in place of some crossed off, while others
ranked equal with the rest though not eligible at first.
One man might be delayed by illness or his personal
affairs, another held up by rivers or sea, but his share
awaited him, to ensure that no one was left out for
being sick, or too busy, or too far away. Everyone
was to come when he wished or when he could. It
was your special distinction, Caesar, to join, as it
were, far distant lands by the ingenuity of your
generosity, to contract vast spaces in the exercise
of your liberality, to overcome hazards and oppose
fortune, to use all your resources, in fact, to ensure
that as regards your bounty every humble Roman
should feel he was born a citizen as much as a man.

26. On the day for the distribution it had been the
custom for swarms of children, the populace of the
future, to watch for the emperor's public appearance
and line his path. Every parent's concern was to
show his little ones mounted on his shoulders, to teach
them flattering words and fawning phrases, while
they repeated their lessons, their vain pleas mostly
falling on the emperor's deaf ears, to be brushed
aside in their ignorance of what they asked and what
was refused, until the day would come when they
would understand all too well. You, however, would
permit no requests. Though your eyes might be
gladdened by the sight of the rising generation of
Rome, you gave orders that every child must be
admitted and enrolled before seeing or approaching
you, so that henceforward reared on your bounty

tionis experirentur, crescerent de tuo qui crescerent
tibi, alimentisque tuis ad stipendia tua pervenirent,
tantumque omnes uni tibi quantum parentibus suis
4 quisque deberent. Recte, Caesar, quod spem Romani nominis sumptibus tuis suscipis. Nullum est
enim magno principe immortalitatemque merituro
impendii genus dignius, quam quod erogatur in
5 posteros. Locupletes ad tollendos liberos ingentia
praemia et pares poenae cohortantur, pauperibus
6 educandi una ratio est bonus princeps. Hic fiducia
sui procreatos nisi larga manu fovet auget amplectitur, occasum imperii occasum rei publicae
accelerat, frustraque proceres plebe neglecta ut
desectum corpore caput nutaturumque instabili
7 pondere tuetur. Facile est coniectare quod perce-
peris gaudium, cum te parentum liberorum, senum infantium[1] clamor exciperet. Haec prima parvulorum
civium vox aures tuas imbuit, quibus tu daturus
alimenta hoc maximum praestitisti, ne rogarent.

27. Super omnia est tamen quod talis es, ut sub te
liberos tollere libeat expediat. Nemo iam parens
filio nisi fragilitatis humanae vices horret, nec inter
insanabiles morbos principis ira numeratur. Magnum quidem est educandi incitamentum tollere
liberos in spem alimentorum, in spem congiariorum;
maius tamen in spem libertatis, in spem securitatis.
2 Atque adeo nihil largiatur princeps dum nihil auferat,
non alat dum non occidat; nec deerunt qui filios

---

[1] infantium *H*: infantium puerorum *X*.

---

[1] By the *Lex Iulia de maritandis ordinibus* of 18 B.C. and
the *Lex Papia Poppaea* of A.D. 9.

from their earliest days, all should know you as the
Father of the people; they should grow at your expense while they were growing up to serve you, pass
from a child's allowance at your hands to a soldier's
pay, each owing as much to you as to his own parents.
You were right, Caesar, to cherish at your expense
the future of the name of Rome. No expenditure is
so worthy of a great prince destined for immortality
as what is disbursed for posterity. The rich are encouraged to rear children by high rewards and comparable penalties:[1] the poor have only one induce-
ment—a good prince. Unless he makes generous
provision for the children born through his people's
confidence in him, unless he cherishes them with
loving care, he hastens the downfall of empire and
realm; if he neglects his poorer subjects he protects
in vain his leading citizens, who will become a head
cut from a body, top-heavy, soon to fall. It is easy
to imagine your pleasure when the cheers of fathers
and children, old and young, rang in your ears—the
first you heard of your youngest subjects, on whom
you had bestowed something even greater than their
allowance: the right to receive it unasked.

27. Above all, you are a prince whose reign makes
it both pleasure and profit to rear children. No
father now need fear more for his son than the
hazards of human frailty—among fatal illnesses he
need not count his emperor's wrath. There is indeed great encouragement to have children in the
promise of allowances and donations, but greater still
when there is hope of security and freedom from fear.
It may be that a ruler gives nothing, supports no one,
but so long as he neither takes nor destroys he will

concupiscant. Contra largiatur et auferat, alat et occidat: ne ille id iam[1] brevi tempore effecerit, ut omnes non posterorum modo sed sui parentumque 3 paeniteat. Quocirca nihil magis in tota tua liberalitate laudaverim, quam quod congiarium das de tuo, alimenta de tuo, neque a te liberi civium ut ferarum 4 catuli sanguine et caedibus nutriuntur; quodque gratissimum est accipientibus, sciunt dari sibi quod nemini sit ereptum, locupletatisque tam multis pauperiorem esse factum principem tantum. Quamquam ne hunc quidem: nam cuius est quidquid est omnium, tantum ipse quantum omnes habet.

28. Alio me vocat numerosa gloria tua. Alio autem? quasi vero iam satis veneratus miratusque sim quod tantam pecuniam profudisti, non ut flagitii tibi conscius ab insectatione eius averteres famam, nec ut tristes hominum maestosque sermones laetiore 2 materia detineres. Nullam congiario culpam, nullam alimentis crudelitatem redemisti, nec tibi bene faciendi fuit causa ut quae male feceras impune fecisses. Amor impendio isto, non venia quaesita est, populusque Romanus obligatus a tribunali tuo, 3 non exoratus recessit. Obtulisti enim congiarium gaudentibus gaudens securusque securis; quodque antea principes ad odium sui leniendum tumentibus

---

[1] id iam *Mynors, alii alia*: in tam *M*.

not lack subjects who desire sons. On the other hand, if he gives and then takes away, supports and then destroys, all too soon he will make men regret they had children, regret even that they had parents and are alive themselves. And so nothing in your generosity commands my admiration so much as the fact that these donations and allowances are paid from your own purse, so that the nation's children are not fed like wild beasts' cubs on blood and slaughter; and what is most welcome to the recipient is his knowledge that no one has been robbed to provide for him, that there is one alone who is the poorer for so many thus enriched—his prince. And perhaps not even he—for anyone with a share in a common wealth is as rich or as poor as the whole.

28. Your many claims for recognition beckon me elsewhere—but no; I have not paid admiring homage to the fact that you poured out these generous sums in no consciousness of crime committed, no desire to avert notoriety's pursuit, nor to provide more cheerful topics to divert grim suspicions from men's tongues. No fault in you had to be redeemed by your donation, no act of cruelty bought off by allowances; your benefactions were not inspired by hope of impunity for your misdeeds. By this expenditure you sought the affection, not the forgiveness of your subjects; the people of Rome heard no entreaties at the tribunal, but stepped down conscious only of their debt to you. For your donation was gladly offered and as gladly received, without apprehension on either side; what your predecessors had thrown as a sop to the surging anger of the populace, to appease the general hatred of them-

plebis animis obiectabant, id tu tam innocens populo
4 dedisti, quam populus accepit. Paulo minus, patres
conscripti, quinque milia ingenuorum fuerunt, quae
liberalitas principis nostri conquisivit invenit adscivit.
5 Hi subsidium bellorum ornamentum pacis publicis
sumptibus aluntur, patriamque non ut patriam
tantum, verum ut altricem amare condiscunt; ex
his castra ex his tribus replebuntur, ex his quandoque
6 nascentur, quibus alimentis opus non sit. Dent tibi,
Caesar, aetatem di quam mereris, serventque
animum quem dederunt: et quanto maiorem infantium turbam iterum atque iterum iubebis incidi!
7 Augetur enim cotidie et crescit, non quia cariores
parentibus liberi, sed quia principi cives. Dabis
congiaria si voles, praestabis alimenta si voles: illi
tamen propter te nascuntur.

29. Instar ego perpetui congiarii reor adfluentiam
annonae. Huius aliquando cura Pompeio non minus
addidit gloriae quam pulsus ambitus campo, exactus
hostis mari, Oriens triumphis Occidensque lustratus.
2 Nec vero ille civilius quam parens noster auctoritate
consilio fide reclusit vias portus patefecit, itinera
terris litoribus mare litora mari reddidit, diversasque

---

¹ Pompey was given charge of the *annona* for five years in
57 B.C. (Cic. *ad Att.* IV. 1. 6). He passed the *Lex Pompeia de
ambitu* in 52; rid the seas of pirates in 67; celebrated a triumph
in 81 B.C., for quelling the " Marians " in Africa; another in 71
after overcoming Sertorius and his successor in Spain; and a
third in 61 after settling the affairs of Asia.

² Trajan was actively engaged on public works from the
start of his reign; *e.g.* repairs to the Via Appia, Via Aemilia,
and Via Puteolana; the harbours at Ostia, Terracina, and
Ancona (cf. *Ep.* VI. 31. 15 for Centum Cellae, under construction in 106); and in 110 the Decemnovium which crossed the

selves, you gave freely to the people, as innocent in your giving as they were in receiving. Nearly five thousand free-born children, Conscript Fathers, were sought out and found, to be entered on the lists through the generosity of their prince, to safeguard the state in war and adorn it in peace, supported by their country while they learn to love her not only as their homeland but as a nurse. The army and citizen body will be completed by their numbers, and they will have children one day whom they will support themselves without any need of allowances. Let the gods only grant you, Caesar, the long life which you deserve and preserve the spirit you owe to them, and the lists of children entered at your bidding will ever multiply! These grow increasingly day by day, not so much because parents care more for children, as because every citizen is cared for by his prince. Go on with subsidies and allowances if it is your wish; but the true reason for these births lies in yourself.

29. Now for the corn-supply, equivalent in its generosity, I believe, to a perpetual subsidy. Nothing so much as this[1] once brought Pompey such great honour, though he swept bribery from elections, rid the high seas of pirates, and strode in triumph across East and West. Herein he proved himself no finer citizen than our Father, who in his wisdom and authority and devotion to his people has opened roads, built harbours, created routes overland, let the sea into the shore and moved the shore out to sea,[2]

Pontine marshes from Forum Appii to Terracina. Pliny, however, speaks here only in general terms. Cf. *Ep.* X. 18. 3 and note.

gentes ita commercio miscuit, ut quod genitum esset
3 usquam, id apud omnes natum videretur. Nonne
cernere datur ut sine ullius iniuria omnis usibus
nostris annus exuberet? Quippe non ut ex hostico
raptae perituraeque in horreis messes nequiquam
4 quiritantibus sociis auferuntur. Devehunt ipsi quod
terra genuit, quod sidus aluit, quod annus tulit, nec
novis indictionibus pressi ad vetera tributa deficiunt;
5 emit fiscus quidquid videtur emere. Inde copiae,
inde annona de qua inter licentem vendentemque
conveniat, inde hic satietas nec fames usquam.

30. Aegyptus alendis augendisque seminibus ita
gloriata est, ut nihil imbribus caeloque deberet,
siquidem proprio semper amne perfusa, nec alio
genere aquarum solita pinguescere, quam quas ipsa
devexerat, tantis segetibus induebatur, ut cum
feracissimis terris quasi numquam cessura certaret.
2 Haec inopina siccitate usque iniuriam sterilitatis
exaruit, quia piger Nilus cunctanter alveo sese ac
languide extulerat, ingentibus quidem tunc quoque
3 ille fluminibus, tamen conferendus. Hinc pars
magna terrarum, mergi repararique amne consueta,
alto pulvere incanduit. Frustra tunc Aegyptus
nubila optavit caelumque respexit, cum ipse fecunditatis parens contractior et exilior isdem ubertatem

---

[1] The earliest reference to *indictiones*, taxes exacted from
the provinces at irregular intervals to meet special needs of
Rome and the army; here contrasted with the regular *tributa*.
[2] For Egypt, cf. Pliny, *NH* V. 47 ff. and XVIII. 167.

and linked far distant peoples by trade so that
natural products in any place now seem to belong to
all. It is plain to see that every year can abun-
dantly supply our needs—and without harm to
anyone. Harvests are not snatched as if from enemy
soil to perish in our granaries, carried off from allies
who lament in vain; instead, these bring of their
own accord the produce of their soil, the year's harvest nurtured by their climate; unburdened by fresh
impositions[1] they can meet long-standing obligations,
and the imperial exchequer pays openly for its purchases. Hence these provisions and the corn-supply,
with prices agreed between buyer and seller; hence,
without causing starvation elsewhere, we have plenty
here in Rome.

30. It was once Egypt's[2] boast that she owned
nothing to rain and weather to nurture and mature
the seeds in her soil; watered as she always was by
her own river and accustomed to a fertility depen-
dent only on the water flowing through her, she was
clad in crops so rich that she could rival the most fertile lands with never a thought that this could cease.
Then she was struck by sudden disaster, dried and
burnt up, left well-nigh barren, when the Nile turned
lazy, sluggish and reluctant to stir out of its bed,
so that though still one of the world's great rivers it
could not now be thought incomparable. Thus a
great area of land which used to be flooded and refreshed by the river became a scorching furnace of
thick dust. All in vain the native Egyptian prayed
for rain-clouds and watched the heavens, now that
the author of productiveness had shrunk and
dwindled and confined the fertile regions within the

eius angustiis quibus abundantiam suam cohibuisset.
4 Neque enim solum vagus ille ⟨cum⟩[1] expandatur
amnis intra usurpata semper collium substiterat
atque haeserat, sed supino etiam ac detinenti solo
non placido se mollique lapsu refugum abstulerat
necdum satis umentes terras addiderat arentibus.
5 Igitur inundatione, id est ubertate, regio fraudata
sic opem Caesaris invocavit, ut solet amnem suum,
nec longius illi adversorum fuit spatium quam dum
nuntiat: tam velox, Caesar, potestas tua est, tamque
in omnia pariter intenta bonitas et accincta, ut
tristius aliquid saeculo tuo passis ad remedium
salutemque sufficiat ut scias.

31. Omnibus equidem gentibus fertiles annos
gratasque terras precor; crediderim tamen per hunc
Aegypti statum tuas fortunam vires experiri,
tuamque vigilantiam spectare voluisse. Nam cum
omnia ubique secunda merearis, nonne manifestum
est, si quid adversi cadat, tuis laudibus tuisque
virtutibus materiam campumque praesterni, cum
2 secunda felices, adversa magnos probent? Percre-
bruerat antiquitus urbem nostram nisi opibus
Aegypti ali sustentarique non posse. Superbiebat
ventosa et insolens natio, quod victorem quidem
populum pasceret tamen quodque in suo flumine in
suis navibus vel abundantia nostra vel fames esset.
3 Refundimus Nilo suas copias: recepit frumenta quae
miserat, deportatasque messes revexit. Discat igitur
Aegyptus credatque experimento, non alimenta se

---

[1] cum *add. corrector cod. Vat.: om. M.*

narrow limits of its own fullness. For not only did
the Nile (which normally spreads far afield) stop short
of and fall below the level it usually occupied in the
hills, but even on level ground which should have
retained them, its waters rapidly retreated instead
of maintaining their usual even, gentle flow; and the
soil was left insufficiently soaked, to be added to the
parched areas. Therefore the country, denied
the flood which is its fertility, looked to Caesar for
aid instead of to their river; and no sooner had he
heard their appeal than their troubles were at an
end. So prompt is your power, Caesar, so prepared
and ready for all alike your goodness of heart, that
if any of your subjects suffers misfortune he has only
to tell you to find help and security in you.

31. It is of course my own prayer that every nation
shall enjoy fruitful seasons and fertile soil, but I
should like to think that Fortune chose Egypt's
plight to test your resources and witness your vigilance. Though you deserve prosperity everywhere,
in everything, chance adversity clearly provides a
field of opportunity for your gifts and talents; for
prosperity proves men to be fortunate, while it is
adversity which makes them great. For long it was
generally believed that Rome could only be fed and
maintained with Egyptian aid, so that this vain and
presumptuous nation used to boast that they must
still feed their conquerors, that their river and their
ships ensured our plenty or our want. Now we have
returned the Nile its riches, sent back the corn we
received; it has had to take home the harvests it
used to dispatch across the sea. Let this be a lesson
to Egypt; let her learn by experience that her

nobis sed tributa praestare; sciat se non esse populo
4 Romano necessariam, et tamen serviat. Post haec,
si volet, Nilus amet alveum suum et fluminis modum
servet: nihil hoc ad urbem ac ne ad Aegyptum
quidem, nisi ut inde navigia inania et vacua et
similia redeuntibus, hinc plena et onusta et qualia
solent venire mittantur, conversoque munere maris
hinc potius venti ferentes et brevis cursus optentur.
5 Mirum, Caesar, videretur, si desidem Aegyptum
cessantemque Nilum non sensisset urbis annona;
quae tuis opibus, tua cura usque illuc redundavit, ut
simul probaretur et nos Aegypto posse et nobis
6 Aegyptum carere non posse. Actum erat de
fecundissima gente, si libera fuisset; pudebat
sterilitatis insolitae nec minus erubescebat fame
quam torquebatur, cum pariter a te necessitatibus
eius pudorique subventum est. Stupebant agricolae
plena horrea quae non ipsi refersissent, quibus de
campis illa subvecta messis, quave in Aegypti parte
alius amnis. Ita beneficio tuo nec maligna tellus, et
obsequens Nilus Aegypto quidem saepe, sed gloriae
nostrae numquam largior fluxit.

32. Quam nunc iuvat provincias omnes in fidem
nostram dicionemque venisse, postquam contigit
princeps, qui terrarum fecunditatem nunc huc nunc

business is not to allow us food but to pay a proper tribute; let her realize that she is not indispensable to the people of Rome although she is their servant. Henceforth, if it wishes, the Nile can stick to its bed and content itself with a river's proper form—it will make no difference to Rome, nor to Egypt either, except that ships will leave her country cargoless and empty, as once they used to return, while from Rome they will sail filled with the cargo they once brought to us. The sea's function thus reversed, it will be from here that a following wind and a shortened voyage are the object of the sailors' prayer. It might seem a miracle, Caesar, that the city's corn-supply had been unaffected by Egypt's shortcomings and the defection of the Nile, but thanks to your vigilance and bounty it has been dispensed so freely that two points are proved: we have no need of Egypt, but Egypt must always need us. She is finished—that country which might have been so productive had she been free. Humiliated by her strange sterility she blushed for her famine as much as she suffered thereby, when your intervention not only answered her needs but also pricked her self-esteem. Her farmers stared in amazement at granaries filled by other hands than theirs: what fields had produced such a harvest? Where in Egypt was there another river? Thus by your gracious aid the earth has not begrudged her fruits, and if the Nile has often shown itself more propitious to Egypt, it has never flowed more generously for our glory.

32. What a benefit it is for every province to have come under our rule and protection when we are blessed with a prince who could switch earth's bounty

illuc, ut tempus et necessitas posceret, transferret referretque, qui diremptam mari gentem ut partem aliquam populi plebisque Romanae aleret ac tueretur!

2 Et caelo quidem numquam benignitas tanta, ut omnes simul terras uberet foveatque: hic omnibus pariter si non sterilitatem, at mala sterilitatis exturbat, hic si non fecunditatem, at bona fecunditatis importat, hic alternis commeatibus Orientem Occidentemque conectit, ut quae ferunt quaeque expetunt opes [1] gentes, discant invicem capiant, quanto libertati discordi servientibus sit utilius unum esse cui

3 serviant. Quippe discretis quidem bonis omnium sua cuiusque ad singulos mala, sociatis autem atque permixtis singulorum mala ad neminem, ad omnes omnium bona pertinent. Sed sive terris divinitas quaedam, sive aliquis amnibus genius, et solum illud et flumen ipsum precor, ut hac principis benignitate contentum molli gremio semina recondat, multi-

4 plicata restituat. Non quidem reposcimus fenus: putet tamen esse solvendum, fallacemque unius anni fidem omnibus annis omnibusque postea saeculis tanto magis quia non exigimus excuset.

33. Satis factum qua civium qua sociorum utilitatibus. Visum est spectaculum inde non enerve nec fluxum, nec quod animos virorum molliret et frangeret, sed quod ad pulchra vulnera contemptumque mortis accenderet, cum in servorum etiam noxiorumque corporibus amor laudis et cupido victoriae

2 cerneretur. Quam deinde in edendo liberalitatem,

---

[1] opes *M*: omnes *Puteolanus*.

here and there, as occasion and necessity require,
bringing aid and nourishment to a nation cut off by
the sea as if its people were numbered among the
humbler citizens of Rome! Even the heavens can
never prove so kind as to enrich and favour every
land alike; but he can banish everywhere the hardships if not the condition of sterility, and introduce
the benefits of fertility, if not fertility itself. He
can so join East and West by convoys that those
peoples who offer and those who need supplies can
learn and appreciate in their turn, after experienc-
ing licence and discord, how much they gain from
having one master to serve. Divide a common
property, and each individual must bear his own
losses; but where everything is jointly held, no one
suffers personal loss and all share in the common
wealth. Yet if there be divinities in earth and spirit-
powers in streams, this is my plea to the soil and
river of Egypt: ask no more of our prince's generosity, take the seed sowed in your soft embrace and
return it multiplied. We ask no interest, but remember that you have a debt to repay; redeem the
broken promise of a single year in all the years and
all the centuries to come, the more so as we are making no demands.

33. Citizens and allies alike had had their needs
supplied. Next came a public entertainment—
nothing lax or dissolute to weaken and destroy the
manly spirit of his subjects, but one to inspire them
to face honourable wounds and look scorn on death,
by exhibiting love of glory and desire for victory
even in the persons of criminals and slaves. What
generosity went to provide this spectacle! and what

quam iustitiam exhibuit omni adfectione aut intactus
aut maior! Impetratum est quod postulabatur,
oblatum quod non postulabatur. Institit ultro et
ut concupisceremus admonuit, ac sic quoque plura
3 inopinata plura subita. Iam quam libera spectan-
tium studia, quam securus favor! Nemini impietas
ut solebat obiecta, quod odisset gladiatorem; nemo
e spectatore spectaculum factus miseras voluptates
4 unco et ignibus expiavit. Demens ille verique
honoris ignarus, qui crimina maiestatis in harena
colligebat, ac se despici et contemni, nisi etiam
gladiatores eius veneraremur, sibi male dici in illis,
suam divinitatem suum numen violari interpreta-
batur, cumque se idem quod deos, idem gladiatores
quod se putabat.

34. At tu Caesar, quam pulchrum spectaculum pro
illo nobis exsecrabili reddidisti! Vidimus delatorum
agmen[1] inductum, quasi grassatorum quasi latronum.
Non solitudinem illi, non iter sed templum sed forum
insederant; nulla iam testamenta secura, nullius
status certus; non orbitas, non liberi proderant.
2 Auxerat hoc malum partim ⟨. . . partim⟩[2] avaritia.
Advertisti oculos atque ut ante castris, ita postea

---

[1] agmen *Cuspinianus*: om. *M*.
[2] partim *M*: principum *Puteolanus*: partim *add. Mynors*:
lacuna nondum expleta.

---

[1] A further reference to Domitian.

impartiality the Emperor showed, unmoved as he was by personal feelings or else superior to them. Requests were granted, unspoken wishes were anticipated, and he did not hesitate to press us urgently to make fresh demands; yet still there was something new to surpass our dreams. How freely too the spectators could express their enthusiasm and show their preferences without fear! No one risked the old charge of impiety if he disliked a particular gladiator; no spectator found himself turned spectacle, dragged off by the hook to satisfy grim pleasures, or else cast to the flames! He [1] was a madman, blind to the true meaning of his position, who used the arena for collecting charges of high treason, who felt himself slighted and scorned if we failed to pay homage to his gladiators, taking any criticism of them to himself and seeing insults to his own godhead and divinity; who deemed himself the equal of the gods yet raised his gladiators to be his equal.

34. But what a splendid spectacle *you* showed us, Caesar, by contrast with that hateful scene! There we saw the informers marched in, like a band of robbers or brigands—only their haunts had not been at the roadside or in lonely spots, but in temple [2] and forum. No will was safe from them, no position secure; to be childless or a parent was equally of no avail. It had been a growing evil, partly through . . .,[3] partly through greed. Then you turned your attention to it, and peace was restored

---

[2] Possibly the Temple of Saturn is meant, *i.e.* the treasury. Cf. 36. 1.

[3] Some word is needed to express Domitian's fear or suspicion.

pacem foro reddidisti; excidisti intestinum malum
et provida severitate cavisti, ne fundata legibus
3 civitas eversa legibus videretur. Licet ergo cum
fortuna tum liberalitas tua visenda nobis praebuerit,
ut praebuit, nunc ingentia robora virorum et pares
animos, nunc immanitatem ferarum, nunc mansuetudinem incognitam, nunc secretas illas et arcanas
ac sub te primum communes opes, nihil tamen
gratius, nihil saeculo dignius, quam quod contigit
desuper intueri delatorum supina ora retortasque
4 cervices. Agnoscebamus et fruebamur, cum velut
piaculares publicae sollicitudinis victimae supra
sanguinem noxiorum ad lenta supplicia gravioresque
5 poenas ducerentur. Congesti sunt in navigia raptim
conquisita ac tempestatibus dediti: abirent fugerent
vastatas delationibus terras, ac si quem fluctus ac
procellae scopulis reservassent, hic nuda saxa et
inhospitale litus incoleret, ageret duram et anxiam
vitam, relictaque post tergum totius generis humani
securitate maereret.

35. Memoranda facies, delatorum classis per-
missa omnibus ventis, coactaque vela tempestatibus
pandere iratosque fluctus sequi, quoscumque in scopu-
los detulissent. Iuvabat prospectare statim a portu
sparsa navigia, et apud illud ipsum mare agere principi

to the forum as it had been to the army-camps. You cut out the canker in our midst; your stern providence ensured that a state founded on laws should not appear to perish through the laws' abuse. So although your high estate and generosity enabled you to present the spectacle we saw, first men whose spirit matched their mighty physique, then animals in their natural state of savagery and also tamed in unexpected degree, then the riches hitherto kept hidden in secret and now, in your reign, to be shared by all; yet nothing was so popular, nothing so fitting for our times as the opportunity we enjoyed of looking down at the informers at our feet, their heads forced back and faces upturned to meet our gaze. We knew them and rejoiced; like victims chosen to atone for the sufferings of their country, treading in the blood of the criminals before them, they were led to long-lasting punishment and more fearful retribution. Ships were hastily produced, and they were crowded on board and abandoned to the hazard of wind and weather. Well, let them go, and flee from the lands their informing had left desolate; and if the stormy sea casts anyone alive on the rocks, let him eke out a wretched existence on the bare crags of a hostile shore, and suffer in the knowledge that by his departure the entire human race is relieved of its cares.

35. The sight was unforgettable: a whole fleet of informers thrown on the mercy of every wind, forced to spread sail before the tempests, driven by the fury of the waves on to the rocks in their course. What joy for us to watch the ships scattered as soon as they left harbour, and on the very water's edge to render

gratias, qui clementia sua salva ultionem hominum
2 terrarumque dis maris commendasset. Quantum
diversitas temporum posset, tum maxime cognitum
est, cum isdem quibus antea cautibus innocentissimus
quisque, tunc nocentissimus adfigeretur, cumque
insulas omnes, quas modo senatorum, iam delatorum
turba compleret; quos quidem non in praesens tantum,
sed in aeternum repressisti, mille poenarum indagine
3 inclusos. Ereptum alienas pecunias eunt; perdant,
quas habent. Expellere penatibus gestiunt: suis
exturbentur neque ut antea exsanguem illam et
ferream frontem nequiquam convulnerandam prae-
beant punctis, et notas suas rideant, sed exspectent
paria praemio damna, nec maiores spes quam metus
habeant, timeantque quantum timebantur.
4   Ingenti quidem animo divus Titus securitati
nostrae ultionique prospexerat, ideoque numinibus
aequatus est: sed quanto tu quandoque dignior
caelo, qui tot res illis adiecisti, propter quas illum
deum fecimus! Id hoc magis arduum fuit, quod
imperator Nerva te filio, te successore dignissimus
perquam magna quaedam edicto Titi adstruxerat,
nihilque reliquisse nisi tibi videbatur, qui tam multa
excogitasti, ut si ante te nihil esset inventum.
Quae singula quantum tibi gratiae dispensata

---

¹ Pliny has forgotten that many of the *delatores* were
senators; *e.g.* Messalinus, Regulus, and Veiento.

thanks to our ruler who in his unfailing mercy had preferred to entrust vengeance over men on earth to the gods of the sea! Then indeed we knew how times had changed; the real criminals were nailed to the very rocks which had been the cross of many an innocent man; the islands where senators were exiled were crowded with the informers[1] whose power you had broken for all time, not merely for a day, held fast as they were in the meshes of punishments untold. They set out to rob other men of money: now let them lose their own. They sought to evict men from their homes: let them be homeless too. Let them stop presenting a brazen and unblushing front, unmarked by any disgrace, stop laughing off all reproaches. Now they can expect losses in proportion to their rewards, and know apprehension to match their former hopes; now they can feel the fear they once inspired.

It is true that the divine Titus[2] in the nobility of his spirit had taken measures for our security and need for vengeance, and because of this was placed among the gods; but how much more will you one day deserve your seat in heaven, for all your additions to those measures for which we recognized his godhead! And your achievement was the more difficult because the Emperor Nerva,[3] worthy as he was of you as his son and successor, had himself made notable additions to Titus's edict, so that it seemed that nothing was left—except for you, whose ideas were so many that nothing might have been thought of before. Had you dispensed these favours singly

[2] Suetonius, *Titus* 8. 5.
[3] Dio, LXVIII. 1. 2.

5 adiecissent! At tu simul omnia profudisti,[1] ut sol
et dies non parte aliqua sed statim totus, nec uni aut
alteri sed omnibus in commune profertur.

36. Quam iuvat cernere aerarium silens et quietum,
et quale ante delatores erat! Nunc templum illud
nunc vere dei ⟨sedes⟩,[2] non spoliarium civium
cruentarumque praedarum saevum receptaculum, ac
toto in orbe terrarum adhuc locus unus in quo
2 optimo principe boni malis impares essent. Manet
tamen honor legum, nihilque ex publica utilitate
convulsum, nec poena cuiquam remissa, sed addita
est ultio, solumque mutatum, quod iam non delatores
3 sed leges timentur. At fortasse non eadem severitate fiscum qua aerarium cohibes: immo tanto
maiore quanto plus tibi licere de tuo quam de publico
credis. Dicitur actori atque etiam procuratori tuo:
4 " In ius veni, sequere ad tribunal." Nam tribunal
quoque excogitatum principatui[3] est par ceteris,
nisi illud litigatoris amplitudine metiaris. Sors et
urna fisco iudicem adsignat; licet reicere, licet
exclamare: " Hunc nolo, timidus est et bona saeculi
parum intellegit; illum volo, qui Caesarem fortiter
amat." Eodem foro utuntur principatus et libertas;
quae praecipua tua gloria est, saepius vincitur fiscus,
cuius mala causa numquam est nisi sub bono principe.

---

[1] profudisti *Catanaeus*: perfudisti *M*.
[2] dei sedes *Schwarz*: deus *M*.
[3] principatui *Lipsius*: cruciatum *M*.

---

[1] The *Digest* (I. 2. 2. 32) says that Nerva set up a special
praetor's court to judge cases between individuals and the *fiscus*.
(Under Hadrian the creation of equestrian *advocati fisci* made
this court superfluous. *S.H.A. Hadr.* 20. 6.) It is implied here
that litigants were free to use which court they preferred.

our gratitude would be immense; instead, you chose to pour them out together, like the light of day or the sun, shining not partially on one man or another, but instantly as a bright whole over all alike.

36. It is a pleasure to see peace and quiet restored to the treasury, to see it as it was before the days of informers. Now it is a real temple and sanctuary of a god, not a mortuary of citizens and a grim depository for blood-soaked spoils, no longer the one place left in the world where even under an excellent ruler the good were still at the mercy of the wicked. The laws still command respect, and public utility is in no way diminished; but a new vengeance is added to existing penalties, and the sole innovation lies in the fact that men no longer go in fear of informers: instead, they fear the law. It may be thought that you are less strict in your control of the imperial exchequer than of the treasury, but in fact you are all the stricter through believing that you have a freer hand to deal with your own money than with the public's. Anyone may call your procurator or his agent to justice, to appear in court—for an emperor's court[1] is set up which differs from the rest only in the eminence of the person concerned in its workings. Lots drawn from the urn assign the exchequer its magistrate, who can be rejected at any one's protest: " Not him, he's weak and out of touch with the spirit of the age—that's the man, independent and loyal subject of Caesar! " The same court serves the principate and the cause of liberty; and nothing brings you greater honour than the fact that it is the exchequer which often loses its case— for only under an honest ruler is defeat possible.

5 Ingens hoc meritum; maius illud quod eos pro-
curatores habes, ut plerumque cives tui non alios
iudices malint. Liberum est autem discrimini suo
locum[1] eligere. Neque enim ullam necessitatem
muneribus tuis addis, ut qui scias hanc esse beneficiorum principalium summam, si illis et non uti
licet.

37. Onera imperii pleraque vectigalia institui ut
pro utilitate communi ita singulorum ⟨cum⟩[2] iniuriis
coegerunt.[3] ⟨In⟩ his[4] vicesima reperta est, tributum
tolerabile et facile heredibus dumtaxat extraneis,
2 domesticis grave. Itaque illis inrogatum est, his
remissum, videlicet quod manifestum erat quanto
cum dolore laturi seu potius non laturi homines
essent destringi aliquid et abradi bonis, quae sanguine gentilitate sacrorum denique societate meruissent, quaeque numquam ut aliena et speranda sed ut
sua semperque possessa ac deinceps proximo cuique
3 transmittenda cepissent. Haec mansuetudo legis
veteribus civibus servabatur: novi, seu per Latium

[1] discriminis volo cum *M*: corr. *Madvig.*
[2] cum *add. Baehrens*: non sine *post* ita *Keil*: om. *M.*
[3] coegerunt *Catanaeus*: cogerentur *M.*
[4] in his *Keil*: his *M.*

---

[1] The *vicesima hereditatum*, created by Augustus in A.D. 6,
which, with the *centesima rerum venalium*, was the chief source
of income of the *aerarium militare*. P. devotes five chapters

And there is even greater merit in your choice of procurators, the sort of men whom most of your subjects choose to try their cases in preference to anyone else, although they are free to take these to any court they wish. For you lay no one under obligation to use the amenities you provide, being well aware that a prince's benefactions reach their highest point when he permits his subjects to dispense with them at will.

37. The burdens of empire have necessitated the introduction of several taxes, at the expense of the individual in order to benefit the country as a whole. Among these is the five per cent inheritance tax,[1] one which is more readily acceptable when it is confined to distant heirs, but which weighs heavily on direct heirs within the family. And so hitherto it was applied to the former cases and remitted in the latter, doubtless because it was obvious how hardly men would accept—or rather, not accept—any reduction and diminution of the property assured them through ties of blood and kinship and the bond of family rites, something which they had never considered as an expectation from another's hands but as their own permanent possession, to be passed on one day to their nearest relative in their turn. This legal concession was reserved for citizens of long standing; recent ones, whether they had been granted citizenship after holding Latin rights[2] or

to a colourful account of beneficial changes, but as an ex-treasury official he could well have been more precise.

[2] *Ius Latii* was normally an intermediate stage in the promotion to full citizenship. For imperial gifts of citizenship cf. Tacitus, *Ann.* XI. 23–4 (Claudius and the Aedui).

in civitatem seu beneficio principis venissent, nisi simul cognationis iura impetrassent, alienissimi habe-
4 bantur, quibus coniunctissimi fuerant. Ita maximum beneficium vertebatur in gravissimam iniuriam, civitasque Romana instar erat odii et discordiae et orbitatis, cum carissima pignora salva ipsorum pietate
5 distraheret. Inveniebantur tamen, quibus tantus amor nominis nostri, ut Romanam civitatem non vicesimae modo verum etiam adfinitatum damno bene compensari putarent; sed his maxime debebat gratuita contingere, a quibus tam magno aestima-
6 batur. Igitur pater tuus sanxit, ut quod ex matris ad liberos, ex liberorum bonis pervenisset ad matrem, etiamsi cognationum iura non recepissent, cum civitatem apiscerentur, eius vicesimam ne darent. Eandem immunitatem in paternis bonis filio tribuit, si modo reductus esset in patris potestatem, ratus improbe et insolenter ac paene impie his nominibus inseri publicanum, nec sine piaculo quodam sanctissimas necessitudines velut intercedente vicesima scindi; nullum tanti esse vectigal, quod liberos ac parentes faceret extraneos.

38. Hactenus ille, parcius fortasse quam decuit optimum principem, sed non parcius quam optimum patrem, qui adoptaturus hoc quoque parentis indul-

---

[1] *Iura cognationis.* Pliny is far from clear, but presumably means that for the exemptions to operate both testator and heir had to be citizens of long standing unless the newly-created citizen had his *ius cognationis* with his relative explicitly recognized.   [2] *I.e.* Nerva.

through gift of the Emperor, unless at the same time they had received rights of kinship,[1] were treated as a wholly different category from those with whom they had the closest ties. As a result, what should have been a considerable benefit turned into a grave injustice, and Roman citizenship came to stand for hatred, dissension, and deprivation, since it parted relatives who were dear to each other, regardless of their ties of affection. Even so, people were found for whom the name of Roman meant so much that it seemed adequate compensation not only for a five per cent tax but even for the wrong done their kindred; though the value they put on citizenship gave them the best claim to enjoy it tax-free.

Consequently, your father[2] decreed that any property passing from a mother to her children, or from children to their mother, even in the absence of kindred rights, provided that they were citizens, should be exempt from the five per cent tax. He extended the same exemption to a son in respect of his father's property, provided that he was still under his father's authority, thinking that it was excessive, unprecedented, and might even be called impious for a tax-collector's name to be associated with theirs; and that it was positively sacrilegious for a relationship so sacred to be severed by the intervention of an inheritance tax. Indeed, he thought that no tax was worth the cost of estranging parents and children.

38. That was as far as he went; a perfect ruler might possibly have been more generous, but not a perfect father; for it was his intention to adopt you, and he gave indication of his parental indulgence by

gentissimi fecit, quod delibasse[1] quaedam seu potius demonstrasse contentus, largam ac prope intactam

2 bene faciendi materiam filio reservavit. Statim ergo muneri eius liberalitas tua adstruxit, ut, quemadmodum in patris filius, sic in hereditate filii pater esset immunis, nec eodem momento quo pater esse desisset, hoc quoque amitteret quod fuisset.

3 Egregie, Caesar, quod lacrimas parentum vectigales esse non pateris. Bona filii pater sine deminutione possideat, nec socium hereditatis accipiat, qui non habet luctus; nemo recentem et attonitam orbitatem ad computationem vocet, cogatque patrem quid

4 reliquerit filius scire. Augeo, patres conscripti, principis munus, cum ostendo liberalitati eius inesse rationem. Ambitio enim et iactantia et effusio et quidvis potius quam liberalitas existimanda est, cui

5 ratio non constat. Dignum ergo, imperator, mansuetudine tua minuere orbitatis iniurias, nec pati quemquam filio amisso insuper adfici alio dolore. Sic quoque abunde misera res est pater filio solus

6 heres: quid si coheredem non a filio accipiat? Adde quod cum divus Nerva sanxisset, ut in paternis bonis liberi necessitate vicesimae solverentur, congruens erat eandem immunitatem parentes in liberorum

7 bonis obtinere. Cur enim posteris amplior honor quam maioribus haberetur, curve non retro quoque recurreret aequitas [non][2] eadem? Tu quidem,

---

[1] delibasse *Cuspinianus*: deliberasse *M*.
[2] non *M*: del. *Puteolanus*.

doing no more than touch on or outline what was needed while leaving to his son free and ample opportunity for doing good. Accordingly, without delay, your generosity built on his foundations by extending the immunity enjoyed by a son in regard to his father's property to a father on inheriting his son's, so that the loss of his status of fatherhood should not end its privileges. It was nobly done, Caesar, to refuse to tax a father's tears—a father should take possession of his son's property without forfeiture, and not have to share his inheritance with those who cannot share his grief. No one should demand accounts from one suffering from the recent shock of bereavement, nor compel a father to estimate what he has been left by his own son. And I can emphasize the generosity of our prince's gift, Conscript Fathers, by pointing out that it was thoughtfully planned; for without thought there is no true generosity, only extravagance, ostentation, and the desire to please. It was, then, an act worthy of your clemency to soften the pangs of bereavement and not to permit further sorrows to add to the grief of losing a son. It is grief enough already for a father to outlive his son as his sole heir; what if he has to share the inheritance with another not of his son's choosing? Besides, when the divine Nerva decreed that children should be exempt from the five per cent tax on their father's property it was only logical that the immunity should be extended to fathers with regard to the property of their children. Why should the younger generation be held in higher honour than the older one? And why should justice not equally apply to old and young

407

Caesar, illam exceptionem removisti, " si modo filius
in potestate fuisset patris," intuitus, opinor, vim
legemque naturae, quae semper in dicione parentum
esse liberos iussit, nec uti inter pecudes sic inter
homines potestatem et imperium valentioribus dedit.

39. Nec vero contentus primum cognationis
gradum abstulisse vicesimae, secundum quoque
exemit cavitque ut in sororis bonis frater, et contra
in fratris soror, utque avus avia in neptis nepotisque,
2 et invicem illi servarentur immunes. His quoque
quibus per Latium civitas Romana patuisset, idem
indulsit omnibusque inter se cognationum iura com-
misit, simul et pariter et more naturae, quae priores
principes a singulis rogari gestiebant, non tam
3 praestandi animo quam negandi. Ex quo intellegi
potest quantae benignitatis quanti spiritus fuerit,
sparsas atque, ut ita dicam, laceras gentilitates
colligere atque conectere et quasi renasci iubere,
deferre quod negabatur, atque id praestare cunctis,
quod saepe singuli non impetrassent; postremo
ipsum sibi eripere tot beneficiorum occasiones, tam
4 numerosam obligandi imputandique materiam. Indignum, credo, ei visum ab homine peti quod di
dedissent. Soror estis et frater, avus et nepotes:
quid est ergo cur rogetis ut sitis? Vobis est is,[1]

---

[1] est is *Scaliger*: estis *M*.

alike? You also removed the clause "provided that he was still under his father's authority", in the belief, I imagine, that there is a natural law compelling children always to be obedient to their fathers, one which does not reduce the human race to the level of the animal world, where power and authority go to the stronger.

39. Nor was he satisfied with removing the tax from the first degree of kinship; he also exempted the second degree, and granted immunity to brothers and sisters in respect of each others' property, and to grandparents and grandchildren in the same way. Furthermore, he granted the same concession to those who had gained Roman citizenship through their Latin rights, while at a single stroke to all alike were granted according to Nature's law the rights of kinship which his predecessors had preferred to leave for individual petitions, though not so much with the intention of granting these as of dismissing them with a refusal. Here is clear proof of his imagination and his benevolence—to gather up and reunite the torn and scattered members of a family, to breathe into it new life, to concede what was hitherto refused, and grant to all what individuals had often failed to obtain: in short, to deny himself so many chances of showing himself a benefactor, so many opportunities for gaining credit and putting his subjects in his debt. No doubt he thought it unsuitable that a man should have to ask for what the gods had bestowed. You are brother and sister, grandparent and grandchild; what need is there to ask permission to be what you are? You are blessed with a ruler who with his usual forbearance finds it

qui [1] pro cetera sua moderatione non minus invidio-
5 sum putat dare hereditatem quam auferre. Laeti
ergo adite honores, capessite civitatem; neminem
hoc necessitudinis abruptum velut truncum amputa-
tumque destituet; isdem omnes quibus ante pignori-
bus, sed honestiores perfruentur.

Ac ne remotioris quidem iamque deficientis
adfinitatis gradus a qualibet quantitate vicesimam
ut prius inferre cogentur. Statuit enim communis
omnium parens summam, quae publicanum pati
possit. 40. Carebit onere vicesimae parva et exilis
hereditas, et si ita gratus heres volet, tota sepulcro
tota funeri serviet; nemo observator nemo castigator
adsistet. Cuicumque modica pecunia ex hereditate
alicuius obvenerit, securus habeat quietusque possi-
2 deat. Ea lex vicesimae dicta est, ut ad periculum
eius perveniri nisi opibus non possit. Conversa est
iniquitas in gratulationem, iniuria in votum: optat
3 heres ut vicesimam debeat. Additum est, ut qui
ex eius modi causis in diem edicti vicesimam deberent,
nondum tamen intulissent, non inferrent. At in
praeteritum subvenire ne di quidem possunt: tu
tamen subvenisti cavistique ut desineret, quisque
debere, quod ⟨nemo⟩[2] esset postea debiturus, idem
4 effecisti ne malos principes habuissemus. Quo in-

---

[1] qui *M*: quippe *Keil*: quibus *Kukula*.
[2] nemo *Mynors*: non *Puteolanus*: om. *M*.

---

[1] Dio (LV. 25. 5) says that the tax was paid by all except
close relatives and poor persons. Nothing is known of the
value of the small estates exempt.

no less distasteful to have to permit enjoyment of an inheritance than to appropriate it. You can accordingly seek office and welcome citizenship without misgivings, confident that these new obligations will leave no one broken and desolate, like a tree shorn of its boughs. All may delight in their family ties as before, while enjoying increase of status.

Moreover, even in cases of remoter degrees of kinship, where ties are correspondingly weaker, there will no longer be the same liability as before to the inheritance tax on any and every sum. 40. The amount which shall be subject to taxation has been fixed by the common Father of us all. Small estates,[1] with no large sums involved, will be exempt from the tax; if the grateful heir so wishes, he can devote everything to the costs of funeral rites and a tomb—no one will stand over him to witness and censure what he does. Anyone then who inherits a modest sum will be able to enjoy it without care or anxiety. Since wealth alone is affected under the express terms of the inheritance law, the unequal burden of taxation has become a source of congratulations and its hardships to be desired: every heir positively hopes to be liable to tax. A further clause allows exemption to all who were liable under the old law but only up to the day of the new act, and have not yet paid.[2] Even the gods lack the power to remedy the past; yet this is precisely what you have done, in providing for the cancellation of debts which would cease to exist in future; thanks to you, we might never have had

[2] Two reliefs from the Forum show the burning of registers, which may illustrate this.

genio, si natura pateretur, quam libenter tot spoliatis
5 tot trucidatis bona et sanguinem refudisses! Vetuisti
exigi quod deberi non tuo saeculo coeperat. Alius
ut contumacibus irasceretur, tarditatemque solvendi
dupli vel etiam quadrupli irrogatione multaret; tu
nihil referre iniquitatis existimas, exigas quod deberi
non oportuerit, an constituas ut debeatur.

41. Feres, Caesar, curam et sollicitudinem consularem. Nam mihi cogitanti eundem te collationes
remisisse, donativum reddidisse, congiarium obtulisse,
delatores abegisse, vectigalia temperasse, interro-
gandus videris, satisne computaveris imperî reditus.
An tantas vires habet frugalitas principis, ut tot
2 impendiis tot erogationibus sola sufficiat? Nam quid
est causae cur aliis quidem, cum omnia raperent et
rapta retinerent, ut si nihil rapuissent nihil retinuis-
sent, defuerint omnia; tibi cum tam multa largiaris
et nihil auferas, ut si nihil largiaris et auferas omnia,
3 ⟨omnia⟩[1] supersint? Numquam principibus de-
fuerunt, qui fronte tristi et gravi supercilio utilitatibus fisci contumaciter adessent. Et erant principes
ipsi sua sponte avidi et rapaces et qui magistris non
egerent; plura tamen semper a nobis contra nos
didicerunt. Sed ad tuas aures cum ceteris omnibus

---

[1] omnia *add. Schwarz*: om. M.

the evil emperors before you. In this spirit, had it
been possible, how gladly would you have restored
their life-blood and their fortunes to so many victims
of butchery and spoilation! You forbade the collection of debts contracted before your reign; but
another would have suspected a refusal to submit,
vented his anger accordingly, and punished delay in
payment by exacting twice or four times the amount.
You find nothing to choose between the unfair
exaction of debts which should never have been
contracted and their unjust imposition.

41. You will bear with my anxieties, Caesar, my
concern as consul. Your refusal to accept gifts of
money, your distribution of the military bonus and
civilian largess, dismissal of informers and reduction
of taxes—the thought of all this makes me feel I
should ask you whether you have given due thought
to the Empire's revenues. Are there sufficient
resources to support the Emperor's economy and
enable it to bear unaided the cost of paying out
such sums? Others were robbers on a large scale
and kept their ill-gotten gains, yet they might have
taken and kept nothing, for they were always penni-
less; whereas you have given so much and taken
nothing; but always have enough and to spare as if
you had given nothing and taken all. What is the
explanation? Our rulers have always had people
at their side who were all too ready to keep a stern
and unremitting eye on the needs of the exchequer.
There were even emperors whose personal cupidity
and greed for gain needed no teaching, though in
most cases instruction—to our own detriment—has
come from us. But to your ears the approach is

tum vel maxime avaris adulationibus obstructus est
4 aditus. Silent ergo et quiescunt, et postquam non
est cui suadeatur, qui suadeant non sunt. Quo
evenit ut, cum plurimum tibi pro tuis, plus tamen
pro nostris moribus debeamus.

42. Locupletabant et fiscum et aerarium non tam
Voconiae et Iuliae leges, quam maiestatis singulare
et unicum crimen, eorum qui crimine vacarent.
Huius tu metum penitus sustulisti, contentus magnitudine qua nulli magis caruerunt, quam qui sibi
2 maiestatem vindicabant. Reddita est amicis fides,
liberis pietas, obsequium servis: verentur et parent
3 et dominos habent. Non enim iam servi nostri
principis amici sed nos sumus, nec pater patriae
alienis se mancipiis cariorem quam civibus suis credit.
Omnes accusatore domestico liberasti, unoque salutis
publicae signo illud, ut sic dixerim, servile bellum
sustulisti. In quo non minus servis quam dominis
praestitisti: nos enim securos, illos bonos fecisti.
4 Non vis in te ea laudari, nec fortasse laudanda sint;
grata sunt tamen recordantibus principem illum in
capita dominorum servos subornantem, monstran-
temque crimina quae tamquam delata puniret,
magnum et inevitabile ac totiens cuique experiendum

---

¹ The law of the tribune Titus Voconius of 169 B.C. restrict-
ing the rights of inheritance of daughters; for the *Lex Iulia*
cf. ch. 26. 5, and note.

closed for insinuating counsel of every kind, and especially that of avarice. It dries up and falls silent, for where there is no one to hear advice, soon there is none to proffer it. Consequently we are deeply in your debt, and doubly so—for your own character, and even more for the improvement it has made in our own.

42. Both exchequer and treasury used to be enriched not so much by the Voconian[1] and Julian laws as from the charges of high treason, the unique and only way of incriminating men who had committed no crime. You completely removed our dread of this, content to show the nobility which none had lacked so much as those who used to pretend to majesty. Loyalty is restored among friends, a sense of duty to freedmen and obedience to slaves—who can now respect and obey and keep their masters. Henceforth it is we who are the Emperor's friends, not our slaves, and the Father of our country puts his own subjects' affection above that of persons held in bondage to other men. You have freed us all from the accuser in our homes, and by raising the standard of public safety have effectively suppressed what might be called a servile war—thereby doing a service to slaves by making them better men as well as to their masters in ridding us of our fears. You seek no praise for this, and perhaps it should not be offered, but how welcome it is for those of us who remember that emperor who suborned slaves against the very lives of their masters[2] and told them the charges he proposed to punish before their information was laid—an evil as fearful as it was unavoidable.

---

[2] Cf. Tacitus, *Hist.* I. 2. 6.

malum, quotiens quisque similes principi servos haberet.

43. In eodem genere ponendum est, quod testamenta nostra secura sunt, nec unus omnium nunc quia scriptus, nunc quia non scriptus heres. Non tu falsis non tu iniquis tabulis advocaris. Nullius ad te iracundia nullius impietas nullius furor confugit, nec quia offendit alius nuncuparis, sed quia ipse meruisti. 2 Scriberis ab amicis, ab ignotis praeteriris, nihilque inter privatum et principem interest, nisi quod nunc 3 a pluribus amaris; nam et plures amas. Tene, Caesar, hunc cursum, et probabitur experimento, sitne feracius et uberius non ad laudem modo sed ad pecuniam principi, si herede illo mori homines velint, 4 quam si cogantur. Donavit pater tuus multa, ⟨multa⟩[1] et ipse donasti. Cesserit parum gratus: manent tamen hi qui[2] bonis eius ⟨fruuntur⟩,[3] nihilque ex illis ad te nisi gloria redit. Nam liberalitatem iucundiorem debitor gratus, clariorem ingratus 5 facit. Sed quis ante te laudem istam pecuniae praetulit? quotus quisque principum ne id quidem in patrimoniis nostris suum duxit, quod esset de suo? Nonne ut regum ita Caesarum munera illitos cibis hamos, opertos praeda laqueos aemulabantur, cum

[1] multa *add. Ernesti*: *om. M.*
[2] hi qui *M*: aeque in *Mommsen.*
[3] fruuntur *Keil*: fruantur *Catanaeus*: *om. M.*

---

[1] Cf. Suetonius, *Dom.* 12. 2; *Nero* 32. 2.

from which there was no escape as long as there was nothing to choose between emperor and slave.

43. In the same category must be placed the new security for wills. No longer can a single heir inherit all, sometimes under the pretext that his name is there in writing, sometimes that it is not.[1] Your own name is not invoked to support forged and unjust documents, nor can anyone make you the excuse for his anger, folly, or neglect of duty. You are not named as heir because someone else has given offence, but on your own merits, set down by your personal friends and passed over by strangers. The only difference in fact between your former private life and your present supreme position lies in the greater number of those who love you, as your own affections are more widely spread. Only continue on this course, Caesar, and experience will show whether the reputation and the purse alike of a prince are not better enriched when his subjects make him their heir at their death from choice rather than from compulsion. Your father was generous with his gifts, and you have been equally generous. If someone dies now without showing gratitude, still he leaves heirs to his property, and nothing comes to you but an increase in reputation: for generosity may be more fortunate when it receives recognition, but is more glorious when it does not. Yet who before you chose this distinction in preference to additional wealth? How many emperors refused (like you) to consider as theirs even that portion of our patrimony which originally came from them? Is it not true to say that the gifts of emperors like those of kings used to resemble baited hooks or hidden snares, so that

privatis facultatibus velut hausta et implicita retro
secum quidquid attigerant referrent?

44. Quam utile est ad usum secundorum per
adversa venisse! Vixisti nobiscum, periclitatus es,
timuisti, quae tunc erat innocentium vita. Scis et
expertus es, quanto opere detestentur malos principes, etiam qui malos faciunt. Meministi quae
2 optare nobiscum, quae sis queri solitus. Nam
privato iudicio principem geris, meliorem immo te
praestas, quam tibi alium precabare. Itaque sic
imbuti sumus ut, quibus erat summa votorum melior
pessimo princeps, iam non possimus nisi optimum
3 ferre. Nemo est ergo tam tui, tam ignarus sui, ut
locum istum post te concupiscat. Facilius est ut esse
4 aliquis successor tuus possit, quam ut velit. Quis
enim curae tuae molem sponte subeat? quis comparari tibi non reformidet? Expertus et ipse es,
quam sit onerosum succedere bono principi, et
5 adferebas excusationem adoptati. An párva prona-
que sunt ad aemulandum quod nemo incolumitatem
turpitudine rependit, salva est omnibus vita et
dignitas vitae, nec iam consideratus et sapiens, qui
6 aetatem in tenebris agit? Eadem quippe sub
principe virtutibus praemia quae in libertate, nec
bene factis tantum ex conscientia merces. Amas
constantiam civium, rectosque ac vividos animos non

---

1 A Stoic concept. Seneca, *Ep. ad Luc.* 81.; Pliny, *Ep.* I.
8. 14.

once entangled with private fortunes they drew out
with them whatever they touched?

44. What an advantage it is to have attained success through adversity! You shared our lives, our
dangers, our fears, the common lot at that time of
all innocent men. You know from experience how
bad rulers come to be hated even by those who have
corrupted them. You can remember how you joined
in our prayers and protests—witness the fact that
your sentiments have remained those of a citizen
since you become prince, while your merits have
proved greater than anything you could have hoped
for in another. You have inspired us not to be
satisfied with less than perfection in our ruler,
whereas hitherto we prayed only for someone who
would prove better than the worst. Consequently
everyone knows you—and himself—too well to covet
your position after you; a willing successor might
even be harder to find than a capable one, for who
would voluntarily shoulder your burden of responsibility or readily stand comparison with you? Experience has taught you how difficult it is to succeed
a good emperor—and you could plead the fact of your
adoption. No one could imagine it easy for any
comer to repeat a situation where no one need purchase security by disgrace, where everyone's life is
safe and safe with honour, where foresight and pru-
dence no longer prompt men to spend a lifetime
keeping out of sight. The rewards of virtue are now
the same under an emperor as they were in times of
liberty, and good deeds win more solid recognition
than the mere consciousness of having performed
them.[1] You value enterprise in your subjects, you

419

ut alii contundis ac deprimis, sed foves et attollis.
7 Prodest bonos esse, cum sit satis abundeque, si non
nocet; his honores his sacerdotia, his provincias
offers, hi amicitia tua hi iudicio florent. Acuuntur
isto integritatis et industriae pretio similes, dissimiles
adliciuntur; nam praemia bonorum malorumque
8 bonos ac malos faciunt. Pauci adeo ingenio valent
ut non turpe honestumque, prout bene ac secus
cessit, expetant fugiantve; ceteri, ubi laboris inertiae
vigilantiae somno, frugalitatis luxuriae merces datur,
eadem ista quibus alios artibus adsecutos vident
consectantur, qualesque sunt illi, tales esse et videri
volunt, et dum volunt fiunt.

45. Et priores quidem principes, excepto patre tuo,
praeterea uno aut altero (et nimis dixi), vitiis potius
civium quam virtutibus laetabantur, primum quod
in alio sua quemque natura delectat, deinde quod
patientiores servitutis arbitrabantur, quos non
2 deceret esse nisi servos. Horum in sinum omnia
congerebant, bonos autem otio aut situ abstrusos et
quasi sepultos non nisi delationibus et periculis in
3 lucem ac diem proferebant. Tu amicos ex optimis
⟨sumis⟩,[1] et hercule aequum est esse eos carissimos
bono principi, qui invisissimi malo fuerint. Scis, ut

---

[1] sumis *add. Keil: om. M.*

foster and encourage signs of character and spirit, instead of forcing them into subjection as your predecessors did. People find that honesty pays, now that they are convinced that it does them no harm—indeed, it brings them honours, priesthoods, provinces from your hands, and they flourish in your friendship and favour. This payment for application and integrity spurs on others like them, while encouraging men of different character to mend their ways; for it is the rewards for vice and virtue which make men bad or good. Not many people have a strong enough character to pursue or shun good or evil with no thought of advantage; for the rest, when they see the reward for effort, activity and thrift going to idleness, torpor and extravagance, set about gaining similar advantages by the same devices as they see others use. Their one wish is to resemble such men, be one of them, until their wishing makes them so.

45. Previous emperors, with the exception of your father and one or two more (and that is saying too much), did in fact take more pleasure in the vices of their subjects than in their virtues, first because everyone likes a man after his own heart, then because they supposed that slavery would be more acceptable to people unfitted to be anything but slaves. Such men gathered up all the favours, open-armed; while honest citizens who were forced to bury themselves in retirement were neglected and only saw the light of day at their trials for treason. By contrast, you choose your friends from the best of your subjects, and quite rightly, the affection of a good prince lit on the very men most hated by a bad

sint diversa natura dominatio et principatus, ita non
aliis esse principem gratiorem, quam qui maxime
4 dominum graventur. Hos ergo provehis et ostentas
quasi specimen et exemplar, quae tibi secta vitae,
quod hominum genus placeat; et ideo non censuram
adhuc, non praefecturam morum recepisti, quia tibi
beneficiis potius quam remediis ingenia nostra
experiri placet. Et alioqui nescio an plus moribus
conferat princeps, qui bonos esse patitur quam qui
5 cogit. Flexibiles quamcumque in partem ducimur a
principe atque (ut ita dicam) sequaces sumus. Huic
enim cari, huic probati esse cupimus, quod frustra
speraverint dissimiles, eoque obsequii continuatione
pervenimus, ut prope omnes homines unius moribus
vivamus. Porro non tam sinistre constitutum est,
ut qui malum principem possumus, bonum non
6 possimus imitari. Perge modo, Caesar, et vim
effectumque censurae tuum propositum tui actus
obtinebunt. Nam vita principis censura est eaque
perpetua: ad hanc dirigimur, ad hanc convertimur,
nec tam imperio nobis opus est quam exemplo.
Quippe infidelis recti magister est metus. Melius
homines exemplis docentur, quae in primis hoc in se
boni habent, quod adprobant quae praecipiunt fieri
posse.

46. Et quis terror valuisset efficere, quod reverentia
tui effecit? Obtinuit aliquis ut spectaculum panto-

one. Tyranny and the principate are diametrically opposed; knowing this, you realize how a true prince is most welcome to those who can least endure a tyrant. These then are the men you promote and show as a typical example of the way of life and kind of man you prefer; and if you have not yet assumed the censorship and superintendence of our morals, it is because you would rather test our character by benefits than correctives. Besides, I fancy that a ruler may do more for the morals of his country by permitting good conduct than by compelling it. We are easily led wherever he takes us, following (as it were) in his steps; now we see before us one whose affection and approval we all seek to win, in a way those unlike him can never hope to do; so that by the firmness of our allegiance we are reaching the point when we shall all conform with the ways of a single man. (We are surely not so wrong-headed that we can only copy a bad ruler and not a good one.) You need only continue as you are, Caesar, and the principles of your conduct will have the same effective power as a censorship. Indeed, an emperor's life *is* a censorship, and a true perpetual one;[1] this is what guides and directs us, for example is what we need more than command. Fear is unreliable as a teacher of morals. Men learn better from examples, which have the great merit of proving that their advice is practicable.

46. Could any terror have had the power to effect what has been accomplished through our regard for you? Someone did indeed succeed in suppresssing

---

[1] Domitian was *censor perpetuus* from the end of 85.

mimorum populus Romanus tolli pateretur, sed non
2 obtinuit ut vellet: rogatus es tu quod cogebat alius,
coepitque esse beneficium quod necessitas fuerat.
Neque enim a te minore concentu ut tolleres panto-
mimos, quam a patre tuo ut restitueret exactum est.
3 Utrumque recte: nam et restitui oportebat, quos
sustulerat malus princeps, et tolli restitutos. In his
enim, quae a malis bene fiunt, hic tenendus est
modus, ut appareat auctorem displicuisse non factum.
4 Idem ergo populus ille, aliquando scaenici imperatoris
spectator et plausor, nunc in pantomimis quoque
aversatur et damnat effeminatas artes et indecora
5 saeculo studia. Ex quo manifestum est principum
disciplinam capere etiam vulgus, cum rem si ab uno
fiat severissimam fecerint omnes. Macte hac gravi-
tatis gloria, Caesar, qua consecutus es ut, quod
antea vis et imperium, nunc mores vocarentur.
6 Castigaverunt vitia sua ipsi qui castigari merebantur,
idemque emendatores qui emendandi fuerunt.
Itaque nemo de severitate tua queritur, et liberum
7 est queri. Sed cum ita comparatum sit, ut de nullo
minus principe querantur homines quam de quo
maxime licet, tuo in saeculo nihil est quo non omne

---

[1] Suetonius, *Dom.* 7. 1. The miming actors and dancers
(*pantomimi*) introduced into Rome in 22 B.C. were repeatedly
banished by the emperors, but always reappeared. Trajan
banished them in 99–100, but they were back for the triumph
of the Second Dacian War in 107, and the death of one
maximus pantomimorum is recorded in S. 173 (ILS 5184).

the mimes[1] and persuading the Roman people to put up with this, though he did not succeed in making them willing to do so. But in your case, the people asked you to take the measures which the other had imposed, seeing them now as a public benefit and not an enforced necessity, as unanimous in their demand for you to do away with the mimes as they had been for your father to restore them. They were right in both cases—it was necessary to restore what a bad emperor had suppressed, and once restored, equally necessary to suppress it, for the rule to follow when good deeds are done by bad men is to make it clear that the agent deserves censure, not the act. And so the same populace which once watched and applauded the performances of an actor-emperor[2] has now even turned against the professional mimes, and damns their perverted art as a taste unworthy of our age. This shows that even the vulgar crowd can take a lesson from its rulers, since a reform so sweeping, if once started by an individual, can spread to all. All honour to your noble wisdom, Caesar, for this has enabled you to see an accepted custom take the place of what used to be an arbitrary decree! Of their own accord men who deserved correction have corrected their own faults and proved themselves reformers though previously needing reform. Consequently no one complains of your severity though complaint is open to all. It is always the way that fewest complaints are made about a ruler who allows most freedom to make them, and under your regime there is nothing which can fail to give joy and happiness

[2] Nero. Cf. Tacitus, *Ann.* XVI. 4.

8 hominum genus laetetur et gaudeat. Boni prove-
huntur; mali, qui est tranquillissimus status civitatis,
nec timent nec timentur. Vitiorum paenitentiam
exspectas, mederis erroribus sed implorantium,[1]
omnibusque quos bonos facis hanc adstruis laudem,
ne coegisse videaris.

47. Quid? vitam, quid? mores iuventutis quam
principaliter formas! quem honorem dicendi magistris, quam dignationem sapientiae doctoribus habes!
ut sub te spiritum et sanguinem et patriam receperunt
studia! quae priorum temporum immanitas exsiliis
puniebat, cum sibi vitiorum omnium conscius princeps
inimicas vitiis artes non odio magis quam reverentia
2 relegaret. At tu easdem artes in complexu oculis
auribus habes. Praestas enim quaecumque praecipiunt, tantumque eas diligis quantum ab illis
3 probaris. An quisquam studia humanitatis professus
non cum omnia tua tum vel in primis laudibus ferat
4 admissionum tuarum facilitatem? Magno quidem
animo parens tuus hanc ante vos principes arcem
publicarum aedium nomine inscripserat; frustra
tamen, nisi adoptasset qui habitare ut in publicis
5 posset. Quam bene cum titulo isto moribus tuis
convenit, quamque omnia sic facis tamquam non
alius inscripserit! Quod enim forum, quae templa
tam reserata? Non Capitolium ipsaque illa adoptionis tuae sedes magis publica magis omnium.

---

[1] implorantium *Schwarz*: implorantibus *M*.

---

[1] Cf. *Ep.* III. 11; Tac. *Ag.* 2. 1–2; Suet. *Dom.* 10. 3. Domitian banished the philosophers from Rome and Italy in 93.
[2] The *domus Flavia* on the Palatine; the title is confirmed
by ILS 9358.

to every kind of man. The honest find advancement, while the dishonest are neither feared nor unduly fearful, sure proof of the peace and stability of the realm. You wait for repentance of vice, you remedy faults only at the plea of transgressors, and all whom you have made better men are granted the additional merit of not appearing to owe anything to enforced guidance from you.

47. As for the lives and characters of the young—how you are forming them in true princely fashion! And the teachers of rhetoric and professors of philosophy—how you hold them in honour! Under you the liberal arts are restored, to breathe and live in their own country—the learning which the barbarity of the past punished with exile, when an emperor acquainted with all the vices sought to banish everything hostile to vice, motivated less by hatred for learning as by fear for its authority.[1] But you embrace these very arts, opening arms, eyes and ears to them, a living example of their precepts, as much their lover as the subject of their regard. Every lover of culture must applaud all your actions, while reserving his highest praise for your readiness to give audiences. Your father had shown his magnanimity by giving the title of " open house " to what (before your time or his) had been a stronghold of tyranny [2]— yet this would have been an empty formula had he not adopted a son capable of living in the public eye. Between your habits and that inscription there is perfect accord; every action of yours suggests you might have set it there yourself. No forum, no temple is so free of access: not even the Capitol and the very site of your adoption are more public and

Nullae obices nulli contumeliarum gradus supera-
tisque iam mille liminibus ultra semper aliqua dura
6 et obstantia. Magna ante te, magna post te, iuxta
te tamen maxima quies: tantum ubique silentium,
tam altus pudor, ut ad parvos penates et larem
angustum ex domo principis modestiae et tranquilli-
tatis exempla referantur.

48. Ipse autem ut excipis omnes, ut exspectas!
ut magnam partem dierum, inter tot imperî curas,
quasi per otium transigis! Itaque non albi[1] et
attoniti, nec ut periculum capitis adituri tarditate,
sed securi et hilares cum commodum est convenimus.
2 Et admittente principe interdum est aliquid quod
nos domi quasi magis necessarium teneat: excusati
semper tibi nec umquam excusandi sumus. Scis
enim sibi quemque praestare, quod te videat quod
frequentet, ac tanto liberalius ac diutius voluptatis
3 huius copiam praebes. Nec salutationes tuas fuga
et vastitas sequitur: remoramur resistimus ut in
communi domo, quam nuper illa immanissima belua
plurimo terrore munierat, cum velut quodam specu
inclusa nunc propinquorum sanguinem lamberet,
nunc se ad clarissimorum civium strages caedesque
4 proferret.   Obversabantur foribus horror et minae et
par metus admissis et exclusis; ad hoc ipse occursu

---

[1] albi *Madvig*: anxii, balbi, pallidi *alii*: alii *M*.

---

[1] Cf. Seneca, *de Ben.* VI. 33. 4; 34. 2.
[2] Suetonius, *Dom.* 10. 2 and 15. 1.   Domitian had put to
death the two sons (Flavius Sabinus and Flavius Clemens) of
his father's brother, Sabinus.

open to all. There are no obstacles, no grades of entry to cause humiliation,[1] nor a thousand doors to be opened only to find still more obstacles barring the way. No, everything is peaceful before reaching you and on leaving you and above all, in your presence; such deep silence, such great reverence, that from the prince's house an example of calm and moderation returns to every humble hearth and modest home.

48. And you yourself—awaiting and receiving everyone in person—devote a large part of every day to so many cares of State, while preserving the unhurried atmosphere of a life of leisure. So we gather round you, no longer pale and terrified, slow of step as if in peril of our lives, but carefree and happy, coming when it suits us. And having gained audience, we may at times have something which seems urgent to keep us at home; we are always excused by you, without having to find excuses. Knowing as you do how eager we all are to see and frequent you, you are all the readier to make easy opportunities in advance for this pleasure. Moreover, when our respects are paid, there is no immediate flight to leave the hall empty—we stay behind to linger on as if in a home we share, though this is the place where recently that fearful monster built his defences with untold terrors, where lurking in his den he licked up the blood of his murdered relatives [2] or emerged to plot the massacre and destruction of his most distinguished subjects.[3] Menaces and horror were the sentinels at his doors, and the fears alike

[3] Suet. *Dom.* 10. 2; Tac. *Ag.* 45; Dio LXVII. 13; Pliny, *Ep.* I. 5. 3, III. 11. 3.

quoque visuque terribilis: superbia in fronte, ira in
oculis, femineus pallor in corpore, in ore impudentia
5 multo rubore suffusa. Non adire quisquam non
adloqui audebat, tenebras semper secretumque
captantem, nec umquam ex solitudine sua pro-
deuntem, nisi ut solitudinem faceret.

49. Ille tamen, quibus sibi parietibus et muris
salutem suam tueri videbatur, dolum secum et
insidias et ultorem scelerum deum inclusit. Dimovit
perfregitque custodias Poena, angustosque per aditus
et obstructos non secus ac per apertas fores et
invitantia limina irrupit: longe tunc illi divinitas sua,
longe arcana illa cubilia saevique secessus, in quos
timore et superbia et odio hominum agebatur.
2 Quanto nunc tutior, quanto securior eadem domus,
postquam erus[1] non crudelitatis sed amoris excubiis,
non solitudine et claustris, sed civium celebritate
3 defenditur! Ecquid ergo? Discimus experimento
fidissimam esse custodiam principis innocentiam
ipsius. Haec arx inaccessa, hoc inexpugnabile muni-
mentum, munimento non egere. Frustra se terrore
succinxerit, qui saeptus caritate non fuerit; armis
4 enim arma irritantur. Num autem serias tantum
partes dierum in oculis nostris coetuque consumis?
non remissionibus tuis eadem frequentia eademque
5 illa socialitas interest? non tibi semper in medio

[1] erus *Baehrens*: eius *M*.

[1] Cf. Suetonius, *Dom.* 18. 1; Tacitus, *Ag.* 45. 3.
[2] Domitian was assassinated in his palace; Suet. *Dom.* 17.

of admission and rejection; then himself in person, dreadful to see and to meet, with arrogance on his brow and fury in his eye, a womanish pallor spread over his body but a deep flush to match the shameless expression on his face.[1] None dared approach him, none dared speak; always he sought darkness and mystery, and only emerged from the desert of his solitude to create another.

49. Yet though he thought to protect his life behind walls and masonry, locked in with him were treachery, conspiracy, and the god of retribution for his crimes. Vengeance pushed aside his guards, broke through and burst in by the narrow passages and their barriers, as if the doors stood open and thresholds called her in.[2] Nothing availed him then—not his divinity, nor those secret chambers, those cruel haunts whither he was driven by his fear and pride and hatred of mankind. How much safer is that same dwelling today, and how much happier, now that its master finds protection in popularity instead of cruelty, and seeks the thronging crowds of his subjects instead of solitude behind locked doors! What is the lesson for us? Experience shows that the one guard which a prince can wholly trust is his own innocence. The sole citadel without access, the only defences which can never be breached are—never to need them. It is useless for a man to be armed with terror if he lacks the protection of love; for arms only call out more arms.

Nor is it only the working hours of your day which you spend in our midst for all to see; your leisure hours are marked by the same numbers and friendliness. Your meals are always taken in public and

cibus semperque mensa communis? non ex convictu
nostro mutua voluptas? non provocas reddisque
sermones? non ipsum tempus epularum tuarum,
6 cum frugalitas contrahat, extendit humanitas? Non
enim ante medium diem distentus solitaria cena,
spectator adnotatorque convivis tuis immines, nec
ieiunis et inanibus plenus ipse ⟨et⟩ eructans[1] non
tam adponis quam obicis cibos quos dedigneris
attingere, aegreque perpessus superbam illam con-
victus simulationem, rursus te ad clandestinam
7 ganeam occultumque luxum refers. Ergo non
aurum nec argentum, nec exquisita ingenia cenarum,
sed suavitatem tuam iucunditatemque miramur,
quibus nulla satietas adest, quando sincera omnia et
8 vera et ornata gravitate. Neque enim aut peregrinae superstitionis ministeria aut obscaena petu-
lantia mensis principis oberrat, sed benigna invitatio
et liberales ioci et studiorum honor. Inde tibi parcus
et brevis somnus, nullumque amore nostri tempus
angustius, quam quod sine nobis agis.

50. Sed cum rebus tuis ut participes perfruamur,
quae habemus ipsi, quam propria quam nostra sunt!
Non enim exturbatis prioribus dominis omne stagnum, omnem lacum, omnem etiam saltum immensa
possessione circumvenis, nec unius oculis flumina

---

[1] et eructans *Mynors*: ructans *Livineius*: eructans *M.*

---

[1] In fact, Trajan drank rather heavily. Cf. SHA *Hadr.* 3. 3;
Alex. Sev. 39. 1.
[2] Domitian favoured strange cults, and coins of c. 95 show

your table open to all, the repast and its pleasures
are there for us to share, while you encourage our
conversation and join in it. As for the length of
your banquets, polite manners prolong what frugality [1] might cut short. You do not arrive already
gorged with a solitary feast before midday, to sit
menacingly over your guests, watching and marking
all they do, nor when they are fasting and hungry
do you belch from a full stomach and present
or rather throw at them the food you disdain to
touch, and after a pretence at enduring this insult-
ing mockery of a banquet take yourself back to
secret gluttony and private excesses. And so it is
not the plate of gold and silver, nor the ingenuity of
the dishes served which command our admiration
so much as your own courtesy and charm, of which
we can never have too much, for all is genuine and
sincere and conducted with true dignity. The Emperor has rid his tables of the ministrants of an
oriental superstition [2] and the indecent antics of im-
pudent buffoons; in their place is warm hospitality,
love of culture and civilized wit. Then afterwards
your sleep is short and sparing, for in your love of us
there is no period of your time so short as that you
spend alone.

50. Yet while we enjoy your possesssions as if we
had a share in them, our personal property is truly
our own. You do not dispossess existing owners in
order to add to your vast domains every marsh and
lake, and even pasture-land; rivers, mountains and
seas are no longer reserved for the eyes of one man

temples of Cybele and Serapis; cf. Dio LXVII. 9.   For Pliny's
dislike of such entertainment, cf. *Ep.* IX. 17.

2 montes maria deserviunt. Est quod Caesar non
suum videat, tandemque imperium principis quam
patrimonium maius est. Multa enim ex patrimonio
refert in imperium, quae priores principes occupa-
3 bant, non ut ipsi fruerentur, sed ne quis alius. Ergo
in vestigia sedesque nobilium immigrant pares
domini, nec iam clarissimorum virorum receptacula
habitatore servo teruntur, aut foeda vastitate pro-
4 cumbant. Datur intueri pulcherrimas aedes deterso
situ auctas ac vigentes. Magnum hoc tuum non
erga homines modo sed erga tecta ipsa meritum,
sistere ruinas solitudinem pellere, ingentia opera
eodem quo exstructa sunt animo ab interitu vindicare.
Muta quidem illa et anima carentia sentire tamen
et laetari videntur, quod niteant quod frequententur,
quod aliquando coeperint esse domini scientis.
5 Circumfertur sub nomine Caesaris tabula ingens
rerum venalium, quo fit[1] detestanda avaritia illius,
qui tam multa concupiscebat, cum haberet supervacua
tam multa. Tum exitialis erat apud principem huic
6 laxior domus, illi amoenior villa: nunc princeps in
haec eadem dominos quaerit, ipse inducit; ipsos illos
magni aliquando imperatoris hortos, illud numquam

---

[1] quo fit *Perizonius*: quod sit *M*.

---

[1] The distinction is drawn between the emperor's *patri-monium* and what was subject to his *imperium*. Cf. Seneca, *de Ben.* VII. 6. 2.

[2] The property of the fiscus was sometimes sold off to

434

alone. The Emperor no longer feels the need to own whatever he sees, and at long last the land subject to his sovereign rights extends farther than his personal property;[1] many of his inherited estates (which his predecessors held not for their own pleasure so much as to deny them to anyone else) are being restored to the State. Thus into the seats and homes of the nobility step new masters equal to the old, and the houses of the great no longer fall to pieces in the hands of a slave for occupant, collapsing in hideous decay. Instead, we may see splendid mansions, extended and flourishing, the dust all swept away: a noble service you render, Caesar, not only to man but to the very buildings, for in checking ruin, banishing neglect, and saving great edifices from destruction, you show the same imaginative spirit as those who built them. And indeed, those dumb inanimate stones seem to sense the happiness of being restored to splendour and frequented once again, now that at last they have a master who appreciates their worth. Under the name of Caesar is published a long list of possessions for sale,[2] which shows up as the more abominable the cupidity of that emperor who possessed far more than he needed, but always wanted more.[3] In those days it was fatal for anyone about him to own a spacious house or attractive property; today our prince looks for owners for those very places, and introduces them

augment the treasury; cf. Suetonius, *Cal.* 38–9; Dio LXVIII. 2 (Nerva).

[3] Suetonius, *Dom.* 12. 1 ascribes this to his need for money. But Syme (*JRS* XX) points out that Domitian's motive in attacking senators was political, not financial.

435

nisi Caesaris suburbanum licemur emimus implemus.
7 Tanta benignitas principis, tanta securitas temporum est, ut ille nos principalibus rebus existimet
dignos, nos non timeamus quod esse digni videmur.
Nec vero emendi tantum civibus tuis copiam praebes,
sed amoenissima quaeque largiris et donas; ista
inquam donas in quae electus, in quae adoptatus es;
transfers quod iudicio accepisti, ac nihil magis tuum
credis, quam quod per amicos habes.

51. Idem tam parcus in aedificando quam diligens
in tuendo. Itaque non ut ante immanium trans-
vectione saxorum urbis tecta quatiuntur; stant
securae domus nec iam templa nutantia. Satis est
tibi nimiumque, cum successeris frugalissimo prin-
2 cipi; magnum reicere aliquid et amputare ex his,
quae princeps tamquam necessaria reliquit. Praeterea pater tuus usibus suis detrahebat quae fortuna
3 imperî dederat, tu tuis quae pater. At quam
magnificus in publicum es! Hinc porticus, inde
delubra occulta celeritate properantur, ut non con-
summata sed tantum commutata videantur. Hinc
immensum latus circi templorum pulchritudinem

---

[1] *e.g.* Lucullus or Pompey. Cf. **63. 4**.

[2] The Circus Maximus, badly damaged in the fire of 64 and
not yet wholly restored. Cf. Dio LXVIII. 7. 2. The façade
along the road between the Circus and the Palatine was 600
metres long.

himself. Even the gardens outside Rome which
had once been owned by a famous general[1] and had
always been in the imperial family are ours; we can
make an offer, buy and occupy them. Such is our
prince's goodness of heart, such the security of our
times, that he believes us worthy of princely possessions and we have no fears about seeming so. Nor
do you give your subjects the opportunity only to
purchase—you have bestowed on us as a gift some
of the loveliest properties, making over to us the
very inheritance for which you were chosen and
adopted, which was made yours by a reasoned decision; for you hold that ownership is best enjoyed
through the persons of your friends.

51. Your interest in preserving what exists is
matched by your restraint over further building.
The walls and roofs in the city have stopped shuddering as they did at the passage of huge blocks of
stone; our houses stand safe and secure, and the
temples are no longer threatened with collapse.
There is enough, and more, for you, although your
predecessor was so careful in his expenditure, and it
is splendid too to have cut down and retrenched even
on what he thought was necessary; especially as in
his case he was denying himself personal enjoyment
of what the hazards of empire had brought him,
whereas your self-denial is applied to what came
from him. But when it comes to public building,
you do it on the grand scale. Here stands a colonnade, there a shrine, rising as if by magic, so rapidly
as to seem remodelled rather than fresh-built. Elsewhere the vast façade of the Circus[2] rivals the beauty
of the temples, a fitting place for a nation which has

437

provocat, digna populo victore gentium sedes, nec
4 minus ipsa visenda, quam quae ex illa spectabuntur,
visenda autem cum cetera specie, tum quod aequatus
plebis ac principis locus, siquidem per omne spatium
una facies, omnia continua et paria, nec magis
proprius spectanti Caesari suggestus quam propria
5 quae spectet. Licebit ergo te civibus tuis invicem
contueri; dabitur non cubiculum principis sed ipsum
principem cernere in publico, in populo sedentem,
populo cui locorum quinque milia adiecisti. Auxeras
enim numerum eius congiarii facilitate maioremque
in posterum suscipi liberalitatis tuae fide iusseras.

52. Horum unum si praestitisset alius, iam dudum
illi radiatum caput et media inter deos sedes auro
staret aut ebore, augustioribusque aris et grandiori-
2 bus victimis invocaretur. Tu delubra non nisi
adoraturus intras, tibi maximus honor excubare pro
templis postibusque praetexi. Sic fit, ut di ⟨tibi⟩[1]
summum inter homines fastigium servent, cum
3 deorum ipse non adpetas.[2] Itaque tuam statuam in
vestibulo Iovis optimi maximi unam alteramve et
hanc aeream cernimus. At paulo ante aditus omnes
gradus totaque area hinc auro hinc argento relucebat,
seu potius polluebatur, cum incesti principis statuis

---

[1] tibi *add. Keil: om. M.*
[2] appetas *Livineius:* adeptus *M.*

---

[1] Confirmed by ILS 286 (S. 374 (*a*)).

conquered the world, a sight to be seen on its own account as well as for the spectacles there to be displayed: to be seen indeed for its beauty, and still more for the way in which prince and people alike are seated on the same level. From one end to the other is a uniform plan, a continuous line, and Caesar as spectator shares the public seats as he does the spectacle. Thus your subjects will be able to look on you in their turn; they will be permitted to see not just the Emperor's box, but their emperor himself, seated among his people—the people to whom you have given an additional five thousand seats.[1] For you had already increased their number by the liberality of your largess, and had encouraged it to be further increased in future on the guarantee of your generosity.

52. If another had boasted a single one of these achievements he would long since have worn a nimbus round his head; a seat of honour wrought in gold or ivory would have been placed for him among the gods, and prayers offered in his name with major victims on the holiest of altars. But you enter the sanctuaries only to offer your own prayers—for you the highest honour is to have your statues placed outside the temples, on guard before the doors. This is why the gods have set you on the pinnacle of human power: they know that you do not covet their own. Of your statues, only one or two are to be seen in the vestibule of the temple of Jupiter Best and Highest, and these are made of bronze; whereas only recently every approach and step, every inch of the precinct was gleaming with silver and gold, or rather, was casting pollution, since the

4 permixta deorum simulacra sorderent. Ergo istae
quidem aereae et paucae manent manebuntque
quam diu templum ipsum, illae autem ⟨aureae⟩[1] et
innumerabiles strage ac ruina publico gaudio
litaverunt. Iuvabat illidere solo superbissimos vultus, instare ferro, saevire securibus, ut si singulos
5 ictus sanguis dolorque sequeretur. Nemo tam
temperans gaudii seraeque laetitiae, quin instar
ultionis videretur cernere laceros artus truncata
membra, postremo truces horrendasque imagines
obiectas excoctasque flammis, ut ex illo terrore et
minis in usum hominum ac voluptates ignibus
6 mutarentur. Simili reverentia, Caesar, non apud
genium tuum bonitati tuae gratias agi, sed apud
numen Iovis optimi maximi pateris: illi debere nos
quidquid tibi debeamus, illius quod bene facias,
7 muneris esse qui te dedit. Ante quidem ingentes
hostiarum greges per Capitolinum iter magna sui
parte velut intercepti devertere via cogebantur, cum
saevissimi domini atrocissima effigies tanto victimarum cruore coleretur, quantum ipse humani
sanguinis profundebat.

53. Omnia, patres conscripti, quae de aliis principibus a me aut dicuntur aut dicta sunt, eo pertinent

---

[1] aureae *add. Catanaeus: om. M.*

---

[1] *Ep.* IV. 11; Suet. *Dom.* 22. Domitian's mistress, Julia,
was the daughter of Titus. (In fact, the *Lex Claudia* had

figures of the gods were defiled by having statues of an incestuous emperor in their midst.[1] And so your few statues of bronze stand and will stand as long as the temple itself, whereas those innumerable golden images, as a sacrifice to public rejoicing, lie broken and destroyed. It was our delight to dash those proud faces to the ground, to smite them with the sword and savage them with the axe, as if blood and agony could follow from every blow. Our transports of joy—so long deferred—were unrestrained; all sought a form of vengeance in beholding those bodies mutilated, limbs hacked in pieces, and finally that baleful, fearsome visage cast into fire, to be melted down, so that from such menacing terror something for man's use and enjoyment should rise out of the flames.

With the same reverence for the gods, Caesar, you will not allow public thanks for your benevolence to be addressed to your genius, but direct them to the godhead of Jupiter Best and Highest; to him, you say, we owe whatever we owe you, and your benefactions are the gift of him who gave you to us. Yet previously the vast herds of victims were often stopped on the Capitoline Way and large numbers forced to turn aside, for in honour of that grim statue of a brutal tyrant[2] the blood of victims had to flow as freely as the human blood he shed.

53. All that I say and have said, Conscript Fathers, about previous emperors is intended to show how

authorized marriage between uncle and niece: Suet. *Claud.* 26. 3; Tac. *Ann.* XII. 5.)

[2] The equestrian statue set up in 89 at the west end of the Forum; cf. Statius, *Silvae* I. 1.

ut ostendam, quam longa consuetudine corruptos
depravatosque mores principatus parens noster
reformet et corrigat. Alioqui nihil non parum grate
2 sine comparatione laudatur. Praeterea hoc primum
erga optimum imperatorem piorum civium officium
est, insequi dissimiles; neque enim satis amarit
3 bonos principes, qui malos satis non oderit. Adice
quod imperatoris nostri non aliud amplius ac diffusius
meritum est, quam quod insectari malos principes
4 tutum est. An excidit dolori nostro modo vindicatus
Nero? Permitteret, credo, famam vitamque eius
carpi qui mortem ulciscebatur, nec ut in se dicta
5 interpretaretur, quae de simillimo dicerentur. Quare
erga[1] te, Caesar, muneribus [omnibus[2]] tuis omnibus
comparo, multis antepono, quod licet nobis et in
praeteritum de malis imperatoribus cotidie vindicari
et futuros sub exemplo praemonere, nullum locum
nullum esse tempus, quo funestorum principum
manes a posterorum exsecrationibus conquiescant.
6 Quo constantius, patres conscripti, et dolores nostros
et gaudia proferamus; laetemur his quibus fruimur,
ingemiscamus illis quae patiebamur; simul utrumque
faciendum est sub bono principe. Hoc secreta nostra
hoc sermones hoc ipsae gratiarum actiones agant,

---

[1] erga *H*: ergo *X*: ego *Keil*.
[2] omnibus *M*: *del corrector cod. Vat.*

our Father is amending and reforming the character of the principate which had become debased by a long period of corruption. Indeed, eulogy is best expressed through comparison, and, moreover, the first duty of grateful subjects towards a perfect emperor is to attack those who are least like him: for no one can properly appreciate a good prince who does not sufficiently hate a bad one. Furthermore, no service of our emperor's has spread so far in its effects as the freedom he allows us to criticize bad rulers with impunity. Have we already forgotten in our troubles how Nero was but lately avenged?[1] Can you imagine that *he* would have allowed the breath of criticism to fall on Nero's life and reputation, when he avenged his death? Would he not guess that anything said against one so like himself could be applied to him? And so in your case, Caesar, alongside all your other benefits and above many of them, I set our freedom to avenge ourselves daily on the evil emperors of the past, and to warn by example all future ones that there will be neither time nor place for the shades of disastrous rulers to rest in peace from the execrations of posterity. With all the more assurance, Conscript Fathers, can we therefore reveal our griefs and joys, happy in our present good fortune and sighing over our sufferings of the past, for both are equally our duty under the rule of a good prince. This then must we make the subject of our private talk, our public conversation

---

[1] In 95 Domitian condemned to death Epaphroditus, who had helped his master Nero to commit suicide (Suet. *Dom.* 14. 4). For an echo of these words cf. Tac. *Hist.* II. 76. 7: " An excidit trucidatus Corbulo? "

meminerintque sic maxime laudari incolumem imperatorem, si priores secus meriti reprehendantur. Nam cum ⟨de⟩[1] malo principe posteri tacent, manifestum est eadem facere praesentem.

54. Et quis iam locus miserae adulationis manebat ignarus, cum laudes imperatorum ludis etiam et commissionibus[2] celebrarentur, saltarentur atque in omne ludibrium effeminatis vocibus modis gestibus frangerentur? Sed illud indignum, quod eodem tempore in senatu et in scaena, ab histrione et a 2 consule laudabantur. Tu procul a tui cultu ludicras artes removisti. Seria ergo te carmina honorque aeternus annalium, non haec brevis et pudenda praedicatio colit; quin etiam tanto maiore consensu in venerationem tui theatra ipsa consurgent, quanto 3 magis de te scaenae silebunt. Sed quid ego istud admiror, cum eos quoque honores qui tibi a nobis offeruntur aut delibare parcissime aut omnino soleas recusare? Nihil ante tam vulgare tam parvum in senatu agebatur, ut non laudibus principum immorarentur, quibuscumque censendi necessitas acci- 4 disset. De ampliando numero gladiatorum aut de instituendo collegio fabrorum consulebamur, et quasi prolatis imperii finibus nunc ingentes arcus excessurosque templorum fastigium titulos, nunc menses

[1] de add. corrector cod. Vat.: om. M.
[2] commissionibus Lipsius: commessacionibus M.

and our speeches of thanks, never forgetting that an
emperor is best praised in his lifetime through
criticism of his predecessors according to their deserts. For when an evil ruler's survivors hold their
peace, it is clear that his successor is no better.

54. Could any spot remain ignorant of the lamentable spirit of adulation in the country, when tribute
to the emperors was paid in the form of shows and
riotous entertainment,[1] where dancing and wailing
ran through every kind of buffoonery and effeminacy,
expressed in rhythmic antics and shrieks? But the
scandal was that everything was approved in the
Senate as well as on the stage, through consul and
actor alike. You cut out all these stage performances from honours paid to you. Thus serious
poetry and the everlasting glory of our historic past
pay you tribute in place of a moment's disgraceful
publicity; furthermore, the whole theatre-audience
will rise to show its respect with all the more un-
animity now that the stage is to say less of you.
But why confine my admiration to this, when the
other honours we offer you are always so sparingly
accepted or else refused?[2] Hitherto, anyone called
on to speak in the Senate, on any subject however
slight and trivial, had to prolong his speech with
adulation of the emperor. We debated the increase
in number of gladiators or the founding of a workers'
union; the boundaries of empire might have been
extended as we discussed colossal arches and inscriptions too long for temple architraves, or else
the months, when more than one were to take the

---

[1] Described in Suetonius, *Dom.* 4.
[2] Confirmed by *Ep.* X. 9. 2.

etiam nec hos singulos nomini Caesarum dicabamus.
Patiebantur illi, et quasi meruissent laetabantur.
5 At nunc quis nostrum tamquam oblitus eius de quo
refertur censendi officium principis honore consumit?
Tuae moderationis haec laus, ⟨non⟩[1] constantiae
nostrae, et tibi obsequimur quod in curiam non ad
certamen adulationum sed ad usum munusque
iustitiae convenimus, hanc simplicitati tuae verita-
tique gratiam relaturi, ut te quae vis velle, quae non
6 vis nolle credamus. Incipimus inde desinimus ibi, a
quo incipi in quo desini sub alio principe non posset.
Nam plerosque ex decretis honoribus et alii non
receperunt, nemo ante tantus fuit ut crederetur
7 noluisse decerni; quod ego titulis omnibus speciosius
reor, quando non trabibus aut saxis nomen tuum sed
monimentis aeternae laudis inciditur.

55. Ibit in saecula fuisse principem cui florenti et
incolumi numquam nisi modici honores, saepius nulli
2 decernerentur. Et sane si velimus cum priorum
temporum necessitate certare, vincemur; ingeniosior
est enim ad excogitandum simulatio veritate, servitus
3 libertate, metus amore. Simul cum iam pridem
novitas omnis adulatione consumpta sit, non alius
erga te novus honor superest, quam si aliquando de
4 te tacere audeamus. Age, si quando pietas nostra

---

[1] non *add. Lipsius*: om. M.

---

[1] Nero gave his name to April, and that of Claudius and
Germanicus to May and June (Tac. *Ann.* XV. 74. 1 and XVI.

names of the Caesars.[1] For their part, the emperors
suffered this and even enjoyed it, believing it their
due. But which of us today spends the proper time
for his speech on praising the emperor as if forgetful
of the subject of debate? The credit here is due to
moderation on your part, not self-restraint on ours;
it is in obedience to your wishes that we assemble in
the House not to compete in flattery but to practise
and render justice, and to pay tribute to your open-
hearted sincerity through our confidence that your
likes and dislikes are genuinely what you say they
are. We start and finish at a point where neither
was possible when another was in power; for though
there have been others who refused most of the
honours offered them, no one was great enough
before for us to believe that he did not want them
offered. This, I think, is more splendid than any
inscription, since your name is engraved not on
beams of wood or blocks of stone but in the records
of imperishable glory.

55. It will go down through the ages that there
has been a prince to whom, in the full vigour of his
lifetime, only modest honours were decreed, and,
more often, none at all. Of course we cannot hope
to compete with the compulsion of former times, for
novelty is more readily devised by simulated than
by genuine feeling, less successfully by freedom and
affection than by servitude and fear. Since, therefore, adulation has exhausted any possibility of innovation, the only new way left for us to do you
honour is to venture sometimes to say nothing. Ah,

12. 2). Domitian gave his title of " Germanicus " to September, and his own name to October (Suet. *Dom.* 13. 3).

silentium rupit et verecundiam tuam vicit, quae
qualiaque aut decernimus nos, aut tu non recusas!—
ut adpareat non superbia et fastidio te amplissimos
honores repudiare, qui minores non dedigneris.
5 Pulchrius hoc, Caesar, quam si recusares omnes;
nam recusare omnes ambitionis, moderatio est eligere
parcissimos. Quo temperamento et nobis et aerario
⟨consulis, nobis quidem quod omni liberas suspicione,
aerario⟩[1] autem, quod sumptibus eius adhibes
modum, ut qui exhaustum non sis innocentium bonis
6 repleturus. Stant igitur effigies tuae, quales olim
ob egregia in rem publicam merita privatis dica-
bantur; visuntur eadem e materia Caesaris statuae
7 qua Brutorum qua Camillorum. Nec discrepat
causa: illi enim reges hostemque victorem moenibus
depulerunt, hic regnum ipsum quaeque alia captivitas
gignit, arcet ac summovet, sedemque obtinet principis
8 ne sit domino locus. Ac mihi intuenti sapientiam
tuam minus mirum videtur, quod mortales istos
caducosque titulos aut depreceris aut temperes; scis
enim ubi vera principis, ubi sempiterna sit gloria.
Hi sunt honores in quos nihil flammis, nihil senectuti,
9 nihil successoribus liceat. Arcus enim et statuas,
aras etiam templaque demolitur et obscurat oblivio,

---

[1] *lacunam explevit corrector cod. Vat.*: om. M.

---

[1] D. Junius Brutus, who expelled the Tarquins in 510 B.C.
had his statue on the Capitol. M. Furius Camillus, who drove

if ever our loyal devotion breaks its silence and over-
comes your hesitation, what honours shall we decree
and you be glad to accept! Then it will be made
plain that it was not pride and contempt which made
you refuse the highest honours while accepting lesser
ones, for this, Caesar, was nobler on your part than
to refuse all: to refuse all would be merely courting
favour, while it is true modesty to choose the lowest.
The same spirit of moderation marks your relations
with us, and with the treasury; we need not feel
that our motives are suspect, and the treasury has a
limit set to its expenditure, since you are not minded
to replenish it (if emptied) from the wealth of innocent
men. And so statues are put up for you as they
were for individuals in times past for their outstanding services to the State; Caesar's portrait is there
for all to see, fashioned from the same bronze as that
of a Brutus or a Camillus, and for the same reason [1]—
for they expelled the tyrant kings and conquering
foe from the walls of Rome, while Caesar sweeps
tyranny away, banishes all that captivity has bred,
and makes sure that the imperial seat he holds shall
never be a tyrant's throne. And knowing your
wisdom as I do, I find it less remarkable that you
set aside or limit those titles which are mortal and
must perish; for you know where lies the true, eter-
nal glory of a prince. Therein are the honours
over which devouring flames, passage of time, the
hands of a successor have no power. Arches and
statues, even altars and temples must all decay, to

the Gauls from Latium in the fourth century, had his in the
Forum. Cf. 13. 4.

449

Q

neglegit carpitque posteritas: contra contemptor ambitionis et infinitae potestatis domitor ac frenator animus ipsa vetustate florescit, nec ab ullis magis laudatur quam quibus minime necesse est. Praeterea ut quisque factus est princeps, extemplo fama eius, incertum bona an mala, ceterum aeterna est. 10 Non ergo perpetua principi fama, quae invitum manet, sed bona concupiscenda est; ea porro non imaginibus et statuis, sed virtute ac meritis pro- 11 rogatur. Quin etiam leviora haec, formam principis figuramque, non aurum melius vel argentum quam favor hominum exprimat teneatque. Quod quidem prolixe tibi cumulateque contingit, cuius laetissima facies et amabilis vultus in omnium civium ore oculis animo sedet.

56. Adnotasse vos credo, patres conscripti, iam dudum me non eligere quae referam. Propositum est enim mihi principem laudare, non principis facta. Nam laudabilia multa etiam mali faciunt, ipse laudari nisi optimus non potest. Quare non alia maior, imperator auguste, gloria tua quam quod agentibus tibi gratias nihil velandum est, nihil omittendum 2 [est].¹ Quid est enim in principatu tuo, quod cuiusquam praedicatio vel transilire vel praetervehi debeat? Quod momentum, quod immo temporis punctum, aut beneficio sterile aut vacuum laude? Non omnia eius modi, ut is optime te laudasse videatur, qui narraverit fidelissime? Quo fit ut prope in immensum diffundatur oratio mea, et

¹ omittendum est quid est *M*: omittendum ecquid *Livineius*.

be lost in oblivion, for posterity to neglect or revile; in contrast, a spirit which is above ambition, which can hold in check the temptations of power unbounded, blossoms as the years go by and hears its praise most often on the lips of those who are least forced to sing it. Moreover, an emperor is no sooner elected than his fame is assured for all time, for better or worse; he need not seek a lasting reputation (it will last in spite of him) but a good one: and this is preserved not in portraits and statues but in virtue and good deeds. His form and features too, so short-lived as they are, are not so well expressed and retained in silver and gold as by his people's love. That happy fortune is yours to enjoy, in every way you could desire, for your radiant face and beloved countenance dwell in the words, the looks, the thoughts of all your subjects.

56. I dare say you have noticed, Conscript Fathers, that I have long since stopped selecting what I shall say; for I set out to praise my prince in person, and not his actions. Many deeds may be admirable though bad men do them, but a man can only win praise for himself if he possesses true virtue. Wherefore, august Emperor, nothing can bring you greater glory than the fact that in expressing our thanks we have nothing to omit or conceal. Is there anything in your principate which a panegyrist must hurry over with a passing word? Any moment or instant of time which has yielded no benefit and commands no approbation? Does not everything combine to make the highest praise of you no more than a faithful record of the truth? And so my speech could be infinitely prolonged, although the period of

3 necdum de biennio loquor. Quam multa dixi de
moderatione, et quanto plura adhuc restant! ut
illud, quod secundum consulatum recepisti, quia
princeps et pater deferebat; at postquam ad te
imperî summam, et cum omnium rerum tum etiam
tui potestatem, di transtulerunt, tertium consulatum
recusasti, cum agere tam bonum consulem posses.
4 Magnum est differre honorem, gloriam maius.
Gestum consulatum mirer an non receptum?—
gestum non in hoc urbis otio et intimo sinu pacis,
sed iuxta barbaras gentes, ut illi solebant, quibus
erat moris paludamento mutare praetextam igno-
5 tasque terras victoria sequi. Pulchrum imperio
gloriosum tibi, cum te socii atque amici sua in patria,
6 suis in sedibus adierunt. Decora facies multa post
saecula consulis tribunal viridi caespite exstructum,
nec fascium tantum sed pilorum signorumque honore
circumdatum. Augebant maiestatem praesidentis
diversi postulantium habitus ac dissonae voces,
7 raraque sine interprete oratio. Magnificum est
civibus iura, quid hostibus reddere! speciosum
certam fori pacem, quid immanes campos sella
curuli victorisque vestigio premere, imminere mina-
cibus ripis tutum quietumque, spernere barbaros

---

¹ Probably Pliny means the period from 28 January 98
when Trajan succeeded Nerva to 1 January 100, when he
assumed his third consulship. He was consul for the second
time on 1 January 98, first with Nerva, then with Sex. Julius
Frontinus.

² Cf. 57. 1. Trajan could have assumed a third consulship
when he became emperor in January 99.

which I speak is less than two years.[1] I have said much about your moderation, but how much more is still unsaid! For example: you accepted a second consulship because an emperor, your father, bestowed it; but later on, when the gods placed supreme authority in your hands, that power to direct your own future as well as everything else, you refused the consulate a third time, although you could have assumed its duties so well.[2] It is noble to postpone a distinction, nobler still to put aside the glory it would bring you. Which commands my admiration more—the consulship you refused or the one you held? and held not in the tranquil atmosphere of the city deep in the embrace of peace, but in the face of savage tribes, like those heroes of old who changed the toga of office for a soldier's cloak and carried victory to lands unknown. It brought honour for the empire and distinction to you, when friends and allies sought audience in their own countries, their native lands; it was a splendid sight after so many years to see green turf piled high for a consul's tribunal, with the soldiers' javelins and standards for a guard of honour alongside the rods of office, and you presiding in person, your majesty enhanced by contrast with the varied garb of your petitioners and their discordant voices, their speeches seldom dispensing with an interpreter. If it is noble to administer justice to fellow-citizens, what is it to enemies! The splendour of occupying a curule chair in the assured peace of the forum pales beside the glory of setting it up in vast open spaces in the conqueror's wake, with calm and security acting as a threat to hostile river-banks; the glory too of scorn-

fremitus hostilemque terrorem non armorum magis
8 quam togarum ostentatione compescere! Itaque
non te apud imagines sed ipsum praesentem audien-
temque consalutabant imperatorem, nomenque quod
alii domitis hostibus, tu contemptis merebare.

57. Haec laus acti consulatus, illa dilati, quod
adhuc initio principatus ut iam exsatiatus honoribus
et expletus consulatum recusasti, quem novi im-
2 peratores destinatum aliis in se transferebant. Fuit
etiam qui in principatus sui fine, consulatum quem
dederat ipse, magna ex parte iam gestum extorqueret
et raperet. Hoc ergo honore, quem et incipientes
principes et desinentes adeo concupiscunt ut auferant,
3 tu otioso ac vacante privatis cessisti. Invidiosusne
erat aut tibi tertius consulatus aut principi primus?
Nam secundum imperator quidem, sub imperatore
tamen inisti, nihilque imputare in eo vel honori potes
4 vel exemplo nisi obsequium. Ita vero, quae civitas
quinquies atque etiam sexies consules vidit, non illos
qui exspirante iam libertate per vim ac tumultum
creabantur, sed quibus sepositis et absentibus in
rura sua consulatus ferebantur, in hac civitate
tertium consulatum princeps generis humani ut

---

[1] Nero, in his panic over the revolt of Vindex (Suet. *Nero* 43).
[2] Cf. 8. 3-4. Pliny speaks in exaggerated terms: Trajan had received the titles of *Caesar, Imperator* and *Germanicus* on his adoption, but was never joint emperor with Nerva.
[3] *e.g.* L. Papirius Cursor, Q. Fabius Maximus, M. Claudius Marcellus (five times); Quinctius Capitolinus (six times).

ing the cries of savages, and displaying the toga
instead of parading arms to quell fear of the foe!
Thus you were hailed as *imperator* not in effigy but in
person, in your own hearing; others had to defeat an
enemy to win this title, but it was yours for your cool
indifference to his threats.

57. So much for the fame of the consulship you
held. Now for the one you postponed, when your
principate had only just begun and (as if sated and
surfeited with honours) you refused the office of consul which newly-elected emperors had previously
claimed even when it was assigned to others. One
of them at the end of his reign had even snatched
away a consulship he had bestowed himself and
which had nearly run its course.[1] This then was a
distinction so coveted by emperors whether beginning or ending their reigns that they could seize
it from its bearers; yet you left it for your subjects,
even when it was vacant and unoccupied. Should
we have begrudged you a third consulship? Or a
first one in your new capacity as our prince? You
were in fact emperor when you entered your second
one, but were still serving under another emperor,[2]
and could only claim credit by setting an example of
obedience. Why, the country has seen men five or
six times consul,[3] and not only those named amid the
violence and confusion of the times when liberty
breathed her last[4] but those to whom the office was
brought at their country homes far away from Rome:[5]
could it look on while a prince and leader of mankind
refused a third consulship as likely to be unpopular

---

[4] Marius, seven times: Caesar, five times consul.
[5] *e.g.* L. Quinctius Cincinnatus, Q. Atilius Regulus.

5 praegravem recusasti? Tantone Papiriis etiam et
Quintiis moderatior Augustus et Caesar et pater
patriae? At illos res publica ciebat. Quid? te non
eadem res publica, non senatus, non consulatus ipse,
qui sibi tuis umeris attolli et augescere videtur?

58. Non te ad exemplar eius voco, qui continuis
consulatibus fecerat longum quendam et sine discrimine annum: his te confero quos certum est,
quotiens consules fuerunt, non sibi praestitisse.
Erat in senatu ter consul, cum tu tertium consulatum
2 recusabas. Onerosum nescio quid verecundiae tuae
consensus noster indixerat, ut princeps totiens consul
esses quotiens senator tuus: nimia modestia istud
3 etiam privatus recusasses. An consularis viri tri-
umphalisque filius cum tertio consul creatur ascendit?
non debitum hoc illi, non vel sola generis claritate
promeritum? Contigit ergo privatis aperire annum
fastosque reserare, et hoc quoque redditae libertatis
indicium fuit quod consul alius quam Caesar esset.
Sic exactis regibus coepit liber annus, sic olim
4 servitus pulsa privata fastis nomina induxit. Miseros
ambitionis, qui ita consules semper, ut semper
principes erant! Quamquam non ambitio quam
livor et malignitas videri potest, omnes annos possi-

---

[1] Domitian was consul 17 times, and in 84 was nominated
for 10 years, though the sequence was broken in 89 (Suetonius,
Dom. 13. 3; Dio LXVII. 4. 3).

[2] Unidentified. Possibly Fabricius Veiento (Syme, *JRS*
XX), consul [3] in 83.

with his people? Are you to be so much more modest than a Papirius or a Quinctius—you who are Augustus and Caesar and the Father of your country? There was a republic then, you say, to summon them; but surely there is still a republic to call on you, as well as a Senate, and the consulate itself, which must be honoured and ennobled if you will shoulder its responsibilities.

58. I am not asking you to model yourself on him[1] whose successive consulships dragged the long year out without a break, only drawing a comparison with those who have thought little of their several consulships. A member of the Senate had been consul three times at the moment when you refused to hold office a third time.[2] Evidently we asked too much of your modesty by our unanimous request that our prince should be consul as often as one of his own senators, but your diffidence about accepting would have been excessive even in an ordinary citizen. Can a third consulship really be promotion for the son of a consular father granted a triumph? Is it not rather his due, his proper reward, if only as a member of a distinguished family? And so ordinary people enjoyed the honour of opening the year and heading the official calendar, and this too was proof of liberty restored: the consul now need not be Caesar. (The year began in freedom in the same way after the kings were expelled, long ago when the appearance of individual names in the calendar marked the end of servitude.) O wretched ambition in those who sought to match their lifelong power with a perpetual consulship! Or perhaps not ambition so much as spiteful jealousy, to appropriate

dere, summumque illud purpurae decus non nisi
5 praecerptum praefloratumque transmittere. Tuam
vero magnanimitatem an modestiam an benignitatem
prius mirer? Magnanimitatis fuit expetito semper
honore abstinere, modestiae cedere, benignitatis per
alios frui.

59. Sed iam tempus est te ipsi consulatui praestare,
ut maiorem eum suscipiendo gerendoque facias.
Nam saepius recusare ambiguam ac potius illam
interpretationem habet, tamquam minorem putes.
Tu quidem ut maximum recusasti; sed hoc persuadere
2 nemini poteris, nisi aliquando et non recusaveris.
Cum arcus cum tropaea cum statuas deprecaris, tribu-
enda est verecundiae tuae venia; illa enim sane tibi
dicantur. Nunc [1] vero postulamus, ut futuros principes doceas inertiae renuntiare paulisper, delicias
differre paulisper, et saltem ad brevissimum tempus
ex illo felicitatis somno velut excitari; induere
praetextam quam cum dare possent occuparint,
ascendere curulem quam detineant, esse denique
quod concupierint, nec ideo tantum velle consules
3 fieri ut fuerint. Gessisti alterum consulatum, scio;
illum exercitibus, illum provinciis, illum etiam exteris
gentibus poteris imputare, non potes nobis. Audimus quidem te omne munus consulis obisse, sed
audimus; diceris iustissimus humanissimus patientis-

---

[1] nunc *Lipsius*: cum *M*.

every year and pass on the official purple only when
its lustre was tarnished after use. Where then shall
I give my highest praise—to the noble spirit in you
which led you to deny an honour always sought after,
to the moderation which made you yield it to others,
or to the benevolence which enabled you to enjoy
it through them?

59. Even so, the time has come for you to offer
yourself for the consulate, and increase its status by
taking and holding it in person. To refuse it too often
can be misinterpreted, or give the impression that
you value it too little. In fact, of course, you refused
because you value it so highly, but you will convince
no one of this unless one day you accept. You may
beg to be spared trophies and statues and arches of
triumph and must be forgiven for your modesty,
for these are clearly offered to you personally. But
what we are asking now is that you teach future
emperors to break away from their inertia and suspend
their pleasures for a while, to rouse themselves for a
moment at least, and not sleep away their good fortune: to put on the toga of office which is already
in their possession as it is in their power to give, to
mount the curule chair which they are keeping
empty: in short, to be what they have really wished
to be, and not to agree to become consul only to say
they have been one. You have held a second consulship, I know, but the armies, the provinces, even
foreigners can be said to have benefited from it, not
any of us. Certainly we have heard it said that you
fulfilled every duty as a consul, but what is hearsay?
And the rumour goes that you were the very soul of
justice, kindness, and consideration, but it is only

simus fuisse, sed diceris. Aequum est aliquando nos
iudicio nostro oculis nostris, non famae semper et
rumoribus credere. Quousque absentes de absente
4 gaudebimus? Liceat experiri an aliquid superbiae
tibi ille ipse secundus consulatus attulerit. Multum
in commutandis moribus hominum medius annus
5 valet, in principum plus. Didicimus quidem, cui
virtus aliqua contingat, omnes inesse; cupimus
tamen experiri, an nunc quoque una eademque res
6 sit bonus consul et bonus princeps. Nam praeter id
quod est arduum, duas easque summas potestates
simul capere, tum inest utrique non nulla diversitas,
cum principem quam simillimum esse privato, consulem quam [1] dissimillimum deceat.

60. Atque ego video proximo anno consulatus
recusandi hanc praecipuam fuisse rationem, quod
eum absens gerere non poteras. Sed iam urbi
votisque publicis redditus, quid est in quo magis sis
adprobaturus, quae quantaque fuerint quae de-
siderabamus? Parum est ut in curiam venias, nisi
et convocas; ut intersis senatui, nisi et praesides;
2 ut censentes audias, nisi et perrogas. Vis illud
augustissimum consulum aliquando tribunal maiestati
suae reddere? ascende. Vis constare reverentiam
magistratibus, legibus auctoritatem, modestiam pos-
3 tulantibus? adire.[2] Quod enim interesset rei publicae, si privatus esses, consulem te haberet tantum

---

[1] simillimum esse privato, consulem quam *Cuspinianus*:
om. M.
[2] adire *codd.*: accipe *Kukula*: audi, adside, adsiste, *alii alia*.

---

[1] A Stoic doctrine. Cf. Cic. *de Off.* II. 35.
[2] Not strictly impossible; cf. Suetonius, *Aug.* 26. 3.

rumour. It is only right that we should be able one
day to trust the evidence of our own eyes and our
own judgement, and not always have to rely on your
reputation and reports. How long are we to rejoice
in your existence without ever having you in our
midst? Let us see whether that second consulship
of yours has not really made you give yourself airs!
A year's interval can make a big difference in a man's
character, and even more in a prince's. We are told
that possession of one virtue means possession of all,[1]
but all the same we want to know whether a good
consul and a good prince are still one and the same
today. For apart from the general difficulty of
exercising two kinds of supreme power at the same
time, there is a certain contradiction between them:
for a prince should resemble as much and a consul
as little as possible an ordinary citizen.

60. I do of course realize that your chief reason
last year for refusing the consulship was the impossi-
bility of holding it in absence.[2] But now that you
are restored to Rome in answer to our prayers, how
else can you give better proof to us of those great
qualities in you which we missed when you were
away? It is not enough for you to enter the House
if you do not bid us assemble; you should not be
present at our meetings without presiding, nor listen
to speeches unless you call on the speakers. Would
you restore its former majesty to the consuls' tribunal, once so much revered? Then mount it. Do
you want to strengthen respect for the magistrates,
spread restraint among litigants, and confirm the
authority of the law? Then let men come before
you. Rest assured that your country's present

461

an et senatorem, hoc nunc scito interesse, principem
4 te habeat tantum an et consulem. His tot tantisque
rationibus quamquam multum reluctata, verecundia
principis nostri tandem tamen cessit. At quemadmodum cessit? Non se ut privatis, sed ut privatos
sibi pares faceret. Recepit enim tertium consulatum,
5 ut daret. Noverat pudorem noverat moderationem
hominum, qui non sustinerent tertio consules esse
nisi cum ter consule. Bellorum istud sociis olim,
periculorum consortibus, parce tamen tribuebatur,
quod tu singularibus viris ac de te quidem bene ac
6 fortiter sed in toga meritis praestitisti. Utriusque
cura utriusque vigilantia obstrictus es, Caesar. Sed
in principe rarum ac prope insolitum est, ut se putet
obligatum, aut si putet amet. Debes ergo, Caesar,
et solvis, et cum ter consules facis non tibi magnus
princeps sed non ingratus amicus videris; quin etiam
perquam modica quaedam civium merita fortunae
7 tuae viribus in maius extollis. Efficis enim ut
tantum tibi quisque praestitisse videatur, quantum
a te recepit. Quid isti benignitati precer, nisi ut
semper obliges obligeris, incertumque facias, utrum
magis expediat civibus tuis debere tibi an praestitisse!
61. Equidem illum antiquum senatum contueri

---

¹ Trajan was consul for the third time in 100, from January
to February with Sex. Julius Frontinus, and from March to
April with someone unidentified (possibly Vestricius Spurinna).
A third consulship was the highest honour possible for a
senator (cf. *Ep.* II. 1. 2).

interest in wanting to see you consul as well as emperor is simply what it would be if you were an ordinary citizen and could be senator and consul as well.

Thus these repeated, cogent arguments have broken down the long resistance of our prince's modesty, and at last he has yielded.[1] In what way? Not by descending to his subjects' level, but by raising them to his; for he accepted a third consulship only to be able to bestow one. He knew the moderation and reluctance of those who would accept a third consulship only as colleagues of another who was three times consul. This honour used to be granted in the past to allies in war and companions in danger, and only in rare cases; yet you bestowed it on two outstanding individuals who had served you well and bravely but as civilians. In both cases, the watchful care of your colleague set a restriction on you, Caesar; but it is rare and almost unknown in a prince to think himself under any restraint, or to welcome it if he does. This then is a debt which you wish to repay, and in doing so by granting a third consulship you see yourself not as a great emperor so much as a not ungrateful friend. Moreover, however modest the services of your subjects, you ennoble them by virtue of your rank, for everyone is made to feel that he has given as much as he has received from you. Your generosity leaves me with nothing to ask, save that you will always create these mutual obligations, and so leave your subjects in doubt whether they do better as your debtors or your creditors.

61. For my part, I thought I had the great Senate

videbar, cum ter consule adsidente tertio consulem
designatum rogari sententiam cernerem. Quanti
2 tunc illi quantusque tu! Accidit quidem ut corpora
quamlibet ardua et excelsa procerioribus admota
decrescant, item ut altissimae civium dignitates
collatione fastigii tui quasi deprimantur, quantoque
propius ad magnitudinem tuam ascenderint, tantum
3 etiam a sua descendisse videantur. Illos tamen tu,
quamquam non potuisti tibi aequare cum velles, adeo
in edito collocasti, ut tantum super ceteros quantum
4 infra te cernerentur. Si unius tertium consulatum
eundem in annum in quem tuum contulisses, ingentis
animi specimen haberetur. Ut enim felicitatis est
quantum velis posse, sic magnitudinis velle quantum
5 possis. Laudandus quidem et ille qui consulatum
tertium meruit, sed magis sub quo meruit: magnus
memorandusque qui tantum praemium cepit, sed
6 maior qui capienti dedit. Quid quod duos pariter
tertio consulatu, duos collegii tui sanctitate decorasti?
ut sit nemini dubium hanc tibi praecipuam causam
fuisse extendendi consulatus tui, ut duorum consulatus amplecteretur collegamque te non uni daret.
7 Uterque nuper consulatum alterum gesserat a patre
tuo (id est quanto minus quam a te!) datum;
utriusque adhuc oculis paulo ante dimissi fasces
oberrabant, utriusque sollemnis ille lictorum et
praenuntius clamor auribus insederat, cum rursus

---

[1] Frontinus was consul for the second time in 98.

of past times before my eyes when I beheld a consul
for the third time seated by your side, and a consul-
elect, again for the third time, called upon to
speak. This was their finest hour, as it was also
yours! Tall men, however erect, normally look
smaller by the side of those who are taller still; in
the same way, your subjects' highest honours are
diminished by comparison with your own exalted
state, and the nearer they approach to your eminence, the more they seem to lose of their own.
Such men could never be made your equal, however
much you wished, but you raised them sufficiently
high for them to stand out above the rest as you did
above them. If you had singled out one person only
for a third consulship during the year you held your
own it would have been clear proof of your magnanimity—for if success means the power to do all one
wishes, magnanimity is the will to do all one can.
In that case there would have been praise for the
man who earned his third consulship, but more for
the prince under whom he earned it; the winner of
such a prize might be great and memorable, but how
much greater the one who awarded it! Well: did
you not choose two for the honour of a third consulship, two for the sacred privilege of being your
colleague? (No one then can doubt that your chief
reason for extending your own consulship was to
cover not one but both of theirs.) Both had recently
held a second consulship, received from your father[1]—
which is not quite the same as having it granted by
you; for both, the rods of office so lately laid aside
were still before their eyes, and the traditional cries
of the lictors heralding their approach still ringing in

curulis rursusque purpura; ut olim cum hostis in
proximo, et in summum discrimen adducta res
publica, expertum honoribus virum posceret, non
consulatus hominibus isdem sed idem homines con-
8 sulatibus reddebantur. Tanta tibi bene faciendi
vis, ut indulgentia tua necessitates aemuletur.
Modo praetextas exuerant: resumant; modo lictores
abire iusserant: revocent; modo gratulantes amici
9 recesserant: revertantur. Hominisne istud ingenium
est, hominis potestas, renovare gaudia redintegrare
laetitiam, nullamque requiem gratulationibus dare
neque alia repetendis consulatibus intervalla per-
10 mittere, nisi dum finiuntur? Facias ista semper,
nec umquam in hoc opere aut animus tuus aut
fortuna lassetur; des quam plurimis tertios consulatus, et cum plurimis tertios consulatus dederis,
semper tamen plures quibus debeas dare supersint.

62. Omnium quidem beneficiorum quae merentibus tribuuntur non ad ipsos gaudium maius quam ad
similes redundat; praecipue tamen ex horum consulatu non ad partem aliquam senatus sed ad totum
senatum tanta laetitia pervenit, ut eundem honorem
2 omnes sibi et dedisse et accepisse videantur. Nempe
enim hi sunt quos senatus, cum publicis sumptibus
minuendis optimum quemque praeficeret, elegit,
et quidem primos. Hoc est igitur hoc est, quod

---

¹ Cf. *Ep.* II. 1. 9, and Dio, LXVIII. 2. 3; also Syme, *JRS*
XX. The effect of this commission was not impressive—some
sacrifices and horse-races were abolished, but its reforms were
confined to the expenditure of the *aerarium Saturni*. There
is no evidence that it continued under Trajan.

their ears when once again they donned the purple and seated themselves in the curule chair; just as in times past, when the enemy at the gates and the republic's gravest hour of peril demanded men tried and tested in office, it was a case of returning the same men to the consulate rather than the consulate to them. Such is your power to do good that your gracious favour has the same effect as stern necessity. These men had just taken off their robes of office when they must put them on again, dismissed their lictors only to call them back; their friends had offered congratulations and taken their leave, and now they must return. Surely some superhuman stroke of genius, some more than mortal power enables you to renew men's times of rejoicing and revive their happiness, to deny all respite to congratulations, and refuse to allow a break before the next consulship beyond the time spent on winding up the one before! May your work continue, and may your spirit and guiding fortune never tire; bestow third consulships on as many of us as possible, and when you have given all you can, may there ever be more of us to whom they should be given!

62. All benefits which are awarded to deserving men give as much pleasure to others like them as to the recipients; yet in particular, the consulship conferred on these two senators delighted the entire Senate (not just one section of it) so much that everyone felt he shared both in the giving of the honour and in receiving it. For these are the men who were the Senate's choice, and indeed its first choice, when it was selecting the best men for the commission to reduce public expenditure;[1] this, then, is what recommended

467

3 penitus illos animo Caesaris insinuavit. An parum
saepe experti sumus hanc esse rerum condicionem,
ut senatus favor apud principem aut prosit aut
noceat? Nonne paulo ante nihil magis exitiale erat
quam illa principis cogitatio: " hunc senatus probat,
hic senatui carus est "? Oderat quos nos amaremus,
4 sed et nos quos ille. Nunc inter principem sena-
tumque dignissimi cuiusque caritate certatur. De-
monstramus invicem, credimus invicem, quodque
maximum amoris mutui signum est, eosdem amamus.
5 Proinde, patres conscripti, favete aperte, diligite
constanter. Non iam dissimulandus est amor ne
noceat, non premendum odium ne prosit: eadem
Caesar quae senatus probat improbatque. Vos ille
praesentes, vos etiam absentes in consilio habet.
Tertio consules fecit quos vos elegeratis, et fecit hoc
6 ordine quo electi a vobis erant. Magnus uterque
honor vester, sive eosdem maxime diligit quos scit
vobis esse carissimos, sive illis neminem praefert,
7 quamvis aliquem magis amet. Proposita sunt
senioribus praemia, iuvenibus exempla. Adeant fre-
quentent securas tandem ac patentes domos. Quisquis probatos senatui viros suspicit, hic maxime
8 principem promeretur. Sibi enim adcrescere putat
quod cuique adstruatur, nullamque in eo gloriam
ponit, quod si omnibus maior, nisi maximi fuerint
9 quibus maior est. Persta, Caesar, in ista ratione

468

them so warmly to Caesar. Has not past experience shown us all too often a situation where the Senate's approval can make or mar a man in the Emperor's eyes? It is only a short time since nothing was so fatal as for him to think that this one or another had the Senate's affection and support. He hated everyone we loved—but we felt the same about his favourites. Today, prince and Senate are rivals in their affection for all who most deserve it; by turns we prove this or accept the proofs he gives us, and—chief indication of our mutual sentiments— we love the same men. Henceforth, Conscript Fathers, you may be open in your favours and steadfast in your affections; there is no need now to conceal your love and hatred for fear the one may bring harm, the other profit, when Caesar's approval and disapproval rests on the same objects as the Senate's. Present or absent, you share his counsels. He granted a third consulship to men of your choosing, and in the same order in which you had chosen them. Whether he has special affection for those who he knows are dearest to your hearts, or whether he will not give precedence to anyone he personally prefers to them, the honour he does you is equally great. Older men can look to rewards, young ones to examples; they can gather on the doorsteps of houses which at last feel free to open wide their doors. Anyone who looks up to the men the Senate admires can be sure of finding favour with a prince who believes that his own status is increased as others advance, and who feels no distinction in standing supreme unless those beneath him stand as high as possible. Continue, Caesar, in the course you have

propositi, talesque nos crede, qualis fama cuiusque
est. Huic aures huic oculos intende: ne respexeris
clandestinas existimationes nullisque magis quam
audientibus insidiantes susurros. Melius omnibus
quam singulis creditur: singuli enim decipere et
decipi possunt, nemo omnes neminem omnes fe-
fellerunt.

63. Praevertor iam ad consulatum tuum, etsi sunt
quaedam ad consulatum quidem pertinentia, ante
consulatum tamen: in primis quod comitiis tuis
interfuisti candidatus, non consulatus tantum sed
immortalitatis et gloria et exempli quod sequerentur
2 boni principes, mali mirarentur. Vidit te populus
Romanus in illa vetere potestatis suae sede; perpessus es longum illud carmen comitiorum nec iam
inridendam moram consulque sic factus es ut unus
3 ex nobis, quos facis consules. Quotus quisque
principum antecedentium honorem istum aut consulatui habuit aut populo? Non alii marcidi somno,
hesternaque cena redundantes, comitiorum suorum
nuntios opperiebantur; alii sane pervigiles et in-
somnes, sed intra cubilia sua illis ipsis consulibus a
quibus consules renuntiabantur, exsilia et caedem
4 machinabantur? O prava et inscia verae maiestatis
ambitio, concupiscere honorem quem dedigneris,
dedignari quem concupieris, cumque ex proximis
hortis campum et comitia prospectes, sic ab illis

---

[1] The *renuntiatio*, the proclamation of the newly-elected
consuls before the *comitia centuriata* assembled in the Campus
Martius.

planned, and believe each one of us to be the equal of
his public reputation; have eyes and ears for that
alone, and pay no attention to furtive suggestions and
whispers which do most damage to those who heed
them. General opinion is more to be trusted than
individual—it is quite possible for individuals to
deceive and be deceived, but no one can dupe every-
body, nor can everyone combine to dupe him.

63. I pass now to your consulship, though there
are certain events relating to it which did in fact
precede it: first of all, you were present in person
at your election, as a candidate not only for the
consulate but for immortality and the fame of setting
an example for good rulers to follow and bad ones to
look on with surprise. The people of Rome saw you
in the ancient seat of their former power, while you
bore patiently with the long ceremonial of the elec-
toral assembly,[1] the slow ritual which this time was
not a farce; and so you were made consul as if one
of us, us who are made consuls by your word. How
many of your predecessors did honour in this way
either to the consulate or to the people? Some of
them, we know, awaited the news of their election
heavy-eyed with sleep, gorged with the banquet of
the day before; others who were certainly alert and
awake in their own rooms were plotting exile and
death for the very consuls who proclaimed their elect-
tion. Vile ambition, blind to the meaning of true
majesty, for a man to covet honours which at heart he
despised, to despise what he coveted, and although his
gardens overlooked the election-field,[2] to keep away

[2] Perhaps the gardens of Lucullus, imperial property since
47, which overlooked the Campus Martius. Cf. 50. 6.

5 abesse, tamquam Danubio Rhenoque dirimare!
Averseris tu honori tuo sperata suffragia, renunti-
arique te consulem iussisse contentus, liberae civitatis
ne simulationem quidem serves; abstineas denique
comitiis abstrusus atque abditus, quasi illic tibi non
6 consulatus detur sed abrogetur imperium? Haec
persuasio superbissimis dominis erat, ut sibi viderentur principes esse desinere, si quid facerent
tamquam senatores. Plerique tamen non tam super-
7 bia quam metu quodam submovebantur. An stupro-
rum sibi incestarumque noctium conscii, auspicia
polluere sacratumque campum nefario auderent
8 contaminare vestigio? Non adeo deos hominesque
contempserant, ut in illa spaciosissima sede hominum
deorumque coniectos in se oculos ferre ac perpeti
possent. Tibi contra et moderatio tua suasit et
sanctitas, ut te et religioni deorum et iudiciis
hominum exhiberes.

64. Alii consulatum ante quam acciperent, tu et
dum accipis meruisti. Peracta erant sollemnia
comitiorum, si principem cogitares, iamque se omnis
turba commoverat, cum tu mirantibus cunctis accedis
ad consulis sellam, adigendum te praebes in verba
principibus ignota, nisi cum iurare cogerent alios.
Vides quam necessarium fuerit consulatum non recu-

---

¹ Sworn by the elected consuls before the consul presiding
over the *comitia*.

as though the Rhine and Danube flowed between!
Would you scorn the votes you hoped would confirm
your election, and think it sufficient to be proclaimed
consul by your own order, without preserving any
semblance of a free state? Would you stand aloof
from the elections, cowering in some hiding-place,
as if they were not there to confer a consulship on
you but to abrogate your supreme power? Earlier
despots, in their overweening pride, held to their
conviction that if ever they acted as senators, they
would cease to be emperors in their own eyes. Most,
however, were influenced not so much by pride as by
a kind of fear; conscious of their vices and their incestuous nights, how could they have dared to defile
the auspices and pollute the sacred field with their
guilty tread? Their contempt for everything human
and divine had not reached the point of steeling them
to stand up in that great open space and face the eyes
of gods and men directed on them. In striking contrast, it was your moderation and your purity of heart
which persuaded you to offer yourself to men's
judgement and the divine presence of the gods.

64. There have been others who merited the consulate before receiving it, but in addition, you proved
your worth at the very moment of doing so. The
election ceremonies were over (for, remember, this
candidate was already emperor) and the entire crowd
was already on the move, when you surprised everyone by going up to the consul's chair and presenting yourself to take the oath,[1] in the words no
emperor had ever used except when compelling
others to swear. Now you see how essential it was
for you not to have refused the consulate: we should

473

sare. Non putassemus istud te facturum fuisse, si
2 recusasses. Stupeo, patres conscripti, necdumque
satis aut oculis meis aut auribus credo, atque identidem me an audierim, an viderim interrogo. Imperator ergo et Caesar et Augustus ⟨et⟩[1] pontifex
maximus stetit ante gremium consulis, seditque
consul principe ante se stante, et sedit inturbatus
3 interritus, et tamquam ita fieri soleret. Quin etiam
sedens stanti praeiit ius iurandum, et ille iuravit
expressit explanavitque verba quibus caput suum
domum suam, si scienter fefellisset, deorum irae
consecraret. Ingens, Caesar, et par gloria tua, sive
fecerint istud postea principes, sive non fecerint.
4 Ullane satis digna praedicatio est idem tertio consulem fecisse quod primo, idem principem quod
privatum, idem imperatorem quod sub imperatore?
Nescio iam, nescio, pulchriusne sit illud quod praeeunte nullo, an hoc quod alio praeeunte iurasti.

65. In rostris quoque simili religione ipse te legibus
subiecisti, legibus, Caesar, quas nemo principi scripsit.
Sed tu nihil amplius vis tibi licere quam nobis: sic
fit, ut nos tibi plus velimus. Quod ego nunc primum
audio, nunc primum disco; non est princeps super

---

[1] et *add. Livineius*: om. *M*.

---

[1] The *votorum nuncupatio* was made on the Capitol by the
consul on the day of his entry into office. Pliny appears,
however, to refer to oaths taken on the rostra in the Forum,
at the beginning and end of the consulship.

not have believed you would act as you did had you
not accepted it. I am still astonished, Conscript
Fathers, still unable to believe the evidence of my
years and eyes; I keep on asking myself whether
I really heard and saw this thing. The Emperor,
Caesar, Augustus, the Chief Pontiff stood before the
seated consul—yes, the consul sat while his prince
stood before him, and remained seated, undisturbed
and unafraid, as if it were normal practice. Moreover, while he sat he repeated the words of the oath
to his prince who remained standing: and the latter
swore. Clearly and explicitly he pronounced the
words whereby he consigned his life and household
to the wrath of heaven if knowingly he swore false.
Great is your glory here, Caesar, and so it will remain, whether your successors follow your example
or not. A man three times consul acted as he did
at his first election: a prince showed himself no
different from a commoner, an emperor no different
from one of his subjects: this surely is beyond all
praise. For my part, I cannot judge which is the
more splendid: the fact that you took the oath with
no precedent before you, or that you took the words
from another's lips.

65. In the Forum, too, you mounted the platform
of your own accord and were equally scrupulous to
submit yourself to the laws.[1] No one had intended
these laws to apply to the Emperor, Caesar, but you
were unwilling for your privileges to extend beyond
our own. The result is that we are all the more
willing for them to do so. There is a new turn of
phrase which I hear and understand for the first
time—not " the prince is above the law " but " the

leges sed leges super principem idemque Caesari
2 consuli quod ceteris non licet. Iurat in leges
attendentibus dis (nam cui magis quam Caesari
attendant?), iurat observantibus his quibus idem
iurandum est, non ignarus alioqui nemini religiosius
quod iuraverit custodiendum, quam cuius maxime
interest non peierari. Itaque et abiturus consulatu
iurasti te nihil contra leges fecisse. Magnum hoc
erat cum promitteres, maius postquam praestitisti.
3 Iam totiens procedere in rostra, inascensumque illum
superbiae principum locum terere, hic suscipere hic
ponere magistratus, quam dignum te quamque
diversum consuetudini illorum, qui pauculis diebus
gestum consulatum, immo non gestum abiciebant
per edictum! Hoc pro contione pro rostris, pro iure
iurando, scilicet, ut primis extrema congruerent,
utque hoc solo intellegerentur ipsi consules fuisse,
quod alii non fuissent.

66. Non transilui, patres conscripti, principis nostri
consulatum, sed eundem in locum contuli, quidquid
de iure iurando dicendum erat. Neque enim ut in
sterili ieiunaque materia eandem speciem laudis
deducere ac spargere atque identidem tractare
2 debemus. Inluxerat primus consulatus tui dies,
quo tu curiam ingressus nunc singulos, nunc universos
adhortatus es resumere libertatem, capessere quasi

law is above the prince "; Caesar bows to the same restrictions as any other consul. He takes the oath of obedience to the law with the gods as witness (for who if not Caesar can command their attention?)— he takes it under the watchful eye of those who must take it too, well aware that no one must be more scrupulous about keeping to his oath than the man most concerned that there should be no perjury.

Then, at the moment of laying down your consulship, you swore a similar oath that you had done nothing contrary to the law; and this, as a statement of achievement, was even finer than your earlier promise. To appear on the platform so often, to frequent a place shunned by the pride of princes, there to assume and there to lay down your offices: how this conduct becomes you, and how it contrasts with the conduct of those who took up a consulship for a day or two—or, rather, failed to take it up— only to issue a proclamation that they had flung it aside! That was what took the place of the assembly, the platform and their oath, doubtless to make their consulship end as it had begun, and to provide the only indication that they had been elected at all: namely, the absence of any other consul.

66. I have not left out our prince's consulship, Conscript Fathers, but I wanted all I had to say about oaths to be dealt with at once, for this is no barren, empty subject in which a single facet of his glory must be broken up into fragments and handled several times. The first day of your consulship had hardly dawned before you entered the Senate-house and exhorted us, individually and collectively, to resume our freedom, to take up the responsibilities

477

communis imperî curas, invigilare publicis utilitati-
3 bus et insurgere. Omnes ante te eadem ista
dixerunt, nemini tamen ante te creditum est. Erant
sub oculis naufragia multorum, quos insidiosa tranquillitate provectos improvisus turbo perculerat.
Quod enim tam infidum mare quam blanditiae
principum illorum, quibus tanta levitas tanta fraus,
ut facilius esset iratos quam propitios cavere? Te
4 vero securi et alacres quo vocas sequimur. Iubes
esse liberos: erimus; iubes quae sentimus promere
in medium: proferemus. Neque enim adhuc ignavia
quadam et insito torpore cessavimus: terror et
metus et misera illa ex periculis facta prudentia
monebat, ut a re publica (⟨ubi⟩[1] erat autem omnino
res publica?) oculos aures animos averteremus. At
5 nunc tua dextera tuisque promissis freti et innixi,
obsaepta diutina servitute ora reseramus, frena-
tamque tot malis linguam resolvimus. Vis enim
tales esse nos quales iubes, nihilque exhortationibus
tuis fucatum, nihil subdolum, ⟨nihil⟩[2] denique quod
credentem fallere paret non sine periculo fallentis.
Neque enim umquam deceptus est princeps, nisi qui
prius ipse decepit.

67. Equidem hunc parentis publici sensum cum
ex oratione eius tum pronuntiatione ipsa perspexisse

---

[1] ubi *add. Mynors*: nulla *Kukula*: om. *M*.
[2] nihil *add. Burnouf*: om. *M*.

of the power we might be thought to share,[1] to watch over the interests of the people, and to take action. All your predecessors had said the same, but none had been believed. In our mind's eye were the shipwrecks of the many who had advanced in a hazardous period of calm, only to be sunk by an unforeseen storm; for no sea could be more treacherous than the flattery of those emperors whose instability and guile made it more difficult to be on guard against their favour than their wrath. But in your case, we have no fears, and are all eagerness to follow your lead. You bid us be free, and we shall be free; you tell us to express ourselves openly, and we shall do so, for our previous hesitation was due to no cowardice or natural inertia, but to fear and apprehension, and the lamentable caution born of our perils which bade us turn eyes and ears and minds from our country, from that republic which was utterly destroyed. Today we can place our trust and reliance on your promises and sworn oath, and open our lips long sealed by servitude, loosen our tongues which were bound to silence by so many evils; for you truly wish us to be what you bid us, and your exhortations are free from all overtones of deception. In short, no traps are laid today for the trustful, bringing their own dangers for those who set them—for no prince has ever been deceived unless he led the way in deception.

67. For my part, I believe I have formed this impression of the Father of us all as much from the

---

[1] Durry compares *Ep.* IX. 2. 3, and thinks the " quasi " a Tacitean comment on the Senate's diminished powers. Cf. **63.** 5 (*liberae civitatis simulatio*).

videor. Quae enim illa gravitas sententiarum, quam inadfectata veritas verborum, quae adseveratio in voce, quae adfirmatio in vultu, quanta in oculis 2 habitu gestu, toto denique corpores fides! Tenebit ergo semper quid suaserit, scietque nos, quotiens 3 libertatem quam dedit experiemur, sibi parere. Nec verendum est ne incautos putet si fidelitate temporum constanter utamur, quos meminit sub malo principe aliter vixisse. Nuncupare vota et pro aeternitate imperii et pro salute principum, immo pro salute principum ac propter illos pro aeternitate 4 imperii solebamus. Haec pro imperatore nostro in quae sint verba suscepta, operae pretium est adnotare: " Si bene rem publicam et ex utilitate omnium ⟨rexerit⟩[1]." Digna vota quae semper suscipiantur 5 semperque solvantur. Egit cum dis ipso te auctore, Caesar, res publica, ut te sospitem incolumemque praestarent, si tu ceteros praestitisses; si contra, illi quoque a custodia tui capitis oculos dimoverent teque relinquerent votis, quae non palam susci- 6 perentur. Alii se superstites rei publicae optabant faciebantque; tibi salus tua invisa est, si non sit cum rei publicae salute coniuncta. Nihil pro te pateris optari, nisi expediat optantibus, omnibusque annis in consilium de te deos mittis, exigisque ut sententiam

---

[1] rexerit *add. Keil (cf 68. 1)*: rexeris *Puteolanus*: *om. M.*

---

[1] For the annual renewal of vows throughout the empire, see *Ep.* X. 35–6 and X. 100–1 (3 January in successive years).

manner of his delivery as from the words he has said.
Only consider the seriousness of his sentiments, the
unaffected candour of his words, the assurance in his
voice and decision in his countenance, and the complete sincerity of his gaze, his pose and gestures, in
fact of his entire person! So, we may be sure, he
will always remember the advice he gave us, and will
always understand that in making use of the freedom
he granted we are acting only in obedience to him.
We need have no fears that he will think us improvi-
dent if we show no hesitation in profiting by the
security of the times, since he remembers how differently we lived under a wicked emperor. We were
accustomed to offering vows[1] to ensure the eternity
of the empire and the safety of the emperors, or,
rather, the safety of the emperors and thereby the
eternity of the empire. But in the case of our present emperor, it is worth noting the wording of these
vows, and the clause " if he has ruled the State well
and in the interests of all." Such vows are indeed
worthy of being always renewed and always discharged. At your instigation, Caesar, the State has
struck a bargain with the gods that they shall preserve your health and safety as long as you do the
same for everyone else; otherwise they are to turn
their attention from protecting your life, and to
abandon you to such vows as are taken in secret.
Others used to wish to outlive the State, and took
steps to do so; but for you, the thought of personal
safety is hateful unless it be bound up with the
safety of us all. You permit no prayers on your
behalf unless they benefit their authors, and every
year you set the gods to reconsider you, insisting that

481

suam mutent, si talis esse desieris qualis electus es;
7 sed ingenti conscientia, Caesar. quasi pacisceris cum
dis, ut te si mereberis servent, cum scias an merearis
8 neminem magis quam deos scire. Nonne vobis,
patres conscripti, haec diebus ac noctibus agitare
secum videtur: "Ego quidem in me, si omnium
utilitas ita posceret, etiam praefecti manum armavi;
sed ne deorum quidem aut iram aut neglegentiam
deprecor, quaeso immo et obtestor, ne umquam pro
me vota res publica invita suscipiat, aut si susceperit
ne debeat"?

68. Capis ergo, Caesar, salutis tuae gloriosissimum
fructum ex consensu deorum. Nam cum excipias ut
ita demum te dei servent, si bene rem publicam et
ex utilitate omnium rexeris, certus es bene te rem
publicam et ex utilitate omnium regere cum servent.
2 Itaque securus tibi et laetus dies exit, qui principes
alios cura et metu distinebat, cum suspensi et
attoniti, parumque confisi patientia nostra, hinc
atque inde publicae servitutis nuntios exspectarent.
3 Ac si forte aliquos flumina nives venti praepedissent,
statim hoc illud esse credebant quod merebantur;
nec erat discrimen ullum pavoris, propterea quod
cum a malo principe tamquam successor timeatur
quisquis est dignior, cum sit nemo non dignior, omnes
4 timentur. Tuam securitatem non mora nuntiorum,
non litterarum tarditas differt. Scis tibi ubique

---

[1] Sex. Attius Suburanus was commander of the Guard (cf.
Dio LXVIII. 16. 1). He was soon promoted to the Senate
(consul in 101 and again in 104).

they must revise their opinion if you have changed since the time of your election. But you act with full knowledge, Caesar, in your pact with the gods to preserve you if you deserve it; you are well aware that no one can judge this better than the gods themselves. Can you not imagine, Conscript Fathers, how his thoughts run, night and day: " I have put arms to be used against me, if public interest demands, in the hands of my own prefect;[1] but when it comes to the gods, I will never seek to avert either their wrath or their indifference, rather will I beg and pray that my country shall never have to offer vows on my behalf against its will, or if it has already done so, that they shall not be binding."

68. Thus, Caesar, from your agreement with the gods you have a glorious reward in your continued safety. For by stipulating that the gods shall preserve you only " if you have ruled the State well and in the interests of all " you can be confident that you are ruling well, as long as they are preserving you. And so you can be carefree and happy all through that day which was fraught with fear and anxiety for the other emperors, who spent it racked by suspense, uncertain how far to try our patience, awaiting from all quarters the messages of our common servitude. And if perchance some of these were delayed by rivers, snow, or adverse winds, they jumped to the conclusion that they would get their just deserts. Their apprehensions were always the same; for a bad ruler fears anyone worthier than himself as a likely successor, so when all are worthier, all are feared. Your own tranquillity is not interrupted either by belated messages or slow delivery of letters;

iurari, cum ipse iuraveris omnibus. Nemo hoc non
5 sibi praestat. Amamus quidem te in quantum
mereris; istud tamen non tui facimus amore sed
nostri, nec umquam inlucescat dies quo pro te
nuncupet vota non utilitas nostra sed fides, Caesar.
6 Turpis tutela principis, cui potest imputari. Queri
libet quod in secreta nostra non inquirant principes
7 nisi quos odimus. Nam si eadem cura bonis ac malis
esset, quam ubique admirationem tui, quod gaudium
exultationemque deprenderes, quos omnium cum
coniugibus ac liberis, quos etiam cum domesticis aris
focisque sermones! Scires mollissimis istis auribus
parci. Et alioqui, cum sint odium amorque contraria,
hoc perquam simile habent, quod ibi intemperantius
amamus bonos principes, ubi liberius malos odimus.

69. Cepisti tamen et adfectus nostri et iudicii
experimentum, quantum maximum praesens capere
potuisti, illo die quo sollicitudini pudorique candidatorum ita consuluisti, ne ullius gaudium alterius
tristitia turbaret. Alii cum laetitia, alii cum spe
recesserunt; multis gratulandum, nemo consolandus
2 fuit. Nec ideo segnius iuvenes nostros exhortatus
es, senatum circumirent, senatui supplicarent, atque
ita a principe sperarent honores, si a senatu petissent.
3 Quo quidem in loco, si quibus opus exemplo, adiecisti

----

¹ The *nominatio* by the emperor of eligible candidates,
sometime in mid-January.

you can be sure that everywhere the oath is being taken for you, as you have taken it for us all, for no one would deny himself this pleasure. The fact is, we love you as you deserve—but in our own self-interest rather than in yours. The day will never dawn when we offer vows on your behalf only from a sense of duty, with no benefit to ourselves. (There is no virtue in supporting a prince who can claim the credit for our support.) We may well complain that it is only the rulers we hate who violate our privacy, for if good and bad were equally inquisitive, what universal admiration for yourself you would find, what delight and rejoicing, what conversations you would hear everywhere between us and our wives and children, and even before the hearths and altars of our homes! You would then understand how we are sparing those sensitive ears of yours. But however different love and hatred may be, they have one close resemblance: we give our love more unrestrainedly to good princes in this very place where we have freely hated bad ones.

69. You have, however, had proof of our affection and our sentiments, as far as you could in person, on the day[1] when your thoughtfulness for the anxieties and personal feelings of candidates was at pains not to let anyone's pleasure be marred by another's disappointment. Some departed full of happiness, others full of hope; there were many to congratulate, but none to console. You were none the less active in urging our young men to canvass the Senate, address their pleas to the senators, and not to hope for advancement from the Emperor unless they had sought it here. If anyone needed an

ut te imitarentur. Arduum, Caesar, exemplum, et
quod imitari non magis quisquam candidatorum
quam principum possit. Quis enim vel uno die
reverentior senatus candidatus, quam tu cum omni
vita tum illo ipso tempore quo iudicas de candidatis?
4 An aliud a te quam senatus reverentia obtinuit, ut
iuvenibus clarissimae gentis debitum generi honorem,
5 sed ante quam deberetur offerres? Tandem ergo
nobilitas non obscuratur sed inlustratur a principe,
tandem illos ingentium virorum nepotes, illos posteros
libertatis nec terret Caesar nec pavet; quin immo
festinatis honoribus amplificat atque auget, et
maioribus suis reddit. Si quid usquam stirpis
antiquae, si quid residuae claritatis, hoc amplexatur
6 ac refovet, et in usum rei publicae promit. Sunt in
honore hominum et in ore famae magna nomina
⟨excitata⟩ [1] ex tenebris oblivionis indulgentia
Caesaris, cuius haec intentio est ut nobiles et con-
servet et faciat.

70. Praefuerat provinciae quaestor unus ex candidatis inque ea civitatis amplissimae [2] reditus egregia
2 constitutione fundaverat. Hoc senatui adlegandum
putasti. Cur enim te principe, qui generis tui

---

[1] excitata *Keil, alii alia*: om. *M*.
[2] civitatis amplissimae *Lipsius*: civitas amplissima *M*.

---

[1] *Nobilitas* was never legally defined. It is used by Pliny
and Tacitus to refer to the descendants of the consular families
of the Republic, and also, probably, to those of the period
before A.D. 14, when the consular elections were transferred to
the Senate and the Republic might be said to have ended.
Cf. *Ep.* V. 17. 6.

example at this point, you added that he had only to
follow yours—a difficult example for anyone to follow, no easier for a candidate than for a prince!
Where is the candidate who can show greater respect
for the Senate for a single day than you have done
throughout your life, and particularly on the day
when the candidates were subject to your decision?
What else was it but respect for the Senate which
made you offer young men of noble birth the position
which was their family right, but earlier than it was
due? So at long last the light of the nobility[1] is not
dimmed by Caesar but made to shine more brightly;
at last the grandsons of great men, the descendants
of liberty, need not tremble in fear before the Emperor; instead, he exalts and honours them by early
distinctions, and restores them to their ancestral
glory. Any remnant of an ancient house, any lingering spark of former splendour he revives and
cherishes and promotes to the service of the State.
The great names are held in honour among men;
they are on the lips of fame, brought back from the
shades of oblivion by the graciousness of Caesar,
whose intention is not only to preserve our noble
families but to create them.

70. One of the candidates[2] had been responsible
for a province as quaestor, and there had settled
the finances of an important city by a remarkable
piece of planning. This, you thought, should be put
before the Senate; for while you are emperor—you,

[2] Possibly Sextus Quinctilius Valerius Maximus, born in
Alexandria Troas in Mysia, given *latus clavus* by Nerva;
quaestor in Bithynia in 97. trib. pleb. in 100, praetor 103, then
corrector of Achaia (*Ep.* VIII. 24; S. 235).

claritatem virtute superasti, deterior esset condicio
eorum qui posteros habere nobiles mererentur,
quam eorum qui parentes habuissent? O te dignum
qui de magistratibus nostris semper haec nunties,
nec poenis malorum sed bonorum praemiis bonos
3 facias! Accensa est iuventus erexitque animos ad
aemulandum quod laudari videbat, nec fuit quisquam quem non haec cogitatio subiret, cum sciret
quidquid a quoque in provinciis bene fieret, omnia
4 te scire. Utile est, Caesar, et salutare praesidibus
provinciarum hanc habere fiduciam, paratum esse
sanctitati industriae suae maximum praemium,
5 iudicium principis suffragium principis. Adhuc autem
quamlibet sincera rectaque ingenia, etsi non de-
torquebat, hebetabat tamen misera sed vera re-
6 putatio: "Vides enim: si quid bene fecero sciet
7 Caesar? aut si scierit testimonium reddet?" Ita
eadem illa seu neglegentia seu malignitas principum,
cum male consultis impunitatem, recte factis nullum
praemium polliceretur, nec illos a crimine et hos
8 deterrebat a laude. At nunc si bene aliquis provinciam rexerit, huic quaesita virtute dignitas offertur.
Patet enim omnibus honoris et gloriae campus: ex
hoc quisque quod concupiit petat et adsecutus sibi
debeat. Provinciis quoque in posterum et iniuriarum
metum et accusandi necessitatem remisisti. Nam si

whose virtues have gone far beyond the distinction
of your origin—why should the status of those who
deserve to have descendants among the nobility be
inferior to that of those whose parents were already
ennobled? You are indeed well fitted to report on
our magistrates in this way on all occasions, and by
rewarding the good instead of punishing the bad so
make them better men. The country's youth was
fired with inspiration to imitate what it saw winning
recognition; none could fail to share this thought,
knowing that anything done well by anyone in the
provinces was fully known to you. There is profit
now and advantage for those with responsible posi-
tions in the provinces; they can rest assured that
incorruptibility and application on their part can
expect the highest reward in the Emperor's judgement and support. Hitherto, however honest and
upright his nature, a man's views were distorted, or
at any rate weakened, by the reflection—lamentable
but true—that even if he did well, would Caesar
know? And if he knew, would he show it? And so
the emperors in their malice or their indifference
allowed evil counsels to go unpunished, while promising no rewards to deeds well done; thus they de-
terred some from seeking distinction but no one from
crime. Things are different today. Anyone who
has governed a province well is offered the position
his merits demand; the field of promotion and fame
lies open to all; everyone can set out to achieve his
aspirations, and owes his success to his own efforts.
The provinces too have been relieved by you of their
fears for the future, the danger of malpractices and
the need to bring prosecutions; for if they can ad-

profuerint quibus gratias egerint, de nullo queri
cogentur; ⟨sciunt⟩[1] et alioqui nihil magis prodesse
candidato ad sequentes honores quam peractos.
Optime magistratus magistratu, honore honor petitur.
9 Volo ego, qui provinciam rexerit, non tantum codi-
cillos amicorum nec urbana coniuratione eblanditas
preces sed decreta coloniarum decreta civitatum
adleget. Bene[2] suffragiis consularium virorum urbes
populi gentes inseruntur. Efficacissimum pro candidato genus est rogandi gratias agere.

71. Iam quo adsensu senatus, quo gaudio excep-
tum est, cum candidatis ut quemque nominaveras
osculo occurreres, devexus quidem in planum et
2 quasi unus ex gratulantibus! Te magis mirer, an
improbem illos qui effecerunt ut istud magnum
videretur, cum velut adfixi curulibus suis manum
tantum et hanc cunctanter et pigre et imputantibus
3 similes promerent? Contigit ergo oculis nostris
antiqua[3] facies, princeps aequatus candidatis,[4] et
simul stantis intueri parem accipientibus honorem
4 qui dabat. Quod factum tuum a cuncto senatu
quam vera acclamatione celebratum est: " Tanto
maior, tanto augustior"! Nam cui nihil ad augen-

---

[1] lacunam statuit Keil, Mynors: sciunt add. Baehrens: om. M.
[2] bene Lipsius: ne M.
[3] antiqua Mynors: insolita Catanaeus: alta Kukula: ante M.
[4] equitus candidatus M: aequatus candidatis editores:
principis aequati candidatis Kukula, Durry.

---

[1] Contrast the views of Thrasea Paetus, expressed in
Tacitus, Ann. XV. 21.
[2] There is no mention here of the usual commendatio, the
emperor's recommendation of some of the nominated candidates, nor of voting by the Senate (as in Ep. III. 20). Trajan
appears to do no more than make his wishes known (cf. 71. 7).

vance the career of those whose services have won
their thanks, they will not be compelled to lodge
complaints against anyone, and besides, they know
now that nothing helps a candidate for future
honours better than the ones he has already held.
It is an excellent thing for office to be sought through
office, and honour as a result of honour already bestowed. For my part, I should like to see a provincial governor citing not only the recommendations
of his friends and the support on his behalf he has
coaxed out of city factions, but also the civic resolutions of the Roman townships and cities where he has
served.[1] It is good that cities, peoples and nations
play their part in casting votes for the men they knew
as governors, and the most effective way of petition-
ing on behalf of a candidate is to express your gratitude to him in thanks.

71. Again, with what applause and delight the
Senate acclaimed you, when you embraced each
candidate as you named him,[2] stepping down to our
level as if your intention was to join in our congratulations! Which am I to do—admire you, or blame
those who made your behaviour exceptional by
contrast with their own: when they sat as if rooted
to their chairs of office, offering only a hand so slowly
and reluctantly, and apparently seeing merit in doing no more than that? Our eyes have been fortunate to behold the old-style form of ceremony, the
prince as equal with the candidates, to see him
standing with them, conferring honour and yet
standing no higher than those who received it from
him; so that with sincere admiration the entire
Senate acclaimed you as the more noble and revered.

dum fastigium superest, hic uno modo crescere potest,
si se ipse summittat securus magnitudinis suae.
5 Neque enim ab ullo periculo fortuna principum
longius abest quam humilitatis. Mihi quidem non
tam humanitas tua quam intentio eius admirabilis
6 videbatur. Quippe cum orationi oculos vocem
manum commodares, ut si alii eadem ista mandasses,
omnes comitatis numeros obibas. Atque etiam, cum
suffragatorum nomina honore quo solent exciperentur,
tu quoque inter excipientes eras, et ex ore Caesaris
7 ille senatorius adsensus audiebatur, quodque apud
principem perhibere testimonium merentibus gaude-
bamus, perhibebatur a principe. Faciebas ergo,
cum diceres optimos; nec ipsorum modo vita a te
sed iudicium senatus comprobabatur, ornarique se,
non illos magis quos laudabas, laetabatur.

72. Iam quod precatus es ⟨caelites⟩,[1] ut illa ipsa
ordinatio comitiorum bene ac feliciter eveniret nobis
rei publicae tibi, nonne tale est ut nos hunc ordinem
votorum convertere debeamus, eosdemque[2] obsecrare
ut omnia quae facis quaeque facies prospere cedant
tibi rei publicae nobis, vel si brevius sit optandum,
2 ut uni tibi in quo et res publica et nos sumus? Fuit
tempus, ac nimium diu fuit, quo alia adversa alia
secunda principi et nobis: nunc communia tibi
nobiscum tam laeta quam tristia, nec magis sine te
3 nos esse felices quam tu sine nobis potes. An si

---

[1] caelites *add. Mynors*: *om. M.*
[2] eosdemque *codex Londiniensis*; eos denique *M.*

For when a man can improve no more on his supreme position, the only way he can rise still higher is by stepping down, confident in his greatness. (There is nothing the fortune of princes has less to fear than the risk of being brought too low.) For me, even your courtesy seemed less remarkable than your anxiety to make it felt. In adapting your expression, your voice and gestures to your words, as if this was some commission you had to entrust to another, you ran through the whole gamut of politeness. Similarly, when the names of the sponsors were received with the usual cries of acclamation, your voice could be heard among them; from Caesar's lips was heard the Senate's assent, and the tribute we were happy to pay to merit in the Emperor's presence was voiced by him with us. Thus by hailing these men as the best choice, you made them so; nor was it only their life which won your approval, but also the judgement of the Senate: which rejoiced to find itself honoured no less than those who received your praise.

72. Next, you offered prayers to the gods, that the elections, thus duly performed, should bring success and happiness to us, to the State, and to yourself. Should we not rather reverse this order, and beg the gods to grant that all your actions, present and future, prove successful for yourself, for the State, and for us, or, to shorten our prayers, for yourself alone, on whom the State and ourselves alike depend? There was a time (which lasted all too long) when the Emperor's successes and misfortunes did not coincide with ours; but now we share with you both joys and sorrows, and we cannot be happy without you

posses in fine votorum adiecisses ut ita precibus tuis
di adnuerent, si iudicium nostrum mereri perseve-
rasses? Adeo nihil tibi amore civium antiquius, ut
ante a nobis deinde a dis, atque ita ab illis amari
4 velis, si a nobis ameris. Et sane priorum principum
exitus docuit, ne a dis quidem amari nisi quos
homines ament. Arduum erat has precationes tuas
5 laudibus adaequare; adaequavimus tamen. Qui
amoris ardor, qui stimuli, quae faces illas nobis
exclamationes subiecerunt! Non nostri, Caesar,
ingenii, sed tuae virtutis tuorumque meritorum
voces fuerunt, quas nulla umquam adulatio invenit,
6 nullus cuiquam terror expressit. Quem sic timuimus
ut haec fingeremus? quem sic amavimus ut haec
fateremur? Nosti necessitatem servitutis: ecquando
7 simile aliquid audisti, ecquando dixisti? Multa
quidem excogitat metus, sed quae adpareant quaesita
ab invitis. Aliud sollicitudinis aliud securitatis ingenium est; alia tristium inventio, alia gaudentium:
neutrum simulationes expresserint. Habent sua
verba miseri, sua verba felices, utque iam maxime
eadem ab utrisque dicantur, aliter dicuntur.

73. Testis ipse es quae in omnium ore laetitia.
Non amictus cuiquam non habitus quem modo
extulerat. Inde resultantia vocibus tecta, nihilque
2 tantis clamoribus satis clausum. Quis tunc non e

---

[1] Cf. the coin legend *Felicitas*.

any more than you can without us.[1] Or should you
(if it were possible) have ended by asking the gods
to grant your prayers only so long as you continued
to merit our esteem? Nothing stands higher with
you than your subjects' affection: so much so, that
you would put our love before that of the gods, and
desire theirs only if you have ours. Certainly the
fate of your predecessors has taught you that no one
can expect the gods to love him when men do not.
It was difficult for us to match these prayers of yours
with appropriate acknowledgement, but we man-
aged to do so; such was the warmth of our feeling
and our enthusiasm, which set a torch to our cries
of acclamation! No mental power on our side
prompted these words, Caesar, but your own virtue,
your own merits—words such as no adulation has ever
devised nor terror wrung out. Whom have we feared
so as to conjure up these expressions, or loved so as
to produce an avowal like this? You know the exi-
gencies of servitude; have you ever heard or said the
like? Fear may indeed be inventive, but the result
is far-fetched and constrained. The very nature of
anxiety is not that of security, and misery has quite
different resources at its command from joy: neither
can be prompted by pretended emotion. Unhappi-
ness has its own language, and so has good fortune,
and even if what they say is identical, it is differently
worded.

73. You witnessed yourself the happiness in the
faces of us all. None kept his cloak or dress as when
he lately left his home, as we raised the roof with our
cheers; nothing could shut in such cries. Not a man
but leapt to his feet, unconscious of having done so,

vestigio suo exsiluit? quis exsiluisse sensit? Multa
fecimus sponte, plura instinctu quodam et imperio;
3 nam gaudio quoque cogendi vis inest. Num ergo
modum ei tua saltem modestia imposuit? Non
quanto magis a te reprimebatur exarsimus? non
contumacia, Caesar; sed ut in tua potestate est an
4 gaudeamus, ita in quantum nec in nostra. Com-
probasti et ipse acclamationum nostrarum fidem
lacrimarum tuarum veritate. Vidimus humescentes
oculos tuos demissumque gaudio vultum, tantumque
5 sanguinis in ore quantum in animo pudoris. Atque
hoc magis incensi sumus ut precaremur, ne quando
tibi non eadem causa lacrimarum, utque numquam
6 frontem tuam ⟨adduceres⟩.[1] Hoc ipsum has nos
sedes quasi responsuras interrogemus, viderintne
umquam principis lacrimas; at senatus saepe
viderunt. Onerasti futuros principes, sed et posteros
nostros. Nam et hi a principibus suis exigent, ut
eadem audire mereantur, et illi quod non audiant
indignabuntur.

74. Nihil magis possum proprie dicere, quam quod
dictum est a cuncto senatu: " O te felicem "! Quod
cum diceremus, non opes tuas sed animum mira-
bamur. Ea enim demum vera felicitas, felicitate
2 dignum videri. Sed cum multa illo die dicta sunt
sapienter et graviter, tum vel in primis: " Crede
nobis, crede tibi." Magna hoc fiducia nostri, maiore

---

[1] adduceres *add. Schuster*: *om. M*.

for we did much self-prompted, and still more by
some instinct or authority—even behind rejoicing
there is a driving force. No thought for your
modesty could restrain us—our fervour leapt into
flames the more you would have damped it down.
This was no wilful disobedience, Caesar; yours is the
power to release our joy, but its extent is beyond our
control. On your part, too, you confirmed the sincerity of our acclamation by the unfeigned shedding
of your tears. We saw your eyes wet, your face
overcome by joy; we saw your blushes give outward
expression to the sense of unworthiness in your heart.
This fired us the more to pray that you would never
have a different cause for tears or anything to cloud
your face. And to these seats of ours we must put a
question, as if they could make reply: have they
ever seen an emperor's tears? (The Senate's they
have witnessed often enough.) You have laid a
heavy burden on emperors to come, and no less on
our successors, who will expect their princes to be
worthy to receive a similar acclamation; while these
princes will feel slighted because they do not.

74. I can find no more appropriate word than the
one voiced by the entire Senate in hailing you as
" fortunate." Here we were referring not to your
material wealth but to your inner self, for genuine
good fortune lies in being judged worthy of enjoying
it. But among the many words of weight and wisdom spoken on that day,[1] these must be singled out:
" Trust us, trust yourself." This was said with great

[1] These are the *acclamationes* greeting the proposals of the
emperors. Examples are quoted at length in *SHA. Alex. Sev.*
6–7, *M. Claud. Tac.* 4–5.

3 tamen tui diximus. Alius enim fortasse alium, ipsum
se nemo deceperit, introspiciat modo vitam seque
quid mereatur interroget. Proinde dabat vocibus
nostris fidem apud optimum principem, quod apud
malos detrahebat. Quamvis enim faceremus quae
amantes solent, illi tamen non amari se credebant
4 sibi. Super haec precati sumus, ut sic te amarent
di quemadmodum tu nos. Quis hoc aut de se aut
principi diceret mediocriter amanti? Pro nobis ipsis
quidem haec fuit summa votorum, ut nos sic amarent
di quomodo tu. Estne verum, quod inter ista
clamavimus: " O nos felices "? Quid enim felicius
nobis, quibus non iam illud optandum est, ut nos
diligat princeps, sed di quemadmodum princeps?
5 Civitas religionibus dedita, semperque deorum indulgentiam pie merita, nihil felicitati suae putat
adstrui posse, nisi ut di Caesarem imitentur.

75. Sed quid singula consector et colligo? quasi
vero aut oratione complecti aut memoria consequi
possim, quae vos, patres conscripti, ne qua inter-
ciperet oblivio, et in publica acta mittenda et
2 incidenda in aere censuistis. Ante orationes principum tantum eius modi genere monimentorum
mandari aeternitati solebant, acclamationes quidem
nostrae parietibus curiae claudebantur. Erant enim
quibus nec senatus gloriari nec principes possent.

---

[1] The *acta diurna*; cf. *Ep.* V. 13. 8. Inscribing on bronze,
Dio LX. 10. 2.; LXI. 3. 1.

confidence in ourselves, but greater still in you; for a man may deceive another, but no one can deceive himself, so long as he looks closely at his life and asks himself what are his true deserts. Moreover, our words carried conviction in the ears of the best of princes through the very factor which made them unconvincing to his evil predecessors; for though we went through the motions of affection before them, they could never believe that they were genuinely liked. Furthermore, we prayed that the gods should love you as you do ourselves, and who would say this of himself or to his prince if either were only moderately loved? On our own account, the sum of our prayers was simply that the gods should love us as you do. Amidst our acclamation of yourself we declared ourselves happy too: has this not the ring of truth? How could we be happier? Secure in our prince's love, we have only to hope that the gods will love us in the same way. And so this city which has always shown its devotion to religion and earned through piety the gracious favour of the gods has only one thought for the completion of its happiness: the gods must follow where Caesar shows the way.

75. But why trouble to assemble all these details? I could hardly hope to keep in mind or cover in a speech all that you, Conscript Fathers, decided to save from oblivion by publishing in the official records and inscribing on bronze.[1] Hitherto, only the speeches of the emperors were made safe for all time by records of this kind, while our acclamations went no farther than the walls of the senate-house; and indeed, these were such that neither Senate nor prince could take pride in them. Today these have

3 Has vero et in vulgus exire et posteris prodi cum ex
utilitate tum ex dignitate publica fuit, primum ut
orbis terrarum pietatis nostrae adhiberetur testis et
conscius; deinde ut manifestum esset audere nos de
bonis malisque principibus non tantum post ipsos
iudicare; postremo ut experimento cognosceretur
et ante nos gratos, sed miseros fuisse, quibus esse nos
4 gratos probare antea non licuit. At qua contentione,
quo nisu, quibus clamoribus expostulatum est, ne
adfectus nostros ne tua merita supprimeres, denique
5 ut in posterum exemplo provideres! Discant et
principes acclamationes veras falsasque discernere,
habeantque muneris tui quod iam decipi non poterunt.
Non instruendum illis iter ad bonam famam, sed non
deserundum; non submovenda adulatio sed non
reducenda est. Certum est et quae facere et quae
6 debeant audire si faciant. Quid nunc ego super ea,
quae sum cum toto senatu precatus, pro senatu
precer, nisi ut haereat animo tuo gaudium, quod
tunc oculis protulisti; ames illum diem et tamen
vincas, nova merearis, nova audias? eadem enim
dici nisi ⟨ob eadem⟩[1] facta non possunt.

76. Iam quam antiquum quam consulare, quod
triduum totum senatus sub exemplo patientiae tuae
sedit, cum interea nihil praeter consulem ageres!
2 Interrogatus censuit[2] quisque quod placuit; ⟨licuit⟩[3]

---

[1] ob eadem *add. Catanaeus, om. M. lacunam post* nisi
statuit Keil, Mynors.
[2] interrogatus censuit *Mueller:* interrogavit *M.*
[3] licuit *add. Haupt, om. M.*

---

[1] The final summing-up at the trial of Marius Priscus (cf.
Ep. II. 11).

been sent out into the world and passed on to posterity both in the general interest and to do honour to us all; firstly, so that the world could be summoned as an active witness to our loyalty, secondly to demonstrate that we were not afraid to pass judgement on good and bad rulers even in their lifetime, finally to give proof that though previously we were not ungrateful, we were unhappy so long as we were denied the opportunity of making our gratitude known. Now we are all eagerness and determination, clamouring for you not to set limits to our feelings or your own merits, in a word, to remember the example you owe to posterity! Let future princes too learn to distinguish between true acclamation and false, and owe it to you that they can no longer be deceived. The road to good repute need not be made for them, they have only to follow it; they have not to clear their path of adulation, only to guard against its return. There is no uncertainty about how they must act nor how their actions will be received. What then can I add, in the name of the Senate, to the prayers I shared with the whole Senate, except this? May your heart never lose the joy which showed in your eyes on that occasion, may you always think of that day with affection, and yet go on to greater things, to win fresh rewards and hear new acclamation; for the same words can only be repeated about the same deeds.

76. It was in accordance with the best traditions of the consulate that the Senate should continue in a three-day sitting,[1] following your own example of patience, and that during that time you acted solely in your capacity as presiding consul. Each senator

dissentire discedere, et copiam iudicii sui rei publicae
facere; consulti omnes atque etiam dinumerati
3 sumus, vicitque sententia non prima sed melior. At
quis antea loqui, quis hiscere audebat, praeter
miseros illos qui primi interrogabantur? Ceteri
quidem defixi et attoniti ipsam illam mutam ac
sedentariam adsentiendi necessitatem quo cum
dolore animi, quo cum totius corporis horrore per-
4 petiebantur! Unus solusque censebat, quod sequerentur omnes et omnes improbarent, in primis ipse
qui censuerat. Adeo nulla magis omnibus displicent,
quam quae sic fiunt tamquam omnibus placeant.
5 Fortasse imperator in senatu ad reverentiam eius
componebatur; ceterum egressus statim se recipiebat
in principem, omniaque consularia officia abicere
6 neglegere contemnere solebat. Ille vero ita consul,
ut si tantum consul foret, nihil infra se putabat, nisi
7 quod infra consulem esset. Ac primum ita domo
progrediebatur, ut illum nullus adparatus adrogantiae
principalis, nullus praecursorum tumultus detineret.
Una erat in limine mora consultare aves revererique
8 numinum monitus. Nemo proturbabatur, nemo
submovebatur; tanta viatoribus quies, tantus pudor
fascibus, ut plerumque aliena turba subsistere et
9 consulem et principem cogeret. Ipsius quidem

---

¹ It was in fact the first (that of Cornutus Tertullus, *Ep.*
II. 11. 19–22), and Pliny must mean that the voting showed
it was also the best.
² Cf. *Ep.* VIII. 14. 8. This account is one of the most

when called on for his opinion spoke as he thought
fit; he was free to disagree, to vote in opposition, and
to give the State the benefit of his views. We were
all consulted and even reckoned with, and the sentence which carried the day was the better one, and
not merely the first proposed.[1] Contrast the previous reign: who dared then to open his mouth or
say a word except the poor wretches called on for the
first speech? The rest, too terrified to move, en-
dured the forced necessity of giving assent in silence,
without rising from their seats, their mental anguish
as painful as their physical fears.[2] A solitary senator expressed a single view for all to follow, though
none approved, and least of all the speaker. (People
detest nothing so much as measures which pretend to
be the general will.) Maybe the Emperor put on an
attitude of respect for the Senate in its presence, but
once out of the House he was emperor again, throw-
ing off all his consular obligations with careless contempt. But Caesar has conducted himself as if he
were *only* consul, thinking nothing beneath him unless
it were beneath a consul too. In the first place, he
would leave his home without the delays caused by
the pomp which accompanies imperial pride, or by
the commotion of attendants who must clear his
path; he paused only once on his threshold to take
the auspices and receive with proper reverence the
directions of the gods. No one was jostled or pushed
aside, and his official escort was so unobtrusive and
his lictors so restrained that several times the prince

" Tacitean " in the speech, ending with an apt *sententia*. The
phrase *adsentiendi necessitas* was used by Tacitus in *Ann.* III.
22. 4 for the senate of Tiberius.

officium tam modicum temperatum, ut antiquus
aliquis magnusque consul sub bono principe incedere
videretur.

Iter illi saepius in forum, frequenter tamen et in
campum. 77. Nam comitia consulum obibat ipse;
tantum ex renuntiatione eorum voluptatis, quantum
2 prius ex destinatione capiebat. Stabant candidati
ante curulem principis ut ipse ante consulis steterat,
adigebanturque in verba in quae paulo ante ipse
iuraverat princeps, qui tantum putat esse in iure
iurando, ut illud et ab aliis exigat. Reliqua pars diei
3 tribunali dabatur. Ibi vero quanta religio aequitatis,
quanta legum reverentia! Adibat aliquis ut princi-
4 pem: respondebat se consulem esse. Nullius ab eo
magistratus ius, nullius auctoritas imminuta est,
aucta etiam: siquidem pleraque ad praetores re-
mittebat, atque ita ut collegas vocaret, non quia
populare gratumque audientibus, sed quia ita
5 sentiebat. Tantum dignationis in ipso honore
ponebat, ut non amplius esse censeret, quod aliquis
collega adpellaretur a principe, quam quod praetor
esset. Ad hoc tam adsiduus in tribunali, ut labore
6 refici ac reparari videretur. Quis nostrum idem
curae, idem sudoris insumit? quis adeo expetitis

---

[1] Cf. 63. 2 and note. This is the *renuntiatio* of the suffect
consuls for 100. As Tertullus is referred to as *consul designatus*
at the trial of Priscus, the ceremony probably took place
before the trial.

and consul was forced to wait for another passing crowd. As for his own entourage, it was so modest and disciplined that it might have been accompanying the progress of some great consul of the past in the service of an honest ruler.

Usually he proceeded to the forum, but quite often to the Field of Mars. 77. There he was present in person at the consular elections,[1] and took as much pleasure in hearing the consuls proclaimed as he did in their designation. The candidates stood before the prince's chair, as he had previously stood himself before the consul's, and were directed to take the oath in the same words as their prince had recently used—for he believes the act of swearing so important that he expects everyone to do as he did. The rest of the day was devoted to the administration of justice, and there he gave proof of his scrupulous attitude towards equity and his deep reverence for the letter of the law. If approached as emperor, he simply replied that he was consul. No magistrate had his rights or authority diminished; indeed, he took pains to increase these, by delegating the majority of the cases to the praetors and addressing them as his colleagues, not with any idea of courting popularity among his audience, but because these were his genuine sentiments—for such was the value he put upon the praetor's office that in his estimation to be called the Emperor's colleague added nothing to its status. In addition, his application to the task of administering justice made it appear that he was refreshed and restored by hard work. Which of us takes the same trouble or makes so much effort? Who devotes himself to the duties of the offices he

7 honoribus aut deseruit aut sufficit ? Et sane aequum
est tantum ceteris praestare consulibus ipsum qui
consules facit: quippe etiam fortuna videbatur
indignum, si posset honores dare qui gerere non
8 posset. Facturus consules doceat, accepturisque
amplissimum honorem persuadeat scire se, quid sit
quod dabit ; sic fit ut illi quoque sciant quid acceperint.

78. Quo iustius senatus ut susciperes quartum
consulatum et rogavit et iussit. Imperî hoc verbum,
non adulationis esse obsequio tuo crede, quod non
alia in re magis aut senatus exigere a te aut tu
2 praestare senatui debes. Ut enim ceterorum hominum ita principum, illorum etiam qui sibi di videntur,
aevum omne et breve et fragile est. Itaque optimum quemque niti et contendere decet ut post se
quoque rei publicae prosit, moderationis scilicet
iustitiaeque monimentis, quae prima statuere consul
3 potest. Haec nempe intentio tua ut libertatem
revoces ac reducas. Quem ergo honorem magis
amare, quod nomen usurpare saepius debes, quam
quod primum invenit reciperata libertas ? Non est
minus civile et principem esse pariter et consulem
4 quam tantum consulem. Habe etiam rationem
verecundiae collegarum tuorum, collegarum inquam :
5 ita enim et ipse loqueris et nos loqui vis. Onerosa
erit modestiae illorum tertii consulatus sui recordatio,

---

¹ Trajan held the consulate a fourth time 1–12 January 101.
Evidently at this date (September 100) he is not yet *designatus*.
² Cf. Suetonius, *Dom.* 13. 2.

sought or fulfils expectations like this? It is of course only proper that he should stand out above the other consuls, when it was he who made them, for it would be an insult to his position if office could be bestowed by one incapable of filling it. The creator of consuls must also instruct them, and show those who are going to receive the highest office from him that he knows the value of his gifts; in this way they will also come to know the value of what they have been given.

78. With all the more justice then, did the Senate ask you to bow to its wishes and accept the consulate for a fourth time.[1] That it speaks with the voice of authority and not of flattery is proved by your own attitude of deference; there is no demand which the Senate has a better claim to make of you or you to grant. For the prince no less than for the common man the thread of life is short and easily snapped, even when he deems himself the equal of the gods;[2] and thus it is only proper that the best among us should apply his efforts to leaving records of his justice and moderation which will be of service to his country even after death. None can achieve this better than the consul. We know that your intention is to set up liberty in our midst again. What distinction should find more favour with you, what title should you bear more often than that which was the first creation of liberty restored? It is just as democratic to be prince as well as consul as to be consul alone. Take thought too for the feelings of propriety of your colleagues (yes, colleagues; for that is how you refer to them and wish us to do the same); it will be painful for modest men to recall their own

donec te saepius consulem videant. Neque enim
potest non nimium esse privatis, quod principi satis
est. Adnuas, Caesar, optantibus, quibusque apud
deos adesse consuesti, quorum potes ipse votorum,
compotes facias.

79. Tibi fortasse sufficiat tertius consulatus, sed
nobis tanto minus sufficit. Ille nos instituit induxit,
ut te iterum iterumque consulem habere cupiamus.
2 Remissius istud contenderemus, si adhuc nesciremus
qualis esses futurus: tolerabilius fuit experimen-
3 tum tui nobis quam usum negari. Dabiturne
rursus videre consulem illum? Audiet reddet quas
proxime voces, praestabitque gaudium quantum ipse
percipiet? Praesidebit laetitiae publicae auctor
eius et causa, temptabitque adfectus nostros ut solet
4 cohibere nec poterit? Pietati certe senatus cum
modestia principis felix speciosumque certamen, seu
fuerit victa seu vicerit. Equidem incognitam quandam proximaque maiorem praesumo laetitiam.
Quis enim est tam modicilli ingenii qui non tanto
meliorem consulem speret, quanto saepius fuerit?
5 Alius se a continuo labore, etsi non desidiae ac
voluptati dedisset, otio tamen et quiete recreasset;
hic consularibus curis exsolutus principales resumpsit,
tam diligens temperamenti, ut nec consulis officium
6 princeps nec principis consul adpeteret. Videmus

third consulship unless they see you consul once
again. What is sufficient for the prince cannot help
but be excessive for his subjects. Grant these
prayers, Caesar, and gratify the wishes of those for
whom it is your custom to intercede with the gods;
for this is in your power.

79. Perhaps in your own eyes a third consulship is
enough, but this is all the more reason for its not
sufficing our demands. It only formed the habit in
us of wanting to see you consul again and again. We
might be less pressing if we had yet to learn what
sort of consul you would be; refusal of a chance to
test you would be more easily accepted than the
denial of continuing with you whom we know. Shall
we be permitted to see him as consul once again?
Will he hear and repeat the formula of yesterday,
and give us pleasure equal to his own? Will he
preside over our public rejoicing, as its author and its
object, attempt (as is his wont) to check our outbursts
of enthusiasm—and fail to do so? The Senate's
loyal devotion will match itself against the prince's
moderation in a splendid struggle, happy in its out-
come whether it triumphs or not. For my part, I
anticipate some form of happiness as yet unknown and
even greater than before, for no one is so unimagina-
tive as not to hope for a consul to prove all the better
for repeated experience. Another man, though he
did not abandon himself to the delights of idleness,
would at least have sought relief from continuous
service by an interval of peaceful retirement; but he
rid himself of a consul's cares only to resume those of
empire, so balancing his responsibilities that as
prince he never sought to be consul, nor as consul to

ut provinciarum desideriis, ut singularum etiam
civitatum precibus occurrat. Nulla in audiendo
difficultas, nulla in respondendo mora. Adeunt
statim, dimittuntur statim, tandemque principis
fores exclusa legationum turba non obsidet.

80. Quid? in omnibus cognitionibus quam mitis
severitas, quam non dissoluta clementia! Non tu
locupletando fisco operatus sedes, nec aliud tibi
sententiae tuae pretium quam bene iudicasse.
2 Stant ante te litigatores non de fortunis suis sed de
tua existimatione solliciti, nec tam verentur, quid
3 de causa sua quam quid de moribus sentias. O vere[1]
principis atque etiam dei curas,[2] reconciliare aemulas
civitates, tumentesque populos non imperio magis
quam ratione compescere; intercedere iniquitatibus
magistratuum, infectumque reddere quidquid fieri
non oportuerit; postremo velocissimi sideris more
omnia invisere omnia audire, et undecumque invo-
4 catum statim velut adesse et adsistere! Talia esse
crediderim, quae ille mundi parens temperat nutu,
si quando oculos demisit in terras, et fata mortalium
5 inter divina opera numerare dignatus est; qua
nunc parte liber solutusque tantum caelo vacat,
postquam te dedit, qui erga omne hominum genus
vice sua fungereris. Fungeris enim sufficisque
mandanti, cum tibi dies omnis summa cum utilitate
nostra, summa cum tua laude condatur.

81. Quodsi quando cum influentibus negotiis

---

[1] vere *M*: veras *R*.
[2] dei curas *Keil*: decoras *H*: decoris *X*.

---

[1] Cf. *Ep.* VI. 31, where Trajan presides over cases heard at
Centum Cellae.

be prince. We see how he hastens to fulfil the desires of the provinces, the prayers too of every city, with no difficulties over giving audience nor delays in making reply. Admission is immediate, dismissal prompt; at last there is an end of closed doors and crowds of delegates waiting on the palace steps.

80. Now let me turn to judicial matters,[1] where you showed how strictness need not be cruel nor mercy weak. You did not mount the tribunal for the purpose of enriching your private exchequer, and the only reward you sought in passing sentence was the knowledge that justice had been done. Before you stood the litigants, concerned more for your opinion of them than for their fortunes, fearful of your judgement on their character rather than on their case. This is indeed the true care of a prince, or even that of a god, to settle rivalry between cities, to soothe the passions of angry peoples less by exercise of power than by reason: to intervene where there has been official injustice, to undo what should never have been done: finally, like a swift-moving star, to see all, hear all, and be present at once with aid wherever your help is sought. It is thus, I fancy, that the great Father of the universe rules all with a nod of the head, if he ever looks down on earth and deigns to consider mortal destinies among his divine affairs. Now he is rid of this part of his duties, free to devote himself to heaven's concerns, since he has given you to us to fill his rôle with regard to the entire human race. And you are filling it, worthy of his trust in you: since every passing day brings every advantage for us and the greatest glory for you.

81. But whenever you have succeeded in stemming

paria fecisti, instar refectionis existimas mutationem
laboris. Quae enim remissio tibi nisi lustrare saltus,
excutere cubilibus feras, superare immensa montium
iuga et horrentibus scopulis gradum inferre, nullius
manu nullius vestigio adiutum, atque inter haec pia
2 mente adire lucos et occursare numinibus? Olim
haec experientia iuventutis, haec voluptas erat, his
artibus futuri duces imbuebantur, certare cum fuga-
cibus feris cursu, cum audacibus robore, cum callidis
astu; nec mediocre pacis decus habebatur submota
campis inruptio ferarum et obsidione quadam libera-
3 tus agrestium labor. Usurpabant gloriam istam illi
quoque principes qui obire non poterant; usurpabant
autem ita ut domitas fractasque claustris feras, ac
deinde in ipsorum (quidni?) ludibrium emissas,
mentita sagacitate colligerent. Huic par capiendi
quaerendique sudor, summusque et idem gratissimus
4 labor invenire. Enimvero, si quando placuit idem
corporis robur in maria proferre, non ille fluitantia
vela aut oculis sequitur aut manibus, sed nunc
gubernaculis adsidet, nunc cum valentissimo quoque
sodalium certat frangere fluctus, domitare ventos
reluctantes remisque transferre obstantia freta.

82. Quantum dissimilis illi, qui non Albani lacus
otium Baianique torporem et silentium ferre, non

the tide of your engagements, the form of recreation you prefer is simply this—a change of work. Your only relaxation is to range the forests, drive wild beasts from their lairs, scale vast mountain heights, and set foot on rocky crags, with none to give a helping hand or show the way; and amidst all this to visit the sacred groves in a spirit of devotion, and present yourself to the deities there. In the days of old this was the training and the delight of youth, these were the skills which formed the leaders of the future—to pit speed against an animal's swift-footedness, and strength and dexterity against its courage and cunning; while in times of peace it brought no small honour to sweep marauding wild beasts from the plains and raise the siege they laid to the farmers and their work. Then this distinction was also claimed by those emperors who lacked the ability to win it, claimed by a mere pretence of skill, as they rounded up animals who had been tamed and weakened by captivity and then let loose to provide them (of course!) with amusement. But Caesar puts just as much effort into the chase as he does into making a capture, while the hardest task of hunting out a quarry is what delights him most. And, indeed, does he ever decide to display the same physical energy on sea, he is not one to follow the sails afloat only by eye or pointing finger; one moment he sits at the helm, at another he matches the sturdiest of his comrades in mastering the waves, taming the opposition of the winds, and forcing a passage by oar against a racing current.

82. How different he is from that man who could not bear the calm of the Alban lake, or the still

pulsum saltem fragoremque remorum perpeti poterat, quin ad singulos ictus turpi formidine horre-
2 sceret! Itaque procul ab omni sono inconcussus
ipse et immotus, religato revinctoque navigio non
3 secus ac piaculum aliquod trahebatur. Foeda facies,
cum populi Romani imperator alienum cursum
alienumque rectorem velut capta nave sequeretur.
4 Nec deformitate ista saltem flumina carebant, atque
etiam Danubius ac Rhenus tantum illud nostri dede-
coris vehere gaudebant, non minore cum pudore
imperî, quod haec Romanae aquilae, Romana signa,
Romana denique ripa, quam quod hostium prospec-
5 taret, hostium quibus moris est eadem illa nunc
rigentia gelu flumina aut campis superfusa, nunc
liquida ac deferentia lustrare navigiis nandoque
6 superare. Nec vero per se magno opere laudaverim
duritiam corporis ac lacertorum; sed, si his validior
ipso corpore animus imperitet, quem non fortunae
indulgentia emolliat, non copiae principales ad
segnitiem luxumque detorqueant, tunc ego seu
montibus seu mari exerceatur, et laetum opere cor-
7 pus et crescentia laboribus membra mirabor. Video
enim iam inde antiquitus maritos dearum ac deum
liberos nec ⟨parentum divinitate nec⟩[1] dignitate
nuptiarum magis quam his artibus inclaruisse.
8 Simul cogito, cum sint ista ludus et avocamentum,

[1] *lacunam explevit Schnelle.*

---

[1] Lake Lucrinus. Domitian had houses on the shores of
both lakes.

silence of the lake at Baiae,[1] nor even endure the
sound and splash of an oar without shivering in disgraceful terror at each stroke! So it was that, far
removed from the slightest sound, sheltered from
every shock and movement, his vessel firmly held in
tow, he was brought like a victim to the sacrifice.
Disgraceful scene, for the emperor of the Roman
people to follow behind with another to steer his
course and direct his helm, as if held prisoner in his
own ship! Rivers also witnessed this shameful
travesty; the Danube and Rhine[2] were delighted for
their waters to play their part in our disgrace, and it
was no less a blot on the empire for this to be seen
by Roman eagles, Roman standards, and the Roman
river-bank, than by the other side, the bank of the
enemy—the enemy whose habit it was to navigate or
swim across these same rivers, whether blocked with
ice-floes or flooding the plains when ice is melted and
passage is free. Not that I think so highly of hard-
ness of physique and muscle as such, unless the body
is ruled by a mind more powerful than itself, one
which is neither softened by fortune's favour nor
led astray by imperial riches into idleness and excess;
in this case a body which thrives on work and sinews
developed by service, whether trained on mountain
or at sea, will win my admiration. I have observed
that since ancient times, the husbands of goddesses
and the sons of gods have won fame less through the
glory of their marriages or the divinity of their fathers
than by skills such as these; at the same time I ask

[2] Here, as usual, Pliny belittles Domitian's military activity
both in Germany and in the Suebian–Sarmatic wars. Cf.
11. 4, 14. 5, 20. 4 and notes.

quae quantaeque sint huius curae seriae et intentae,
et a quibus se in tale otium recipit. Voluptates sunt
enim voluptates, quibus optime de cuiusque gravitate

9 sanctitate temperantia creditur. Nam quis adeo
dissolutus, cuius non occupationibus aliqua species
severitatis insideat? Otio prodimur. An non
plerique principes hoc idem tempus in aleam stupra
luxum conferebant, cum seriarum laxamenta cura-
rum vitiorum contentione supplerent?

83. Habet hoc primum magna fortuna, quod nihil
tectum, nihil occultum esse patitur; principum vero
non domus modo sed cubicula ipsa intimosque
secessus recludit, omniaque arcana noscenda famae
proponit atque explicat. Sed tibi, Caesar, nihil
accommodatius fuerit ad gloriam quam penitus

2 inspici. Sunt quidem praeclara quae in publicum
profers, sed non minora ea quae limine tenes. Est
magnificum quod te ab omni contagione vitiorum
reprimis ac revocas, sed magnificentius quod tuos;

3 quanto enim magis arduum est alio praestare quam
se, tanto laudabilius quod, cum ipse sis optimus,

4 omnes circa te similes tui fecisti. Multis inlustribus
dedecori fuit aut inconsultius uxor adsumpta aut
retenta patientius; ita foris claros domestica destrue-
bat infamia, et ne maximi cives haberentur, hoc

myself what, if these are Caesar's recreation and amusements, must be the extent of his serious interests and preoccupations, from which he turns to relaxation like this. For it is a man's pleasures (yes, his pleasures) which tell us most about his true worth, his moral excellence, and his self-control. No one is so dissolute that his occupations lack all semblance of seriousness; it is our leisure moments which betray us. This is the very time which the majority of his predecessors used to spend on gambling, debauchery and extravagance, thus replacing what should have been the relaxation of their serious concerns by a different form of tension—their pursuit of vice.

83. One of the chief features of high estate is that it permits no privacy, no concealment, and in the case of princes, it flings open the door not only to their homes but to their private apartments and deepest retreats; every secret is exposed and revealed to rumour's listening ear. But in your case, Caesar, nothing could better redound to your credit than a searching inspection of this kind. Your public conduct is indeed remarkable, but no less so your private life. Splendid though it is to keep yourself thus unspotted by any form of vice, it is even more so to do the same for the members of your family, for the more difficult it is to vouch for others rather than oneself, the more honour is due to you for combining your own excellence with making all those around you reach the same high standard. Many distinguished men have been dishonoured by an ill-considered choice of a wife or weakness in not getting rid of her; thus their fame abroad was damaged by their loss of

efficiebatur, quod mariti minores erant. Tibi uxor
5 in decus et gloriam cedit. Quid enim illa sanctius,
quid antiquius? Nonne si pontifici maximo eligenda
sit coniunx, aut hanc aut similem (ubi est autem
6 similis?) elegerit? Quam illa nihil sibi ex fortuna
tua nisi gaudium vindicat! Quam constanter non
potentiam tuam, sed ipsum te reveretur! Idem
estis invicem quod fuistis; probatis ex aequo, nihilque vobis felicitas addidit, nisi quod scire coepistis,
quam bene uterque vestrum felicitatem ferat.
7 Eadem quam modica cultu, quam parca comitatu,
quam civilis incessu! Mariti hoc opus, qui ita
imbuit ita instituit; nam uxori sufficit obsequî gloria.
8 An, cum videat quam nullus te terror, nulla comitetur
ambitio, non et ipsa cum silentio incedat, ingredient-
emque pedibus maritum, in quantum patitur sexus,
imitetur? Decuerit hoc illam, etiamsi diversa tu
facias; sub hac vero modestia viri quantam debet
verecundiam uxor marito, femina sibi!

84. Soror autem tua ut se sororem esse meminit!
ut in illa tua simplicitas, tua veritas, tuus candor
agnoscitur! ut si quis eam uxori tuae conferat, du-
bitare cogatur, utrum sit efficacius ad recte viven-
2 dum bene institui an feliciter nasci. Nihil est tam
pronum ad simultates quam aemulatio, in feminis
praesertim: ea porro maxime nascitur ex coniunc-

---

1 The empress Pompeia Plotina; cf. *Ep.* IX. 28. 1.
2 The *pontifex maximus* was of course the emperor himself.
3 Ulpia Marciana.

reputation at home, and their relative failure as
husbands denied them complete success as citizens.
But your own wife[1] contributes to your honour and
glory, as a supreme model of the ancient virtues; the
Chief Pontiff himself,[2] had he to take a wife, would
choose her, or one like her—if one exists. From
your position she claims nothing for herself but the
pleasure it gives her, unswerving in her devotion not
to your power but to yourself. You are just the
same to each other as you have always been, and
your mutual appreciation is unchanged; success has
brought you nothing but a new understanding of
your joint ability to live in its shadow. How modest
she is in her attire, how moderate the number of her
attendants, how unassuming when she walks abroad!
This is the work of her husband who has fashioned
and formed her habits; there is glory enough for a
wife in obedience. When she sees her husband
unaccompanied by pomp and intimidation, she also
goes about in silence, and as far as her sex permits,
she follows his example of walking on foot. This
would win her praise even if you did the opposite,
but with a husband so moderate in his habits, how
much respect she owes him as his wife, and herself as
a woman!

84. Your sister,[3] too, never forgets that she is your
sister, and your own frank sincerity and candour can
be clearly recognized in her, so that if comparison
were drawn between her and your wife, one could
only wonder which is the more conducive to an upright life, good training or fortunate birth. Nothing
leads to dissension so readily, especially between
women, as the rivalry which is most likely to arise

ctione, alitur aequalitate, exardescit invidia, cuius
3 finis est odium. Quo quidem admirabilius existi-
mandum est, quod mulieribus duabus in una domo
parique fortuna nullum certamen nulla contentio
4 est. Suspiciunt invicem invicem cedunt, cumque
te utraque effusissime diligat, nihil sua putant interesse utram tu magis ames. Idem utrique propositum, idem tenor vitae, nihilque ex quo sentias duas
5 esse; te enim imitari, te subsequi student. Ideo
utraque mores eosdem, quia utraque tuos habet;
inde moderatio, inde etiam perpetua securitas.
Neque enim umquam periclitabuntur esse privatae,
6 quae non desierunt. Obtulerat illis senatus cognomen Augustarum, quod certatim deprecatae sunt,
quam diu adpellationem patris patriae tu recusasses, seu quod plus esse in eo iudicabant, si uxor
7 et soror tua quam si Augustae dicerentur. Sed,
quaecumque illis ratio tantam modestiam suasit, hoc
magis dignae sunt, quae in animis nostris et sint et
8 habeantur augustae, quia non vocantur. Quid enim
laudabilius feminis, quam si verum honorem non in
splendore titulorum, sed in iudiciis hominum repon-
ant magnisque nominibus pares se faciant, et dum
recusant?

85. Iam etiam et in privatorum animis exoleverat
priscum mortalium bonum amicitia, cuius in locum
migraverant adsentationes blanditiae et peior odio

---

¹ Trajan had in fact accepted the title of *pater patriae* before
the consular elections of October 98 (57. 4), but the first
inscription recording the title *Augusta* (ILS 288, S. 106) can

from close proximity, to be fed on similarity of status and inflamed by jealousy until it ends in open hatred; all the more remarkable then must it appear when two women in the same position can share a home without a sign of envy or rivalry. Their respect and consideration for each other is mutual, and as each loves you with all her heart, they think it makes no difference which of them stands first in your affection. United as they are in the purpose of their daily life, nothing can be shown to divide them; their one aim is to model themselves on your example, and consequently their habits are the same, being formed after yours. Hence their quiet contentment and untroubled serenity—they run no risk of being no more than your subjects, for that is what they have always been. The Senate had offered them the title of *Augusta*,[1] which both made haste to refuse, unwilling to bear it so long as *you* refused to be known as the Father of your country, or else believing it a greater honour to be spoken of simply as your wife and sister. But whatever the reason for such modesty on their part, this is the title they deserve; this is how we think of them in our hearts, the more because it is left unspoken. Nothing can be more glorious for women than to value true distinction through the opinion of the world instead of by the magnificence of titles, and to make sure they are worthy of a great name though they may not wish to bear it.

85. Furthermore, even in the hearts of ordinary men, humanity's former blessing of friendship had

be dated between December 104 and 105, and Pliny's evidence is explicit that it was not held in 100.

amoris simulatio. Etenim in principum domo nomen tantum amicitiae, inane scilicet inrisumque
2 remanebat. Nam qui poterat esse inter eos amicitia, quorum sibi alii domini alii servi videbantur?
Tu hanc pulsam et errantem reduxisti: habes amicos
3 quia amicus ipse es. Neque enim ut alia subiectis,
ita amor imperatur, neque est ullus adfectus tam
erectus et liber et dominationis impatiens, nec qui
4 magis vices exigat. Potest fortasse princeps inique,
potest tamen odio esse non nullis, etiamsi ipse non
5 oderit: amari nisi ipse amet non potest. Diligis
ergo cum diligaris, et in eo quod utrimque honestissimum est, tota gloria tua est; qui superior factus
descendis in omnia familiaritatis officia, et in amicum
ex imperatore submitteris, immo tunc maxime im-
6 perator cum amicum agis. Etenim cum plurimis
amicitiis fortuna principum indigeat, praecipuum
7 est principis opus amicos parare. Placeat tibi semper
haec secta, et cum reliquas virtutes tuas tum hanc
constantissime teneas, nec umquam tibi persuadea-
tur humile esse principi nisi odisse. Iucundissimum
est in rebus humanis amari, sed non minus amare.
8 Quorum utroque ita frueris ut, cum ipse ardentissime
diligas, adhuc tamen ardentius diligaris, primum

---

[1] A reference to the precarious position of the *amici
principis*.
[2] Cf. Tacitus, *Hist*. IV. 7.

withered and died, and in its place had sprung up
flattery and adulation, and worse even than hatred,
the false semblance of love; while in the Emperors'
palace nothing remained of friendship but the name,
now empty and derided.[1] For how could friendship survive between men thus divided, the one half
feeling themselves the masters, the other half their
slaves? It was you, Caesar, who brought her back
from exile, to find a home again; you have friends
because you know how to be one. Love cannot be
demanded of subjects, as other things can; there is
no sentiment so lofty and independent, so impatient
of tyranny, so uncompromising in its expectations of
a return. It is possible for a prince to incur hatred
(though perhaps unjustly) from many of his subjects,
though he feels none himself; it is not possible for
him to win affection unless he shows it too. And so
you love as you are loved; all honour to both sides,
though the glory is all yours, since it is you who step
down from your superior status to carry out all the
duties of friendship, descend from being emperor to
be a friend—though in fact you are never more emperor than when you fill the rôle of friend, for a
prince needs every kind of friendship to maintain his
position,[2] and so his first care is to provide himself with
friends. May you ever follow this line of conduct,
never fail to practise this among your other virtues:
and never let yourself be persuaded that a prince
demeans himself unless he hates. There is nothing
more delightful in human affairs than to inspire love,
unless it is to feel it, and you can enjoy both, seeing
that the warmth of your own affection kindles even
more in your friends. The reasons are two: it is

quia facilius est unum amare quam multos, deinde quia tibi amicos tuos obligandi tanta facultas inest, ut nemo te possit nisi ingratus non magis amare.

86. Operae pretium est referre quod tormentum tibi iniunxeris, ne quid amico negares. Dimisisti optimum virum tibique carissimum invitus et tristis, et quasi retinere non posses, quantumque amares eum, desiderio expertus es, distractus separatusque,

2 dum cedis ut vinceris. Ita quod fando inauditum, cum princeps et principis amicus diversa velletis, id potius factum est quod amicus volebat. O rem memoriae litterisque mandandam, praefectum praetorii non ex ingerentibus se, sed ex subtrahentibus legere, eundemque otio quod pertinaciter amet reddere, cumque sis ipse distentus imperî curis, non

3 quietis gloria[1] cuiquam invidere! Intellegimus, Caesar, quantum tibi pro laboriosa ista statione et exercita debeamus, cum otium a te tamquam res optima et petatur et detur. Quam ego audio confusionem tuam fuisse, cum digredientem prosequereris! Prosecutus es enim nec temperasti tibi, quo minus exeunti in litore amplexus, in litore

4 osculum ferres. Stetit Caesar in illa amicitiae specula, stetit precatusque est abeunti prona maria celeremque, si tamen ipse voluisset, recursum nec

---

[1] gloria *codex unus, Mynors*: gloriam *R, M.*

---

[1] Unidentified.

easier to love one man than many, and your opportunities for putting your friends under obligation to
you are so great that no one, without ingratitude,
can fail to make sure that his love exceeds your own.

86. At this point I must recall the personal distress
you chose to undergo rather than refuse anything
to a friend. You released from office a man of the
highest merit,[1] one of your dearest friends, in spite of
your grief and reluctance, as if there was no possibility of your retaining him. How much you felt
for him was shown by the extent of your regret;
your heart was torn and broken as you yielded to his
pressure. The situation was unheard-of: for an
emperor and his friend to have conflicting desires,
and the friend's wishes to take precedence. Here
then is something to go down on record for all to remember—a prefect for the praetorian guard was
chosen not from those who put themselves forward
but from those who held back, and once chosen was
allowed to return to the retirement he so obstinately
preferred: occupied as you were by the cares of empire, you begrudged no one an honourable release.
We can appreciate the extent of our debt to you,
Caesar, for all the hardships and vexations of the
responsibilities you bear, when retirement is sought
and granted by you as the greatest of blessings.
Your distress, I am told, was undisguised, as you
saw him on to the boat; yes, you saw him off, and
there on the shore you were not ashamed to give him
your embrace and kiss of farewell. There on a
watchtower, the witness of his friendship, stood
Caesar, and prayed for a calm sea for his departing
friend, prayed too for a speedy return (if that was to

sustinuit recedentem non etiam atque etiam votis
5 et lacrimis sequi. Nam de liberalitate taceo.
Quibus enim muneribus aequari haec cura principis
haec patientia potest, qua meruisti ut ille sibi
nimium fortis ac prope durus videretur? Nec dubito
quin agitaverit secum, an gubernacula retorqueret,
et fecisset nisi quod paene ipso contubernio principis
felicius iucundiusque est, desiderare principem de-
6 siderantem. Et ille quidem ut maximo fructu suscepti ita maiore depositi officii gloria fruitur; tu
autem facilitate ista consecutus es, ne quem retinere
videaris invitum.

87. Civile hoc et parenti publico convenientissimum nihil cogere, semperque meminisse nullam
tantam potestatem cuiquam dari posse, ut non sit
2 gratior potestate libertas. Dignus es, Caesar, qui
officia mandes deponere optantibus, qui petentibus
vacationem, invitus quidem sed tamen tribuas, qui
ab amicis orantibus requiem non te relinqui putes,
qui semper invenias et quos ex otio revoces, et quos
3 otio reddas. Vos quoque quos parens noster familiariter inspicere dignatur, fovete iudicium eius quod
4 de vobis habet: hic vester labor est. Princeps enim,
cum in uno probavit amare se scire, vacat culpa si
alios minus amat. Ipsum quidem quis mediocriter

be his desire); nor could he help following him into the distance with repeated prayers and tears. Of your generosity I say nothing. No services could approach princely solicitude and endurance like yours, which merited some recognition on his side that his determination came too near obstinacy. No doubt he debated in his heart whether to swing round his helm, and would have done so, if there were not more joy and happiness than even what a prince's intimacy can bring, in missing him in absence with the knowledge that he feels the same. And so he enjoys both the high reward of having accepted office and the greater honour which came to him from laying it down; while your readiness to fall in with his wishes has at least made it clear that you cannot be suspected of retaining anyone against his will.

87. To use no force, to remember at all times that whatever the powers anyone is granted, liberty will always be dearer to men's hearts—this is indeed democratic and proper for one who is father to us all. It is your prerogative, Caesar, to confer office on those who may desire to relinquish it, to grant exemption to any who seek it, though it may be against your own wishes, to understand that your friends are not deserting you if they want to retire, to be always finding people whom you recall from private life or send back to it. And to those of you in the Senate whom our Father deems worthy of his friendship and regard, I say: cherish the high opinion he has of you; this is your concern not his, for a prince may show that he can feel affection in one case without being blamed for not doing as much for others. But which

527

diligat, cum leges amandi non det sed accipiat?
Hic praesens ille mavult absens amari; uterque
ametur, ut mavult; nemo in taedium praesentia,
5 nemo in oblivionem absentia veniat. Tenet quisque
locum quem semel meruit, faciliusque est ut oculis
eius vultus absentis, quam ut animo caritas excidat.

88. Plerique principes, cum essent civium domini, libertorum erant servi: horum consiliis horum
nutu regebantur; per hos audiebant per hos loque-
bantur, per hos praeturae etiam et sacerdotia et
2 consulatus, immo ab his petebantur. Tu libertis
tuis summum quidem honorem, sed tamquam
libertis habes abundeque sufficere his credis, si probi
et frugi existimentur. Scis enim praecipuum esse
3 indicium non magni principis magnos libertos. Ac
primum neminem in usu habes nisi aut tibi aut patri
tuo aut optimo cuique principum dilectum aestimatumque;[1] hos ipsos cotidie deinde ita formas,
ut se non tua fortuna sed sua metiantur, et tanto
magis digni, quibus honor omnis praestetur a nobis,
4 quia non est necesse. Iustisne de causis senatus
populusque Romanus Optimi tibi cognomen adiecit?
Paratum id quidem et in medio positum, novum
tamen. Scias neminem ante meruisse, quod non

---

[1] aestimatumque *Gruter*: statimque *M*.

---

[1] Cf. Suetonius, *Claud.* 28–9, *Galba* 15; Pliny, *Ep.* VII. 29,
VIII. 6. There is little evidence for Trajan's attitude to the
imperial freedmen. Vitellius' policy of reserving administrative posts for knights (Tac. *Hist.* 1. 58) had been continued by
Domitian (Suetonius, *Dom.* 7. 3) and was firmly established
by Hadrian (SHA *Hadr.* 22. 8.). For freedmen who are
procurators under Trajan, cf. *Ep.* VI. 31. 8, X. 27 and 85.

[2] Cf. 2. 7 and note.

of you could be lukewarm in his feelings towards one who accepts the rules of friendship instead of imposing his own? One man may seek Caesar's affection in person, another when he is away; let both receive it according to his preference. No one becomes irksome by his presence, no one is forgotten in absence; everyone retains his position once he has won it, and Caesar can more easily forget the face of an absent friend than let the love he bears him fade from his heart.

88. Most of the emperors, though masters of their subjects, were the slaves of their freedmen, at the mercy of their counsels and their whims.[1] Through them they spoke and were spoken to; through them priesthoods, prefectures and consulships were sought—through them, or rather, from them. By contrast, you hold your freedmen in high honour, but as freedmen only, and believe that a reputation for honesty and good character is all they should expect, for you know that the chief indication of weakness in a ruler is the power of his freedmen. In the first place, you employ no one unless he was considered and chosen for you or your father or for one of the better emperors; then you train these men daily in such a way that they measure themselves against their own position, not yours: with the result that they prove all the more worthy of our high regard because it is not forced on us.

Is there not just reason for the title bestowed on you by the Senate and people of Rome—the title of *Optimus*, Best?[2] It may seem ready-made and commonplace, but in fact it is something new. No one is known to have merited it before, though it was

5 erat excogitandum si quis meruisset. An satius fuit
Felicem vocare? quod non moribus sed fortunae
datum est. Satius Magnum? cui plus invidiae
quam pulchritudinis inest. Adoptavit te optimus
6 princeps in suum, senatus in Optimi nomen. Hoc
tibi tam proprium quam paternum; nec magis distincte definiteque designat, qui Traianum quam qui
Optimum adpellat, ut olim frugalitate Pisones,
sapientia Laelî, pietate Metelli monstrabantur;
quae simul omnia uno isto nomine continentur. Nec
videri potest optimus, nisi qui est optimis omnibus
7 in sua cuiusque laude praestantior. Merito tibi ergo
post ceteras adpellationes haec est addita ut maior.
Minus est enim imperatorem et Caesarem et Augustum quam omnibus imperatoribus et Caesaribus et
8 Augustis esse meliorem. Ideoque ille parens
hominum deorumque Optimi prius nomine, deinde
Maximi colitur. Quo praeclarior laus tua, quem
non minus constat optimum esse quam maximum.
9 Adsecutus es nomen, quod ad alium transire non
possit, nisi ut adpareat in bono principe alienum, in
malo falsum, quod licet omnes postea usurpent,
10 semper tamen agnoscetur ut tuum. Etenim ut

---

¹ Sulla and Pompey were given the names Felix and Magnus.
² Since the time of L. Calpurnius Piso Frugi, who as tribune
in 149 B.C. introduced the *Lex de pecuniis repetundis*.
³ C. Laelius, a member of the Scipionic circle and the leading
figure in Cicero's *De Amicitia*, called *Sapiens* for his Stoic
inclinations; Q. Metellus (cos. 80 B.C.) called *Pius* for his
efforts to recall his father from exile.

there to be used if someone proved worthy. Would
it have been better to call him " Fortunate "?
This is a tribute to his luck, not his character. What
about " the Great "?[1] This has a ring of envy
rather than renown. In adopting you, the best of
emperors gave you his own name, to which the
Senate added that of *Optimus*, to be as much your
personal name as the one your father gave. Thus
you are as clearly designated and defined by the
name of *Optimus* as by that of Trajan; just as formerly the house of Piso was known for frugality,[2] and
those of Laelius and Metellus for wisdom and filial
piety.[3] All these virtues are contained in the single
name which is yours, for " the Best " can only refer
to the man who outstrips all others who are best in
their own distinctive ways. And so it was only
proper to place this at the end of your other titles,[4]
as being the greater one, for it means less to be
Emperor and Caesar and Augustus than to be better
than all those who have borne those titles before
you. For the same reason, the Father of gods and
men is worshipped under the title *Optimus* followed
by *Maximus*, Best and Highest, and the more
honour is due to you, who in the eyes of all are
equally Highest and Best. You have won a title
which cannot pass to another without seeming bor-
rowed, in the case of a good prince, and false, in the
case of a bad one; and though all in future may claim
it, it will always be recognized as yours. Just as the

---

[4] At this time Trajan was still officially called *Imperator
Caesar Nerva Traianus Augustus Germanicus, pontifex maximus, pater patriae. Optimus* appears after *Traianus* in
inscriptions of 113/14. (S. 99–101.)

nomine Augusti admonemur eius cui primum dica-
tum est, ita haec Optimi adpellatio numquam
memoriae hominum sine te recurret, quotiensque
posteri nostri Optimum aliquem vocare cogentur,
totiens recordabuntur quis meruerit vocari.

89. Quanto nunc, dive Nerva, gaudio frueris, cum
vides et esse optimum et dici, quem tamquam
optimum elegisti! quam laetum tibi, quod com-
paratus filio tuo vinceris! Neque enim alio magis
adprobatur animi tui magnitudo, quam quod optimus
2 ipse non timuisti elegere meliorem. Sed et tu, pater
Traiane, (nam tu quoque, si non sidera,[1] proximam
tamen sideribus obtines sedem) quantum percipis
voluptatem, cum illum tribunum, illum militem tuum
tantum imperatorem, tantum principem cernis,
cumque eo qui adoptavit amicissime contendis, pul-
3 chrius fuerit genuisse talem an elegisse! Macte
uterque ingenti in rem publicam merito, cui hoc
tantum boni contulistis! Licet alteri vestrum filii
virtus triumphalia, caelum alteri dederit,[2] non minor
tamen vestra laus, quod ista per filium, quam si ipsi
meruissetis.

90. Scio, patres conscripti, cum ceteros cives, tum
praecipue consules oportere sic adfici, ut se publice
2 magis quam privatim obligatos putent.[3] Ut enim

---

[1] On 16 January 27 B.C.
[2] Cf. 15. Evidently Trajan's father is dead.
[3] Cf. 14. 1 and note.

name of Augustus reminds us of the man to whom it was first decreed,[1] so this title of *Optimus* will never return to the memory of man without recalling you, and whenever our descendants are called on to bestow it, they will always remember who it was whose merits won it as his due.

89. What happiness you must feel today, divine Nerva, on beholding him whom you judged the best candidate for your choice proving that he is best, and being addressed as such! What joy for you to stand second in comparison with your son! There can be no better indication of your greatness of soul than the fact that though so good yourself you did not hesitate to choose a better man. You also, father Trajan (for you too, though not raised to the stars, must surely occupy the nearest place), must know such delight when you see your son who was tribune and soldier under you[2] now risen to be supreme commander and emperor, when you enter into friendly rivalry with his adopter so as to determine where the greater glory must be assigned—to his begetter or to the one who made him his choice. All honour to you both for the immense service you have done your country and the great benefit you have conferred on it. Though it was your son's merits which brought one of you triumphal ornaments[3] and the other his place in heaven, your glory for owing these to him is what it would be had you won them yourselves.

90. I am well aware, Conscript Fathers, that the consuls should feel a sense of obligation (in their public rather than their private capacity) which goes beyond that of any other citizen. For just as the

533

malos principes rectius pulchriusque est ex communi-
bus iniuriis odisse quam ex propriis, ita boni speciosius amantur ob ea quae generi humano quam quae
3 hominibus praestant. Quia tamen in consuetudinem
vertit, ut consules publica gratiarum actione per-
lata, suo quoque nomine quantum debeant principi
profiteantur, concedite me non pro me magis munere
isto quam pro collega meo Cornuto Tertullo claris-
4 simo viro fungi. Cur enim non pro illo quoque
gratias agam, pro quo non minus debeo? praesertim
cum indulgentissimus imperator in concordia nostra
ea praestiterit ambobus, quae si tantum in alterum
contulisset, ambos tamen aequaliter obligasset.
5 Utrumque nostrum ille optimi cuiusque spoliator et
carnifex stragibus amicorum et in proximum iacto
fulmine adflaverat. Isdem enim amicis gloriabamur,
eosdem amissos lugebamus, ac sicut ⟨nunc⟩[1] spes
gaudiumque, ita tunc communis nobis dolor et metus
6 erat. Habuerat hunc honorem periculis nostris
divus Nerva, ut nos, etsi minus ⟨notos⟩,[2] ut bonos
promovere vellet, quia mutati saeculi signum et
hoc esset, quod florerent quorum praecipuum votum
ante fuerat, ut memoriae principis elaberentur.

91. Nondum biennium compleveramus in officio

---

[1] nunc *add. cod. Londiniensis*: *om. M.*
[2] notos *add. Lipsius*: *om. M.*

hatred roused by the evil emperors was more right and honourable if prompted by general rather than personal injustices, so it is nobler to love the good ones for their services to the human race and not to any particular men. But it has become customary for the consuls, once their official speech of thanks is finished, to go on to express their personal debt to their prince. Allow me then to perform this duty, as much on behalf of my distinguished colleague, Cornutus Tertullus,[1] as for myself. I should surely speak for us both when my debt of thanks is due as much on his account as on my own, especially when the supreme generosity of the Emperor took note of our intimacy and conferred on us jointly what would have won the gratitude of us both had it been as-signed only to one. Both of us had suffered from that robber and assassin of every honest man through the massacre of our friends, as the hot breath of his falling thunderbolt passed close by our heads;[2] for we took pride in having the same friends and mourned their loss together, and just as today we share the same hopes and joys, at that time we were one in grief and terror. The divine Nerva had recom-pensed us for our times of peril in expressing his wish to promote us as being honest citizens, though as yet unknown; for the advancement of those whose only prayer hitherto had been to remain forgotten by the Emperor was a further indication that times had changed.

91. We had not yet completed our second year in

[1] Cf. *Ep.* V. 14 and Index.
[2] Cf. *Ep.* III. 11. 3 and VII. 27. 14: the " reign of terror " under Domitian in 93.

laboriosissimo et maximo, cum tu nobis, optime principum fortissime imperatorum, consulatum obtulisti,
2 ut ad summum honorem gloria celeritatis accederet:
tantum inter te et illos principes interest, qui beneficiis suis commendationem ex difficultate capta-
bant, gratioresque accipientibus honores arbitrabantur, si prius illos desperatio et taedium et similis
repulsae mora in notam quandam pudoremque
3 vertissent. Obstat verecundia quo minus percen-
seamus, quo utrumque nostrum testimonio ornaris,
ut amore recti amore rei publicae priscis illis con-
4 sulibus aequaveris. Merito necne, neutram in
partem decernere audemus, quia nec fas est ad-
firmationi tuae derogare, et onerosum confiteri vera
esse quae de nobis praesertim tam magnifica dixisti.
5 Tu tamen dignus es, qui eos consules facias, de quibus ista possis praedicare. Tribuas veniam quod
inter haec beneficia tua gratissimum est nobis, quod
6 nos rursus collegas esse voluisti. Ita caritas mutua,
ita congruens tenor vitae, ita una eademque ratio
propositi postulabat, cuius ea vis ut morum simili-
tudo concordiae nostrae gloriam minuat, ac perinde
sit mirum, si alter nostrum a collega ac si a se ipse
7 dissentiat. Non ergo temporarium et subitum est,
quod uterque collegae consulatu tamquam iterum

---

[1] The *praefectura aerarii Saturni* (*Ep.* V. 14, X. 3a) to which
Pliny and Tertullus were nominated in January 98, before
Nerva's death on the 27th. In *Ep.* X. 3a and X. 8. 3. Pliny
says that the appointment was made jointly by Nerva and
Trajan.

an exacting and important office[1] when you offered
us the consulate, and this you did, noblest of princes
and most valorous of emperors in the field, so that to
its supreme honour might be added the further distinction of rapid promotion. This marks the gulf
between you and those among your predecessors
who sought to recommend their benefits by hedging
them with difficulties, and believed that honours
would be more acceptable to their recipients if hope
long deferred, exasperation and endless delays tanta-
mount to a rebuff, had first turned them into a mark
of ignominy. Modesty prevents us from quoting
in detail your recommendation whereby you did
honour to our love of virtue and the State by com-
paring us with the great consuls of the past—whether
justly or not we cannot venture to decide, for it
would be improper for us to disparage your expressed
opinion, and an embarrassment to admit to any
truth in such a splendid tribute to ourselves. You,
on the other hand, are fully worthy to bestow the
consulate on such men as you can extol in terms like
these. Forgive me for saying that the most welcome
feature to us of the favours you bestow is your intention that we should be colleagues once again. That
was demanded by our mutual affection, the harmony
of our way of life, and the uniformity of our principles,
which is so marked that the similarity of our habits
detracts from the merit of our close agreement; for
either of us to disagree with his colleague would be
as surprising as if he were at odds with himself.
Thus there is nothing incidental or transitory in the
pleasure which each of us feels in the consulship of
his colleague; it might be a second one of his own,

suo gaudet, nisi quod tamen qui rursus consules
fiunt, bis quidem sed temporibus diversis obligantur,
nos duos consulatus simul accepimus, simul gerimus
alterque in altero consules et[1] iterum et pariter sumus.

92. Illud vero quam insigne, quod nobis praefectis
aerario consulatum ante quam successorem dedisti!
Aucta est dignitas dignitate, nec continuatus tantum
sed geminatus est honor, finemque potestatis
⟨altera[2]⟩ alterius tamquam parum esset excipere
2 praevenit. Tanta tibi integritatis nostrae fiducia
fuit, ut non dubitares te salva diligentiae tuae
ratione facturum, si nos post maximum officium
privatos esse non sineres. Quid quod eundem in
annum consulatum nostrum ⟨in quem tuum[3]⟩
contulisti? Ergo non alia nos pagina quam te consulem accipiet, et nostra quoque nomina addentur
3 fastis, quibus ipse praescriberis. Tu comitiis nostris
praesidere, tu nobis sanctissimum illud carmen
praeire dignatus es; tuo iudicio consules facti, tua
voce renuntiati sumus, ut idem honoribus nostris
suffragator in curia, in campo declarator exsisteres.
4 Iam, quod ei nos[4] potissimum mensi attribuisti quem
tuus natalis exornat, quam pulchrum nobis! quibus
edicto, quibus spectaculo celebrare continget diem

---

[1] consules et *Baehrens*: consul sed *M*.
[2] altera *ante* alterius *add. Mynors*: *post* alterius *Keil*: *om. M*.
[3] in quem tuum (*sed ante* consulatum) *add. Schnelle*: *ita Mynors*: *om. M*.
[4] ei nos *Schwarz*: eos *M*.

---

[1] *i.e.* they continued in office until the end of August and
immediately entered on their consulship.

only with this difference: those who hold office twice
are indeed honoured twice, but on different occasions, whereas we have received our two consulships
together and hold them together, and through the
person of the other each feels that we are consuls at
the same moment and for a second time.

92. It is no less remarkable that you bestowed
the consulate on us while we were prefects of the
treasury before you appointed a successor there.
Honour has been heaped on honour, and our responsibilities not only prolonged without a break but
doubled, now that a second office has anticipated the
end of the first as if it were not enough for it to follow
in succession. Such was your faith in our integrity
that you were confident that it would do no damage
to your principles of close surveillance if you did not
permit us to retire into private life when we laid
down an office of such importance.[1] Nor must I neglect to mention that you conferred a consulship on
us in the same year as you held your own,[2] and so
our consulship will be recorded on the same page as
yours, and our names will appear on the calendar
headed by your own. It was not beneath your dignity to preside in person at our election and to pro-
nounce the sacred formula of the oath; it was your
decision to make us consuls, and your voice which
proclaimed us; you sponsored our candidature in the
senate-house and announced its success on the
election-field. Moreover, what an honour it is for
us of all men to be assigned to the month which is distinguished by your birthday! It will be our good
fortune to celebrate by public games and official

[2] Cf. 60. 4 and note.

539

illum triplici gaudio laetum, qui principem abstulit
pessimum, dedit optimum, meliorem optimo genuit.
5 Nos sub oculis tuis augustior solito currus accipiet,
nos inter secunda omina et vota certantia, quae
praesenti tibi conferentur, vehemur alacres et incerti,
ex utra parte maior auribus nostris accidat clamor.

93. Super omnia tamen praedicandum videtur,
quod pateris consules esse quos fecisti; quippe
nullum periculum, nullus ex principe metus consu-
lares animos debilitat et frangit, nihil invitis audiendum, nihil coactis decernendum erit. Manet mane-
bitque honori veneratio sua nec securitatem auctori-
2 tate perdemus. Ac, si quid forte ex consulatus
fastigio fuerit deminutum, nostra haec erit culpa
non saeculi. Licet enim quantum ad principem,
licet tales consules agere, quales ante principes erant.
3 Ullamne tibi pro beneficiis referre gratiam parem
possumus? nisi tamen illam, ut semper nos meminerimus consules fuisse et consules tuos; ea sentia-
mus, ea censeamus quae consularibus digna sunt;
ita versemur in re publica ut credamus esse rem
publicam; non consilium nostrum, non operam sub-
trahamus, nec defunctos nos et quasi dimissos con-

---

[1] Trajan was born on 18 September (?) 53; Domitian was
assassinated on 18 September 96 and Nerva proclaimed
emperor the same day. (S. 148d.)

[2] In the second half of October; on the *dies imperii* of Trajan
(cf. 8).

announcement that day of triple rejoicing which saw
the removal of the worst emperors, the accession of
the best, and the birth of one even better than the
best.[1]   It will be our lot to mount (beneath your own
eyes) a chariot even nobler than usual, and amid the
cries of good omen and clamour of competing vows
offered in your presence,[2] we shall be carried gladly
along, unable to judge from which quarter the louder
cheering strikes our ears.

93. There is still something which demands praise
beyond all else: the fact that when you have made
consuls you allow them to act without interference,
by which I mean that there are no fears nor perils as
regards the Emperor to weaken and destroy their
spirit; the consuls will not have to listen to anything
against their will nor have decisions forced on them.
Our office retains and will retain the respect due to
it, and in exercising our authority we need lose none
of our peace of mind.   Moreover, if the high dignity
of the consulate should chance to be diminished, the
fault will not be found in the times we live in but in
ourselves.   So far as rests with our prince, the consuls are free to fill their rôle as they did before the
days of emperors.   Is there any proper return we
can make you, to match all you have done for us?
Only perhaps by remembering all our lives that we
have been consuls, your consuls: by ensuring that
our opinions and pronouncements are worthy of the
office we once held: by playing an active part in
public affairs to show we believe that the republic
still exists: by not withholding our aid and counsel,
and by not imagining ourselves rid of the consulate
and dismissed from office, but believing ourselves

sulatu sed quasi adstrictos et devinctos putemus,
eundemque locum laboris et curae quem reverentiae dignitatisque teneamus.

94. In fine orationis praesides custodesque imperî
divos ego consul pro rebus humanis, ac te praecipue,
Capitoline Iuppiter, precor, ut beneficiis tuis faveas,
tantisque muneribus addas perpetuitatem. Audisti
quae malo principi precabamur: exaudi quae pro
2 dissimillimo optamus. Non te distringimus votis;
non enim pacem, non concordiam, non securitatem,
non opes oramus, non honores: simplex cunctaque
ista complexum omnium votum est, salus principis.
3 Nec vero novam tibi iniungimus curam. Tu enim
iam tunc illum in tutelam recepisti, cum praedonis
avidissimi faucibus eripuisti; neque enim sine auxilio
tuo, cum altissima quaeque quaterentur, hic, qui
omnibus excelsior erat, inconcussus stetit: praeteritus est a pessimo principe, qui praeteriri ab optimo
4 non poterat. Tu clara iudicii tui signa misisti, cum
proficiscenti ad exercitum tuo nomine tuo honore
cessisti. Tu voce imperatoris quid sentires locutus,
filium illi nobis parentem tibi pontificem maximum
5 elegisti. Quo maiore fiducia isdem illis votis, quae
ipse pro se nuncupari iubet, oro et obtestor, " si

---

[1] Cf. *Ep.* X. 52.

always closely bound up with it in some way, so that we continue to uphold by our efforts and devotion the position which brought us so much honour and respect.

94. To end my speech, I call on the gods, the guardians and defenders of our empire, speaking as consul on behalf of all humanity: and to you in particular, Capitoline Jupiter, I address my prayer that you shall continue your benefits, and augment the great gifts you have bestowed by making them perpetual. You heard our prayers under a bad prince; now give ear to our wishes on behalf of his opposite. We are not burdening you with vows—we do not pray for peace, concord, and serenity, nor for wealth and honours: our desire is simple, all-embracing, and unanimous: the safety of our prince.[1] This is no new concern we ask of you, for it was you who took him under your protection when you snatched him from the jaws of that monster of rapacity; for at the time when all the peaks were tottering to their fall, no one could have stood high above them all and remained untouched except by your intervention. So he escaped the notice of the worst of emperors, though he could not remain unnoticed by the best. It was you too who gave him clear signs of your interest as he set out to join his army,[2] when you yielded to him your own name and glory; and you who spoke your opinion through the voice of the Emperor, when you chose a son for him, a father for us, a Chief Pontiff for yourself. It is therefore with increased confidence, using the same form of vow that he asked to be made on his behalf, that I make

[2] Cf. 5. 2-4 and notes.

bene rem publicam, si ex utilitate omnium regit,"
primum ut illum nepotibus nostris ac pronepotibus
serves, deinde ut quandoque successorem ei tribuas,
quem genuerit quem formaverit similemque fecerit
adoptato, aut si hoc fato negatur, in consilio sis
eligenti monstresque aliquem, quem adoptari in
Capitolio deceat.

95. Vobis, patres conscripti, quantum debeam,
publicis etiam monimentis continetur. Vos mihi
in tribunatu quietis, in praetura modestiae, vos in
istis etiam officiis, quae studiis nostris circa tuendos
socios iniunxeratis, cum ⟨fidei⟩[1] tum constantiae
2 antiquissimum testimonium perhibuistis. Vos proxime destinationem consulatus mei his acclamationi-
bus adprobavistis, ut intellegam etiam atque etiam
enitendum mihi, ut hunc consensum vestrum com-
plectar et teneam, et in dies augeam. Etenim
memini tunc verissime iudicari, meruerit quis
honorem necne, cum adeptus est. Vos modo favete
3 huic proposito et credite, si cursu quodam provectus
ab illo insidiosissimo principe, ante quam profiteretur
4 odium bonorum, postquam professus est substiti,
cum viderem quae ad honores compendia paterent
longius iter malui; si malis temporibus inter maestos

---

[1] fidei *add. Keil: om. M.*

---

[1] Cf. 8. 1.
[2] The *acta diurna* or the *acta senatus*; cf. 75. 1.
[3] Cf. *Ep.* I. 23.
[4] Cf. *Ep.* VII. 16.

this my earnest prayer: "If he rules the State well
and in the interests of all," first preserve him for our
grandsons and great-grandsons, then grant him one
day a successor born of him and formed by him in the
image of the adopted son he is, or if fate denies him
this, guide and direct his choice to someone worthy
to be adopted in your temple on the Capitol.[1]

95. To you, Conscript Fathers, my debt is great,
and this is published in the official records.[2] You it
was who paid me tribute according to the best
traditions, for my orderly conduct as tribune,[3] my
moderation as praetor,[4] my integrity and determination in carrying out the requests you made of
my professional services for the protection of our
allies.[5] More recently, you hailed my designation
as future consul with such acclamation that I am well
aware that I must redouble my efforts if I am to receive your continued approval, and retain and increase it day by day; I do not forget that the truest
judgement on whether a man merits an office or not
is passed at the moment of his assuming it. All I
ask is your support in my present undertaking and
your belief in what I say. If then it is true that I
advanced in my career under that most treacherous of emperors before he admitted his hatred for
honest men, but was halted in it once he did so,[6]
preferring a longer route when I saw what the short
cuts were which opened the way to office; that in

[5] Cf. *Ep.* X. 3a and VI. 29.
[6] Pliny held his quaestorship, tribunate, and praetorship
under Domitian, and also the *praefectura aerarii militaris*;
the check in his career must therefore refer to his consulship,
if indeed there was one. See Introduction, p. xi.

545

et paventes, bonis inter securos gaudentesque numeror; si denique in tantum diligo optimum principem, in quantum invisus pessimo fui. Ego 5 reverentiae vestrae sic semper inserviam, non ut me consulem et mox consularem, sed ut candidatum consulatus putem.

bad times I was one of those who lived with grief and
fear, and can be counted among the serene and happy
now that better days have come; that, finally, I love
the best of princes as much as I was hated by the
worst: then I shall act not as if I consider myself
consul to day and ex-consul tomorrow, but as if I
were still a candidate for the consulate, and in this
way shall minister at all times to the reverence which
is due to you all.

Translator's note. Where *princeps* is translated as
' prince ' it is because no other English word seems
to combine the emphasis of a monosyllable with the
patriotic feeling which inspires the speech.

APPENDIX A

INSCRIPTIONS

There are a few fragmentary inscriptions referring to Pliny, the longest of which (C.I.L.v. 5262: ILS 2927: S. 230) is known only from a fifteenth-century copy and one fragment remaining in Milan. The whole had evidently stood over the baths at Comum, but was afterwards cut up to make a tomb and sent to Milan in the middle ages, where it was found in the church of St. Ambrose.

1.
C.   PLINIVS· L· F· OVF·   CAECILIVS   *secundus*
AVGVR· LEGAT· PRO PR· PROVINCIAE· PON *ti*   *et*   *bithyniae*   *cos*
CONSVLARI· POTESTA*t.* IN· EAM· PROVINCIAM· E *x*   *s.*   *c.*   *missus*   *ab*
IMP· CAESAR· NERVA· TRAIANO· AVG· GERMAN *ico*   *dacico*   *p.*   *p.*
5 CVRATOR· ALVEI· TI*b*ERIS· ET· RIPARVM· E *t*   *cloacar.*   *p.*   *urb.*
PRAEF· AERARI· SATV*r*NI· PRAEF· AERARI· MIL *it.*   *pr.*   *trib.*   *pl.*
QVAESTOR· IMP· SEVIR·   EQVITVM   *romanorum*
TRIB· MILIT· LEG· *III* GALLICA*e*   X *vir stli*

TIB· IVDICAND·   THERM *as ex* HS · · · · · · · · ADIECTIS ·   IN
10 ORNATVM· HS   CCC · · · · · *et eo amp* LIVS · IN · TVTELA*m*
HS· CC· T· F· I· *item in alimenta* LIBERTOR· SVORVM· HOMIN· C'
HS· [XVIII] LXVI DCLXVI· REI *p. legavit quorum inc* REMENT· POSTEA· AD· EPVLVM
*pl*EB·VRBAN·VOLVIT·PERTIN *ere* · · · · *item vivu* S· DEDIT·IN ALIMENT·PVEROR
ET·PVELLAR· PLEB·VRBAN· HS*d̄* *item bybliothecam et* IN TVTELAM· BYBLIOTHE
15 CAE· HS· C̃

APPENDIX A

1. Gaius Plinius Caecilius Secundus, son of Lucius of the tribe Oufentina, consul: augur: praetorian commissioner with full consular power for the province of Pontus and Bithynia, sent to that province in accordance with the Senate's decree by the Emperor Nerva Trajan Augustus, victor over Germany and Dacia, the Father of his Country: curator of the bed and banks of the Tiber and sewers of Rome: official of the Treasury of Saturn: official of the military Treasury: praetor: tribune of the people: quaestor of the Emperor: commissioner for the Roman knights: military tribune of the Third Gallic legion: magistrate on board of Ten: left by will public baths at a cost of . . . and an additional 300,000 sesterces for furnishing them, with interest on 200,000 for their upkeep . . . and also to his city capital of 1,866,666 2/3 sesterces to support a hundred of his freedmen, and subsequently to provide an annual dinner for the people of the city. . . . Likewise in his lifetime he gave 500,000 sesterces for the maintenance of boys and girls of the city, and also 100,000 for the upkeep of the library. . .

APPENDIX A

2.
C· PLINIO· L· F
OVF CAECILIO
SECVNDO COS
AVG· CVR· ALVEI· TIBER
ET RIP*ar et cloac*Ar VRB

3.
C· PLINI*o* *l.* .
OVF . CAEC*ilio*
SECVNDO . *c* O S
AVGVR· CVR· ALV· TIB
E*t ri*P. ET CLOAC· VRB
Praef. *a*ER· SAT· PRAEF
AER· MIL· / / / / Ɔ IMP
SEVIR· EQ· R· TR· M *i* L
LEG· III· GALL· X· VIRO
STL· IVD· FL· DIVI· T· AVG
VERCELLENS*es*

APPENDIX A

The following fragment can still be seen, built into the wall of Como Cathedral (C.I.L.v. 5263):

2. To Gaius Plinius Caecilius Secundus, son of Lucius of the tribe Oufentina, consul: augur: curator of the bed and banks of the Tiber and sewers of Rome. . . .

The following inscription was found at Fecchio, a small village near Como, and sent to the Brera Museum in Milan (C.I.L.v. 5667):

3. To Gaius Plinius Caecilius Secundus, son of Lucius of the tribe of Oufentina, consul: augur: curator of the bed and banks of the Tiber and sewers of Rome: official of the Treasury of Saturn: official of the military Treasury: . . . quaestor of the Emperor: commissioner for the Roman knights: military tribune of the Third Gallic legion: magistrate on board of Ten: priest of the deified Emperor Titus: dedicated by the citizens of Vercellae.

This is the only reference we have to a priesthood which must have been held in Pliny's native Comum; another inscription records that Calpurnius Fabatus held a similar one.

APPENDIX B

PLINY'S HOUSE AT LAURENTUM

A reconstructed plan taken from Clifford Pember's
model in the Ashmolean Museum, Oxford.

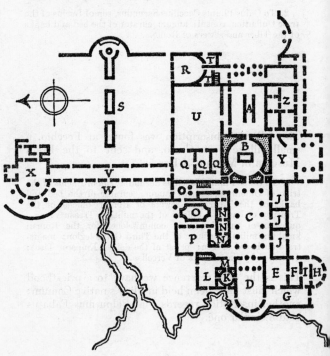

APPENDIX B

A. Entrance Hall
B. Courtyard
C. Inner hall
D. Dining-room
E. Bedroom
F. Bedroom
G. Gymnasium
H. Bedroom
I. Bedroom
J. Slaves' rooms
K. Bedroom
L. Small dining-room

M. Rooms and antechambers
N. Bathrooms
O. Heated swimming-bath
P. Ball court
Q. Suite with upper storey
R. Dining-room, with stores above
S. Garden with vine pergola
T. Rooms behind dining-room
U. Kitchen garden
V. Covered arcade
W. Terrace
X. Pliny's private suite
Y–Z. Kitchens and storerooms, not mentioned by Pliny

BIOGRAPHICAL INDEX

Italics indicate that person is recipient of the letter referred to.

557

BIOGRAPHICAL INDEX

BIOGRAPHICAL INDEX

BIOGRAPHICAL INDEX

legate of Dacia (ILS 2417, S. 192) later *amicus* and victim of Hadrian (SHA *Hadr.* 7. 1); as tribune in 105 attacks advocates for money-making and collusion, V. 13. 6; speaks against Varenus Rufus at trial, V. 20. 6; requests him to produce accounts, VII. 6. 2.

T. AVIDIUS QUIETUS, of Faventia, suff. cos. 93, later legate of Britain; brother of Avidius Nigrinus (i); friend of Thrasea Paetus, VI. 29. 1; supports P.'s attack on Publicius Certus in 97, IX. 13. 15.

AVITUS, *v.* Julius; Junius; Octavius.

BAEBIUS HISPANUS, unknown friend of P.; advice on buying property for Suetonius, I. 24; news of disappearance of Robustus, *VI.* 25.

Q. BAEBIUS MACER, suff. cos. 103, praetorian procos. of Baetica, curator of Appian Way (Martial, X. 17, XII. 98., *praefectus urbis* 117 (SHA *Vit. Hadr.* 5. 5); as cos. elect proposes sentence for J. Bassus, IV. 9. 16; proposes settlement in case of Egnatius Marcellinus, IV. 12. 4; letter on Elder Pliny, *III.* 5.

BAEBIUS MASSA, praetorian proconsul of Baetica, *c.* 91–2, *delator* under Domitian (Tac. *Hist.* IV. 50; *Agr.* 45); Herennius Senecio and P. prosecute him on behalf of Baetica in 93, III. 4. 4; VI. 29. 8; VII. 33. 4.

BAEBIUS PROBUS, native of Baetica, accused with Caecilius Classicus, otherwise unknown, III. 9. 12 ff.

BAETICA, province of Spain, BAETICI. P.'s close connexion, 1. 7. 2; P. acts for them in case against Massa in 93, III. 4. 4; VI. 29. 8; VII. 33. 4; and against Classicus in 103, III. 4; III. 9; VI. 29. 8; birthplace of Herennius Senecio, VII. 33. 5; province of Calestrius Tiro, VI. 22. 7; VII. 16. 3.

BAIAE, resort in Campania, IX. 7. 3; *Pan.* 82. 1.

BALLOT ACT, its effects on senatorial elections and abuses, III. 20; IV. 25.

BASILICA JULIA, Centumviral Court sits there, V. 9. 1.

BASSUS, *v.* Annius; Asinius; Aufidius; Gavius; Julius; Pomponius.

BITHYNIA, BITHYNIANS, bring case against J. Bassus, IV. 9. 2; and against Varenus Rufus, V. 20; VI. 13; VII. 6. 1; VII. 10. 1; Valerius Maximus quaestor there, VIII. 24. 8; P. arrives as *legatus*, X. 17a; b; 18. 1; See also X. 41. 4; 65. 2; 66. 2; 77. 3; 79. 1; 87. 2; 108; 109; 112; 113; 114.

BITTIUS PRISCUS, unknown, to appear before Centumviral Court, VI. 12. 2.

(Q. FULVIUS GILLO) BITTIUS PROCULUS, suff. cos. 98, husband of Pompeia Celerina and so stepfather to P.'s second wife; treasury colleague of Publicius Certus in 97, IX. 13. 13; and cos. elect, IX. 13. 23.

BLAESUS, *v.* Velleius.

BOARD OF FIVE, set up by Nerva to reduce public expenditure, II. 1. 9; *Pan.* 62.

BOSPORUS, expected embassy from, X. 63; 67. 2.

BRIXIA (Brescia) in Transpadane Italy, birthplace of Minicius Acilianus, I. 14. 4.

BROCCHUS, *v.* Armenius.

BRUCTERI, tribe of central Germany (Tac. *Germ.* 33); their chief established in his territory by Vestricius Spurinna, II. 7. 2.

BRUTTIANUS, *v.* Lustricius.

BRUTTIUS PRAESENS, *v.* Praesens.

M. (JUNIUS) BRUTUS, the tyrannicide; his bust preserved, I. 17. 3; his statue on the Capitol, *Pan.* 55. 6; his light verse, V. 3. 5.

BYZANTIUM, administered with Bithynia; its expenditure on delegates to be reduced, X. 43; 44; legionary centurion sent there from Moesia, X. 77; 78.

CAECILIUS CELER, senator, intervenes between P. and Regulus, I. 5. 8; perhaps recipient of letter on value of reading aloud, *VII.* 17.

CAECILIUS CLASSICUS, proconsul of Baetica, 97–8, born in Africa, III. 9. 2, husband of Casta, III. 9. 29; prosecuted after his death by P. on behalf of Baetici in 101, III. 4;

VI. 29. 8; details of case, III. 9; otherwise unknown.

CAECILIUS MACRINUS, friend of P., possibly Transpadane; letters on triumphal honours for Spurinna, *II.* 7; trial of Classicus, *III. 4*; trial of Varenus Rufus, *VII. 6*; *10*; floods in Tuscany, *VIII.* 17; speech sent, *IX. 4.*

C. CAECILIUS STRABO, suff. cos. 105; proposes settlement in case of Egnatius Marcellinus, IV. 12. 4; as cos. elect, intends to bring case against Corellia, IV. 17. 1.

(A.) CAECINA PAETUS, suff. cos. 37, husband of elder Arria, father of younger Arria; his part in Scribonianus' abortive rising, (Suet. *Claud.* 13), illness and death of his son, suicide with Arria in 42, III. 16.

CAECINIA, *v.* Arria, the younger.

CAELIANUS, *v.* Sempronius.

M. CAELIUS (RUFUS), the orator, defended by Cicero in *Pro Caelio*; cited as example of the grand style, I. 20. 4.

CAELIUS CLEMENS, relative of Pompeia Celerina, sent out to serve under P. in Bithynia, X. 51.

(Ti.) CAEPIO HISPO, suff. cos. c. 101 (ILS 1027); his proposal for lenient sentence on J. Bassus carried, IV. 9. 16 ff.

CAESENNIUS SILVANUS, relative of Suetonius, who asks for his military tribunate to be transferred to him, III. 8.

CAESAR, *v.* Julius; Domitian; Trajan.

P. CAESIUS PHOSPHORUS, freedman; request for citizenship for him, X. 11. 2.

CALESTRIUS TIRO, praetorian, he or his son cos. 122 (S. 348, 362), friend and colleague of P. as quaestor and praetor, VII. 16; native of Picenum(?) *VI. 1*; governor of Baetica, 107/8, *VI. 22.* 7; letter of advice, *IX. 5*; visits Calp. Fabatus at Comum on way out, VII. 16; 23; 32; letter on d. of Corellius Rufus, *I.* 12.

CALLIDROMUS, slave of Laberius Maximus, captured in Dacian wars, X. 74. 1.

CALLIMACHUS, Alexandrian poet, model for Arrius Antoninus, IV. 3. 4.

CALPURNIA, P.'s third wife, granddaughter of Calp. Fabatus, IV. 1. 1; her character and affection, IV. 19; much missed by P. in absence, *VI. 4*; 7; *VII.* 5; her miscarriage, VIII. 10; 11; returns from Bithynia on d. of grandfather, X. 120; 121.

CALPURNIA HISPULLA, daughter of Calpurnius Fabatus of Comum, aunt of P.'s third wife; letters praising her niece, *IV. 19*; and reporting a miscarriage, *VIII. 11*; outlives her father, X. 120; 121.

(L.) CALPURNIUS FABATUS, Roman knight of Comum (career in ILS 2721; Tac. *Ann.* XVI. 8), grandfather of P.'s wife, Calpurnia; manages P.'s estates, *VI. 30. 1*; presents colonnade to Comum, *V. 11*; owns property in Campania, *VI. 30*; and near Ameria, VIII. 20. 3; visited by P., *IV. 1*; V. 14. 8; and by Calestrius Tiro, *VII. 16*; *23*; *32*; letters promising support for Bittius Priscus, *VI. 12*; on land sale to Corellia, *VII. 11*; on his granddaughter's miscarriage, *VIII. 10*; his death, X. 120.

(CALPURNIUS FABATUS?), son of above, died before P. married his daughter, V. 11. 2.

CALPURNIUS FLACCUS, unknown friend of P., sends fieldfares to Laurentum, *V. 2.*

P. CALPURNIUS MACER, suff. cos. 103, *legatus propraetore* of Lower Moesia while P. is in Bithynia (S. 196); to supply P. with engineer, X. 42; 61; 62; sends centurion to Byzantium, 77; letters on his country house, *V. 18*; and, perhaps, bravery of woman of Comum, *VII. 24.*

C. CALPURNIUS PISO, young literary friend of P., possibly cos. 111 and grandson of the Neronian conspirator; reads poem *Legends of the Stars*, V. 17.

(L. CALPURNIUS) PISO, *trib. plebis* 149 B.C., called Frugi, *Pan.* 88. 6.

L. (CALPURNIUS) PISO, cos. 27 (Tac. *Ann.* IV. 62) quoted, III. 7. 12.

BIOGRAPHICAL INDEX

BIOGRAPHICAL INDEX

his name linked with Calvus, I. 16
5; IV. 27. 4; *Carmen* XVI. 5
quoted, IV. 14. 5.

(L. VALERIUS) CATULLUS MESSALINUS,
cos. with Domitian in 73 and 85;
the notorious blind *delator* used by
Domitian, IV. 22. 5 (Tac. *Agr.* 45;
Juv. 4. 113).

Q. (LUTATIUS) CATULUS, cos. 102 B.C.;
his light verse, V. 3. 5.

CELER, unknown Roman knight
charged by Domitian with violating
Vestal Cornelia, IV. 11. 10; *v.*
Caecilius; Nonius.

CELERINA, *v.* Pompeia.

CELSUS, *v.* Juventius.

CENTUM CELLAE (Civita Vecchia) in
Etruria; P. assessor to Trajan
there; building of harbour, VI. 31.

CENTUMVIRAL COURT. P. starts
career there, I. 18. 3; his special
sphere, VI. 12. 2; applauded there,
IV. 16; IX. 23. 1; addresses four
panels sitting jointly, IV. 24. 1;
VI. 33. 3; Regulus sets trap
for P., I. 5. 4; adjournments not
granted, I. 18. 6; disputed will,
V. 1. 6; praetor's edict suspends
sitting, V. 9; appearance of hired
audiences, II. 14. 4ff.

CERES, Temple on P.'s property at
Tifernum to be rebuilt, IX. 39. 1.

CERIALIS, *v.* Tuccius (Tullius?);
Velius.

CERTUS, *v.* Publicius.

CHRIST, CHRISTIANS; Trajan's and
P.'s attitude, X. 96; 97 (cf. Euse-
bius, *Hist. Ecc.* III. 33; Tertullian,
Apol. II. 6–10.

CHRYSIPPUS, relative of P.'s doctor;
request for citizenship, X. 11. 2.

(M. TULLIUS) CICERO, the orator, cos.
63 and augur 53 B.C., IV. 8. 4; P.'s
model in eloquence, I. 2. 4; 5. 11–
12; 20; his mastery of grand style,
IX. 26. 8; his light verse, V. 3. 5;
criticized by Asinius Gallus, VII. 4.
3 ff.; epigram on favourite Tiro,
VII. 4. 6; generous encouragement
of poets, III. 15. 1; wider choice of
subject than P., IX. 2. 2; quotations from *Ep. ad Att.*, I. 2. 4; *In
Verrem*, I. 20. 10; *de Oratore*, VII.
17. 13; *Tusc. Disp.*, IX. 23. 6;
references to *Pro Cluentio*, *Pro*

Cornelio, *Pro Murena*, *Pro Vareno*,
I. 20. 7–8.

CITY PREFECT, P. acts as assessor,
VI. 11. 1.

CLARIUS, unknown, defended by P.,
IX. 28. 5.

CLARUS, *v.* Erucius; Septicius.

CLASSICUS, *v.* Caecilius.

CLAUDIOPOLIS, (Bolu) city in Bithynia; P. reports public bath started
on unsuitable site, X. 39; 40.

CLAUDIUS, Emperor 41–54; attends
reading by Servilius Nonianus, I.
13. 3; revolt against him of Scribonianus, legate of Illyricum in 42,
III. 16. 7, 9; his freedman Pallas
honoured in Senate, VII. 29. 1;
VIII. 6 (Suet. *Claud.* 28); is left
house for a shrine at Prusa, X. 70;
71; deified by Nero, *Pan.* 11. 1.

(Ti.) CLAUDIUS ARISTION, leading citizen of Ephesus (and president of
Provincial Council of Asia), cleared
of charge heard at Centum Cellae,
VI. 31. 3.

CLAUDIUS CAPITO, represents Bithynians in their continued attack on
Varenus Rufus, VI. 13. 2.

CLAUDIUS EUMOLPUS, local senator of
Prusa, charges Dio Cocceianus, X.
81.

CLAUDIUS FUSCUS, son-in-law of
Caecilius Classicus, acquitted in
trial, III. 9. 18.

CLAUDIUS MARCELLINUS, unknown
senator, defends Flavius Marcianus
at trial of Marius Priscus, II. 11.
15.

(Ti.) CLAUDIUS POLLIO, Roman knight
(ILS 1418), biographer of L. Annius
Bassus, member of Nerva's land
commission; *praefectus equitum* in
Syria during P.'s military service;
now wants friendship of Cornutus
Tertullus, VII. 31.

CLAUDIUS POLYAENUS, citizen of
Prusa, left house and contents to
Emperor Claudius; copy of will
sent to Trajan, X. 70; 71.

CLAUDIUS RESTITUTUS, senator, probably born in Africa; defends Hispanus and Probus at trial of Classicus, III. 9. 16; letter on bad
behaviour at readings, *VI. 17.*

CLEMENS, *v.* Attius; Caelius.

BIOGRAPHICAL INDEX

565

BIOGRAPHICAL INDEX

DIOMEDES, Homeric hero; reference to *Iliad* VI. 235, V. 2. 2.

DIONYSIUS, baker of Nicomedia, X. 74. 1. *V.* Valerius.

DOMITIA LUCILLA, daughter of Cn. Domitius Lucanus and Curtilia, heiress of her grandfather, Curtilius Mancia, her uncle and her father, VIII. 18. 4–7.

DOMITIAN, Emperor 81–96; prosecutions during his reign, I. 5. 5; III. 9. 31, 33; IV. 9. 2; banishment of philosophers, III. 11. 2; *Pan.* 47; Corellius Rufus determined to outlive him, I. 12. 8; execution of Vestal virgin, IV. 11. 5 ff.; use of informers, I. 5; IV. 22. 5; *Pan.* 34; Senate under D., VIII. 14. 8; *Pan.* 76. 3; Senate's reaction after death, IX. 13. 2; *Pan.* 52; P.'s career under D., III. 11; VII. 27. 14; *Pan.* 90. 5; 95. 3; D.'s official letters quoted, X. 58; 60; 66; 72; deifies Titus, *Pan.* 11. 1; journey from Suebian War, *Pan.* 20. 4; avenges Nero, *Pan.* 53. 4; successive consulships, *Pan.* 58; behaviour at elections, *Pan.* 63. 4; misuse of arena, *Pan.* 38. 4; slaves suborned, *Pan.* 42. 4; relatives murdered, *Pan.* 48. 3; confiscation of property, *Pan.* 50; suppression of mimes, *Pan.* 46. 1; incestuous marriage, IV. 11. 6; *Pan.* 52. 3; appearance, *Pan.* 48. 4; cowardice, *Pan.* 82; cupidity, *Pan.* 50; his statue in Forum, *Pan.* 52.7; his murder, *Pan.* 49. 1.

(Cn. DOMITIUS) AFER, the celebrated orator, of Nîmes, d. 59 (Tac. *Ann.* IV. 52; 60; XIV. 19; Quint. *Inst. Orat.* X. 1. 118; XII. 11. 3); interrupted in court by hired applause, II. 14. 10; adopts Cn. Domitius Lucanus and Cn. Dom. Tullus, who inherit his wealth, VIII. 18. 5.

(L.) DOMITIUS APOLLINARIS, suff. cos. 97, friend of Martial; as cos. elect defends Publicius Certus, IX. 13. 13; letters asking for support for Sextus Erucius, *II. 9*; describing P.'s house in Tuscany, *V. 6* (his own house at Formiae, Martial X. 30).

(Cn.) DOMITIUS LUCANUS, perhaps of Gallia Narbonensis, suff. cos. 79,

died *c.* 94 (ILS 990, MW 299; Martial, I. 36; IX. 51); married daughter of T. Curtilius Mancia, father of Domitia Lucilla, VIII. 18. 4–5.

(Cn.) DOMITIUS TULLUS, suff. cos.[2] in 98, younger brother of Dom. Lucanus, adopted with him by Dom. Afer, VIII. 18. 4–5; adopted his brother's daughter, to whom he left his fortune; his paralysis and death *c.* 108, VIII. 18 (ILS 991, MW 300; Martial, I. 36; III. 20; IX. 51).

NERO (CLAUDIUS) DRUSUS, 38–9 B.C., stepson of Augustus, brother of Tiberius; his victories and death in Germany, III. 5. 4.

(M.) EGNATIUS MARCELLINUS, later suff. cos. 116, as quaestor in province, tried to have late secretary's salary paid to heirs, IV. 12.

EGYPT, its marvels, VIII. 20. 2; P. sends his freedman there for his health, V. 19. 6; P.'s therapist Egyptian, X. 6. 2; Pompeius Planta prefect, IX. 1. 1; X. 6. 7; 10. 2; drought in Egypt, *Pan.* 30–1.

ENCOLPIUS, slave or freedman serving P. as reader, spits blood on journey, VIII. 1. 2.

Q. ENNIUS, the poet; his light verse, V. 3. 6.

EPHESUS, capital of province of Asia; charges its leading citizen, Claudius Aristion, VI. 31. 3; P. arrives there, X. 15. 17a; travels on to Pergamum, X. 18. 1.

EPIGONUS, son of Chrysippus, X. 11. 2.

EPIMACHUS, freedman assistant to procurator of Trajan in Bithynia, X. 84.

(M.) ERUCIUS CLARUS, Roman knight and advocate, married to sister of C. Septicius Clarus, II. 9. 4; letter on talents of Pompeius Saturninus, *I. 16*.

(SEX.) ERUCIUS CLARUS, son of above, later cos. 117, legionary legate under Trajan in Parthian War, captured Seleucia (Dio LXVIII. 30), and City Prefect, 146; given *latus clavus*

BIOGRAPHICAL INDEX

by Nerva at P.'s request, and stands for tribunate about 101, II. 9.

ESQUILINE HILL, where P. has his town house, III. 21. 5.

EUBOEA, called by Demosthenes the bulwark of Attica, IX. 26. 8.

EUMOLPUS, v. Claudius.

EUPHRATES, Stoic philosopher of Tyre, enemy of Apollonius of Tyana, pupil of Musonius, *m.* daughter of Pompeius Julianus; known to P. in Syria, then teaching in Rome; expelled by Domitian in 93 but back in Rome, I. 10 (died by suicide in Rome in 119, Dio LXIX. 8).

EUPHRATES, river; *Pan.* 14. 1.

EUPOLIS, Athenian comic poet, *Frag.* 94 quoted on Pericles, I. 20. 17.

EURIPIDES, the Greek dramatist; *Hecuba* 569 and *frag.* 812N² quoted, IV. 11. 9; 27. 6.

EURYTHMUS, freedman and procurator of Trajan, charged with forging a will, VI. 31. 8 ff.

FABATUS, v. Calpurnius.

FABIUS (or FLAVIUS) APER, senator, proposes penalty in case of Tuscilius Nominatus, V. 13. 5.

FABIUS HISPANUS, native of Baetica, charged with Caecilius Classicus, III. 9. 12 ff.

(L.) FABIUS JUSTUS, suff. cos 102; Tacitus' *Dialogus* dedicated to him; *legatus* of Lower Moesia 105 to probably 108 (S. 302, Syme JRS XLIX. 28 ff.) and governor of Syria 109 (S. 421). Two notes received, *I. 11*; *VII. 2.*

FABIUS POSTUMINUS, suff. cos. 96, defends Publicius Certus, IX. 13. 13.

FABIUS RUSTICUS, historian, from Spain, a master of style (Tac. *Agr.* 10. 3; Quint. *Inst. Orat* X. 1. 104); quoted by Tacitus on Nero's reign (Tac. *Ann.* XIII. 20; XIV. 2; XV. 61); P. writes justifying his own variations of style, *IX. 19.*

FABIUS VALENS (i), receives letter on vicissitudes of Fortune, *IV. 24.*

FABIUS VALENS (ii), (perhaps recommended to Trajan, X. 86. b). Both

(i) and (ii) are otherwise unknown, possibly the same man.

C. FABRICIUS, the victor over Pyrrhus, *Pan.* 13. 4.

(A. DIDIUS GALLUS) FABRICIUS VEIENTO, cos.³ in 83, *amicus* of Nero and the Flavians and a *delator* under Domitian, IV. 22. 4 (ILS 1010, MW 155; Tac. *Ann.* XIV. 50; Juv. *Sat.* IV. 113 ff.); later dines as friend of Nerva, IV. 22. 4; defends Publicius Certus against P., and shouted down, IX. 13. 13, 19.

(L.) FADIUS RUFINUS, suff. cos. 113, points out P. to provincial friend, IX. 23. 4; letter on will of Domitius Tullus, *VIII. 18.*

FALCO, v. Pompeius.

FANNIA, daughter of Thrasea Paetus and younger Arria, granddaughter of elder Arria, III. 16. 2; second wife of Helvidius Priscus and twice banished with him, VII. 19. 4; on her request his *Life* written by Herennius Senecio, VII. 19. 5; banished again and possessions confiscated in 93, III. 11. 3; VII. 19. 6; returns from exile in 97, IX, 13. 5; her last illness and death, VII, 19.

C. FANNIUS, perhaps related to Thrasea Paetus, biographer of victims of Nero; his dream of Nero and death, *c.* 105, V. 5.

FEROX, v. Julius.

FESTUS, v. Valerius.

FIRMUM (Fermo), in Picenum, native town of P.'s friend Statius Sabinus; P. to take on case, VI. 18.

FIRMINUS, v. Hostilius.

FIRMUS, v. Romatius; Saturius.

FLACCUS, v. Ammius; Calpurnius.

FLAMEN; Voconius Romanus *flamen* in Hither Spain, II. 13. 4; P. *flamen divi Titi* in Comum, Appendix A. 3, S. 230.

FLAVIUS APER, v. Fabius A.

FLAVIUS ARCHIPPUS, of Prusa, teacher of philosophy; claims exemption from jury service, and charged with escaping from prison; previously sentenced for forgery but favoured by Domitian, X. 58; 59; 60; charges Dio Cocceianus with treason, X. 81; 82.

567

BIOGRAPHICAL INDEX

Priscus and Anteia; Cornutus Tertullus her guardian, IX. 13. 16; dies in childbirth with her sister of the same name, IV. 21.

C. HELVIDIUS PRISCUS (i), native of Cluviae, son-in-law of Fannia, son-in-law of Thrasea Paetus, VII. 19. 3, praetorian senator and leader of Stoic opposition (his career, Tac. *Hist.* IV. 5); exiled by Nero in 66, VII. 19. 4, recalled by Galba, exiled again 74–5 and executed by Vespasian (Suet. *Vesp.* 15), III. 11. 3; his *Life* by Herennius Senecio, VII. 19. 5, and eulogy by Junius Arulenus Rusticus (Suet. *Dom.* 10).

(C.) HELVIDIUS (PRISCUS) (ii), son of above by former marriage, cos. before 86 at date unknown, husband of Anteia, IX. 13. 4; condemned to death by Domitian in 93 on instigation of Publicius Certus, III. 11. 3; IX. 13 (Tac. *Agr.* 45; Suet. *Dom.* 10); death of his two daughters, IV. 21; P.'s vindication of him in Senate in 97, afterwards published, IV. 21; VII. 30. 4; IX. 13.

(HELVIDIUS), surviving son of above and Anteia, IV. 21.

HERACLEA, *civitas stipendiaria* of Pontus, to benefit by a legacy, X. 75. 4.

(HERCULES), Trajan compared, *Pan.* 14. 5.

HERENNIUS POLLIO, consular senator, speaks for prosecution at trial of J. Bassus, IV. 9. 14, otherwise unknown.

HERENNIUS SENECIO, native of Baetica and quaestor there, VII. 33. 5, with no subsequent advancement (Dio, LXVII. 13); defends Valerius Licinianus, IV. 11. 12; acts with P. against Baebius Massa in 93, VII. 33; unsuccessfully impeached by Massa for treason; his opinion of Regulus, IV. 7. 8; writes *Life* of Helvidius Priscus, for which he is accused by Mettius Carus and condemned to death in 93, I. 5. 3; III. 11. 3; VII. 19. 5 (Tac. *Agr.* 2 and 45); his memory abused by Regulus, I. 5. 3.

HERENNIUS SEVERUS, senatorian scholar asking for portraits of Corn.

Nepos and T. Catius, IV. 28; letter on illness of Passennus Paulus, *IX.* 22.

HERMES, freedman of P.; sells land at Comum to Corellia on P.'s orders, VII. 11. 1, 6; 14. 1.

HERODAS, Greek mimiambic poet; Arrius Antoninus compared, IV. 3. 4.

(HESIOD) *Works and Days* quoted, III. 7. 15.

HIPPO (DIARRHYTUS), coastal colony in Africa (Bizerta); dolphin appears there, IX. 33. 2 ff.

HISPANUS, *v.* Baebius; Fabius.

HISPELLUM (Spello) in Umbria, presented with source of the Clitumnus and provides amenities, VIII. 8. 6.

HISPO, *v.* Caepio.

HISPULLA, wife of Corellius Rufus, summons P. at his death, I. 12. 9, 10.

HISPULLA, *v.* Calpurnia; Corellia.

HOMER, first read in school, II. 14. 2; his poetic devices, III. 9. 28; describes Achilles' arms at length, V. 6. 43; modifies Greek to suit verse, VIII. 4. 4; a master of grand style, IX. 26. 6. *Iliad* quoted, I. 7. 1; 7. 5; 18; 20. 22; IV. 2. 3; 11. 12; V. 2. 2; VI. 8. 3; VIII. 2. 8; IX. 13. 20; 26. 6. *Odyssey* quoted, V. 19. 2; 20. 7; IX. 1. 4. (Refs. in text.)

(M. JUNIUS) HOMULLUS, suff. cos. 102, later legate of Cappadocia, defends J. Bassus against the Bithynians, IV. 9. 15, and later, Varenus Rufus, V. 20. 6; makes proposal in debate on election expenditure, VI. 19. 3.

HONORATUS, *v.* Vitellius.

HORACE, the poet, his lyric poetry the model for Passennus Paulus, IX. 22. 2; possible reference to *Ars Poetica* 28, IX. 26. 2.

Q. HORTENSIUS, the orator, opponent of Cicero; his light verse, V. 3. 5.

HOSTILIUS FIRMINUS, legate and accomplice of Marius Priscus, tried and sentenced, II. 11. 23; 12. 2.

HYPERIDES, Greek orator, his ample style, I. 20. 4.

ICARIA (Nicaria), Aegean island; P. wrote elegiacs when weatherbound there, VII. 4. 3.

BIOGRAPHICAL INDEX

BIOGRAPHICAL INDEX

V. 21. 3; candidature for quaestor-
ship supported by P. and Tacitus,
VI. 6; 9; news of storm damage,
IV. 6.

JULIUS PISO, citizen and public benefactor of Amisus, charged with having received money grant from local
senate, X. 110; 111.

(L.) JULIUS (URSUS) SERVIANUS, cos.
before 97, 102, 134 (S. 305, and ILS
4271); m. Domitia Paulina, sister
of Hadrian, executed by him in 136
(SHA *Vit. Hadr.* 15, 23–5); legate of
U. Germany, then Pannonia, 98–100,
VIII. 23. 5; obtains *ius trium
liberorum* for P., X. 2. 1; assigned
as *iudex* by Trajan in case, VII. 6. 8;
absent from Rome, in Dacia(?),
III. 17; his daughter marries
Fuscus Salinator. *VI. 26.*

JULIUS SPARSUS, perhaps the suff.
cos. 88 and friend of Martial (Mart.
XII. 57); letters on the success of
P.'s speeches, *IV. 5;* *VIII. 3.*

JULIUS TIRO, unknown; his will con-
tested at Centum Cellae, VI. 31. 7 ff.

JULIUS VALENS, unknown, incurably
ill in Rome, V. 21. 2.

JULIUS VALERIANUS, unknown senator; letters on his Marsian estates,
II. 15; on case of Tuscilius Nominatus, *V. 4;* *13.*

JUNIA, Vestal Virgin, perhaps related
to Junius Mauricus; relative of
Fannia, nursed in illness by her,
VII. 19. 1.

JUNIUS AVITUS, quaestorian, given
lacus clavus by Trajan, legionary
tribune under J. Servianus in Germany and Pannonia; his death as
aedile elect, VIII. 23; letter on
snobbery, *II. 6.*

JUNIUS MAURICUS, senator, brother
of Jun. Arulenus Rusticus and
guardian of his children, *I. 14;*
II. 18; banished by Domitian in 93,
III. 11. 3; returns in 97, I. 5. 10,
15; friend of Nerva, member of
Trajan's *consilium;* his outspoken-
ness, IV. 22. 3 ff. (cf. Tac. *Hist.*
IV. 40); his house at Formiae
visited by P., *VI. 14.*

JUNIUS PASTOR, unknown, defended
by P. at start of his career, I. 18.
3.

JUPITER, his powers in *Iliad* XVI.
250, I. 7. 1; temple at Comum, to
which P. presents statue, III. 6. 5;
temple on the Capitol, *Pan.* 8. 3;
16. 1; as father of Hercules, *Pan.*
14. 5; P.'s invocation to him and
final prayer, *Pan.* 1. 5, 6; 94. 1.

JUSTUS, *v.* Fabius; Minicius; Tullius.

(P.) JUVENTIUS CELSUS, jurist, head
of Proculian School, later suff. cos.
117, 129, and member of Hadrian's
consilium with Neratius Priscus
(SHA *Vit. Hadr.* 18); as praetor in
106 attacks Licinius Nepos, VI. 5.
4 ff.

(M'.) LABERIUS MAXIMUS, cos. 89,
103, legate in Moesia in 100 (S. 441),
fought in First Dacian War (Dio
LXVIII. 9. 4); later exiled (SHA
Vit. Hadr. 5. 5); his former slave
brought to P., X. 74. 1.

C. LAELIUS, the Stoic, called Sapiens,
Pan. 88. 6.

(A.) LAPPIUS MAXIMUS (NORBANUS),
suff. cos. 86 and 95, as legate of
Lower Germany put down revolt of
Saturninus in 88 (ILS 1006, MW.
60); proconsul of Bithynia, 85–6,
X. 58. 6.

LARCIUS LICINUS, advocate, author of
Ciceromastix; started practice of
inviting audiences in time of Claudius, II. 14. 9; as praetorian legate
in Spain *c.* 73 wished to buy Elder
Pliny's notebooks when latter procurator there, III. 5. 17.

LARCIUS MACEDO, praetorian senator,
son of a freedman, murdered by his
slaves, III. 14.

LARGUS, *v.* Julius.

LARIUS LACUS, *v.* Como, lake.

LATIN, epigrams, IV. 18. 2; elegiacs,
VII. 4. 3; language, II. 13. 7; IV.
11. 3; VII. 4. 9; 25. 4; rhetoric,
III. 3. 3; speech, IX. 36. 3; translation, VII. 9. 2.

LATIN FREEDMEN (*Latini Iuniani*),
VII. 16. 4; X. 104.

LATIN RIGHTS, *Pan.* 37. 3; 39. 2.

LAURENTUM, near Ostia; P.'s house
there fully described, II. 17; road
from Rome, II. 17. 2; P.'s writing

BIOGRAPHICAL INDEX

Pan. 35. 4; changes in inheritance tax, *Pan.* 37–8; a good ruler, *Pan.* 45. 1; restores mimes, *Pan.* 46. 2; makes palace *aedes publicae, Pan.* 47. 4; cuts down expenditure on building, *Pan.* 51; bestows 2nd consulship on Trajan, *Pan.* 56. 3; and 3rd on his colleagues, *Pan.* 61. 7.

NESTOR, Homeric hero; Arrius Antoninus compared, IV. 3. 3.

NICAEA, one of chief cities in Bithynia (Iznik); *servi poenae* acting as *servi publici,* X. 31. 2; theatre and gymnasium begun and abandoned, X. 39; 40; P. awaits embassy from Bosporus there, X. 63; 67. 1; P. hears case involving Dio Cocceianus, X. 81. 4; Nicaeans claim property of intestate citizens, X. 83; 84.

NICETES SACERDOS, rhetorician from Smyrna (criticized in Tac. *Dial.* 15. 3); his lectures attended by father of J. Naso and by P., VI. 6. 3.

NICOMEDIA, capital city of Bithynia (Izmit); P.'s legate arrives, X. 25; *servi poenae* acting as *servi publici,* X. 31; request for fire service refused, X. 33; 34; money wasted on abandoned aqueduct, X. 37; 38; proposed canal to connect Lake Sophon with sea, X. 41; 42; 61; 62; soldier Appuleius stationed there, X. 74. 1; new forum, X. 49; 50.

C. NIGRINUS, *v.* C. (Avidius) Nigrinus.

NILE, river, fails to flood the land of Egypt, *Pan.* 30–1.

NOMINATUS, *v.* Tuscilius.

M. (SERVILIUS) NONIANUS, cos. 35, famous orator and historian (Tac. *Ann.* XIV. 19); his reading attended by Emperor Claudius, I. 13. 3.

NONIUS, unknown friend of Rosianus Geminus, IX. 30. 1.

NONIUS CELER, unknown senator(?), to whose intended wife P. gives a dowry, VI. 32. 1.

NORBANUS LICINIANUS, native of Baetica, representing his country; previously exiled by Caecilius Classicus, III. 9. 31; found guilty of collusion at trial of Classicus, and of acting as *delator* against Salvius Liberalis, III. 9. 29 ff.

NOVEMBER, month; P.'s legate arrives in Bithynia 24 November, X. 25.

NOVIUS MAXIMUS, literary friend of P.; letters on hired audiences in Court, *II. 14;* on merits of his book, *IV. 20;* on death of C. Fannius, *V. 5;* urged to publish his attack on late Pompeius Planta, *IX. 1.*

NUMANTINUS, title of Scipio Aemilianus, VIII. 6. 2.

NYMPHIDIUS LUPUS (i), ex-chief centurion on P.'s staff in Bithynia; *praefectus cohortis* during P.'s military service in Syria, X. 87. 1.

NYMPHIDIUS LUPUS (ii), son of above, *praef. cohort.* under J. Ferox and Fuscus Salinator, recommended for promotion, X. 87. 3.

OCRICULUM (Otricoli) in Umbria; Pompeia Celerina has house there, I. 4. 1; Robustus disappears there, VI. 25. 1.

OCTAVIUS AVITUS, *legatus proconsule* of Hippo Diarrhytus in Africa, inadvertently kills the dolphin, IX. 33. 9 (cf. Pliny *NH.* IX. 26).

OCTAVIUS RUFUS, literary friend of P.; letter agreeing not to act against Baetici, *I. 7;* and on his delay in reading and publishing his verses, *II. 10.*

OLYMPUS, Mount, near Prusa, X. 81. 1.

OSTIA, in Latium, the road from Rome to it, II. 17. 2; supplies P.'s house at Laurentum, II. 17. 26.

PACORUS, king of Parthia, died *c.* 112, sent gift by Decebalus, king of Dacia, X. 74. 1; his portrait on a missing jewel, X. 74. 3.

PAETUS, *v.* Caecina; Thrasea.

PALATINE, hill, imperial palace there, I. 13. 3.

PALLAS, freedman and *a rationibus* of the Emperor Claudius (Suet. *Claud.* 28), executed by Nero (Tac. *Ann.* XIV. 65); awarded insignia of praetor and money, and refuses the money, VIII. 6 (Tac. *Ann.* XII. 53); the Senate's decree inscribed on his tomb, VII. 29.

PANCHARIA SOTERIS, to be granted citizenship, X. 11. 2.

[PANEGYRICUS], text of speech sent to

Voconius Romanus, III. 13; expanded version read to friends, III. 18.

PANNONIA, Danube province; J. Servianus legate there, VIII. 23. 5; laurels of victory sent from there in 98, *Pan.* 8. 2.

PAPHLAGONIA, coastal region of Bithynia-Pontus, supplies corn, X. 27.

(L.) PAPIRIUS (CURSOR), five times consul, *Pan.* 57. 3.

PARTHIA, escaped slave from Parthia appears before P., X. 74. 1; nugget from gold-mines sent to Trajan, X. 74. 3.

(C.) PASSENNUS PAULUS (PROPERTIUS BLAESUS) of Asisium, poet, Roman knight and descendant of Propertius (ILS 2925); gives public reading of his verse, VI. 15; his illness, IX. 22.

(C.) PASSIENUS CRISPUS, cos. 27 and 44, married Nero's aunt, Domitia, and then his mother, Agrippina, orator and wit (Tac. *Ann.* VI. 20. 1; Sen. *de Ben.* I. 15. 5); witticism quoted, VII. 6. 11.

PASTOR, *v.* Junius.

PATAVIUM (Padua), in Transpadane Italy, known for its provincial virtues, I. 14. 6.

PATERNUS, *v.* Plinius.

PATROCLUS, Homeric hero, *Iliad* XVIII. 20 quoted, IV. 11. 12.

PAULINUS, *v.* Valerius.

PERGAMUM, city in Asia, P. detained there by illness, X. 17a. 1.

PERICLES, the Athenian statesman, praise of his eloquence, I. 20. 17 ff.

PERUSIA (Perugia) in Umbria; Pompeia Celerina has house there, I. 4. 1.

PHILIP II, of Macedon, mentioned in quotations from Demosthenes, IX. 26. 8–9.

PICENUM, coastal region in NE. Italy, native place(?) of Calestrius Tiro, VI. 1. 1.

PISO, *v.* Calpurnius; Julius.

PLANTA, *v.* Pompeius.

PLATO, the philosopher, Euphrates compared, I. 10. 5; *Phaedo* 95b quoted, IV. 25. 5.

PLAUTUS, the comic dramatist, imitated by Pompeius Saturninus, I.

16. 6; and by Vergilius Romanus, VI. 21. 4.

(PLINIA), mother of P., sister of Elder P., friend of Calpurnia Hispulla, IV. 19. 7; with P. at Misenum during eruption of Vesuvius, VI. 16; 20.

PLINIUS PATERNUS, unknown literary friend of P., possibly a relative; letters on buying slaves, *I. 21*; P.'s book of verse sent, *IV. 14*; illness in P.'s household, *VIII. 16*; on the authority of history, *IX. 27*.

C. PLINIUS SECUNDUS, of Comum, P.'s maternal uncle and father by adoption, V. 8. 5; born A.D. 23 4, III. 5. 7; Roman knight, *amicus* of Vespasian, III. 5. 7, 8, 18; commander of fleet at Misenum, VI. 16. 4; death in the eruption of Vesuvius in 79, VI. 16; 20; his service in Germany and Spain, administrative and literary career and bibliography, III. 5.

C. PLINIUS SECUNDUS, the author, born late 61 or early 62, VI. 20. 5; native of Comum, Verginius Rufus his guardian, II. 1. 8; wrote a "tragedy" at fourteen, VII. 4. 2; studied at Rome under Nicetes Sacerdos and Quintilian, VI. 6. 3; adopted by his uncle, V. 8. 5; at Misenum for eruption of Vesuvius, VI. 16; 20; began career at bar at eighteen, V. 8. 8, in Centumviral Court, I. 18. 3, his special sphere, IV. 24; VI. 12. 2; *decemvir stlitibus iudicandis*, ILS 2927, S. 230, Appendix A. 1; *tribunus militum* of 3rd Gallic Legion, in Syria, auditing accounts, VII. 31. 2; III. 11. 5; *sevir equitum Romanorum*, S. 230; *quaestor Augusti* VII. 16. 2; *tribunus plebis* I. 23, 2; VII, 16. 2; praetor, III. 11. 2; VII. 16. 2; prosecutes Baebius Massa in 93, VI. 29. 8; VII. 33. 4; *praefectus aerarii militaris*, S. 230; death of second wife, vindicates Helvidius Priscus in 97, IX. 13; *praef. aer. Saturni* 98–100, V. 14. 5; X. 3a, 1; *Pan.* 91. 1; prosecutes Marius Priscus, 99–100, II. 11; 12; suff. consul with Cornutus Tertullus Sept.–Oct. 100, III. 13. 1; *Pan.* 90–1; married third wife, Calpurnia, IV. 19; granted *ius*

trium liberorum by Trajan, X. 2; prosecutes Caecilius Classicus 100–1, III. 9; defends J. Bassus, 102–3, IV. 9; elected *augur* in 103, IV. 8; *curator alvei Tiberis et riparum et cloacarum urbis*, 104–6, V. 14. 2; S. 230; *flamen divi Titi* (in Comum), App. A. 3; defends Varenus Rufus, 106–7, V. 20; arrives in Bithynia as *legatus propraetore consulari potestate* (S. 230) on 17 September, X. 17b; presumed death after 28 January and before 18 September, X. 102; 121.

His properties, at Comum, II. 1. 8; 15; IX. 7; at Laurentum, I. 9; II. 17; IV. 6; IX. 40; at Tifernum (*mei Tusci*), III. 19; IV. 6; V. 6; VIII. 2; IX. 15; 16; 36; 37.

His benefactions, to Comum, I. 8; III. 6; IV. 13; V. 7; VII. 18; App. A. 1, S. 230; to Tifernum, III. 4; IV. 1; X. 8. His personal generosity, I. 19; II. 4; III. 21; V. 19; VI. 3; 25; 32; VII. 11; VIII. 2; 16; requests on behalf of others, I. 24; II. 9; 13; III. 2; 8; IV. 4; 15; 28; VI. 6; 8; 23; VII. 7; 8; 22; literary interests, I. 13; 16; 20; II. 5; II. 19; III. 13; 15; IV. 27; V. 8; 15; 17; VI. 21; VII. 9; 17; 20; VIII. 4; 19; 21; IX. 22; 26; his own verse, IV. 14; V. 3; 15; VII. 4; 9; scientific interests, VII. 27; VIII. 8; 20; IX. 33; X. 41; 61; 90. His dislike of snobbery, II. 6; of affectation, IV. 2; 7; VI. 17; of intolerance, IX. 12; 17; of the Races, IX. 6. His difficulties with his farms, II. 4; 15; III. 19; VIII. 2; IX. 20; 37; X. 8.

(POMPEIA) PLOTINA, Empress, wife of Trajan; eulogy of her virtues, *Pan.* 83; offered title of *Augusta, Pan.* 84; letter forwarded to her, IX. 28. 1.

PO, river (Padus); P. staying N. of it (at Comum?). VI. 1. 1.

POLLIO, *v.* Asinius; Claudius; Herennius.

POLYAENUS, representative of Bithynia, acting in case against Varenus Rufus, VII. 6. 6, 14; 10. 1. Perhaps related to Claudius Polyaenus, X. 70. 1.

POLYCLITUS, Greek artist, mentioned by Cicero, I. 20. 10.

POLYCLITUS, notorious freedman of Nero (Tac. *Ann.* XIV. 39; *Hist.* II. 95) referred to by Trajan, VI. 31. 9.

POMPEIA CELERINA, mother of P.'s second wife, apparently remarried to Bittius Proculus, IX. 13. 13; her readiness to lend capital to P., III. 19. 8; visited by P. at Alsium, VI. 10. 1; death of her daughter, P.'s wife, IX. 13. 4; her relative sent out to P. in Bithynia, X. 51; letter on her various properties, *I. 4.*

(Cn.) POMPEIUS COLLEGA, suff. cos. 73, legate of Galatia (ILS 8904, MW 86), speaks as consular at trial of Marius Priscus, II. 11. 20 ff. (Or his son, Sex. Pompeius Collega, cos. 93, ILS 9059.)

(Q.) (ROSCIUS COELIUS MURENA) POMPEIUS FALCO, suff. cos. 108, consular legate of Trajan and Hadrian, (ILS 1035, S. 231), son-in-law of Sosius Senecio; letters on whether to practise in courts while tribune, *I. 23;* on poems of Sentius Augurinus, *IV. 27;* requests for military tribunate for Cornelius Minicianus, *VII. 22;* and for city news, *IX. 15. V.* Murena.

POMPEIUS JULIANUS, leading citizen of Syria, father-in-law of Euphrates, I. 10. 8.

Cn. POMPEIUS MAGNUS, *v.* Pompey.

(C.) POMPEIUS PLANTA, Roman knight, *amicus* of Trajan, X. 7. 3, procurator of Lycia under Vespasian, prefect of Egypt 97–100, IX. 1. 1; X. 7; 10. 2 (ILS 8907, S. 273); attacked by Novius (?) Maximus, after death, *c.* 108, IX. 1.

POMPEIUS QUINTIANUS, unknown, his early death lamented, IX. 9.

POMPEIUS SATURNINUS, advocate and author of history and verse, otherwise unknown, I. 16; friendship with Neratius (?) Priscus, *VII. 7;* VII. 8; *VII. 15;* letter with speech on opening of library, *I. 8;* on death of Julius Avitus, *V. 21;* on book by Rufus, *IX. 38.*

POMPEY, the Great, a national hero, VIII. 6. 2; draws up code of law for Bithynia, X. 79; 80; 112; 114;

115; his achievements, *Pan.* 29. 1;
addressed as *Magnus, Pan.* 88. 5.

POMPONIA GALLA, makes P. her joint
heir after disinheriting her son, V.
1.

POMPONIANUS, friend of Elder Pliny,
cut off by eruption at Stabiae, VI.
16. 11, 16.

(T.) POMPONIUS BASSUS, cos. 94,
legate of Cappadocia and Galatia
95–100 (S. 417); *curator alimentorum* in Florence 102 (ILS 6675,
6106, S. 436–7); letter on his plans
for retirement, *IV. 23.*

(Q.) POMPONIUS RUFUS, suff. cos. 95,
legate of Lower Moesia in 99 (ILS
1999–2000, S. 350–1) and later of
Tarraconensis (ILS 1014); as consular gives evidence in trial of
Classicus, III. 9. 33; and opens
prosecution of J. Bassus, IV. 9. 3.
(Possibly C. Pomponius Rufus, cos.
98.)

(P.) POMPONIUS SECUNDUS, cos. 44,
friend of Elder Pliny (*NH* VII. 80;
XIII. 83) who wrote his biography,
III. 5. 3; poet and tragedian, VII.
17. 11; imprisoned by Tiberius (Tac.
Ann. V. 8) but survived, and later
legate of U. Germany (Tac. *Ann.*
XII. 28).

PONTIC SHORE, Gavius Bassus prefect
of, X. 21. 1; 86a.

PONTIFFS, College of; Domitian
chief pontiff, IV. 11. 6; Trajan chief
pontiff, X. 68; 69.

PONTIUS ALLIFANUS, literary friend,
resident in Campania; letters on
appointment of Cornutus Tertullus
to the Via Aemilia, *V. 14*; on his
hospitality to P., *VI. 28*; on P.'s
efforts as a poet, *VII. 4.*

PONTUS, province administered with
Bithynia, X. 108; 109; 112; P.
tours there, X. 67. 1; home of J.
Largus, X. 75. 1.

POPILIUS ARTEMISIUS, probably freedman, introduced to P. by his patron
Voconius Romanus, IX. 28. 2.

POSTUMINUS, *v.* Fabius.

POSTUMIUS MARINUS, P.'s doctor,
attends him in illness; citizenship
for his relatives requested, X. 11. 1.

PRAENESTE (Palestrina) in Latium; P.
prefers his Tuscan home, V. 6. 45.

(C. BRUTTIUS) PRAESENS (L. FULVIUS
RUSTICUS), probably praetorian,
native of Lucania, unwilling to
come to Rome, *VII. 3.* Cos. 119
and 139: his belated but distinguished career, S. 193.

PRIMA, *v.* Furia.

PRISCUS, friend of Pompeius Saturninus, VII. 7; 8; 15 (perhaps Neratius). *V.* Bittius; Cornelius; Javolenus; Marius; Neratius; Stilonius.

PROBUS, *v.* Baebius.

PROCULA, *v.* Serrana.

PROCULUS, *v.* Bittius; Silius.

(SEXTUS) PROPERTIUS, the poet, of
Asisium, the ancestor and model of
the poet Passennus Paulus, V I. 15;
IX. 22.

PRUSA, *civitas stipendiaria* near Mt.
Olympus in Bithynia, birthplace of
Dio Cocceianus; P. inspects the
town's accounts, X. 17a; 17b; need
for new public bath, X. 23; 24;
site must be cleared for it, X. 70;
71; case of Flavius Archippus, X.
58; 59; 60; case involving Dio
Cocceianus, X. 81; 82.

PUBLICIUS CERTUS, praetorian senator
and *praefectus aerarii*; prosecuted
Helvidius Priscus in 93, IX. 13. 2;
attacked by P. in Senate in 97, IX.
13. 13 ff.; loses normal advancement to consulate, dies soon after,
IX. 13. 22–3.

PUDENS, *v.* Servilius.

PYRENEES, mountains, crossed by
Trajan on march to Germany, *Pan.*
14. 2.

PYTHON, ambassador of Philip of
Macedon, cited by Demosthenes,
IX. 26. 9.

QUADRATILLA, *v.* Ummidia.

QUADRATUS, *v.* Ummidius.

QUIETUS, *v.* Avidius.

QUINCTIUS CAPITOLINUS, six times
consul, *Pan.* 57. 5.

QUINTIANUS, *v.* Pompeius.

QUINTILIAN (M. Fabius Quintilianus)
of Tarraconensis, appointed Professor of Rhetoric by Vespasian, the
author of *Institutio Oratoria* etc.;
in early days worked under Domitius Afer, II. 14. 10; P.'s tutor, II.

BIOGRAPHICAL INDEX

14. 9; his lectures, VI. 6. 3; *Inst. Orat.* X. 1. 9 quoted, IV. 11. 12 (cf. Juv. *Sat.* 7. 186–9; *Inst Orat.* 1. preface).

QUINTILIANUS, unknown, husband of Tutilia, offered dowry for his daughter, *VI. 32.*

RACES (Circenses), their futility, IX. 6; Tacitus present, IX. 23. 2.

RECTINA, wife of Tascius, living on slopes of Vesuvius, asks for help from Elder Pliny, VI. 16. 8.

REGIA, palace, the official meeting place of the *pontifices*, IV. 11. 6.

M. (AQUILIUS) REGULUS, praetorian senator, half-brother of Vipstanus Messalla (Tac. *Hist.* IV. 42), *delator* in Nero's and Domitian's reign, I. 5. 15; P. considers prosecuting him in 97, I. 5. 15; P.'s judgement on his style of oratory, I. 20. 14; IV. 7; VI. 2; his instability of character, II. 11. 22; his legacy-hunting, II. 20; wealth and extravagant mourning for his son, IV. 2; IV. 7; his death, *c.* 104, VI. 2. (Contrast Martial, I. 82; 111; II. 74; VI. 38.)

RESTITUTUS, *v.* Claudius.

RHINE, river, *Pan.* 14. 1; 63. 4; 82. 4.

RHODES; Aeschines read one of Demosthenes' speeches there, II. 3. 10; IV. 5.

ROBUSTUS, unknown Roman knight, disappears on a journey, VI. 25.

ROMANUS, *v.* Vergilius; Voconius.

ROMATIUS FIRMUS, *decurio* of Comum; P. offers to make up capital qualification for status as Roman knight, *I. 19;* P. urges him to perform his duties as magistrate, *IV. 29.*

ROME, I. 7. 4; 17. 4; II. 3. 1; 11. 19; 17. 2; III. 9. 27; 14. 6; 16. 7; IV. 18. 4; 22. 3; V. 4. 4; 6. 4; VI. 1. 2; 6. 1; 9. 1; VII. 27. 2; 29. 2; VIII. 20. 2; X. 8. 6; 10. 2; 18. 3; 26. 2; 40. 3; 63; 68.

(T. PRIFERNIUS PAETUS) ROSIANUS GEMINUS, P.'s consular quaestor in 100; unspecified military post; suff. cos. not till 125 (ILS 1067, S. 228) though recommended to Trajan, *c.* 111, X. 26; in Lyons *c.* 108/9, *IX. 11;* letters on his health, *VII. 1;* on death of Ummidia Quadratilla, *VII. 24;* on death of wife of Minicius Macrinus, *VIII. 5;* on tolerance, *VIII. 22;* on generosity, *IX. 30.*

RUFINUS, *v.* Fadius; Trebonius.

RUFUS, unknown friend of late son of Calpurnius Fabatus, now in Campania (?), VI. 30. 5, perhaps Sempronius Rufus *q.v.*

RUFUS, *v.* Acilius; Asinius; Calvisius; Caninius; Corellius; Curtius; Minicius; Octavius; Pomponius; Satrius; Sempronius; Varenus; Verginius.

RUSO, *v.* Cremutius.

RUSTICUS, *v.* Arulenus; Fabius.

SABINA, perhaps a relative of Statius Sabinus of Firmum; makes P. her heir, VII. 10.

SABINIANUS, unknown, is persuaded to forgive his erring freedman, *IX. 21;* 24.

SABINUS, *v.* Statius.

SACERDOS, *v.* Nicetes.

SACERDOTAL GAMES, in Rome, started by a performance of mime, VII. 24. 6.

SALINATOR, *v.* Fuscus.

(C.) SALVIUS LIBERALIS (NONIUS BASSUS) suff. cos. *c.* 84, distinguished advocate (cf. Suet. *Vesp.* 13; ILS 1011, MW 311); banished by Domitian, III. 9. 33; defends Marius Priscus, II. 11. 7; eloquent at trial of Classicus, III. 9. 36.

SARDUS, unknown; receives letter of thanks for his tribute to P., *IX. 31.*

L. SATRIUS ABASCANTUS, request for Roman citizenship for him, X. 11. 2.

SATRIUS RUFUS, senator, career unknown, sneered at by Regulus when acting with P., I. 5. 11; speaks in defence of Publicius Certus in 97, IX. 13. 17.

SATURIUS FIRMUS, son-in-law of Asinius Rufus, IV. 15. 3; otherwise unknown.

SATURNALIA, festival (17 December), kept by P., VIII. 7. 1; his slaves allowed their celebrations, II. 17.

579

BIOGRAPHICAL INDEX

24; a time for exchanging gifts, IV. 9. 7.

SATURNINUS, unknown native of Comum, intends legacy for his city and makes P. his heir, V. 7.

SATURNINUS, v. Pompeius.

(Ti. JULIUS) SAUROMATES, King of the Cimmerian Bosporus, client-kingdom of Rome (S. 52); sends courier and embassy to Trajan passing through Nicaea, X. 63; 64; 67.

Q. (MUCIUS) SCAEVOLA, jurist, probably the cos. of 95 B.C.; his light verse, V. 3. 8.

SCAURUS, v. Atilius; Terentius.

SCIPIONES, as national heroes, VIII. 6. 2; *Pan.* 13. 4.

(L. ARRUNTIUS CAMILLUS) SCRIBONIANUS, cos. 32, *legatus propraetore* of Illyricum in 42; his abortive revolt against Claudius and death, III. 16. 7, 9 (cf. Tac. *Hist.* I. 89; Suet. *Claud.* 13).

SECUNDUS, v. Plinius; Pomponius.

SEMPRONIUS CAELIANUS, military tribune *angusticlavius* serving in Bithynia, reports slaves among his recruits, X. 29; 30.

SEMPRONIUS RUFUS, suff. cos. 113, perhaps of Comum and friend of Calpurnius Fabatus's son, VI. 30. 5; letters on abolishing the Games at Vienna, *IV.* 22; on the praetor's edict against fees for counsel's services, *V.* 9.

SEMPRONIUS SENECIO, unknown Roman knight, charged at Centum Cellae with forging a will, VI. 31. 8.

SENATE, hears cases of Marius Priscus, II. 11; 12; *Pan.* 76. 1; of Caecilius Classicus, III.9; of J. Bassus, IV. 9; of Tuscilius Nominatus, V. 4; 13; of Varenus Rufus, V. 20; VI. 5; 13; of freedmen of Afranius Dexter, VIII. 14; P. delivers *Panegyricus* in Senate, III. 18. 1; *Pan. passim*; consulted by Egnatius Marcellinus, IV. 12; and by Sollers, V. 4. 1; P. undertakes cases at request of Senate, VI. 29. 7 ff.; X. 3a; 3b; Senate under Claudius votes honours to Pallas, VII. 29; VIII. 6; Senate under Nero, III. 7. 10 ff.; Senate under Domitian, VIII. 14.

8–9; *Pan.* 76. 3; Senate under Trajan, *Pan.* 23; 61; 69; 75.

SENECA, v. Annaeus.

SENECIO, v. Herennius; Sempronius; Sosius.

(Q. GELLIUS) SENTIUS AUGURINUS, young senator and poet, relative of Vestricius Spurinna (later procos. of Achaia or Macedonia under Hadrian, ILS 5947a, S. 447); gives poetry reading; tribute to P. quoted, IV. 27; receives note of praise, *IX. 8.*

SEPTEMBER, month; celebration at T. of Ceres on the Ides, IX. 39. 2; contains many public holidays, X. 8. 3; P. arrives in Bithynia 17 September, X. 17a. 2; 17b.

SEPTEMVIRI EPULONUM, one of the four priestly colleges; Marius Priscus a member, II. 11. 12; P. asks to be given vacancy, X. 13.

(C.) SEPTICIUS CLARUS, Roman knight, friend of P. and Suetonius, who dedicated *De Vita Caesarum* to him; later prefect of praetorian guard under Hadrian, and subsequently regarded an an enemy (SHA *Hadr.* 9. 5; 11. 3); uncle of Sextus Erucius, II. 9. 4; receives dedicatory letter, *I. 1*; dinner invitation, *I. 15*; letters on P.'s view of friendship, *VII. 28*; on illness of P.'s reader, *VIII. 1.*

SERRANA PROCULA, native of Patavium, grandmother of Minicius Acilianus, I. 14. 6.

(Q.) SERTORIUS, the republican ruler of Spain; the well-known story of pulling off the horse's tail, III. 9. 11.

SERTORIUS SEVERUS, praetorian senator, joint heir with P. of Pomponia Galla, V. 1. 1.

SERVIANUS, v. Julius.

P. SERVILIUS CALVUS, proconsul of Bithynia 109–10 (?), otherwise unknown; men banished by him and still at large claim their sentence reversed, X. 56; Trajan will question Calvus, X. 57.

SERVILIUS PUDENS, P.'s legate in Bithynia, arrives 24 November, X. 25.

SEVERUS, v. Annius; Catilius; Herennius; Sertorius; Vettenius; Vibius.

BIOGRAPHICAL INDEX

BIOGRAPHICAL INDEX

BIOGRAPHICAL INDEX